Build Over There

Understanding the Government's role in shaping our cities

Hamish Barrell is an experienced town planner and a contributing author to the International Manual of Planning Practice 2015. Having worked near London for the last nine years he also has previous work experience in the United States of America and New Zealand, both in private and public capacities. He has almost 20 years of experience, through changing economic conditions, in roles as diverse as inner city development, coastal planning and regularising major infrastructure. He is well placed to offer insights into both the worthy and negative elements of the different planning systems around.

Build Over There

Understanding the Government's role in shaping our cities

Hamish Barrell

Arena Books

First published in 2017 by Arena Books

Arena Books
6 Southgate Green
Bury St. Edmunds
IP33 2BL

www.arenabooks.co.uk

Distributed in America by Ingram International, One Ingram Blvd., PO Box

3006, La Vergne, TN 37086-1985, USA.

Hamish Barrell
   Build Over There *Understanding the Government's role in shaping our
   cities*

British Library cataloguing in Publication Data. A catalogue record for this book is
available from the British Library.

ISBN-13   978-1-909421-88-2

BIC classifications:- AMA, AMCR, RPC, RNF, TNH, RND, KNJC.

Printed and bound by Lightning Source UK

Cover design
By Jason Anscomb

Typeset in
Times New Roman

BUILD OVER THERE

UNDERSTANDING THE GOVERNMENT'S ROLE IN SHAPING OUR CITIES

In an age of virtual communication, globalisation and technological advance, does the issue of where we build, or not build, really matter? Described as a code that is to the city what an operating system is to the computer, the evolution of the planning system is a story that can be traced from antiquity, through the industrial revolution to the present day crisis in the welfare state.

Typically delivered through a hierarchical set of institutions, it has implications for the economy, human rights, land values, sustainability, social cohesion, disasters and even military campaigns. Its shortcomings, tensions and contradictions play out in both strange and familiar issues; from the wasted space embodied in costly new skyscraper proposals to the eviction of residents, ownership of public assets, lack of affordable housing and highway congestion.

The town planning system is currently on trial, and at stake is the importance we, as a society, attach to the location and form of our built environment. Does the system really need a re-boot and if so what would it look like? Given that there are similar urban issues experienced the world over, it's necessary to search out the reasons for why is it so difficult to get agreement on the best way to address them.

In memory of
Alastair Wright
who always sought the best outcomes when intervening
on behalf of regional government in his local community.
In addition, I would like to thank
My family
for their support in getting this written.

CONTENTS

PART I:
PROGRESS, URBANISATION AND ITS CONSEQUENCES

1.0 Introduction

We live at a time in history when a number of trends or processes affecting humanity are converging. Economies are becoming increasingly interconnected and interdependent in economic, cultural and environmental matters. Conversely, ecological systems are being increasingly fragmented. Damage is occurring at such an alarming rate that it is claimed we are witnesses of the sixth great extinction, with more species becoming extinct today than at any time since dinosaurs were wiped off the face of the Earth by an asteroid 65 million years ago. Inequality of human wealth has become extreme, with more than half of it owned roughly by just one per cent of the population (Oxfam, 19 Jan 2015).

It is more than mere coincidence that there has never been a greater percentage of the world's population living in urban areas, and this is expected to rise to three quarters by 2050. In 1900, only 10% of the world's 1.8 billion people lived in cities. The percentage increased steadily over the next 50 years to 500 million or 30%. It was between 1957 and 2007 that the most dramatic change occurred, with a quadrupling of the world's urban population. Studies from UN-Habitat have revealed that the 40 largest 'super cities' occupy a tiny fraction of the Earth's habitable area, yet they contain 18% of the world's population, 66% of the world's economic activity and 85% of the global, scientific and technological innovation. Given their density, more than half of the world's population is squeezed into just 2.8% of the planet's land surface. Urban centres that dwarf those of past times are now accepted, even encouraged, as being inevitable; promoting everything from higher productivity, incomes, creativity, democracy, social cohesion and equality.

Due to a lack of resources and employment, or because they are seeking to improve themselves, people will migrate from one place to another. Cities are the major destination for them to fulfil their needs, as they act as a pull factor. Urbanisation effectively amounts to humanities' choice to 'live and work in close proximity.' Generally, state authorities' have seen fit to intervene to improve outcomes. In advanced economies, not only are large budgets spent on roads and infrastructure but the location of buildings and other activities are controlled through a complex system of regulations. Yet far from there being a set approach, or 'right way,' the level of intervention varies not just from country to country but also city to city. Different principles have been put forward that are considered to be universal. Understandings have changed over time. Underpinning it all, is a political dimension that pervades these attitudes.

Almost every day the media spotlight is shone on some facet of the planning system. It might be a housing crisis, infrastructural failure, community opposition to a development proposal, or the perceived failings of the State, charged with addressing urban issues. Are there common reasons underlying these situations? What mandate does Government have to resolve these issues? Is the level of intervention about right, or should it increase or decrease? When ideologies clash over technical wisdom, or the rights of individuals clash in communities due to common urban issues, who should prevail? What are the alternatives and when do they get considered? To answer these questions, it's necessary to understand the nature of the economic order which dictates so many urban development outcomes (Part I). The next Part sets out the reasons why settlements developed and how they depend upon the resources around them (Part II). Then it's possible to compare and contrast how cities were shaped from the industrial revolution onwards. In particular, how the 'modernist project' shapes cities differently by state intervention under capitalism and communist / central planning. Part III concerns itself with the origins and different types of planning systems. Part IV examines the institutional arrangements and planning practice. Specific themes are examined in Part V, VI and VII which the planning system either has as its goals or key matters of consideration. For each, I discuss the merits of different approaches that can be taken by the planning system. Finally, I conclude by examining where 'state control' should fit in today's world based on the different contexts of The West, the industrialised East and the Third World.

2.0 The Traditional Community

It's a truism that we are all in the end dependent on the land for our survival. The basic physiological needs for human existence of drink, food and adequate shelter stay constant over time. Without land, cities and communities cannot exist. Buildings, streets and public spaces are the external representation of the city. They are formed by communities coming together to a particular place in time. Those communities themselves may have been formed over generations.

If we went right back to our distant ancestors, then we'd be plunged into an existence where survival in the wilderness was the norm. Rural living encourages independence. Yet what people have discovered, is that co-operation makes the hard work of survival easier. Contrary to popular wisdom, it's interaction and co-operation and not selfishness, that best explains the human condition. It relates to our ability to communicate, recognise, evaluate, bond, co-operate and compete. In the end, it is the sense of belonging that comes from association with your own special group. According to the American researcher, Edward Wilson (2014), social intelligence, enhanced by group selection, made Homo Sapiens the first, fully dominant species in Earth's history.

At its most basic level, a community is no more than a group of people with something in common, which brings them (and keeps them) together. A community is a group, which is larger than a household and has a sharing of values among the individual members. It could be a geographic location, historical identity, fear of a common enemy, place of worship, shared interest, common employer or a bond that grows out of solidarity.

Community life is essential for human fulfilment. Humans need to relate to others on a sustained basis to develop their experiences of life, collaborate in discovery of truths, show justice and expand on opportunities for genuine fulfilment. Without being part of community, human beings cannot develop linguistically, culturally or morally. What defines us as human is only realised when people interact with each other, as members of shared communities (Taylor, 1990; and Bell, 1993).

With limited options for transport, communities in the past were typically small and tied to geographic areas. This is the so-called age where everyone living in an area knew and trusted each other – local relations were based on shared activities, particular common understandings and congruent values. Average village size in 1086, according to The Domesday Book, was around 150 inhabitants. According to Robin Dunbar (Oxford evolutionary anthropologist), what hasn't changed in the following 1,000 years is that 150 is the maximum number of friends an individual can handle. Communities or groups of friends grow too large and fall apart with more than 150 inhabitants.

In contrast, societies are groups (or communities) of people who share things. These include geographical and virtual territory, social values, political authority and dominant cultural expectations. Like groups, societies were once based on proximate face-to-face community. French sociologist,

Emile Durkheim (1984) referred to this as 'mechanical solidarity'. Human societies can be characterised on the basis of their culture. That includes a high level of taste in fine arts and humanity, shared institutions and also religion. About the latter, Durkheim differentiated between 'private' belief and 'social' religion. In the absence of modern transport and communications, religion gave a set of practices which maintained complex social relations over large areas. There was no need for the modern nation state. Religion was, as it were, the original Non-Government Organisation. It therefore sits at the seat of culture and identity (as noted by German philosopher, Max Muller, 1823 - 1900). Social cohesion is reinforced through ritual institutions that assert values and offer recognition to personal events. This includes birth or marriage.

The production, distribution and consumption of resources within a group or society, comes down to the underlying economic system. Prior to industrialisation, it was based within Europe on feudalism. People were born into certain 'stations' and stayed there for the rest of their lives. The 'system' lacked both class and individual economic mobility. Stability was prioritised and change seen negatively. The American economist Rostow referred to this as the so called 'traditional society' stage in his economic growth and development model. Following the Black Death in the mid-1300s the feudal system began to decline but lingered on in parts of Eastern Europe until the 19th Century.

Needless to say, this society was associated with significant inequality and the associated tensions this created between certain groups. The source of this inequality was directly related to the prevailing patterns of land ownership. Under Feudalism, all the land in a kingdom was typically the reigning Monarch's, who then distributed it to the Lords or Nobles. They in turn gave it to their vassals, while serfs, at the bottom tier, worked for their Lords.

In England, the countries' history has been defined by three sweeping changes in land ownership patterns:

- William the Conqueror's first act upon defeating the Anglo-Saxons in 1066/67 was to declare that all land in England now belonged to the Monarch. This was unprecedented. Whereas England had earlier been a mosaic of landowners, all land ended up being held by just one person overnight. William then proceeded to parcel much of that land out to those who had fought with him at the Battle of Hastings. This was the beginning of feudalism, the legacy of which continues to this day. It forms the basis of the landowning culture that has plagued the United

Kingdom ever since. An example is the ongoing debate on whether to abolish 'manorial rights.' Many see such rights as an outdated concept which hark back to the Middle Ages. Those opposed to its abolishment, consider that it would simply transfer rights from one group of property owners to another.

- Henry VIII's dissolution of the monasteries. At the time, the Church owned between one-fifth and one-third of all the land in all England. A significant portion (about one third) of which was being used for charitable purposes. This land grab by Henry VIII allowed him to sell it to the highest bidder amongst members of the aristocracy; and
- Enclosure, during the 18th and 19th Centuries. This is where rich landowners used their control of state processes to appropriate public land for their private benefit (Inclosure Acts). This created a landless working class. They would form the labour force for the new factories emerging in the north of England at the start of the industrial revolution.

The pattern of land ownership remains a powerful societal force. Ownership gives a certain degree of power over those who must live upon the land. Increased demand and competition for the land gives the owner power to take a larger and larger share of the earnings of labour. It is this power that gives land its value; the ability of the owner to reap what he or she does not work to produce (for example, extracting rent from the labourer). This principle stays true, whether it's for a farm cottage in the 19th Century, or a modern apartment (flat) in the city.

3.0 Nature of Progress

Change from the 'traditional society,' to the modern world is the result of progress. This is the idea that the world can become increasingly better. Sidney Pollard (1968) described progress as an 'assumption that a pattern of change exists in the history of mankind … that it consists of irreversible changes in one direction only, and that direction is towards improvement.'

Progress began in the renaissance enlightenment. The associated values of science, reason, liberation and freedom changed the way people thought. It has been described as a partnering of intellectual imagination and free will, which allowed scientific thought (Schouls P. 2000).

At this time, the role of human intervention in the physical world was debated. The German philosopher, Leibniz thought that the problem of divine justice was to discover God's hidden plan through reason and then complete it. French Enlightenment writer, historian, and philosopher, Voltaire criticised God for wasting nature through catastrophes and senseless destruction. Meanwhile, René Descartes, looked to the application of science as a way to 'regain paradise.'   By gaining mastery over nature, humanity could progressively improve the human condition.   Out of such debates, came the idea of a role for human beings in correcting and improving an imperfect world.

Material progress has coincided closely with the rise of science and industry:

(1) Industrialisation was founded on the principles of progress, including separation and domination of nature (Descartes).

(2) Proto sciences claimed to give new scientific knowledge about what society was like, and how one may change it for the better (which in the end went onto form the origins of planning theory).

Industrial societies' increased well-being came about through two factors. The first was exploiting carbon usage and the second human ingenuity. This was all undertaken within expanded urban environments. The ancient world, had been largely powered by human or animal labour. Industrialisation, on the other hand, was only possible through the development of new energy sources. The first of these new sources was waterpower. Shearing frames within mills were used to produce textiles and replace workers. Iron was produced using automated techniques.

A far more significant development was that of steam power, created through the burning of wood and later, coal. A key development was the invention of coke at Coalbrookdale (Shropshire, England) in the early 18th Century. This could be used to make pig iron in blast furnaces. The most revolutionary source of all though, was the introduction of electricity in the late 19th Century. This gave further impetus for further industrialisation. It also enabled the production of a vast new array of goods and services unavailable to traditional society.   Food production changed with the introduction of tin cans and refrigeration – cities would still rely on the agricultural surplus but with the newfound benefits of long-term storage (stockpiling), they could now take advantage of trade from around the world.

There was also a range of new labour saving devices, for example, from the domestic hoover and fridge through to the electric elevator.   It was Sprague and Elisha Otis's safety brake that enabled the effective servicing of

New York high rises from the 1880s. New buildings were also needed to serve new functions. It was necessary to understand where machinery would go in factory layouts, its orientation and access arrangements.

The building construction process itself was transformed. Nothing symbolised this more than the change from vernacular building materials to new technologies, such as concrete and steel. Concrete has become the second most widely used material on earth, after water. Over 2.5 tonnes of concrete is produced each year for every person on earth.

Building techniques have also changed. Pilkington's float glass process allowed for very big windows in buildings, such as skyscrapers. Just as Henry Ford (1863 – 1947) revolutionised the mass production of motorcars, the American real estate developer William Levitt (1907 - 1994) did the same for mass housing. Levitt applied techniques of mass production to the construction of entire neighbourhoods, such as Levittown on Long Island.

3.1 Transport

Traditional society was based around limited mobility and narrow horizons. (Chang, 2011). New technologies have created the possibilities for increasing inter-connectedness throughout the world – through travel, trade and communications. Transport networks allow for more cohesive societies. This was seen with the construction of decent roads across the Roman Empire.

A key to the success of industrialisation and the resulting urbanisation were the means to connect peoples and territories together. This included trade, migration and investment. In 1492, Columbus reached the America's and after that time new colonies began to be set up. Colonisation was dependent upon setting up new coastal cities, based on port facilities. The city of Bombay in India is a good example.

Inland canal projects formed an extension to coastal shipping routes (such as that of the Grand Union project in England, or the Erie Canal project of the American mid-west). They allowed freight and goods to by-pass an often run down and unreliable road network. With the introduction of the steam engine and use of rail lines, the canal system was quickly surpassed. Beginning in north England, the rail system had an even more dramatic impact in the United States. As it was rolled out from the settled east, it allowed new towns and cities to be set up in the interior. Eventually, rail stretched across the continent, providing a link with the western coast.

Rail not only gave the catalyst for whole new settlements, it also allowed existing ones to expand. For London, keeping the circulation going was vital for the functioning of the city. Its population had expanded from 1 million to 7 million in the space of 100 years, as a result of the early industrial revolution. Once in place, railways then began to support the growth of linear, urban development which allowed residents to live close to rail lines. The development of suburbs in London was initially predicated in parallel, with over-ground lines.

The steam engine had its drawbacks. The next step was development of the electric subway (by Sprague), that avoided choking fumes and gave traction on all wheels. Extending these urban rail networks often necessitated overcoming significant natural barriers. A notable triumph of engineering against the odds, was the extension of Metro Line 4 across the River Seine, in Paris (1905). Generally, such limitations reinforced distinct differences in urban connectivity. In London, development of the tube was better on the north bank. It had gravel capped hills, better subsoil and relatively drier positions than the marshy areas south of the River Thames.

The means of accessing the road network was the next to be transformed. Initially, it was a race between motor vehicles (both electric and petrol) to vie for the replacement of horses. The Model T car (from 1908), by Ford stood for the convergence of petrol, motor technology and assembly line, mass production. Private motor vehicles went on to offer freedom, flexibility, convenience and comfort to the masses. In particular, it allowed commuters to live further away from their places of work. In contrast to rail, motor vehicles allowed for a more dispersed urban development including the 'filling in of the urban gaps.' Cars also offer status to their owners. More than one billion vehicles populate the earth today, with that number rising.

The final transformation came through the development of air transport links in the 20th Century. This gave an unprecedented means of global travel at speed. Airports based in and around cities developed quickly.

Overlooked, but by no means less significant, was the bicycle, which came into being during the 19th Century. It enabled the rider to do much greater travel distances than previously possible. Bicycles are human powered. As such, they aren't dependent upon the resource hungry infrastructure necessary for trains, cars and planes to function.

3.2 Communication

Cities have always been meeting places of people and ideas. No less important in connecting peoples, cities and territories together was the invention of new technologies for communication. Telecommunication and the wireless enabled instantaneous communication. These technological advances paralleled transport:

- 1880- 1910: Telephone and commuter railway;
- 1920- 1940: Radio and automobile or airplane;
- 1950 – 1970: Television (TV), transistor radio and motorway and jet

Having televisions in almost every house, has been significant. This is not only for communication, but in changing popular consciousness. Coverage of the Apollo 11 moon landings (1969) was a milestone in bringing society together to view one single live event.

The advent (1980s and 1990s) of computers and multi-media now has the ability to make entertainment and information instantly available. Having all information instantaneously available is in many ways the goal of, what has been termed, the information revolution.

The impact of this on urbanisation is potentially huge. In fact commentators talked early on about this potentially reversing urban 'agglomeration.' During earlier technological cycles no reduction in travel or face to face contact was ever observed. The third Kondratiev wave, for instance, comprised steel and heavy engineering. The fourth wave was about oil, electricity, automobile and mass production. The result of this information technology wave (media, computers and internet) now sees Third World IT technicians fixing Anglo-American software. Experts interact with clients for everything from distance learning to remote medical diagnosis. The internet revolution has enabled many types of work from home. This reduces the need for 'mechanical solidarity.' Information technologies and communication networks have removed the spatial obstacles that hinder capital circulation. Marxist commentators describe this as the 'annihilation of space by time.'

Needless to say, face-to-face communication hasn't been extinguished. Virtual communication can't substitute for all the benefits of direct socialisation which have been observed. In one study, an organisation's office was split up physically. This resulted in the decline and break-down of communication and began a silo mentality. In fact, organisations have sought greater face-to-face interaction through the 'open office' plan. Drawn from sharemarket trading floors, this format offer workers unimpeded flows of information.

Locational criteria for new offices remains important. Even multi-media firms have found homes in the centres of established cities, as well as in newer, high tech enclaves. The best example is Silicon Valley which began with the nurtured innovation of Stanford University back in the mid-20th Century. This set the scene for huge, local urbanisation. Similarly, London dominates informational employment. Significant development by companies engaged in IT operations has taken place along the M4 motorway corridor.

These patterns can be explained by the continuing need for jobs that use theoretical, abstract intelligence. These jobs, and the deep, specialised education and knowledge that go alongside them stay firmly locked in the cores of large cities in The West. Information and communication technology don't eliminate differences between places. In fact, they can permit the exploitation of differences between areas (for example, local labour market conditions). The digital revolution and its technologies haven't allowed developing countries to close the gap with richer nations (World Bank report 'Digital Dividends,' January 2015). Given the ability to copy technological advances elsewhere, the dominant centres of innovation and patterns of emulation may not always stay static. But whether places in the Third World can compete and then rival established centres remains to be seen.

3.3 Means of Production

All organisations, public or private, engage in forms of planning. They seek to transform their activities or environment to achieve certain outcomes. Means of production include entrepreneurship, labour, capital (factories, machines and tools) and land. The 'means of production' can also include the 'means of distribution'. This encompasses stores, banks, the internet and railroads.

There are important differences to note between the economic sectors. The primary sector is tied to the land (an unmoveable commodity), such as farming, forestry and mining. The secondary sector is defined by what is done to primary products. It covers transportation, manufacturing and distribution. The tertiary sector is the financial services that give the capital to make the primary and secondary sector function more smoothly.

Treasury ignores these sectoral distinctions when calculating the 'Gross Domestic Product' (GDP). GDP measures economic performance and record of income produced by commercial transactions. It doesn't distinguish whether production covers guided missiles, skyscrapers or widgets. They're all counted indifferently. The problem is that if no value and surplus value was being produced in production generally, then those sectors couldn't exist by themselves. The Marxist academic David Harvey (2012), puts it like this: if no shirt and shoes were produced, what would retailers sell?

3.4 The Nature of Work

The biggest structural change introduced by capitalist thinking is seeing the worker as separate from his tools. This is encapsulated through the principles of scientific management and Ford's assembly line mass production methods. The specialisation of labour that accompanied this, means that no one person produces anything. Admittedly, the shift towards use of machinery has made many tasks easier. It means freedom for workers to move elsewhere, but also the ability of owners to displace them. Whatever is produced by a single individual can be quite unskilled, repetitive and easily replaced. The greatest benefits for workers occur where there is competition for their labour and higher wages by one employer are necessary to offset competitors' offers.

Since the Industrial Revolution, those societies which have adapted their divisions of labour most effectively to new technologies are the ones that have succeeded. This is in terms of enhancing their well-being as defined by life expectancy, literacy, diversity of goods, reliability of services and numerous other indicators.

Distinction between hidden vs. non-hidden work

There are many tasks that aren't necessarily well paid. Like Engels before him, Orwell addressed the theme of hidden work, and the desire for society to ignore the essential but undesirable aspects of labour. In 'The Road to Wigan Pier,' Orwell wrote:

'Down there where the coal is dug it is a sort of world apart which one can quite easily go through life without ever hearing about. Probably a majority of people would even prefer not to hear about it. Yet it is the absolutely necessary component of our world above.'

Coal mining is out of sight and out of mind because its natural location is underground. Importantly, Orwell recognised that where location is transportable it can also be hidden as a matter of convenience. Certain Indian Castes that perform manual labour are an example. This is often the mentality that goes into locating such activities within cities. For those in charge of capital or machinery the incentive is to use it as efficiently as possible. Marx identified a link between such high productivity and worker exploitation. It is more realistic to say that the means of production uses the labourer.

Technology has played its part. Enabled by the gaslight, then electric light the working day could be stretched beyond dusk and carry on regardless of the season. Most fair-trade-minded Americans would not have bought things made by their own grandfathers, who worked extremely long hours, under inhumane conditions. Until the beginning of the 20th Century, the average work week in the United States was around sixty hours. Despite the benefits of 'labour saving machinery,' workers in service industries still toil for long hours. They may also be subjected to video surveillance and other measures of monitoring.

Most workers in the West now spend their time in offices. The East India Company was one of the first examples of a large company associated with an office block. This was built in 1729 in Leadenhall Street, London. The East India Company was a complex bureaucracy. It did lots of paperwork for the processing of information and making decisions about things that were taking place on the other side of the world.

Increased industrial production supported classes of non-productive workers. Their responsibilities included both the organisation of production and the organisation of social reproduction, for example, managers. As the nature of work has changed over time, so have the needs of management. There has been a shift from functional (operational) structures to matrix (project based) structures. The difference between productive and unproductive labour is whether it produces surplus value. Part is accumulated or invested to exploit more resources. The rest is spent on unproductive expenditures.

Adam Smith (1723 – 1790), leader in the Scottish Enlightenment and champion of capitalism, linked productive labour to the production of things. In his time, most unproductive workers simply gave personal services. Marxists would argue that only some workers are producing surplus value. Unproductive workers are being supported by a part of the surplus value produced (which doesn't mean that they don't work hard). Investors can therefore either invest it to further exploit workers to get surplus value (in which case productive labour is performed), or spend it on unproductive labour. That is 'wine, women or song.'

What is unproductive labour for one, is productive for another investor. There are long established and honoured industries where workers toil productively to produce all kinds of items that are essentially useless. However, society none-the-less wastes its money on them. The investor who produces these commodities, like any other, does so to make surplus value. In other words, profit is related to their turnover of stock, rather than the labour force. The wages they pay out are just another cost, like the cost of IT equipment, desks or warehouse shelving. The same is true of bank workers. They may work hard, but the banks' profits are based on the rate of interest, not their unpaid labour. So workers employed in circulation are thus not considered productive.

In Marx's time unproductive workers were mainly the 'flunkeys of the rich.' When he wrote Das Capital (1867), there were more domestic servants than industrial workers in the country. The present age is characterised by a huge increase in unproductive expenditure. This acts as a dead weight on the system, or an involuntary levy upon the profits of individual investors. The difference between workers needed to physically transport goods and get them in a form available for consumption, are the costs of capitalist circulation. Capitalism suggests individuals should be rewarded according to their achievements, not their birth. It deliberately promotes the use of incentives for people to become educated, to save and invest, to innovate and adopt new technologies. For workers, as well as entrepreneurs, there is (financial) motivation to better ones self, relative to others. In doing so, workers themselves create a form of inequality.

All economic systems need to transform resources and produce goods. They depend on labour and seek to encourage high levels of worker motivation. Under capitalism, the focus is on incentives (rather than punishment) to work. The motivation for rewards, whether it be wages or profit, is that they're necessary to buy things. If these include investments such as property and are held in enough quantity, it can mean it's possible not to have to work. In each case, 'property' is a necessary requirement to make sure there's a reason for the proceeds of profit and wages to be invested.

A significant factor in all of this is the role of the state - even under a capitalist society. While the techniques of mass production and work discipline originated in the democratic West, they were pursued just as thoroughly under Lenin's Soviet Union. Individuals living under that system were still expected to work and act to promote the betterment of the party and community. Often there were punishments for those seen not to be working hard enough.

Even so, it was apparent that work ethic and motivation varied, even though everyone was assigned some task or job. For example, in a study conducted in the Soviet Union, over 50% of the work force admitted to drinking alcohol while on the job. Furthermore, unbeknown to the communist party, nearly 40% chose to work a second job privately to attain more wealth.

A structural reason for this failure in work ethics and motivation was the necessity that all communists had to be employed. The trouble with over-manning positions trivialised the work needed to be performed. It placed the concentration on quantity, rather than quality. The relative scarcity of 'good' jobs under capitalism is supposed to motivate workers.

3.5 The Logic of Capital

Stockpiling or wealth creation is not a new phenomenon. Sociologists refer to it as the 'ceremonial fund' of past civilisations. It stands for the proportion of labour product that was given for the intensification of relationships. It ensures social cohesion at a more global level than basic economic groups.

Money is perhaps the best way of representing the concept of stockpiling. Marx referred to it as representing the 'congealed sweat' of labour. Capitalism, as a mode of production, is embodied in its drive to reproduce and increase capital. It has always been apparent, but the higher productivity of industrialisation allows for much greater concentrations of wealth. Under a capitalist system, the wealth is held as individual private property.

In the narrow, traditional sense, capital is defined as the machines used to enhance an individual's power to do economically viable work. New types of recognised capital include: social capital, cultural capital, human capital, manufactured capital, natural capital and financial capital. The latter, typically supplied by banks, is the main constraint on the ability to start construction.

Financial capital will influence the cultural capital one receives. Cultural capital is the shared outlook, beliefs, knowledge, and skills that are passed between generations. Cultural capital influences human capital, which refers to the education and job training a person receives. Human capital creates the ability for one to attain social capital, which is essentially the social network to which one belongs. Social capital can largely influence one's ability to find an internship or job. These are, in particular, voluntary associations including family. Their knock on effect increases the general welfare of those involved in them. Understanding how social networks and contacts affect the productivity of individuals and groups is complex. It's tied in with cultural factors.

Successful individuals and companies combine the benefits of technology, finance, social institutions and the law. All four forms of capital play a role in social reproduction because capital is passed from generation to generation. Typically they keep people in the same social class as their parents before them.

There have also been many changes to both law and finance to arrive at the common understandings we have today. The Chinese and Romans prevented innovations that might threaten their societal order. In the West, financial capital was much harder to access when the Church actively discouraged usury/ lending (this remains the case in many Muslim countries). Access to credit eventually became easier but an even bigger step forward was the limited liability company in the 19th Century. It didn't just allow entrepreneurs (including property developers) to set up and borrow funds. It also limited their individual personal risk if the company later failed.

The process of innovation is made possible by economic institutions. These encourage private properties, uphold contracts, create a level playing field and so on. Under market forces, the business system is based around four principles:

- Freedom of choice – that is firms setting their own prices and competing against each other.

  In the past, many small firms were protected from competition in local markets by the high cost of transportation. Nineteenth century capitalism was far less competitive than now. The 'ma and pa' business are an example of those who have set up to supply some need in a particular locality and are only seeking to make enough to survive.

  In more complex urban environments, smaller businesses quickly come up against the forces of accumulated capital. These forces operate under strategies for maximising profit. Increased transport inter-connectedness reduced the spatial barriers which had restricted the 'annihilation of space through time'. Many local producers were gradually forced into competition with producers located at increasing distances. To compete, companies must use new technologies to give them a competitive 'supply side' advantage.

Alternatively, the demand side approach of getting ahead is to exploit market niches and new 'vehicles' for making money. This includes seeking out new fads, fashions, innovations and asset types. Investors seek to persuade consumers of the unique and non-replicable qualities of their commodities (brand names, advertising etc).

An example of this is bottled water. Bottled water has been around for years. It took off in the beginning of the 19th Century. That was when new glass technologies made the cost of a bottle affordable and practical for mass production and consumption. Bottled water then went out of style and need in the early 20th Century. That was when the advent of chlorination in municipal drinking water supplies made public water consistently healthy and safe to drink. But in 1977, bottled water made a comeback when Perrier launched a $5 million marketing campaign in the United States for its imported water. Perrier's marketing and timing were perfect. It took advantage of concerns about pollution and poor-quality tap water. But its uptake was driven by new consumer groups (yuppies) who were after 'lifestyle-defining' products. After Perrier's success, a new market was literally created. This led directly to the current growth and bottled water industry we see today.

- Profit motive - The primary driver of economic activity is typically seen to be profit making (the margin between selling and cost price). Profit is accumulated and unless taxed by the state, retained by the owners. For most, the ownership of the Means of Production has come to refer to a cultural practice. This is one where a few individuals within a larger corporation (or company) control and decide what is done with the entire profit created by that corporation.

It's a race to create economies of scale. Companies seek greater access to funds through floating themselves on the sharemarket. Once this has occurred, the new shareholders will often insist the company keep up in terms of the comparative revenue stream. If not other 'competitors' quickly take over. Typically, the need to retain competitiveness with other investments necessitates short term strategies. These include focusing on efficiency ahead of re-investment and reducing operating costs. So it's no surprise that only smaller operators, such as family firms, can avoid a focus on short term profit making.

The profit motive results in 'self perpertualisation' when aggregated across the economy. This is the constant compulsion to speed up the circulation of capital through ever greater spending. Not only does this propel the need to 'change for change sake' but it results in the so called linear economy or 'throw away' society.

- Private Property rights – There are three basic elements of private property. The first is the exclusivity of rights to choose the use of a resource. Second the exclusivity of rights to the services of a resource. Third rights to exchange the resource at mutually agreeable terms. This can be expressed in a number of different ways. Essentially the ownership of private property allows people to seek to maximise their 'utility' (or their wants and desires).

- Owner control – for land it represents an agreed position in law as to what an individual can do. It has a strong cultural element. Under primitive / feudal arrangements the ownership of property involved reciprocal arrangements within the group. That is 'communal ownership' or 'serfdom.' It may come as a surprise, but the general culture heritage of Europe from the medieval era was opposed to individual self-interest and the free operation of markets. Markets and private property were acceptable only so long as social regulation took precedence over sinful motivations such as greed. The modern understanding of freehold title to land came about during the industrial revolution. This is the state saying that an individuals' rights to their property outweighs anything else over that piece of land. That includes the needs of society in the future.

Societies' adherence to the Rule of Law is the product of generations of institution building. This includes an individual's equality before the law. In the past elites have presented arguments that a law does not apply to them. In England, as in other Commonwealth countries, commercial and property disputes are resolved through Common Law.

The main purpose of property rights, and their biggest success, is that they eliminate the destructive competition for the control of economic resources. Well-defined and well-protected property rights replace competition by violence, with competition by peaceful means (foreign invasions aside). The role of the state for private property is all important. The English philosopher Locke (1632 – 1704) advanced the case of the free market[1] but acknowledged the state's key role in protecting private property. There are arguments that private property rights don't just exist for the sake of those people who hold property. Rights exist to serve social purposes and reach far beyond those who exercise those rights. Those contending this see the overall good of society best served by individuals seeking to better their position relative to others. In other words, society needs private property and the inequalities that go with it to maximise production and consumption.

Market economists see individual successes linked to increased societal well-being as a whole. Markets are the best mechanism for allocating resources. Yet problems abound when defining exactly how this success is defined. For instance, is it growth, domination of a market sector or satisfied customers that becomes the focus, or should it be all these factors?

Past thinkers like Karl Marx (1818 – 1883) adopted the converse view of the historical materialist perspective. As illustrated by the examples of conquest above, they noted that patterns of (land) ownership have important consequences for any society. The problem is the very nature of private property. It creates a distinction between those persons who own finite resources such as land and those who don't. A registered Land Title becomes a form of fictitious capital. Economic Marxism goes so far as to claim that history itself is dictated by ownership to the means of production.

3.6 Economic Development

Describing the logic of capitalism is one matter. Academics, economists and decision makers actually wish to understand and then isolate the factors that allow a nation to 'progress.' Increased production, in the West, has brought about increased consumption. There's an understandable temptation for Third World countries to develop and join the 'consumer economy' of the West. This leads to an intense debate as to why, after decades of trying to catch up, inequality remains. Social capital is often used to explain the cultural differences between economically advanced, backward and developing countries. It is seen by many as more efficient than the state.

---

[1] He was known as the 'Father of Liberalism'.

In 1960, the United States economist and political theorist, Rostow, developed one of the major historical models of economic growth. The idea was that there are five distinct stages of development. The final stage culminated in a 'society of mass consumption.' The UK had been the first country to industrialise but it had been a lengthy and, at times, difficult process. Clearly, other countries sought to adopt or use the results reached elsewhere. What was uncertain was whether countries could skip or telescope the development stages other countries had taken. Countries are, for instance, looking to skip industrialisation. They would rather make the transition from agriculture to a service based economy. Those countries that had become newly dominant could aid the progress of others by trade, subsidies and contributing resources. Or these countries could block progress by preventing use of capital, technology, trading routes, labour, land or other resources.

Perhaps the biggest controversy amongst thinkers is whether progress is inevitable. Examining the pre-conditions that existed in the West before the industrial revolution, observers have noted that it only began with the accumulation of capital. This had been helped by the discovery of America (including cheap labour and the importation of its precious metals).

Dependency theory is an inversion to the theories of social capital and Rostow. It suggests that the failure of Third World countries to accomplish development was caused by their forced dependence on the advanced, capitalist world. The Third World may be doomed to underdevelopment. That's because its surplus is appropriated by the advanced, capitalist countries.

Disagreement is not inevitable, even amongst economists as diverse as free-marketers (for example, Ricardo) and ultra Marxists (for example, Preobrazhensky). Both sides can agree that in order to maximise economic growth in the long run, the 'investible surplus' needs to be concentrated in the hands of the investor. It's the capitalist class in the former. It's the planning authority in the latter. The problem with concentrating income in the supposed investor, is that it does not lead to higher growth if the investor fails to invest.

While a communist system will do this, there is no equivalent mechanism in capitalist economies. The best that liberal leaning economists have suggested is to rely on the vagaries of the so called 'trickle down' theory. Marxism sought 'commonly owned' resources to eliminate the power structures of 'class' and inequalities surrounding the use of the 'surplus.' It intended to prevent class conflict that would otherwise arise.

Liberal economists do not prefer the state owning and managing resources. This is precisely because they think the State lacks the profit driven motive.

They are also deemed to be inefficient and unmotivating for the workforce in general. As we saw with the case of workers in communist countries above, even when regime change is successful[2] inevitably inefficiency and waste results. Eventually, countries pursuing such policies become uncompetitive. They then fall behind in their standard of living. This is the primary reason for having as small a state as possible (and by extension, the minimum amount of land in public ownership). This philosophical 'debate' is still played out over the public ownership of resources in advanced, western countries. These include public forestry, national parks and urban open spaces.

It's worth pointing out that Karl Marx and Frederick Engels thought that it was the notion of private property that stifled the motivation to work. Those who acquired anything of significance were then not considered to want to do any further work. This view assumes that resources in the world are finite. If the economy is viewed as infinite,[3] then the sharing of resources becomes somewhat irrelevant. In non-communist societies, people compete ruthlessly to obtain the largest amount of resources and property for the end goal of wealth. As property is scarce (as is the case generally for land), once all capital is privatised, the incentive to work will be non-existent because all resources will be exhausted. Marx and Engels argued that as all non-communist systems would eventually achieve this condition, the only solution was to make sure privatisation of property isn't allowed.

The most clear historical factor in material progress is the link between industrialisation, productivity growth and rising living standards. Yet it is more than that. Productivity in the West comes down to the system not individuals. The systems include better technologies, better organised firms, better institutions and better infrastructure. These are the products of collective actions taken over generations.

The role of the political system of government also plays a fundamental part in material progress. Marx's solution, as with that of the French Revolution before it, was based on the theory of crisis. For Britain, urbanisation and the emergence of a socially conscious middle and working class challenged the political monopoly of the landed aristocracy. The response of the establishment to the revolutionary threat was for greater power sharing with the middle class. This laid the foundations for 'modern democracy.' Over time ever greater segments of the adult population were given the vote. Democracy stands for majority rule and belief that the right to

---

[2] Successful means authoritarian power structures established, class conflict quashed and systems of commonly owned resources installed.

[3] One of the few examples of an infinite economic sector would be software programming.

difference disappears once the majority has spoken. Social institutions have an important role in change, development and democratic and participatory systems. This gives opportunity for the expression of opinion, the choosing of governments, the forging of consensus and the resolution of differences. For instance, as far back as Ancient Greek society, their theatre dramas gave an important participatory forum for freedom of speech.

It goes deeper than the form of Government, to the structure and hierarchy of society. Hierarchies were the assumed order of industrialised, organisational life. This was both politically and in many large companies. In the 1960s, Warren Bennis among others, began landmark studies on how democratic groups compared with hierarchical groups in performing a variety of tasks. The results were startling at the time. Hierarchies were the way to go if the task was a simple one that could be led by a single, decisive authority. But the strong leader, no matter how gifted, was less effective at leading a team through complex tasks. As ambiguity increased the democratic teams, which shared information and authority, proved superior to the hierarchies. Just as importantly, the democratic teams reported widespread engagement among their members. The only engaged persons on the hierarchical teams were those at the top of their hierarchies. Even that was a mixed blessing, with their positions growing shaky as the complexity of the tasks increased.

Bennis argued that democracies were the social organisms most imbued with the ability to adapt to uncertainty. Democracies benefited uniquely from the aggregate perspectives. That is the experiences and wisdom of everyone within a group. An organisational movement was birthed. Organisational pyramids would be flattened including corporations, non-profit organisations and schools.

In 1964, Bennis and collaborator, Philip Slater, authored a Harvard Business Review piece. This argued that democracy is more ruthlessly effective than any hierarchy, autocracy, oligarchy or technocracy over the long term. They then predicted that the United States would emerge as the victor in its rivalry with the Soviet Union. This would come through the natural superiority of democratic processes over autocratic ones. For decades, the Soviet Union maintained a façade of competence, while internally it decayed. When the 'Iron Curtain' did fall in the late 1980s it was seen by many to verify Benin's theories of 'democracy as the best style of government.'

In the end, the view that the main problems of social distribution had been solved by the post-war boom, welfare state, Keynesian macroeconomic regulation and the 'human face' of the managerial revolution were premature. Western, liberal democracies were not immune to economic cycles and class conflict. All these were elements of what became known as 'corporatism'—

big capital and big state, embodied in the idea of the welfare state. This 'post-war consensus' was based on a premise. If the rich were going to benefit the rest of society, they would have to be made to deliver higher investment and growth through policy measures (for example, tax cuts conditional on investment). They would then share the fruits of such growth through the welfare state. This was part of the so called 'historic compromise' between capital and labour (big business and trade unions). With the Great Depression and Second World War still fresh in mind, any other course of action would have seemed unwise. The intent of the welfare state was to produce a viable social order. This included ideas which had evolved over decades, like minimum working standards and in the end, re-distribution of wealth.

Sweden's welfare state, was perhaps the most far reaching. It embodied a distinct, political ideology. The Social democratic project, led by politicians Uno Ahren, Sven Markelius and Lennart Holm, was collectivist. It had an ability to reconcile political freedom, social welfare and social cohesion. Its embodiment in Stockholm (a Model Social Democratic City) was applied to other countries on both sides of the Iron Curtain.

The welfare state has meant much heavier taxation across the board. In the 1890s, 10% of English household income went on Government spending such as the Navy, the Army and the odd infrastructure project. The proportion has increased to above 40%. This is because of healthcare, education, social security, street lighting, pensions and far more besides. It is even higher in Scandinavian countries.

Intimately linked to technology are the education, skills, competencies and know-how of the work force. These are acquired in schools, homes and on the job. Others have noted that universal education, liberation and democracy both feed into, and feed back into, the process. Progress was originally related to the arts and science. It soon spread into technology, modernisation, liberty, democracy, quality of life and so on. Stable government is thought to need advanced, power sharing arrangements (at all levels of government, including local government). Acemoglu and Robinson (2012) took a similar view. They suggested that the most critical factor is whether a state is inclusive or extractive. Inclusive institutions engage in power sharing, productivity, education and technological advances. In fact, they engage in the general well-being of the nation as a whole. Extractive state institutions instead grab wealth and resources from one part of society to benefit another (Acemoglu & Robinson, 2012).

Fukuyama, the former US State Department official, made the ultimate link between progress, capitalism and democracy in 1992 (upon the demise of the 'Iron Curtain' in Eastern Europe). He famously declared capitalism and democracy to be the 'end' of history; its destination and goal. Suffice to say, later events have shown such a declaration to be deceptively simplistic.

3.7 Economic Restructuring and Globalisation

Cheaper products get passed onto consumers through business competition, drive for efficiency and reduced costs amongst producers. There are downsides, not least business leaders, who driven by the profit motive do not care about the impact of their decisions. Joseph Schumpeter uses the term 'creative destruction'. This is to describe the role of new technologies making existing machines and individual workers' skill sets redundant. The original Luddite movements of the 19th Century was carried out by artisans (particularly in towns in northern England). Their manual skills were being replaced by mechanisation (the shearing frames described earlier). They violently opposed the spread of industry and came to epitomise the struggle 'against progress.'

In the last century, labour saving technologies continued to impact workers. Containerisation allowed cargo to be carried more quickly and cheaply. This affected London's Docklands, Liverpool and many other ports around the world. 'Just-in-time' production and supply of inputs could respond quickly to shifts in demand. This enabled companies to hold smaller inventories. Even retained workers were often worse off. Taylorism and his philosophy of manageralism sapped the individual's work initiative. Unions were unsuccessful, as they lacked enough political power to stop this process.

Capitalism ends up not just as a competitive, but a combative environment too. Different companies are competing to produce goods and services more efficiently than each another. Cutting costs on a firm's waste disposal system may save the company money even if it causes pollution. Everything associated with modern management revolves around finance and financial control. What can be measured matters but what cannot be measured has little status. Before the 1970s, companies were mainly run by engineers or production people along with some salesmen and marketers. Accountants have come to dominate the ranks of management ever since. Everything comes down to numbers. This encourages the belief that businesses are machines. Everything can be controlled. Increased amounts of input lead to increasing amounts of outputs. In reality, businesses are biological not mechanical. They represent collections of people whose behaviours can never be predicted.

One company's success can mean another's failure – all cannot win in this race. It is the survival of the fittest. Whole companies fail. In the United States, 10% of companies collapse every year. In fact, whole industries and sectors are vulnerable. This occurred when automobile companies in Detroit needed to be bailed out after the credit crunch. Periods such as the Great Depression saw marked differences between actual and potential outputs. Market failure over time cuts the number of operators in a market. In the end a point comes when the market is dominated by a limited range of largish companies. These will be described as having achieved 'efficient operations.'

The result of competitive collapse is monopolisation of specific markets. Often this is by large, vertically integrated firms. Many view monopolisation as unacceptable. A single competitor can deliberately increase the profit margins for its own benefit. Short of Government intervention, the only way for a monopolist to be beaten is if its goods are replaced by superior products produced by another company (e.g., using new technologies). IBM is an example of a company that dominated its market for computers. That was until the personal computer dramatically changed the rules.

Monopolies are stable but undesirable, except for the owners concerned. Monopolies represent exclusive control. This may be over some directly or indirectly tradeable item that is unique and non-replicable. This could be a special quality resource, commodity or location. An example of locational uniqueness could relate to the proximity of a business to a transport and communication network. Or it may relate to the proximity of some highly concentrated activities i.e., hotels to airports.

Part of the reason monopolies didn't come to dominate all our markets was due to greater competition introduced by trade with other countries. Again, the same logic of competition described above applies. This is symbolised by increasing trade and the associated movement of capital and services beyond traditional, national boundaries. International trade has always been about the exchange of goods. Better technology has enabled ever-greater movements but distance hasn't entirely died. There is relatively little trade between far-flung areas of the world compared to those of close neighbours. Also, exploiting a countries' potential takes the clever use of technology and advances in transport by business people. It also takes the Government to encourage them.

The strategy of the State in its relations with other countries is important. There are significant benefits when the State is proactive in supporting trade routes and innovation. Most importantly, those countries at the forefront have been able to move ahead and dominate others. A dramatic example of this was when US Commodore Perry's 'mission' to Japan in 1854 forced a re-think in the Japanese Government's approach of isolationism (Kaikin). Their foreign policy had survived between 1641 to 1853.

Government strategy has also been of critical importance in other respects. Countries with less efficient industries have still been able to compete through intervention. This includes subsidisation, trade taxes or retreating from trade altogether. After the Second World War, many newly independent nations opted for inward looking industrialisation and import substitution. In contrast, China and Japan specialised their economies on the basis of what they saw as their competitive advantage.

Tokyo was economically successful in the post-Second World War era. This was based, not on immigration, but on developing primary, offshore, low-cost production sites and potential markets initially directed at Korea. With the benefit of generous post-war funding to rebuild, it was able to prosper, despite low levels of natural resources. Its economy was built around the transfer of resources from other countries to its cities. There it was processed, manufactured through innovative high technology enterprises. Modern China began a long series of experiments towards industrialisation under Mao in the 1960s. In the end it transformed a sclerotic command economy into an export-orientated market system. It now has a significant proportion of the world's factories and depends on other countries for supplies of raw materials.

The theme of specialisation has become familiar in every country in the West. Specialisation depends on overseas suppliers. Some countries have selective industries for which the spatial ramifications can be enormous. For example, during the Second World War, British industries continued to rely on the trade of ball bearings with Sweden. Although a neutral country, it was, after the German occupation of Norway, effectively surrounded. Access to ball bearing supplies was an issue of strategic importance. In the end, access depended upon risky naval operations through the Baltic.

The above factors have morphed into the phenomena known as 'globalisation'; a form of economic integration. This term, coined in the 1960s, became prevalent after the end of the Cold War, with the phenomenon of markets. Powered by multi-national corporations they used information systems and communications to operate internationally. Furthermore, globalisation enabled the transfer of capital off shore.

Technology will continue to challenge society. Basic manufactured items such as plastic spoons, are typically made in factories. This is because processes, such as injection moulding are the most efficient means of mass production. In the near future, it may be possible for 3D printers to substitute for this. High street 3D printers use plastics or resins now to build up finished products.   In the near future advanced techniques will use lasers to melt powdered metal and ceramics into ultra-thin layers.

Additive layer manufacturing will see mega-factories being replaced by much smaller ones. These could be located on back lanes, thanks to low-cost, on demand 3D printing.   Personalised products of the future will be manufactured in the street for the customer. For instance, Amazon is hoping to harness advances in 3D printing to fulfil consumers' every desire. It has emerged that the business has filed a patent application in the United States for trucks equipped with 3D printers. These will take orders online and then produce the finished item either at a customer's door, or on the way to it. WikiHouse (www.wikihouse.cc) is a similar project, but this time with implications for housing. It uses collaborative, open source design and 3D printing to make high quality, low-energy, affordable homes more accessible.

In Rostow's fifth and final stage of development, it's the industrial base that is supposed to dominate the economy. The primary sector becomes of greatly reduced significance in the economy and society. In the modern era, it's no longer just about making something. Goods are relatively more expensive to make anyway and industry has declined. De-industrialisation is when industry counts for less than services in the economy. The shift to the service economy has been the means by which consumption and wealth was able to be accompanied by improvements to the environment.

The focus has shifted to 'adding value.' That is by setting goods apart through differentiation. It's better to contract out parts manufacture to a variety of smaller, nimble businesses than a monolithic supply chain within a huge company. Those smaller companies tend to have newer industries, plant and equipment (capital). They are therefore more efficient than their business neighbours. This includes the need for new buildings to house both new teams and technologies. The make up of the economy then feeds back into the function, shape and composition of cities.

There is a strong spatial element in all of this. Markets for goods and services typically have geographic boundaries. Relative transport and labour costs contribute to success or failure. The traditional structures of social and political control over development, work and distribution have been subverted.   Instead we have the placeless logic of an internationalised economy. This is enacted by information flows amongst powerful actors. Being beyond the sphere of state regulations it spells political division (Castells, 1989). The economy of an industrialised city in northern England is thus affected by decisions made elsewhere – be it Westminster, Brussels or

Beijing. The global economy reduces a nation state's ability to control their economy and maintain old continuities.

3.8 Crisis of Progress

Despite the success of the political system of democracy and the associated trappings of the welfare state, the economies of many western states have major issues. After a major loss of dynamism in the 1960s, productivity growth rates fell by half in the United States in the 1970s. They more or less ceased altogether in France, Germany and Britain in the late 1990s. Harvey (1990) indicates that post-modernity began around 1973. This was when capitalism experienced one of its many crises during the first global recession of the post-war period. It is evident when compared alongside other 'harder working' countries (such as those of The East like Japan, Korea, Taiwan, Singapore, Hong Kong and China). These countries have achieved success more recently. Their respective approach is to mix market-based economics with non-democratic politics.

The question is, who is to blame for the situation in the West? Many (neo-liberal) economists put the loss of innovation, which slowed economic productivity, down to the spread of corporatist values. These values are especially associated with the welfare state focus on solidarity, security and stability. Post war politicians had introduced too much regulation. This stifled competition and patronised interest groups through 'pork-barrel' contracts. It also lent direction to the economy through industrial policy.

Being reflective of the western experience, Rostow's model doesn't make predictions for our time. Yet, is it not the fact that western countries have failed to maintain their industrialised status, that is itself to blame? Many Marxist economists[4] seemed to think so. They observed that the tertiary sector (retail, wholesale, warehouses and distribution) had taken over while the primary and secondary sectors, largely outsourced to the Third World, had ground to a halt. The goal of a (Keynesian style) 'consumption economy' is to give consumers low prices and wide variety. There is less concern about jobs and wages.

The 'relative' lack of state economic direction and the desire of industry to cut labour costs has resulted in the casualisation of the middle class. This phenomenon is associated with the end to the traditional, lifelong, secure,

---

[4] Including Hou Yuon and Khieu Samphan who later became involved in the movement to take over Cambodia (Kampuchea).

professional career.   Rather it's replaced by the vagaries of short-term contracts.   Even in advanced economies, most economists say that unequal societies don't prosper.   It apparently takes a large and confident middle class to provide the consumer spending that drives healthy economic growth.

Others have noted that capitalism's economic problems are associated with its need to grow and expand to prevent stagnation and collapse.   Natural resources may be running out (this is covered further on in Part II, Section 2.0).   Finally, the root cause of the problem may be unproductive elements within capitalism itself.   The runaway increase of unproductive expenditure since the Second World War has levered profit rates down.   This includes financial labour, circulation labour (transport), supervisory labour and commercial labour.   Unproductive labour is a deadweight on the system.   It acts as a levy on the bottom line (the cure for this, discussed later, being further automation).

The most common solution is deregulation and additional labour flexibility.   Western democracies have reversed many of their earlier welfare state policies.   Over the last 30 years they have returned to a more market led model (aptly named neo-classical).   Neo-liberal politics have redefined government spending priorities.   There is a lower priority given to the maintenance of public infrastructure.   This is evidenced by declining schools, hospitals and roads.   The welfare state has, in essence, become embroiled in a tug of war between the system of production and social reproduction.   Those in charge of production attack social reproduction viciously, in order to win the battle at the point of production.   This is why public services are cut.   It pushes the burden of care onto individual families.   By cutting social care the entire working class is vulnerable and less able to resist attacks on its workplace.   In many western countries, somewhat paradoxically, opposition is generally anticipated by today's politicians.   Politicians can generally ignore the opposition - provided they are not economic and social actors deemed critical to their re-election.   In any respect, the latest economic cycle of the 1990s and 2000s has not been met by the same level of resistance as that in the past.

Despite market led policies, wealth generation has been somewhat confined to key sectors.   This includes new technologies (for example, information technology).   For westerners, success in business is now hard to come by. Money has become commerce rather than a public utility enabling commerce (witness the rise of the financial sector).   So large numbers are driven to Wall Street and the City of London, where they seek profits from arbitrage and speculation.   Chief executives pump up share prices.   Fund managers demand that managers hit their quarterly earnings targets. These measures stifle innovation and buoy wealth inequality. Many people are left rolling the dice in hopes of a big score. There are bound to be some winners, many losers and an outcome of increased wealth inequality.

3.9 Inequality

Slowdown in productivity growth has been a major contributor to wage stagnation in the West. In spite of this, household and family incomes have continued to increase. This has almost entirely been associated with longer working hours for worker's partners. Even when living standards are rising they're typically uneven. Different classes use time and resources more efficiently. Just as they exploit different freedoms and opportunities, costs and benefits fall differentially. At the top, workers have more freedom, while those at the bottom work longer shifts and more unsocial hours.

In Henry Ford's time, competition and shaving away costs was seen as necessary within business. Now, more attention is given to excellence and innovation and the wider conditions needed for it to flourish. The acceleration of technological development also means it's harder to keep up. Every time a transformative invention took hold over the past two centuries — whether the steamboat in the 1820s, locomotive in the 1850s, the telegraph or the telephone — businesses would disappear and workers would lose jobs. Yet new businesses would emerge that employed even more.

In the last few decades the 'information economy' has dominated. The introduction of the internet has allowed the location of information work to move 'anywhere.' That means 'location' in the information technology revolution isn't as important. This is at least not in theory. Like past cycles of creative destruction, there is no doubt it has destroyed existing jobs, redefined some but created others.

Yet the rise of computer technology poses a threat that earlier generations of machines didn't. The old machines replaced human brawn but created jobs that needed human brains. The new machines threaten both. The vast majority of people do routine work and the human economy has always demanded routine work. The potential is for machines to take away all these routine jobs, with far fewer opportunities left for ordinary workers.

This can be appreciated when successful IT companies are considered. Apple employs 80,000 people worldwide. It's not only a spectacularly profitable creator of innovative products, but a successful retailer too. The company does not, however, manufacture the iPads, iPhones, iPods, and so forth that it creates and sells. It's focused on creation and distribution but not production of item merchandise. Google, employing 54,000 and Facebook, 4,300 are other examples. Combined, those three superstar companies employ less than a quarter of the 600,000 people General Motors had in the 1970s. And today, GM employs just 202,000 people, while making more cars than ever.

Merrill Lynch (2015) has reported that a 'robot revolution' will transform the global economy over the next 20 years. The potential impact of robotics is immense. Offshoring manufacturing jobs to low-cost economies can save up to 65% on labour costs. Replacing human workers with robots, however, saves up to 90%. According to Oxford University research, up to 35% of all workers in the UK and 47% in the United States are at risk of being displaced by technology over the next 20 years. The vast majority of workers won't be able to learn the skills needed to outrun 'job-killing' computers and robots (Beijia Ma, 2015).

The service economy polarises those engaged in the symbolic analysis of information against those with casualised jobs. The former will have a 'busy but nice life' living in suburbs. The latter represent an underclass. They don't know how to use information technology or make products out of it. Generally they live downtown, use public transport and have a tough time.

In Europe, it is estimated that one-quarter of private wealth is held by the richest 1 per cent; in America, the richest 1 per cent hold one-third. This wealth has ballooned, relative to national income, in countries where growth is slow. The share held by the rich has risen in most nations over recent decades.

Prior to the Davos 2014 'get together' of the world's rich and powerful, at a ski resort set in Switzerland, Charity Oxfam raised concerns over inequality. The elite have rigged laws in their own favour, undermined democracy and created a chasm of inequality across the globe. For instance, they note that, 'since the late 1970s, tax rates for the richest have fallen in 29 of the 30 countries for which data are available. This means that in many places the rich not only get more money but also pay less tax on it.' Policies have been successfully imposed by the rich in recent decades. These include financial deregulation, tax havens and secrecy, anti-competitive business practice, lower tax rates on high incomes and investments and cuts or underinvestment in public services for the majority. According to Oxfam, inequality has run out of control. The 85 richest people on the planet 'own the wealth of half the world's population.' The report exposes the 'pernicious impact' of growing inequality. This helps the richest to 'undermine democratic processes and drive policies that promote their interests at the expense of everyone else.'

There's always been a spatial aspect to this. Trotsky (Marxist revolutionary and theorist; 1879 - 1940) noted capitalism's constant reproduction of spatial inequalities and unequal relationships in different settings. What he was saying in effect was that while many people's life in cities might be easier, the system as a whole was making survival harder for others. This could be in the inner city and suburbs of the Western World. Or it could be between different regions (such as that between cosmopolitan London and former industrial cities of the North West). Or it could be between the First and Third World. This sets the scene for mass migration. In China, millions of surplus agricultural labourers have moved to coastal areas. They form the back bone of the migrant labour force, in what is termed the 'Special Economic Zones.' Otherwise they are left to marginal vocations, or worse. Such floating populations are estimated to be as much as 200 million people.

Inequality has recently emerged as a major concern in countries around the world. The government in China has recently cracked down on the elite perks and privileges. Germany has adopted a minimum wage (2014) while Finland is trialling a universal basic income (2016). The universal basic income can help individuals increase their participation in creative activities, democratic processes and make a transition to new skill sets. It may also reduce administration costs. Even the World Economic Forum (WEF), which organises the Davos talkfest, warned in 2014 of the growing gulf between the rich and the poor. This represented the biggest global risk. It stated that 'the chronic gap between the incomes of the richest and poorest citizens is most likely to cause serious damage globally in the coming decade.' Ironically, many of the corporate giants and world leaders that conferred at Davos, were implicitly being pointed at by Oxfam.

4.0 The New Community

Capitalism, as Marx noted, unsettles every aspect of human life. The 'landed aristocracy,' originating from the Middle Ages, fell from their position of power and over time they were replaced. Firstly, by the industrialists and secondly by the new cosmopolitan class. This parallels how monopolist companies fall to new technologies.

The effect on the working classes has been even more startling. There has been a shift from Durkheim's mechanical solidarity to an organic solidarity. This is one in which individuals are dependent upon each other as a result of the division of labour. Just as the meaning of work has changed as a result of technological progress, each generation has become defined by the new jobs. During the industrialising era, work quickly became dictated by mechanical periodicity i.e., clock and calendar. This resulted in the burgeoning urban population's diminished relationship to natural cycles. It also resulted in their disassociation from the natural world. Also, the change to less physical types of work has eroded traditional male advantages of physical strength. Changed work practices also changed the home. With competition and greater mobility came changes to family life, as workers needed to travel. They would leave home at dawn to go to the factory, mine, mill, or increasingly the office. As a result they spent less time with their families.

Finally, modernisation is the great unsettler. It destroys national cultures and replaces them with a universal, homogeneous culture of industrial production. The logic of economic development thus spells the end for local and non-industrialised cultures. This is something documented as much under communism as democratic nations. Stalin's modernisation of the Soviet Union, in the 1930s, caused a rapid mass movement of people from the countryside to towns. The resulting networks, ideas, communication and flood of information was tantamount to the formation of a new society (Alen and Crow, 2000). Mahatma Gandhi described India's soul as residing in the village. Yet the country's more recent rulers have sought to promote unrestricted modernisation. China's culture was traditionally rural-based but modernisation is, again, threatening that too. Many believe that once its villages are gone the culture will be gone too. Rapid urbanisation means village life, the bedrock of Chinese culture, is rapidly disappearing. Along with this goes its traditions and history (Feng Jicai; 2014).

There's a pervasive tendency to explain societal changes as technologically based. Yet there are also important sociological aspects. The way in which work is valued in western society is a case in point. As with GDP, workers get lumped together. This is regardless of whether they're productive, unproductive or based in a different sector. A key difference is the distinction between paid and unpaid work. The logic of capitalism marginalises unwaged workers, as such work has no economic value.

Yet overall productivity of any community does not depend solely on those paid directly for their work. Workers themselves are produced and reproduced outside of capitalist production. That is in a 'kin-based' site called the family. Labour power, in the main, is reproduced by three interconnected processes:

1. By activities that *regenerate* the worker outside the production process and allow him or her to return to it. These include, among a host of others, food, a bed to sleep in, but also care in psychical ways, that keep a person whole.

2. By activities that maintain and regenerate *non-workers* outside the production process. These can be future or past workers. It includes children and adults out of the workforce for whatever reason; be it old age, disability or unemployment.

3. By reproducing *fresh workers*, meaning childbirth.

Paid workers rely on support of others including volunteers, family support and the like. Social reproduction theory, described by Meg Luxton (Professor of Sociology), explains how the 'production of goods and services and the production of life are part of one integrated process'. The formal economy is the production site for goods and services. The people who produce such things are themselves produced outside the ambit of the formal economy. Generally, this occurs at little cost for capital.

A concern about the pursuit of economic efficiency is that it ignores and marginalises the needs of certain sections of the community. The production of goods and services tends to dominate the sphere of reproduction. When a community lessens the importance of such support, and marginalises those who give it, this inevitably creates divisive tensions and cuts overall productiveness. For instance, women's needs around childcare are by definition non-profit making. As such, they become marginalised as merely 'social.' Women become mere 'consumers of the city.' GDP would have been raised by 26%, in 2010, if unpaid domestic work was included in it (Forbes Magazine).

4.1 Consumerism

Mass consumption has had a profound impact on society. It's associated with the introduction of labour saving devices in the home. The term can perhaps be traced back to the 1851 London Exhibition Centre. This was the first large scale showcasing of goods associated with mass production.

Producers have to be able to advertise and sell products across countries. This means reaching potential customers through mass media. This doesn't just mean the same goods and services are available everywhere. It also means that people everywhere begin to want more of the same goods and services. Advertising (linked these days to a celebrity culture) supported the ideal of mass consumption. In the post war era, it promoted the private suburban dwelling which maximised the use of appliance purchases. The occupants of the suburbs were suggestible but consumer credit and home ownership also played their part.

Society has certainly benefited materially from increased goods. Until now this has been as a result of better food, health systems and lowered risk. While birth rates were high and the average age of mortality increased, the population increased. The transition to the leisure society, however, results in couples with far fewer kids. Children are no longer deemed a valuable commodity due to the need for people with skills to work, that in turn need educating. Pressures to put off childbirth, and for women to go back to work sooner after a birth, are all symptoms of both an individualistic society and one without basic support systems.

When people live longer it results in an ageing population. Funded by elites, gene therapy and other life extending biotechnologies may enable the extension of the human lifespan artificially. In the end, elderly people in a society become supported by too few workers. Immigrants with the skill sets associated with caring must be brought in.

Under consumerism, there is a sense in which the goods themselves tend to acquire social meanings. Commentators have noted that in our society, to participate in the consumption of goods, is to join in society itself. There are also profound cultural changes, with Christmas and children becoming linked to consumerism. Ascription of social significance to products may help to produce societal stability. Yet this is only while the system can increase the rate of goods so that enough people take part in the social game of consumption. The recent UK riots in 2011 showed the fickle nature of such a society.

Consumerism also creates competition and conflict for resources. In advanced, capitalist societies housing gets treated as a commodity. For instance, rising incomes induce people to want to live in bigger houses, and own more than one. Society is getting wealthier over time. This means that house prices will rise. That occurs even if the number of households does not increase, unless the number of houses increases at the same time. Demand for services as diverse as highways to electricity supplies increase over time too. Pressure is put on infrastructure at key times. There are many examples. It may be the strain on electrical networks caused by people watching a particular sports game on TV. Another example is when we all drive to work at the same time of day. It creates road congestion and reduces the accessibility to areas of high demand, such as the central city.

With spending power comes the demand for time off work to enjoy the sorts of goods one has purchased. Legislating for such time off had a major impact on society. Sir John Lubbock introduced the 1871 Bank Holidays Act in the UK which gave bank workers a chance to watch a day's cricket. Day trippers, hoping to get out of London, soon overwhelmed Charing Cross and Fenchurch Street train stations. Leisure time also has ramifications for private space and public networks. Rising incomes induced Victorians to go to the theatre and take more holidays.

4.2 Individualism

Some form of temporal order constitutes a powerful basis of solidarity within a group or society, as Sir Lubbock was well aware. Economic growth and automation were predicted by many commentators in the 1970s. Even earlier, science-fiction writers had suggested we'd be living in a 'leisure society.' Yet the benefits of socialisation for society as a whole have been eroded in the modern world. This has been due to trends associated with technology and economic efficiency.

Technology enables communities to move to new orders with more diverse and distributed social connections. In the guise of providing consumers with 'choice' came the shift towards the 24 hour society. This reduces the likelihood of people meeting at the same time and space (particularly in their local context). TV consumes a large amount of an individual's time each day and reduces interaction between family members. Robert Putnam (US political scientist) calculated that TV is responsible for a 25% drop in social interaction.

Technology results in the 'atomisation of society.' This is associated with the loss of social bonding that occurs through shared events which bring people together and give them something in common. Mobile and communication technology promote the shift from place-based communities to communities of interest. In theory, the world is rapidly becoming a single community - a global village. Yet what is most striking is the rise of communities of interest. They operate across spatial scales and engage politically through representative or special interest groups. People are more mobile, diverse and less constrained in expressing difference. Individuals have numerous other opportunities, distractions and resources. These allow relative independence from place, local relations or other ties. So people are more able to ignore local or group sanctions. Community no longer comes to stand for the local population.

As industrial processes increase, people's dissociation with the outside world increases. The internet generation doesn't feel the same way as older people about the real (spatial) world. This has implications for the city including a lack of interest in heritage and the like. Finally, the impact of automation and reliance on IT products will, in the future, end the need for a significant amount of human labour. Rather than the leisure society that was once expected, instead they merely become a cause of unemployment. That raises awkward issues for society in the future. It's considered bad that the masses once had to do menial tasks for the aristocracy. It will be even worse if there is no need for their services to begin with.

4.3 Materialism

There is a postmodern propensity to form market niches in urban lifestyle choices, consumer habits and cultural forms. The market gives freedom of choice, provided you have enough money. People take part in a consumer society through markets. These include labour or credit, services (access to health, education) and spaces (for example political, physical). Such freedom does not necessarily translate into responsibility. Freedom's greatest trade-off is arguably the social side of life including relationships, promises and trust.

Post-war suburbanisation of the United States was intended to absorb surplus production and keep the economy growing. In doing so it entailed a radical transformation in lifestyles and produced a whole new way of life. New products ranged from suburban tract housing to refrigerators and air conditioning, two cars on the driveway and huge oil consumption. This logic resulted in an addiction to materialism or 'affluenza.' Consumption becomes the purpose of economic activity. It allows us to meet our material aspirations in the pursuit of happiness. In the end, it is vastly different from the notion of living within our means (Giles, 2013).

There are differences in social cohesion. One type is based on 'lasting and genuine forms of living together' where 'co-ordinated action is done for the common good' (described as Gemeinschaft). This is compared to 'association,' where individuals engage in 'artificial' relations for their own ends. This is through the market (for example, trade associations) or the state (for example, political associations) described as Gesellschaft by Tonnies (1988).

Economics has invaded almost every decision made in advanced consumer societies. This includes choosing a spouse in the same way we buy car insurance or incentivising blood donors to save lives. Other examples are those free riding enterprises that ignore the environment or selling one's own body parts to buy an iPad (Roscoe, 2014). The change in thought patterns associated with the shift to the new consumer economy has altered our receptivity to thinking about others. This spills over into our support for charity and the third sector. Both religious and secular charities are having to resort to the same salesman-like advertising techniques as those selling consumer products.

In having satisfied western societies' basic needs, people rarely experience real body-weakening poverty or genuine life-threatening danger. Yet our expectations have correspondingly risen. This results in far more work-related stress today than ever before. Such stress can be constant. It's the reason the French Government is considering legislation to ban out of hours' emails (reported May 2016). With time at a premium, there is reduced tolerance when things go wrong. This leads us to lash out and rage about relatively inconsequential and trivial events. It encompasses violent overreactions such as road rage incidents. It also includes outbursts over trivial details such as whether a restaurant meal is warm enough, or how much company bosses get paid (Mann, 2013 and Richardson & Halliwell 2008). Many homes in the West have become so full of 'stuff' that it has spawned de-cluttering experts. Japan's Marie Kondo is one who advises clients how best to keep only what is necessary and organise it in the most space-saving way.

4.4 Secularisation

Modernisation, consumerism and even urban connectivity itself has weakened the power of institutional religion. Churches no longer have a monopoly over defining the beliefs shared by society as a whole. Since the French Revolution, there has been a significant marginalisation of ecclesiastical institutions. Science, particularly in the West, has played its role. Darwin's theory of evolution affected how many people saw religion; particularly perceived contradictions between scientific theories and scripture. Yet, the theory of evolution is less a blow to theology in scientific matters but a radical theological reorientation. It has reduced the expectation that science can be done in a way where there is any intention to enter the mind of God. Divine and human knowledge differ in kind, not degree.

Cities have long freed people from social convention and traditional social mores (Glaser, 2012). Villages can impose rules because people who break them can be cut off from social connection and suffer the pain of solitude. Morality tends to get in the way of the creativity of bohemians and restricting choices is seen to close off economic opportunities.

In a practical sense, the main reason for the decline of religion in the West is the lack of time to join in it. Unlike individualistic spirituality, religion is a social activity. Secularisation creates more issues for society than just reduced congregational attendance and inability to maintain fine Cathedrals and Church buildings. It challenges societal cohesion. That is the nebulas concept, which according to the government-commissioned, State of the English Cities thematic reports, includes five different dimensions. These are material conditions, passive relationships, active relationships, inclusion and equality.

Kant set out to answer how in a bourgeois society self-interest can be pursued by heteronomic individuals while nonetheless maintaining 'coherence' (i.e. the expanded reproduction of society). Andre Gorz (1994), French social philosopher and journalist, asked whether a society could perpetuate itself without direction, orientation, aim or hope. Can it perpetuate itself when its permanent obsession of economic performance and efficiency, has the supreme goal of an excess of comfort?

Others see it differently. For Herbert Spencer, the English liberal and social Darwinist (1820 – 1903), market relations were enough to hold society together. At its core, social cohesion is about relationships. So individualism is a failure of societies' members talking and relating to each other. This is reflected in the growth of those who believe they are spiritual but not religious. People would prefer a reassuring set of beliefs that make them feel better about their own life. That is instead of being challenged to help others or make the world a better place.

Lord Jonathan Sacks (British Rabbi, philosopher and Judaism scholar; 2013) notes how the growth of individualism, over the past 50 years, has been responsible for a pervasive breakdown in trust. 'When trust breaks down, you see institutions break down,' he continued. 'If people work for the maximum possible benefit for themselves, then we will not have trust in industry, in economics, in financial institutions or even our marriages.' Everyone is out to get what they can. Society ends up with envy and division, or worse still, crisis. The dysfunctional diversity of talented individuals maximising their productivity is a beacon for immigrants. Yet those not doing as well are worse off than ever. It shouldn't be forgotten that inequality also reduces social glue. The lack of 'Gemeinschaft' type relationships in society increase our dependence on government.

4.5 Urbanisation

Urbanisation has come to stand for artificiality and a means to escape everyday existence. Yet electric lights are not a full substitute for sunlight. Nor are packaged or processed foods a full substitute for fresh ingredients. The urban draw seems counterintuitive. The spread of high-speed internet and smartphones offer everyone the same access to global culture. Yet social media is clearly not a full substitute for face to face meetings.

The attractions of urbanisation are not always strictly logical. Today consumers are willing to pay for a constant stream of new, high-end experiences which are typically found in big cities. It's impossible to put a price on popular culture; sit-coms, hip-hop, blogging, nightclubbing with their message of being and staying cool. Wanting to live out what's dramatised hourly on computer and television screens is a powerful inducement. What's essential to the neurotic buzz of 24/7 cable news, Twitter, Snapchat and Facebook is an assumption by those who use them. It has to be assumed that those around them have the same time to devote to respond to their messages. They assume that others are not too busy farming sheep, fishing on the high seas, or extracting iron ore from a mine (Davis, 2015).

There is a thirst for new activities, experiences and recreational activities. It is therefore both a substitute and challenge for religion. The problem may be that urbanites have no answers for the existential challenges. They find psychological refuge in obsessing over the trivial. Fredric Jameson, an American literary critic and Marxist political theorist, described postmodern city dwellers as feeling alienated and living in a hallucination. It's an exhilarating blur filled with image addiction. More recently, urban dwellers have experienced greater anxiety related to the phenomena of 'childhood captivity.' This arises from exaggerated health and safety fears and over-protective parents. There are a rising number of people reporting psychological problems. These are due not just to better reporting but also the modern urban lifestyle, despite the benefits from psychological health care. It should, in theory, give clients and society at large the best advice available.

The end result is a city like London. Its a platform for wealth generation on a world scale, but also a place where people do not talk to their neighbours. They identify with largely non-spatial networks of people with common interests and operate in informal territory within 'action spaces.' Identity becomes more focused around the specifics of lifestyle, locality and ethnic group. All associated activity reflects this.

4.6 Politics

Changing attitudes, described above, feed through into the political system. The decades following the Second World War were sometimes known as The Age of Consensus. The maintenance of social peace and prosperity remained the No 1. political aim of both Centre-Left and Centre-Right. The manifestation of widespread social or political dissent was regarded as a direct threat to the prevailing bipartisan consensus. Politicians therefore responded quickly (and often favourably) to protesters' demands.

The pursuit of progress and the unsettling effect of capitalism place social cohesion at stake. Democratic government becomes seen as a periodic allocation of power to a minority of people who seek to rule others. Elections are reduced to what individuals think they can get out of the electoral bargains promised by politicians. Individualism has increased alienation, apathy and indifference within the democratic process. It gives rise to forces that can dislocate traditional bonds, fragment societies and reinforce conflict and division. Freedom becomes associated less with political status and more with greater spending power. Marxist societies were far from being renown for freedoms but their commentators did make some observations of liberal nations. Their so-called 'political and religious freedoms' are hollow, if one did not have the economic freedom to support oneself.

The effect this has on civic society and the democratic system itself is represented in lower voter turnout. Societal fragmentation has broken down any consensus about what human life is for. The only criteria left for political success is an ever increasing standard of life. That is, more consumer goods within secure, national borders.

The social levelling effect of post-war consensus politics were not allowed to undermine the power and persuasiveness of capitalism itself. Under neoliberalist governments,[5] the majority would need to learn to be

---

[5] Including Thatcher's (UK) and Reagan's (United States).

disappointed. Democracy depends on some balance of property ownership. It is threatened by inequality of resource allocation, as groups seek to take resources from others. Those that can fund extensive media campaigns have the edge which undermines the legitimacy of the resulting government.

Commentators[6] saw that in the end only the state can hold society together. The state needs to act as a moral force in promoting core values. The socialist underpinning of the left has traditionally seen its primary concerns as equity and a redistribution of wealth. It is noted though, that once in power, this aspiration is harder to put into practice. Even the Soviet Union was not a classless society. Gerber and Hout (2004) found that social origin played a role in opportunity and status during the Soviet period. The main characteristics that shaped class standing during the Soviet era were Communist Party membership/ position of authority and expertise, skill and ability. Ten percent of the adult population were Communist Party members, Gerber, 2000. These factors decide class standing, access to material possessions and wealth. This social standing was then passed on to children.

4.7 Response of the New Left towards the Outworkings of Capitalism

The Soviet state's crack down on dissident countries[7] disillusioned many in the left wing of western countries with centralised and authoritarian politics. The New Left which emerged post-1968 formed a different agenda. The agenda focused on identity politics, cultural diversity and was built on new societal niches.

There was broad agreement for the post-modernist view[8] that there is no universal truth or single reality. Such thinking has gained widespread influence in academic circles. Drawing from the doctrine of 'nihilism'[9] there emerged new forms, such as existentialism and deconstructionism. These refuse to believe in values and purpose. Instead they contain a preference for emotion ahead of rationality. This concept allows leaders to lie and therefore for society to lose respect in the political process. It ended the debate on what a good society was and generally resulted in any set of ideals.

---

[6] E.g., Auguste Comte (French Philosopher; 1798 – 1857) and Ferdinand Tonnies (German sociologist; 1855-1936).

[7] For example, Hungary 1956.

[8] French Philosopher Michel Foucault is an leading exponent of this view.

[9] Nihilism had suffered a massive setback in the 1940s.

This explains the cultural elites' estrangement from a sense of mission and a lack of clarity about truth with a capital T. Until the 1970s they had operated on the basis that they had a duty to enlighten people. Without a relationship to truth, (academic) knowledge has no intrinsic meaning. The elite's loss of conviction in its own authority is most strikingly reflected in politics. It also has wider implications for professions addressing urban issues. Professions are generally a useful means of holding society together. Yet they can no longer dare claim distinctiveness or superiority. The role of the elite comes to validate and celebrate what society has become.

There are also consequences for the spread of science, technology and progress. Scientists have always been bound to benefit personally from new developments. They are less inclined to know when to stop projects or judge whether innovations will be generally beneficial with a flexible attitude towards values and truth.   In an age where technological change is accelerating, there has been a repeated failure to set up an equivalent Hippocratic Oath for science. This would be where scientists would ban the use of their expertise to do harm. The problem is in attempting to set up an agency to institutionalise it. It would need the moral authority to licence the oath and administer sanctions for violation.

The New Left's most significant legacy on society is its social policy. This was developed during the so called 'Culture Wars' of the 1960s-1980s. Its goal of social inclusion was to address social failures of the market economy and what it saw as causes of public 'intolerance.' This has shaped state relations to stakeholders and planners to the public ever since. It has to be said that this is not a new aspiration. Generations of social reformers, local authorities, and governments have worked to promote a more integrated, cohesive society. The problem is that most of their attempts have failed.

There are three features associated with New Left policy worthy of further comment. The first is that consumerism had eroded traditional class cultures and led to the 'embourgeoisement' of the working class. According to David Burner, one of its founders[10] claimed that the 'proletariat' were no longer the revolutionary force. Instead, the new agent of revolutionary change were young intellectuals around the world. Even earlier, neo-Marxist theorists[11] stated that workers would never see their true class interests (defined by Marxism of course) until they were freed from 'Western Culture.' Religion and culture blind them. The New Left has given up on the old idea of supporting a proletariat take over. That mission is up to the 'new' minorities

---

[10] C. Wright Mills (American sociologist; 1916- 1962)

[11] Antonio Gramsci and Georg Lukacs.

of favour. They still typically reside in inner city environments. Those in the countryside, such as gypsy and travellers, or workers stuck out beyond the suburbs are of less interest. Social inclusion is the Left's grand response theory to capitalism and globalisation. It allows it to bring various marginalised groups out to fight capitalism.

The second feature was the New Left's long-standing quarrel with the traditional Left's base–superstructure narrative. This was based on reductionism and economicism. It was recognised that the cultural and ideological domain was the one in which social change appeared to be most dramatically visible. This manifested itself in the shift of focus away from the poor, to put 'culture' at the centre of politics.

A third, related feature of the New Left was expanding the political-science denotation of hegemony (dominance). It needed to include the cultural domination by a ruling class of a socially stratified society. The ruling class can manipulate the dominant ideology (cultural values and mores) of society, to intellectually dominate the other social classes with an imposed world view (Weltanschauung). This world view was seen as justifying the social, political, and economic status quo of the society. It was as if it were a natural, normal, inevitable and perpetual state of affairs that always has been so.

To the New Left the cultural dimension seems not a secondary, but a constitutive dimension of society. In the US for instance, it proved a useful counter to the one size fits all conformity culture of 'corporate identity.' This had been overtaking rugged individualism in the post war era (Whyte, 1956).

In the advanced states the increase of social pluralism and lifestyle diversity is largely a product of globalisation. Yet in practice it has been reinforced by the New Left philosophies on social policy. The redefinition of 'politics' has put in its place an 'expanded conception of the political.' Its modern social inclusive policies, which seek to address the divisions thrown up by capitalism, are converging. They first shape public taste to the point it becomes standardised and in the end controlled.

The spatial dimensions of privilege, hierarchy and non-hierarchical pan-confederations are often ignored. In terms of the New Left, Henri Lefebvre's[12] ideas informed the Paris uprising in May 1968. This was in part a reaction to the changing residential geography of Paris's workers. Supporters of the New Left have typically heralded from inner city environments. They have become the inheritors of the former 'class struggles.' In capital cities they give the movement political leverage.

---

[12] French Marxist philosopher and sociologist; 1901 - 1991

'Rootless cosmopolitans,' they are ironically more at home in the socially anonymous, metropolitan city culture created by capitalism. Their preference is for a community of interest anchored in 'no particular place.' It's maybe no coincidence that the New Left is relentless in attacking concepts based on local non-cosmopolitan communities. Bauman (2001) provides a good example. He considered these communities as havens for repression, intra-group conflict, lack of privacy and a stifling and normalising effect on [ironically] individuals. The New Left are equally opposed to suburban living. The stronger sense of community is viewed as middle-class communities having greater resources at their disposal.

Unlike earlier ideologies of The Left that ran from a text book, the new version is arguably less certain. It depends upon a power struggle between minorities. They are less inclined to seek a crisis. They are content at working within existing power structures to apply a pluralist management approach. The result is random, contradictory negotiated outcomes with the only constant being the necessity of big government to intervene. Such a system does not necessarily guarantee a fairer society. Without any moral understanding, one can't legitimise which groups fit best. There is nothing particularly virtuous about minorities per se. The tyranny of elitist minorities in recent war torn Syria or Iraq is evidence of this. The effect of the New Left's struggle is not the end of inequality but to flip the table on out-groups. Now those who disrespect the former out-group become themselves the new out-group. In producing new foci for identity and engagement they actively challenge older forms of social cohesion.

After many decades in action, this approach continues to have its detractors. Some should in theory be supportive. Sacks (2013), noted that multiculturalism in Britain has 'had its day.' It has led to 'segregation and inward looking communities.' He likened it to a hotel where 'nobody is at home.' He added: 'It doesn't belong to anyone, we've each got our own room and so long as we don't disturb the neighbours we can do whatever we like.' American cities and schools are now more segregated along racial lines than they were in the 1960s. This is despite decades of effort to promote integration. Perhaps the most damning evidence has come from Putnam (2007). His research had discovered lowered trust in areas with high diversity including:

- Lower confidence in local government, local leaders and the local news media.
- Lower political efficacy – that is, confidence in one's own influence.

- Lower frequency of registering to vote. More interest and knowledge about politics and more participation in protest marches and social reform groups;
- Higher political advocacy, but lower expectations that it will bring about a desirable result.
- Less expectation that others will cooperate to solve dilemmas of collective action. An example is voluntary conservation to ease a water or energy shortage.
- Less likelihood of working on a community project.
- Less likelihood of giving to charity or volunteering.
- Fewer close friends and confidants.
- Less happiness and lower perceived quality of life.
- More time spent watching television. Increased agreement that 'television is my most important form of entertainment.'

By seeking to opt out of 'one rule for all' (universalism), the doctrine of diversity takes a culture away from social inclusion. Rather, it heads towards ever greater fragmentation. In the end, the values being sought are unlikely to reform culture, ensure societal cohesion or any such thing. At worst, it creates a culture of fear and mistrust – destroying loyalties and a communities' ability of its members to relate to one another. Tolerance, that key virtue of the New Left, does not suggest any desire for interaction or pursuance of a common purpose. It merely results in a hollow culture, when anything can become what you like and society remains bereft as to what culture should be.

In the end, the goal of neo-liberal economists is for worker's wages and living standards to be driven down. They should align with the rising standards in China and India. The New Left's preoccupation with 'diversity' has failed as a counteracting force to individualism. The workforce of the world appears increasingly 'proletariat,' but sadly no longer thinks or behaves as if it is.

5.0 The Normative Approach

How people live together, relate to their environment and define a good or bad decision, is arguably the foundation stone of law. Since the enlightenment various thinkers[13] have believed that a free society depends on a moral and

---

[13] For example, Benjamin Franklin 1706- 1790, one of America's founding fathers, and Adam Smith.

virtuous people. The Liberal West is aligned with the regimes of communism and fascism as seeing economic progress as the primary imperative. Soviet Russia's preoccupation with its own success came with a blatant disregard for the social dimension (Lewin, 2015). There had to be a redistribution of wealth, but the social side of communities was largely ignored. Society was viewed more or less as if it was putty. This contributed to the neglect of the deep structural changes in its society. Knowing these is crucial to understanding its achievements, change, crises' and downfall.

In Hayek's Great Society,[14] all can relate to each other but not through agreement on moral ends. Rather they do so through agreement about means. For example, if we agree to live by the market we shouldn't complain if it delivers unpalatable outcomes. This goes someway to explain the 'anything goes' society of Western cosmopolitan cities.

The New left have also undermined the basis on which elites can make judgments. Authorities in the Liberal West therefore suffer from an all embracing scepticism about making normative judgements. This is not surprising given its pre-occupation with market economics and identity politics. Bodies that do criticise on this basis are quickly labelled as paternalistic. As such, moral and political philosophies tend to be fragmented, incoherent, and conflicting (MacIntyre, 1981). Such little thought is given to moral progress that it goes hand in hand with material progress. Rather than the state seeking to improve the people, a democracy is supposed to do what the people want. For most, the only realistic agreement is for a higher standard of living.

The one area where western society has sought social outcomes beyond higher standards of living is in human rights. These are inherently supposed to be based on universal values. In practice they often get carried out as a 'living' concept by activist judges. So they have expanded from liberal conceptions of individual rights into group rights, on the basis of societal changes. There's a distinction between so-called natural rights or civil liberties and human rights. Natural rights are freedom from the state. Human rights are protection by the state. Typically the latter mean that people are deemed irrational and need state intervention.

There is little debate over the desirability of a core set of human rights. This includes the right to life, liberty, privacy and banning slavery, genocide, murder, torture, prolonged arbitrary detention, and systematic racial discrimination. These rights have become part of international customary law. They are not contested in the public rhetoric of the international arena. Of

---

[14] Friedrich Hayek (1899 – 1992). His Great Society was a representation of the market economy.

course many gross violations occur off the record. Human rights groups such as Amnesty International have the task of exposing the difference between public allegiance to rights and the reality. This is, however, largely practical work.

Political thinkers and activists around the world can and do take different sides on concerns falling outside a 'minimal and universal moral code' (Walzer 1987, 24; Walzer 1994). Some people may accept that they should not do anything to harm others (negative freedom). But they don't have an interest in doing anything to help others either. This grey area of debate includes: criminal law, family law, women's rights, social and economic rights, the rights of indigenous peoples, and the attempt to universalise Western-style democratic practices.

Human rights has shifted into giving certain groups in society priority over others. This is not-with-standing the fact that there is little agreement as to what extended human rights should be between different cultures. Standards of justice found in the forms of life and traditions of different societies vary from context to context. When a standard is applied in a new context this may not be accepted. For instance, Asian people often consider that the interests of society should take precedence over that of the individual. This was said by Singapore's first Prime Minister, Lee Kuan Yew (1923 – 2015), who governed for three decades. Asians therefore place a special emphasis on family and social harmony. They would rather articulate for their own long-term interest than follow the path of individualism. Yew considered that this was leading to chaotic and crumbling societies found in the West.

Some approaches to human rights are going to be better than others. Deciding which is better needs robust debate. There remain difficulties, in the West, about making normative judgements and who in particular, might be qualified to do so. Yet such views are a relatively new concern. Aristotle (Greek philosopher 384- 322BC) thought that the responsibility of a ruler was to enable people to live a good life. They should therefore take a moral view of what they were doing. Back in The East, the Chinese government has been attempting to tackle the results of unbridled progress by ordering a 'thorough clean-up' of undesirable work styles. These, according to state newswire Xinhua, include formalism, bureaucracy, hedonism and extravagance. The General Secretary, Xi Jinping, was quoted as saying that to combat decadence, members of the Chinese Communist Party should be striving toward four goals. These are self-purification, self-perfection, self-renewal and self-progression. Hu Jintao's (Chinese politician) fatherly advice, in the form of eight do's and don'ts, was seen as an antidote to the corruption and cynicism spreading across China (refer to Part IV with respect to Corruption). It's a result of the often raw capitalism that has emerged during 25 years of dramatic economic change. Hu's 'Eight Do's and Eight don'ts admonish people to uphold civic harmony and combat hedonism. They should not make 'selfish gains to the detriment of others' or 'wallow in luxuries and pleasures.'

A State's positive role in guaranteeing social justice and suppressing moral and social chaos is best described as corporatism. The Swedish Social Democrats came up with a form of 'corporatism' after the Second World War. Rather than nationalising the means of production, as under communism, the government instead made sure there was fair distribution of private-sector profits and equality for all. It did mean overriding some individual freedoms. The Swedish economy is still characterised by a very high concentration of capital among a handful of companies. Some of the best known are Volvo, Electrolux, Ericsson, Saab-Scania, Hasselblad and IKEA (seen as being able to be competitive in export markets). Yet their capital and business taxes are not significantly higher than those of the United States.

Most of the economies of the world are corporatist in nature. The categories of socialist and pure market economy are almost empty. There are only corporatist economies of various forms. These include the social democratic regimes of Europe and the Americas. They also include the East Asian and Islamic fundamentalist regimes; such as Taiwan, Singapore and Iran. The Islamic socialist states, such as Algeria, are more corporatist than socialist. This was also the case in Iraq under Saddam Hussain and Syria before the start of the 2011 civil war. The formerly communist regimes of Russia and China are now clearly corporatist in economic philosophy, although not in name.

Morality has traditionally been defined by a code. This is acted upon by the individual in treating others with respect, even when one is materially in need. Started by Christianity, morality has been defined and bound up around religious authority. Religion offers a bond between individuals and it helps them form a connection to the wider universe. 'Moral progress' has been usurped by secular authorities (Gray, 2007). The welfare state itself represents the secularisation of control over assistance. As such, much of the individual reforming zeal has been institutionalised. It is now expressed in the voices of professional organisations and local authority committees, if at all. In many countries the effect of institutionalisation was cushioned. In these instances, the welfare system was only professionalised to the degree it did not affect existing institutional networks (Van der Heijden, 2012).

The law is territorial in the secular west and no source of authority higher than the intangible assets that its people share can be invoked. This 'monopoly on morality' within the public arena sidelines participation by religious groups. The liberal state's commitment to dialogue is only to the 'ideal of public reason.' This means, roughly, that citizens in their public capacity can only engage one another in terms of reasons. These reasons are defined as only those considered to be shared. So political reasoning can only go ahead in terms of public reasons. Reasons based upon the interpretation of sacred text are non-public. Their force as reasons relies upon faith commitments. John Rawls[15] illustrated this through a Venn diagram. The public political values will be the shared space. Upon this overlaps numerous reasonable, comprehensive doctrines.

This of course potentially represents a failure of those in power to understand religion. Science is undoubtedly powerful in its applications. Yet rationality is generally recognised as having bounds. A distinction can be drawn between irrationality and trans-rationality. Conversely it's true to say that public spheres still depend on reserves of meaning. For example, the faith of investors plays the same role that bank gold did, without ever being checked by anyone. If that broke down, triggering a run on removing bank savings, then the wider economy would be placed in peril.

Religion need not be placed in the seat of power, as it tends to operate best from sidelines such as where there is a separation of Church from State. It generally has important lessons to teach on progress, consumerism, usury and unrestricted lending. St Francis of Assisi (1181 or 1183 – 1226) attacked the dualism of nature-society which allows for its exploitation. Middle-class morality in the 19th Century defended consumerism and the consumption of new goods. Inequality and the acquisition of a bourgeoisie lifestyle were justified so long as they were achieved with hard work. People like John Ruskin[16] were not above critiquing consumerism given Biblical stories, such as the 'Tower of Babel' (in Genesis).

The struggle for equality caught on more in egalitarian societies than those defined by inequality. This is an age where old moral certainties have collapsed and thinking about right and wrong, good or bad is more confused than ever. Communities will have to look beyond government for guidance.

---

[15] American liberal political philosopher (1921 - 2002).

[16] Leading art critic and social thinker of the Victorian era (1819 – 1900).

PART II:
THE REASON FOR CITIES

1.0 The Location of Settlements

In Part I the main forces at work on our 'post-industrial' society were outlined. In Part II, I move onto discussing the logic behind settlements and the natural and physical resources upon which they depend.

In the pre-industrial era the location of settlements depended upon proximity to the resources the community needed. These included potable water, fertile soils and agricultural produce. The original location for English villages is a case in point. They were not only formed the same size but were roughly equidistant from each other. Distance varied from county to county according to local prosperity and soil fertility. So, in remote Devon and Cornwall, villages were about six miles apart, whilst in East Anglia and the Midlands, the gap was roughly three miles.

Most cities and towns were located on rivers. Not only did this give water but also a means of transportation. In the medieval era, rivers and estuaries functioned much like modern motorways. The limitations of technology were also a major factor or constraint in the location and size of settlements. London was originally located at the most easterly fordable point on the River Thames, before it became too wide to build a bridge.

There are notable exceptions about the criteria for location. Venice was built in a lagoon. This 'bad location' upon which to build was one that nonetheless offered a form of natural protection to its fleeing inhabitants in the first millennium.

There were other reasons for the location of settlements including political, military and religious. Some settlements became 'symbolic' which in turn reinforced the attraction of living there. Dynamic religious leaders were the inspiration for Canterbury in Kent, where St Augustine picked the spot for his church. In the same way, St Mungo picked the site for what later became Glasgow in Scotland. Generally, however, the spatial substance of cities became heavily dependent on socio-economic activities. The nature of employment was important. The market town, granted such status by the King, was an important means of growth and development during the Latin Middle Ages. Towns and cities during the Middle Ages served those on the countryside not the other way around. The rich may have invested in towns, but they lived in manors set within their rural estates.

The industrial era had a marked effect on human settlements. Again, proximity to resources was the key to investment. Yet the types of resources differed from those in the pre-industrial times. An example of this was having a textile mill next to a river. The German Ruhr, for instance, came to be associated with coalmines and steel mills. This was due to its coal and iron ore deposits. The industrial towns of Birmingham and Manchester came to be associated with canals and coal-fired industries in the same manner.

The journey to work by foot was a constraint to urban growth in the pre-industrial era. Industrialisation didn't change the fact that people still needed to live near to where they worked. Over time, these factories became surrounded by workers' houses, forming a town. These new industrial towns were typically 'densely packed' to enable workers to walk to their place of work. In many cases, new industrial towns were based around the classic single town employer. In other cases, the new industrial towns provided for economies of scale. This is encapsulated in the economist Alfred Marshall's (1842 – 1924) idea of agglomeration. This is where particular trades cluster in particular areas of the city (clustering and congregation). Concentrations, or clusters of economic activity, are often a major driver of efficiency, productivity, innovation and growth; even in the internet age.

Successful settlements kept a balance between both 'housing vs employment' and 'labour vs capital.' Urban density enabled trade and markets. The biggest being the labour market. It also allowed for the co-ordination of capital and labour. The evidence points to the greater the density, the greater the opportunities. The relationship, or lack of it, between capital and labour has significant spatial ramifications. There are plenty of historical examples of the following: (1) capital being forced away by labour conditions, (2) capital seeking alternative sources of labour and finally, (3) the inertia of labour to respond to opportunities.

An example of the first is the shift of capital from the US 'rust belt' to the 'sunbelt' states. This took place during the latter half of the 20th Century. It reflected the power of northern trade unions. The Taft Hartley Act 1947 meant sunbelt 'right-to-work' states had unions with much less bargaining power. Firms could always turn to non-unionised workers. So over time, manufacturers slowly drifted away from the northern 'rust belt' states. This both began the decline of many cities, such as Detroit and started the significant urbanisation of cities such as Houston.

Overcoming the inertia of the labour market has taxed even those states possessing great authority in which to impose change. Soviet leadership wanted to induce labour to migrate east to settle beyond the Urals (Lewin, 2005). Siberia contained an enormous wealth of natural resources. Yet the requisite labour to exploit it was found in existing populated regions. It proved impossible to attract labour from better-off European areas unless good wages and suitable supplies were guaranteed. The poorer, central Asian republics regions had huge labour surpluses. Again the authorities struggled to get people to move because of their profound cultural attachment to their traditional environment.

The story of recent de-industrialisation in the West represents the shift of capital to eastern countries (for example, China). This is a result of the relatively more expensive labour in the West. It has been the catalyst for the mass urbanisation of Shanghai, one of China's largest cities, following the 'Cultural Revolution'. The city was able to absorb labour migration from other regions by taking advantage of the Government's relaxation of its former policy for rural living (Hayes, 2012).

In the post-industrialised world of the West no such level of authority exists. The focus seems to be ensuring the attractiveness of existing cities. Cities have become seen as economic growth machines. Success in inter-urban and inter-regional competition needs investment processes. It also needs key public investment to be orchestrated to occur at the right place and time.

The modern, 'creative' city illustrates that capital can flow just as easily into high wage regions as low wage regions. This has allowed many cities in the West to re-invent themselves from their former industrial legacies. Cities and regions in southern Germany, such as Stuttgart, Frankfurt and Munich, have remained prosperous since the Second World War. They have attracted not only displaced industries from the East, but also foreign investment and high-tech job growth (Hall, 1992). In fact Germans speak of a North South gradient (Nord-Süd Gefaelle), similar to that which exists in England between London and the Northern Cities.

The focus in advanced economies has shifted from access to 'natural resources' to access to skilled labour. Entrepreneurs tend to ask where they can find the best workers. For this reason cities, which are by definition expensive to live in such as New York and San Francisco, continue to stay attractive. Markusen (1996) expresses it this way. Cities are 'sticky places,' in the sense that they attract investment and retain employment.

1.1 From the Village to the Mega City

Cities are associated with higher productivity rates, and hence wealth. In general, the greater the urban density, the more social interaction and convenience are given. They also give something else - opportunity. Villages of Dunbar's number, or smaller towns, may allow inhabitants to 'know' each other. Yet their size may not meet all Maslow's hierarchy of needs (economies of scale do not support civic institutions). Despite condemning the industrial city, Karl Marx and Friedrich Engels noted the benefits that the social change had brought. Pre-industrial villagers were seen to have been 'liberated' from 'the idiocy of rural life.' Engels called this a state of, 'isolation and stupor in which *humankind* has vegetated almost unchanged for thousands of years.' Others have suggested a healthy community is one which is liveable, sustainable, equitable and empowered (Barr and Hashagen, 2000 p23; Marmot and Wilkinson 2001; Wilkinson, D., 1999 and Wilkinson, R., 1996). Yet the interactions of individuals within larger cities are going to be more through non-spatial networks. They are always going to be impersonal and brief, with less trust between individuals being shown.

Market Towns

Some towns have continued their existing functions following industrialisation. They continue to specialise in rural services, supporting the agricultural surplus and feeding into higher order cities. The (English) market town continues to survive. This is despite the income of its inhabitants being derived from places of work well beyond the town itself. These towns consistently score well in the indexes of liveability, happiness and unified aesthetics. They are also stable in terms of capital accumulation.

The secret of market towns' high well-being levels is their sense of distinct identity, community spirit and 'perfect size'. They are small enough for people to feel included but large enough to stay private. The UK Government's well-being programme has sought to identify the factors that are linked to high levels of life satisfaction. It concluded that cities and smaller towns should try to copy large rural and market towns in respect of their community spirit, thriving high streets and social networks (Easton, 2013).

Nordic cities are also often quoted as scoring well for liveability (Monacle, 2016). This is partly due to them having avoided over-urbanisation. The two largest cities, Stockholm and Copenhagen are only over 2 million in population.

Ordinary to Mega-Cities

Cities like Paris, Madrid and San Paulo have a national economic role. Others command multi-national roles, like Singapore and Miami. Further down the hierarchy are places such as Chicago and Hong Kong. These articulate important subnational economies. On the world stage, cities are acting as a centre of refuge for expanding populations of the Third World. These include mega-cities which make up populations in excess of 20 million inhabitants. The scale of urban centres doesn't stop at mega-cities. In fact they are evolving into whole new urban networks, corridors and conurbations. Mexico City is an example. It may one day end up incorporating much of central Mexico including cities of Cuernavaca, Puebla, Cuautla, Pachuca and Queretaro (Garza, 1999). Despite the profile of mega-cities, most of the world's population will be based in second-tier cities.

Financial Cities

The 'world city hypothesis states that the final contenders of urban power and influence as being the global financial centres. These are New York, London and Tokyo. They are described by Saskia Sassen (1991) as command and control centres of the global economy. They previously benefitted from being at the centre of trade routes. They now combine generous office blocks in business sectors with attractive urban living found in temperate climates. They have become a place for 'flight capital' where the rich, from emerging market economies, bring their money. They can escape from 'extractive' regimes and local gangs and get protected by political and personal freedoms. There's also benefit found in sound legal systems, a favourable tax environment, good security and schools.

Other cities may one day rival or replace the 'big three.' Shanghai may one day achieve this status on the back of China's economic rise. The dominant culture of world cities is now cosmopolitan. Its defined by their controlling social strata which Sklair (1991) calls the transnational capitalist class. Their lingua franca is English and Ideology is consumerist. Into this mix are drawn the creative classes and low paid service workers. Together they form a trans-territorial marketplace.

The cultural dimension is important for 'world class cities.' It provides the symbolic association previously given to a place by a religious leader. This is derived from whatever is supposedly unique to these places. It includes historical narratives, interpretations, meanings to collective memories and significance of cultural practices. These special marks of distinction attach to some places providing them with 'symbolic capital' which gives them significant drawing power upon the flows of capital. Paris, Athens, New York, Rio de Janeiro, Berlin and Rome have an economic advantage over Baltimore, Liverpool and Glasgow. The branding of cities is big business. This is especially given the loss of other monopoly powers through easier transport, modern communications and other reductions to trade barriers.

Political Cities

Some cities are based around national state administration and power. Centrally governed countries like the UK stay dominated by a single city (London). Federally governed countries, like Australia, tend to find each state being served by a dominant urban entity. These are places where political ideas develop and evolve, political movements form and often demonstrations take place. Their size and importance reflects government spending priorities. Downsizing the state will have a correspondingly greater effect upon these cities, given their greater share of administrative processes.

1.2 The Role of Capital within Cities

The commodification of the urban environment is just as strong as in other sectors of the economy. Under capitalism, a house is no longer a home but a speculative commodity that you happen to live in. There are two aspects to this. The first is development rights or the right to build. The second is private property or ownership of land.

To build is to exert power. This can be over materials, construction workers, land, neighbours and future inhabitants. The assembly of buildings is akin to other manufacturing processes. They need authority, money and ownership. The outputs or buildings are products for the selling and renting of space. They have to be in a package that is attractive enough to be financially successful. It is mainly for incoming uses that redevelopment and the erection of new buildings occurs. Displaced land uses include those that cannot or will not pay the commercial rent. They are more likely to relocate to existing buildings in older areas. Rather than re-developing the site, they would prefer to adapt and convert them.

The land market is considered finite. Unless you happen to be based in the Netherlands, new land isn't created and each parcel is, in a sense, unique in terms of its location. The price of a property is set by the value placed on that location by the community surrounding it. Landowner's have an interest in the potential of their land to be developed for a more profitable activity than its current use. The revenue stream from land is the basis for assigning the capital value upon which it can be traded. They control the 'tap' of land supply. For land owners, scarcity is created by withholding land or assets from current uses and speculating on future values.

1.3 Role of Urban Capital in Economic Growth

Building new houses accounts for a mere 10th of all housing transactions. The chief determinant of house prices is the state of the market in existing property and the cost of finance. In many parts of the world building loans and mortgages are not available. Construction only progresses as fast as the owner's disposable income allows. Construction can be a prolonged affair over years or even decades. Finance is the single most important driver of property prices. There is an important role for the state about a bank's lending policies to finance mortgages and capital. When interest rates are low or falling and when access to finance is easy, prices tend to rise. Yet when faced with increasing interest rates, coupled with constraints on low deposit mortgages, the pressure on prices is removed.

Financial institutions lend to developers, landowners and construction companies to build. Accordingly, they charge a rate of interest. Yet the viability of this sector relies on the assumption that value is not only produced but also realized in the market. Financial institutions take their interest payments firstly, from the developer (the developer pulls out after making a profit). They then take from the purchaser who is assessed as being able to pay off the realisable amount over the lifetime of the mortgage. Nothing gets produced. This amounts to a capitalisation of property ownership or as Harvey describes it, 'fictitious capital' (Harvey, 2012).

As such, the interest paid to finance the development comes from value production. This is produced somewhere else in the economy. The labour process of production is the only place where true value and surplus value gets created. As landowners become more interested in expected capital gains rather than productive activities, property development drops off and valuable land lies idle.

This is why capital financing of urban development is seen as a fundamentally unstable process. The cyclical character of (private) urban investment is well documented but neglected in the post War era because of state-led Keynesian style interventions. These were deemed effective in flattening them out. After the Second World War, US federally backed mortgages for single-family, detached housing supported suburban development. Since private investment is speculative, in the long term it is crisis prone. This impacts upon the character of urban and other forms of physical, infrastructural investment.

Commentators have pointed to the role of speculative property investment as a source of macro-economic instability (Heim, 2000: 162-76). Bank failures, triggered by over-exposure to non-performing property, transmit knock-on effects throughout an economy. The United States property boom and bust in the 1920s and resulting bad debt, was a major factor contributing to bank failures that followed the Wall Street Crash of 1929.

Starting in the 1970s, Keynesian style intervention was abandoned. It is little surprise that 'boom and bust' cycles returned. The sub-prime crisis is the clear example. During the early 2000s, housing markets in Anglo-America experienced extraordinary waves of speculation. Prices soared and expansive urban development resulted. More accurately, this caused urban sprawl as businesses and families were forced to seek cheaper land outside of the urban centres. Low interest rates and cheap money did the damage (Jenkins, 2015). Demand was also influenced by the media's endless reporting of a buoyant property market. This was stoked by what agents constantly reported as an acute shortage of listings.

The interplay between capital accumulation and urban processes is a key area of research. Cities are not only platforms for consumption. They also stand for a way of expending human energy and capital in their remaking and remodelling. Urbanisation is a means of absorbing the capital and labour surpluses throughout capitalism's history. London has become the ultimate 'sponge.' Even foreign criminals who launder money have been cashing in through the purchase of high-end London properties. This pushes up house prices (Toon, 2015).

Harvey devised a 'circuits of capital' model (Harvey, 1984). Capital investment encompasses the primary circuit of capital (production). The secondary circuit of capital is the built environment. The tertiary circuit of capital is through social welfare programmes. He suggested that crises of over-production in the primary circuit, lead to crises of over-investment in the secondary and tertiary circuits. This occurs as assets are redirected in efforts to ameliorate primary circuit over-accumulation.

Long-term investment needs a combination of finance capital and state engagement to function. Government's role has focused on infrastructure provision; for example, in the UK Budget 16-03-2016. The crisis prone character of physical infrastructure investments including railroads, highways, dams and the like is well documented. The Government is also encouraged to give 'added value schemes' that also indirectly benefit private sector investment.

Many economists recognise that urbanisation offers huge potential for generating domestic demand. Seoul increased its income and investment in public projects, such as roads and communications facilities, during the 1980s. China's National Urbanisation Plan (2014) aims to boost consumption from 45 percent to 50 percent of GDP by 2020. This will be achieved through having over 60 percent of the entire population living in cities by 2020. The process is expected to initiate a new round of economic growth.

1.4 Contradictions and divisions through Functionality within Cities

Cities are both places for people to live together, but they are also sources of division. Most academics consider that the first early towns and villages that sprang up were small peasant communities. Everyone worked at similar tasks and had a comparable standard of living (i.e., Neolithic villages of Middle East). Land was communally owned or not thought of as being owned. The concept of kinship flourished. Most researchers believe that differences in wealth and power became entrenched only gradually over time.

Acemoglu and Robinson (2012) have suggested that social divisions may have pre-dated settlement. What is accepted is that conflict resolution is harder for settled groups. Disagreements can be resolved more easily by people moving away. Larger, settled groups, with more permanent buildings and associated assets, are going to find it less attractive to pick up their possessions and move away.

Settlements needed effective ways of resolving conflict and more elaborate notions of property rights. Decisions had to be made about access to land close to the village, who got which trees to pick fruit from and who got which part of a stream to use. Rules developed and institutions were formed. The formation of a political elite emerged to enforce property rights and maintain order. Freedom and social opportunity declined as populations rose and boundaries hardened between groups. Separate functional areas were one means of resolving such matters. Such areas have always been apparent within urban centres. An example of this is the careful subdivision of the cities of Imperial China by codified law derived from Confucian teachings. Recent archaeological studies prove that the construction of the largest, Chang'an, was based on the principle of axial symmetry. This means it was a carefully planned city in a checkerboard pattern, with each walled and gated ward uniformly arranged. It consisted of three sections: the imperial city, the palace city, and the civilian section. This embedded a microcosm of symbolism in Chinese society. It was based on how China was divided into provinces and regions (referred to as jiuzhou). In the Middle Ages of Europe, the local produce market was based at the town centre. As social activities were focused there, the area was associated with the potential for disturbances. As such, it became tightly controlled by the state. In Arabic settlements, houses were situated as far as possible from centres of public and commercial activity. They were typically centred at the heart of blocks located at the ends of cul-de-sacs. These, unlike other streets or thoroughfares, weren't public, but were co-owned by adjoining residents.

The industrial city brought more people closer together (workers and owners of capital). Inevitable tensions resulted from the conflicting goals of individual aggrandisement and profit seeking. Bringing workers together in large numbers exacerbated tensions. So there was a need to avoid the potential for solidarity, collective action and political change.

The Central Business District was the most accessible point and the hub of the transport networks. Competition for sites and the ability of some land uses to outbid others meant land values were at their highest in the centre. Land values and intensity of development declined smoothly with distance from the centre. In industrial Manchester this produced the 'hub and spoke' formation. The Exchange, now the Royal Exchange Theatre on Cross Street, was the centre of business based around the global cotton trade. From the Exchange, tentacle-like streets extended outwards, cutting through the working districts. They provided an uninterrupted link to the suburban bourgeoisie areas. The store fronts on these streets were owned and maintained by the middle classes. Factories and 'slums'[17] (informal settlements) ringed the city centre. It was these that powered the expanding economy and the vast accumulation of wealth in the city.

The street layout of 19th Century Manchester modelled the growing divisions of the emergent society. Divisions existed between wealth and

---

[17] Slums have been defined as, 'a group of individuals living under the same roof. They lack one or more of the following conditions: access to safe water; access to sanitation; secure tenure; durability of housing; and sufficient living area (United Nations Human Settlements Programme).'

poverty, commerce and factory work, bourgeoisie and working class. Such a predicament needed the spatial aggregation of workers to keep the factories going. It also needed the social separation of worker from worker. In the 1840s, Engels noted that urban space in Manchester was so designed that work was being hidden through the very shape of the city itself. Businessmen and factory owners could enter and leave the commercial areas of the city without ever having to view the working slums and factory districts.

The form of modern cities continues to result from the tensions and paradoxes of capitalism. There have been different attempts to understand the functional arrangements of the industrial city. The sociologist, Burgess (1923), suggested the concentric zone model. This proposed a progression from the central business distric, to manufacturing, residential and commuter zones. There was a decrease in land price the further the distance travelled from the centre. This was followed by the economist Hoyt's sector model in 1939. He theorized that cities tended to grow in wedge-shaped patterns or sectors. They emanated from the central business district and centred on major transportation routes. Higher levels of access meant higher land values which better explained how cities' grow.

Peter Mann's (another sociologist) model of the UK city (1956) was essentially a more sophisticated analysis of concentric zones. It is based on evidence from Sheffield, Nottingham and Huddersfield. The prevailing wind was incorporated to explain the relationship between industrial location and residential areas. The concentric change in Mann's model relates more to age instead of type. The age of housing decreases with distance from the CBD. This is logical since all urban areas spreads outwards as more land is needed. Farmland is bought up a piece at a time to do this.

UK commentators have noted how both high rise and garden cities reproduce the social separation of workers from each other. This is through the creation of forms of space that separate at each level of the societal hierarchy. Garden cities represent the disaggregation of cities. They depend upon the power of space to separate and to physically prevent too high a density. The physical design of high rise apartments can also discourage residents being able to meet even their immediate neighbours in the same residential block. This is, for example, through lack of communal space.

The more a system of production dominates over reproduction, it gets expressed through the creation of hard forms of space. These separate at each level of the hierarchical system. This is discussed later in Part V. Physical control is thus applied to make sure that enough of the population is in walking distance of work. In contrast, if a system of reproduction dominates over production then it manifests itself in soft solutions such as small community and dispersion (discussed below). Production and reproduction were fused in the Soviet Union. The policy there was for urban dispersion and hard spatial solutions to be unified.

The lopsidedness in urban development along class lines is a global issue. Its divisive nature forces people to live 'together' where poverty and extreme wealth are juxtaposed. This is reflected in the difference between workers and owners (whose place is now delegated to management). The result is fourfold. First, there is stagnating growth where productivity has peaked. Second, there is remote working where work can be done almost anywhere. Third there is automation. This is associated with the destruction of some manual trades by robotics and also professions by algorithms embedded inside computers. These can do increasingly complex decision making. Fourth are low birth rates compensated for by new, hard-working migrants.

Leisure cities (take the example of New York - the city that never sleeps), almost implies an absence of the need for manual labour. Tensions exist between global elites and the rest. The latter include those 'subaltern classes' who have locally defined territorial interests and whose rise into the transnational class is blocked (Friedman, 2012). Such tensions are played out in terms of urban form. Post-industrial cities are increasingly fragmented. Commentators now reflect on a more chaotic multi-nucleated structure to the post-modern city (Dear 2000; Lees 2002). In the post-industrial world, the difference between retaining mixed uses vs. single uses has reduced. In its place is exclusivity based on the price mechanism and social services for example, schooling. The 'restive impoverished masses' are generally not compensated by gated communities, luxury apartments, golf courses and high end shopping malls.

Like the competition for trade between the merchant cities of medieval Europe, there is intense competition (often unrecognised, as the media focus on the national level) between competing regions and centres for private capital and skilled labour (as mentioned earlier). While the media and politicians may focus on national differences, important internal divisions exist between and within urban centres - even those within a single country.

In the end, the manner in which such tensions are managed is handled through civil authorities. Politics in China is reducible to a form of scientific managerialism. This may have given way to softer forms in the democratic West but the need to exert control remains. The so-called greater freedoms from social convention in cities give rise to the need for more formal rules and laws. Formal norms are needed to maintain a stable, cohesive group. The contradictions are partly addressed through the separate areas of informal and formal functionality within cities. Town planning has an important role in this.

The state also plays a significant role in the investment of soft infrastructure. This includes the welfare state services of health, education and pensions. It goes some way to explain why a lack of employment does not end some settlements. Some post-industrial cities have high proportions of the populations living on benefits. This reflects inertia, where immobile capital is tied to existing cities. There are various explanations for why labour doesn't move on quickly. First, convenience for existing residents. Second, family loyalties. Third, the logic of the democratic political cycle and fourth, the inertia caused by past investments. When (local) government fails, and help from another tier of government doesn't arrive, then a city will quickly succumb to economic decline through the merciless process of competition. Detroit is the ultimate Western symbol of a failed industrial city due to capitalist contradictions.

1.5 Anti-Urban Movement

Different groups of people have, through the ages, sought to leave cities behind. Their reasons include cities representing 'epicentres' of disease, crime, fire, sin and the like. Indeed, there is almost a bias in some religious writings against cities. Throughout history, a common desire has been to start communities from scratch. The sailing of the Mayfair to North America to set up a new colony was one of the most celebrated cases. It attempted to create a new society, away from the old laws where the settlers had come from.

In Germany, the city in the industrial era was to be a place where 'communitarian morality' could be attained. This was a concept espoused by Fichte and Hegel (German philosopher 1770 – 1831), among other late Enlightenment figures. It gave way to the German equivalent of the Dickensian City. This was considered to be non-Germanic, international and the 'home of the Bolshevik and ethnic minorities.' Anti-urban ideologies influenced perceptions of how the city should be treated. Some theorists, like Riehl, Langbehn, LaGarde and Moeller Van den Bruck, considered the city to be culturally evil. They called for a return to the Burg or Mittelalterliche Stadt (castle and Medieval Town). Others, such as Wilhelmi and Damaschke, espoused utopian settlements that would reduce the high density of the city to a more human scale. Still others, like Theodor Fritsch, advocated an accommodation of industry and agriculture. This represented a meeting of field and factory in a Gartenstadt setting. It's a version of the Garden City, predating Howard. While it would be difficult to call the utopians and accommodators anti-urban, they were 'escapist.' They attacked the evils of industrialisation (Manchestertum), highly dense housing (the Mietskaserne) and the attitudes of urban dwellers (Seelische Verstadterung). Rather than advocating programmes to counteract these perceived evils, the escapist theorists recommended the creation of new forms of community.

Leading this movement was the German Garden City Association, founded in 1902. It was based on the principles of Ebenezer Howard, who founded the 'Garden Cities and Town Planning Association' in Britain. The organisation emphasised the need to preserve rural values, return to nature and to recreate a craft/guild society. This strand continues to the present day in arcadia, where rural lifestyle is considered to give the greatest freedom and privacy. That is rural isolation rather than urban interaction. Yet over time, mainstream organisations have replaced these concerns. There's a desire to reform urban housing conditions and to develop balanced satellite cities.

More flexible transport systems were developed from the 1920s. These helped the de-concentration and decentralisation of people and capital from urban centres (counter-urbanisation). First this extended to suburbanisation. Anglo-American culture, in contrast to European, had sought solace in the rural environment since the romantic poets. Various attempts to detach from existing urban forms were expressed. An example was United States architect, Frank Llyod Wright's (1867 – 1959) Broadacre City. Designed for 1,400 families in one acre (4,000m^2) blocks it was set in the open countryside (as based on the 1932 book The Disappearing City). In the post-war era, Melvin Weber[18] extolled the virtues of freedom that the freeway offered. He viewed future cities, not be concentric clusters as in the past, but urban-associational areas. They would be able to avoid the 'location, location, location' mentality of property ownership based on capitalisation.

Even greater possibilities are now realisable through the extensive use of the private motor vehicle coupled with remote working practices. Technological progress first enabled large scale populations to live together. The internet has substituted connection for physical proximity. This allows disaggregation and the dispersal of urban form (the so called 'death of distance').

Post-modern commuters now have access to 'lifestyle blocks' on urban fringes. These properties are far more generously sized than earlier suburbs or even those envisaged in Broadacre City. They came about as part of a

---

[18] Urban designer and theorist.

significant counter-urban movement in the 1990s and 2000s, enabled by
increasing levels of wealth. Like a cultural myth, the return to living in the
rural environment drives many of the successful elites in cities.

Reformers and political movements have also experimented with de-
urbanisation in the modern age. In the West, this has been relatively small
scale. It has taken the form of commune living. The origins go as far back as
the English Revolution re-emerging in the 1960s hippy movements.

Since Marx saw capitalism as being so strongly linked with cities, he
thought they represented a kind of capitalist by-product. It shouldn't come as
a surprise that Communism made the most audacious attempts to reform or
dispense with existing urban forms. There were several 'splinter' communist /
anti-urban movements. A Russian disurbanist school of the 1920s was led by
the theorists M. Okhitovich and M. Ginsberg. They sought the total abolition
of the traditional concept of the town. Instead they proposed the dispersal of
settlements across the whole of the Soviet Union in the form of continuous
ribbon developments. Individual dwellings would be distributed along roads in
natural and rural surroundings. Yet they would be within easy reach of
communal dining and recreation amenities. Employment centres would be
located at road junctions. Bus services would transport workers to them from
their houses. In China, the People's Communes were employed from 1958
under the 'Great Leap Forward' programme. Each commune was a
combination of smaller farm collectives. They consisted of 4,000-5,000
households up to larger communes of 20,000 households. In the commune
everything was shared. Private kitchens, which offer self-containment, were
replaced with communal dining.

The most infamous anti-urban initiative in modern times took place under
the Khmer Rouge regime (in Kampuchea - formerly Cambodia). When they
seized power the regime undertook a forced evacuation of urban residents
from cities. The pretext was a temporary intent to avoid loss of life from
aerial bombing. Behind it all was a whole scale intention to return society to
the countryside. This was not a return to a distant agriculturally based society
of the past. Instead it was a radical vision. A homogeneous, egalitarian
society would be built on an autonomous economy, free from the capitalist
system. The central role of the peasants in national development was espoused
by Hou Yuon in his 1955 thesis.[19] This challenged the conventional view that
urbanisation and industrialisation are necessary precursors of development.

---

[19] The Cambodian Peasants and Their Prospects for Modernisation.

Khieu Samphan's 1959 thesis[20] argued was that the country had to become self-reliant and end its economic dependency on the Developed World. In its general themes, Khieu's work reflected the influence of a branch of the 'dependency theory' school. He blamed lack of development in the Third World on the economic domination of the industrialised nations. He also observed the structural inequity between the 'productive' countryside and 'unproductive' urban areas. Cities were seen to be 'rabbit-warrens of vice, filth, corruption and disease.' They symbolized all that was wrong with Cambodia. Cities were populated by individuals who contributed nothing to society but in return benefited from the exploitation and oppression of rural-based peasants. Agriculture, crafts and small industry were deemed productive. Tertiary industry, especially commerce and banking, was not.

While the reasons can be debated, it is difficult to argue that the history of such movements has been unsuccessful. The 'urbanisation is inevitable' school of thought sees a growing confidence in cities (psychology). This reflects the profoundly social nature of humanity and our ability to connect and learn from each other. From an economic stand-point, the argument for urbanisation was encapsulated by Verbeek for the World Bank and IMF (2014). Almost no country has graduated to a high-income status without urbanising first. Urbanisation rates above 70% are typically found in high-income countries.

The accumulated capital represented in cities resembles a type of market fund. The value of land rises dramatically when land is transferred from agricultural to urban use. Ownership and control of property thus represents a share in the city resource that is greater than the sum of the parts. This type of logic would suggest a trend towards even greater conglomerations in the future, as described earlier. Yet again, it can be argued that urbanisation is not inevitable. The United States property and credit crunch began in 2008 and the effects are ongoing. It may have far reaching consequences in terms of western society's interest in urbanisation and property speculation. The biggest problem is that there is only so much wealth to go around to support urban centres. One view holds that urbanisation is a modern day 'pyramid scheme.' This is the story of the Aztec civilisation, where the economic surplus had been channelled into ambitious building programmes. It is not only possible, but indeed probable, for confidence in urban living to 'disappear' in the near future. It could be the result of some future epidemic, food system break down, urban crisis or the like. This is explored further in Part VII.

---

[20] Cambodia's Economy and Industrial Development.

1.6 Creating the Urban Grid

Personal mobility in traditional communities, certainly at the daily level, was extremely limited. Few people travelled further than 25 miles from their homes during their entire lifetime. For such communities, the built-up area had to broadly match the general pattern of life. The structure of block shapes, their sizes and distribution were important indicators for pre-industrial settlements. They reveal whether the settlement evolved haphazardly or were laid out with a centrally planned intent. This was the finding of a study based on mathematically modelling 131 cities around the world (Barthelemy and Rémi Louf, 2014).

The strongest drive for uniformity in plan and layout probably came from Imperial China. In Han Confucian ideology, the city was a cosmic focal point. From there the forces of nature could be adapted to or controlled in the interests of the whole realm. A capital city therefore became an epicentre of an orderly spatial grid which extended to the boundaries of civilisation. Cardinal orientation, cardinal axiality and square perimeters delimited by a city wall were intended to mark Chinese cities. In practice, large topographical constraints sometimes prevented this outcome.

In the modern world, cars have come to define urban layout. Barthelemy and Louf (2014) note how Asian and European cities were set up before cars were invented. Self-organised, they lead to regular shapes, rectangles and squares of small and medium size. Some East Coast American cities which were set up before the motor vehicle dominated also have the same type of patterns. Examples include Washington and Boston. This could be the reason why people sometimes say they have a 'European feel.' Central planning has different consequences. North American cities which were planned to make driving easier have grid-like patterns. When central planning is superimposed onto an existing layout it typically does not respect the existing geometry. Instead, it creates 'strange' shapes such as elongated triangles. This is the case for example, in Paris, under Haussmann's works of the 19th Century. Large avenues were created to connect important points which resulted in a large variety of block shapes.

There are four categories of urban layout. First, medium-sized rectangular blocks. Buenos Aires was the only city in this category. Second, small blocks with a diversity of shapes such as in Athens. Third, larger, more balanced blocks with a diversity of shapes, as in New Orleans. Finally, a mosaic of small squares, as in Mogadishu.

Pre-industrial settlements stayed small. Not one got over a million people in size. This was not only due to the pressures on food supply and the transport network to move products, but also for public health reasons. The Romans perhaps came closest to achieving modern conveniences with their use of public bathing and toilets. They also had rules designed to keep faeces out of the streets. Yet without advanced scientific knowledge they could not take full advantage of the benefits their infrastructure offered. The application of faeces on soil as a fertilizer on food crops probably resulted in considerable ill health. Without lengthy composting before use it allowed the spread of parasite eggs (Piers Mitchell, 2016).

Industrialisation gave both improved agricultural practices and better means of transportation. Yet as urban numbers swelled conditions quickly proved unsatisfactory. The result was some of the worst of conditions associated with urban form; particularly epidemics of cholera and typhus. This did not escape the notice of intellectuals and the educated. Voltaire noted (1749) that Paris had great monuments but suffered squalor and inadequate infrastructure. He became a campaigner for smallpox inoculation and a cleaner city (Nicholas Papayanis, 2004). These same living conditions of misery and filth would in the end help to give rise to the French Revolution. The new technique of photography[21] helped bring the Five Points neighbourhood tenement slum conditions to the public's attention in New York.

Urban commentators and campaigners have made cities the scene of vigorous class conflicts and struggles. They have often forced urban administrations (over time) to supply public goods to an urbanised working class. This includes affordable public housing, health care, education, paved streets sanitation and water. Often the arguments advanced for intervention were not based on the conditions per se. In Germany, the relative poor health of military recruits was a key stimuli to national government involvement in urban public health improvements.

Solutions to the problems of newly industrialised cities morphed into what we are now familiar with as the urban infrastructure of the 'grid'. This includes water, sewage, stormwater, power, communication and roads. Such infrastructure literally gives the urban glue that binds individual buildings together. Improvements in the quality of urban infrastructure emerged separately and in different settings.

---

[21] Used by crime reporter and reformer Jacob Riis (1895).

Water Supply

The first and most important item of infrastructure was the need for alternative supplies of fresh water. These were needed to augment what smaller populations had. Typically, alternative supplies had to be sourced from further away. This necessitated water catchments and storage lakes. Transport of water from distant reservoirs was nothing new. Roman engineers had overcome the problem in Rome. Haussmann's modernisation of Paris also featured a little known aqueduct which stretched 80 miles across the Yonne Valley to the southwest.

Surrounded by brackish rivers, the island of Manhattan's existing source of potable water from wells, natural springs and other bodies of water proved unsatisfactory. The wealthy could obtain water from elsewhere. The poorer classes had to make do with adding alcoholic spirits to make it palatable. Spurred by the Great Fire of 1835, the city of New York finally undertook action. This became an ambitious project to dam the Crouton River and install a gravity fed aqueduct to import water.

Sanitation

What wasn't appreciated with bringing new water supplies into cities was that it necessitated more effective sewerage. This was in order to avoid the pollution of water supplies. Epidemics led to ground breaking medical / health discoveries. John Snow's map of the 1854 London cholera outbreak helped authorities trace the cause of the problem. In the end, water chlorination resolved such issues (as discussed earlier in Section I for bottled water).

A key event also brought the city of London to a standstill in the summer of 1858. This was due to the overwhelming stench being emitted from the Thames River. The cause was from the ongoing dumping of all of London's various wastes - human, animal, and industrial. Government at Whitehall was barely able to function while ordinary people were urged to leave their homes. The resulting demands for action from the government culminated in an effective sewerage system to address the immediate issue.

Over time, the capacity of even the farsighted Victorian system has reduced. Urbanisation itself, with its new impervious surface cover, has created the demand for more effective drainage solutions. This is because of the increase in downstream flooding.

Migration and urban over-crowding continue to overstretch existing infrastructure outside of the Developed World. In Dharavi it is thought there are 1,000 inhabitants for every working toilet. Sewage lines often spill into water lines and disease is inevitable. In developing countries the number of urban dwellers without access to electricity, sanitation or clean drinking water totals one billion.

Industrialisation, mass consumption and the 'throw-away' (linear) society also produces inevitably large amounts of solid refuse. Until recently, this was dealt with by setting aside land for tipping. Effective waste management continues to be an issue across the modern world. In the UK, recycling rates dropped following the ending of the recession. China is looking to counter trends in industrial symbiosis whereby waste products are re-used (Hook, 2012). These often need committed Government intervention or subsidisation.

Energy

Settlements place huge demands on the provision of energy. Since industrialisation, demand for energy has increased in relation to the number of uses for which it could be put. Paris became a city of light in the 17th Century after its police force launched a vast street-lighting project. The aim was to make the city less dangerous at night.

Development of the sunbelt cities in the post-war period owes much to the availability of air conditioning. Otherwise living conditions would be almost unbearable. Every year, nearly half (47.6%) of all energy produced in the U.S. is consumed by the Building Sector. This amounts to the same energy consumed by both transportation (28.1%) and industry (24.4%) combined.

The energy for Britain's industrial revolution was based on coal production in Wales and the north of the England. Coal consumption grew rapidly as supplies were able to be transported on the newly created railway networks. Coal was not only used in industrial production but also in domestic heating, owing to its low cost and widespread availability. The manufacture of coke also gave coal gas, which could be used for heating and lighting.

Air Pollution

Air pollution affected many people crowded within walking distances of factories and their places of work. There was a strong socio-economic distinction being felt most heavily on those living on the downside of the prevailing wind. London's east is associated with maritime docksides and industrialised areas. Upstream areas tended to be elevated and more embedded in the countryside. So the south-westerly wind across London meant that polluted air was spread east over the poorer half of the city. The social reformer, Charles Booth showed this on his 1889 poverty maps.

Air pollution has proven harder than water and sanitation issues to fully resolve. It stems from the by-products of the combustion process itself. The introduction of electricity helped to alleviate the problem; for example, as a replacement to the use of coal gas. The means of generating electricity was also important. In the United States, Nikola Tesla's (1856 – 1943) coal fired power stations proved a superior design to alternatives. Based on an alternating current light and power system it meant they could be located well beyond the city.

London's famous (coal based) smog was only addressed by draconian measures after the Great Smog of December 1953. Despite heavy de-industrialisation, air pollution continues to exceed ambient health standards. This is mainly the result of the increased use of petrol and diesel motoring. Inner city districts are particularly sensitive, including the ethnically diverse district of Tower Hamlets. Some of the busiest roads in Britain pass close to large, high-density housing estates. Nowhere in the borough is further than 500 metres from a busy road. New housing developments are being targeted at young family's right along main roads. Henshaw (2016) suggests that air pollution is the biggest cause of diagnosed cancer in UK children. This factor is ahead of other modern lifestyle elements.

Yet such exceedances pale into insignificance when compared to industrial based cities. These continue to have compromised health standards (for example, in Asia). In Shanghai, for instance, rich residents are known to have fitted their dwellings with bottled oxygen! More than 80% of people living in urban areas that monitor air pollution are exposed to poor air quality levels. These exceed World Health Organisation recommended limits. While all regions of the world are affected, populations in low-income cities are the most impacted.

The Future of the Grid

Many towns and cities in the Developing World are in a state of having 'little or no planning to accommodate people or give them services' (UN-Habitat, 2003). In contrast, urban areas in developed countries are not just liveable but almost too comfortable (thanks to the 'grid'). This has opened up new opportunities for residents to satisfy their needs and desires. The use of the motor car originally resulted in the growing interdependence of town and country during the 20th Century. Yet it's gone further, in that most towns no longer cater only for the inhabitants of the immediate built up area. This traditional concept is supplemented more by personal habitats than physical factors. A phenomenon of modern times is the location of housing based on its attractiveness, rather than proximity to work. This is expressed in the German notion of Zwischenstadt. It's a term which covers the concept of the 'in-between city.' Its where the widest variety of action spaces and connections are put together, as on an 'a la carte' menu, provided you can afford it. This explains commuter or retirement cities of the first world. Earlier functional relationships between employment and residential uses have blurred, if not disappeared.

A downside to the grid is that industrialisation has caused the convergence and homogenisation of urban patterns and processes. This is due to parallel changes in the economic base, spatial organisation and social structure of cities (Sassen, 2002; Cohen, 1996; Newman & Thornley, 1996). Space can be read and with it the lifestyle of the inhabitants anticipated no matter whether village or suburban.

Technology allows settlements to be large, efficient and to be located almost anywhere. Two such cities typify what has emerged outside of the temperate climatic zones:

- Las Vegas (Nevada, United States). This is the self-proclaimed entertainment city of 1.5 million people. It's located in the middle of the Mojave Desert where there is intense heat and annual rainfall of less than 10cms. Its location assisted in the construction of the nearby Hoover Dam. However, its ability to attract people to support a gambling industry and venues for quick divorces in the 1930s gave real momentum to its growth. These venues were more heavily regulated elsewhere.
- Dubai (United Arab Emirates) – this city, while coastal, is also located within a hot desert climate in the gulf region. The expansion of Dubai

was initially based on the benefits derived from oil discoveries. Its current population is 2 million people. Unlike other towns based on a mineral industry in decline, it has continued to expand. Their leaders employed a shrewd economic strategy. In the knowledge that their oil reserves were going to run out eventually, they diversified. It meant attracting capital and skilled labour to an area that is not in itself particularly attractive to begin with. Its ability to diversify is based not only on the skills of existing residents but also on the sheer concentration of wealth. This allowed Dubai to expand the physical extent of its coastline by creating artificial islands. These provided more shoreline property. Despite significant constraints, Dubai has some of the tallest skyscrapers in the world. Hurdles include the need to mine groundwater. This is essential not just for drinking but also for cooling skyscrapers etc. Also, its underlying geology is unsuited to skyscrapers. Half of construction costs are underground.

Technology raises the potential for science to be applied for even more outlandish proposals. It could be settlements in Antarctica, floating cities on the oceans (Seasteading Institute proposal) and of course, the future possibility of space colonisation. These are mainly private sector initiatives. The Seasteading proposal is in fact attempting to create new forms of self-government. There is a temptation to view cities as complex, adaptive systems. That is, systems existing without a singular form of top-down control. They evolve over time at many scales through an ability to learn. Other examples are the stock market, the biosphere and the ecosystem, the immune system and most human endeavours in a cultural and social system. This includes political parties or communities.

Yet the role of the state in the provision of the grid shouldn't be ignored. This highlights the dependence society has on the infrastructure around us. Former President Obama explained this during his re-election campaign of 2012 as: 'Somebody helped to create this unbelievable American system that we have that allowed *you* to thrive. Somebody invested in roads and bridges.'

The ability of any given piece of urban infrastructure to cope comes down to the level of demand. There is a point at which 'infrastructure' becomes unaffordable, regardless of where it is located. Investments tie capital to urban structures for the long term. Infrastructure is relatively immobile. It comes into conflict with the dynamics of technological innovations, changes in the economy and population.

Urban services become less economical when population density rises above the infrastructural capacity. Highway systems, for instance, have a point of inflection for car use and travel times. Even power grids need to be the subject of investment to avoid power cuts. Examples of failure in the West include North East US in 2003 and Auckland, New Zealand in the 1990s. These events occurred on privatised infrastructure and were caused by the motivation of shareholders not to cut their profit margins.

Population decline and associated urban shrinkage has also become a feature of the de-industrialised West. Japan is an example. Population decrease is a major cause of change. This causes dysfunctions in existing towns and the surrounding areas that had grown rapidly during times of economic expansion. Town centres were drained of their services. Sixty percent of European regions will experience population decline to 2050 unless recent migration levels are maintained. Indeed, in strictly rational economic terms, there is too much built fabric in the West that's used only for short periods of the day and year. Those buildings that are no longer needed can't be easily sold to make a profit. They've become obsolete or are in a 'state of waiting' for an indefinite period. Questions remain as to whether our societies can continue to meet running costs of buildings over the long term. These costs include energy, maintenance, repairs, renovation.

2.0 Resource Use Beyond City

The development of cities has always depended upon their relationship to resources outside the city, particularly, the agricultural surplus. Yet what has become better understood is the linkages to wider ecological support systems. These give society food to eat, water to drink and air to breathe.

It is apparent how significantly modern society has impacted upon the environment beyond the city. Rostow observed that one of the pre-conditions for starting to develop was widespread and enhanced investment to change the physical environment so as to expand production. This included irrigation, canals and ports. Physical infrastructure investments allowed new connections to non-local markets (railroads, highways, dams and the like). Yet this in turn has placed ever greater demands on natural resources.

Industrialisation has resulted in the transformation, rather than adaptation, of the environment. The number of trees in the world has fallen by about 46 percent since the start of human civilization. A research study by Yale University (Crowther, 2015) reported that each year there has been a gross loss of 15 billion trees and a net loss of 10 billion. The new findings leave abundant reason for concern - with people at the root of the problem. Almost everywhere is of use somehow in the process of capital accumulation. This ranges from the Artic to the Antarctic and from the Atlantic to the Pacific. This wasn't necessarily unacceptable from the point of view of alternative economists. Marx viewed exploitation of the environment as preferable to that of labour.

After 200 years of industrialisation there are far fewer new markets in most resource types to exploit. Critical to ongoing economic growth is access to new forms of energy. Our track record of 3% energy growth per year is not sustainable. This comes down to global physical limits including thermodynamic limits, energy return on energy invested, finite arable land, water, fisheries, climate change and others. For this reason, the world cannot keep getting wealthier forever.

2.1 Food Supply

From ancient times, urban settlements have depended on an 'agricultural surplus' for their survival. Researchers, such as Jared Diamond (2006), linked the demise of civilizations to agricultural failure and inappropriate farming practices. Among them were the Sumerians and Inca's who had shown the skills capable of significant building projects. In contrast, Rostow's 'pre-conditions for take-off' from an agricultural to industrial society assumed two factors. First, more productive, commercial agriculture. Second, cash crops that weren't consumed by producers and were largely exported. One of the most significant benefits to Europe from the discovery of the 'New World' was in bringing back maize and potatoes. These crops were twice as productive as existing crops such as wheat and barley. This meant only half the land and workforce were needed to yield the same amount of food. Technological advances have also contributed to rising birth rates and greater populations. In the 1960s the 'green revolution' started. It's focused on the agro-industry replacing subsistence farming practices.

Ownership arrangements also impact food supply. The argument is that profit based farm management arrangements are best. Under collective farm arrangements neither the manager nor those who worked on the farms were entitled to keep even a portion of profit. Such practices existed under the old Soviet communist system. Compared to the manager of a capitalist farm, they had little incentive to put in extra work time or make additional profit for the farm. For instance, it meant they would rather allow wheat to rot than put in extra time to arrange to transport it to Moscow.

When America was formed it took nine farmers to feed one city dweller. Today, one farmer supports 99 urbanites. The success of modern food supply systems means that agricultural practices have become more intensive and also extensive. It is estimated that 40% of the earth's surface is devoted to food production. Agriculture has grown ever more large scale. This includes the rise of the 'mega farm' to the accompanying changes in land uses involved in food chain distribution (warehouses).

Where water is scarce, the inefficiencies of growing commodity crops in semi-arid and arid areas carries strategic implications. This can be shown using the concept of 'virtual' or 'embedded' water. It measures the water that is embedded in the production of foods and industrial products. This term was coined by Professor Tony Allan in 1993.

One of the worst examples is the fate of the Ural Sea in Soviet Russia. Formerly the fourth largest lake in the world, it has shrunk to less than 10% of its original size. This is due to diversions for agricultural irrigation.

Our current food production system is so carbon intensive and wasteful that some estimates credit it with 19%-29% of total greenhouse gas emissions. Estimates range widely. A more conservative estimate puts agriculture emissions at 10%-12% of humanity's total emissions. The rapid increase in meat consumption has driven livestock numbers to contribute 18% of total human-related greenhouse gas emissions (United Nations Food and Agricultural Organisation, 2006). Meanwhile, the Worldwatch Institute (2009) estimated that livestock accounts for at least 51% of those emissions, if indirect emissions are included. Little emphasis is placed on the fact that under a capitalist system, 30%-40% of all food we produce is wasted through the supply chain.

Even now, the promise of an 'end to world hunger' continues to ring hollow. Famine still occurs. 'Land hunger' and a lack of grain supply gives an underlying basis for revolutionary movements. This includes Peru's Shining Path. Global inter-connectivity both assists in meeting demand but also – arguably creates a bigger risk. The 2012 global commodity food price spike was evidence of this. It is estimated that: 'more food will have to be produced worldwide over the next 50 years than has been during the past 10,000 years combined' (Sachs, 2014).

Common ownership of resources is criticised for giving no one a strong incentive to preserve the resource. The 'Tragedy of Commons' is that the unrestricted use of the common resource by individuals devalues it. The only logic remaining is to take as much as can be gained now, rather than wait for what might be given in the future. A fishery that no one owns for example, will be overfished. A fisherman who throws back small fish to wait until they grow is unlikely to get any benefit from waiting. It's assumed that other fisherman will catch those fish. The same holds true for other common resources whether they be herds of buffalo, oil in the ground, or clean air.

2.2 Mining

There is a saying that if it can't be grown it has to be mined. Once mined however, there is no renewal of the resource. This necessitates investigating sources elsewhere. Mining of stone and metal has taken place since pre-historic times. Modern mining operations can be grouped into five major categories in terms of their respective resources. These are oil and gas extraction, coal mining, metal ore mining, non-metallic mineral mining and quarrying (construction). Of all of these categories, oil and gas extraction (see below under energy) remains one of the largest in terms of its global economic importance. Depending of the nature of the operation they are associated with extractive destruction and environmental pollution.

There is a strong link between raw materials and the built environment. China, for instance, has been consuming up to 50% of key global commodities and materials such as cement, steel and coal. The main driver of this consumption is Chinese real estate. Half of the steel consumed ends up in the built environment. Essentially, ¼ of global steel is now absorbed in this activity alone.

Despite all the technological progress since the early industrial revolution, coal is still the largest source of worldwide energy. This is mainly via the generation of electricity. The most significant uses of coal are in electricity generation, steel production, cement manufacturing and as a liquid fuel. Around 6.6 billion tonnes of hard coal were used worldwide last year and 1 billion tonnes of brown coal. Since 2000, global coal consumption has grown faster than any other fuel. The five largest coal users - China, United States, India, Russia and Japan - account for 76% of total global coal use.

The use of metals in modern society is immense. Metals are needed in many of the everyday articles that surround us. Just as importantly they are needed for the manufacture of most other materials and products that people use. Without steel we would not have modern pharmaceuticals or newspapers. Optical lenses and CDs are pressed in steel forms, milk is chilled in steel containers, and the list goes on.

While there are vast amounts of everyday metals available in metal ore, the world's stock of easily accessible supplies are dwindling. There have been ever more ambitious mining operations. The Bingham open-cast copper mine in the United States is the largest, deepest man-made excavation in the world. It supplies between 13- 18% of the United States needs. The pit is over 0.6 miles (0.97 km) deep. It is 2.5 miles (4 km) wide and covers 1,900 acres (770 ha). Such extractive industries also tend to be capital-intensive, employing far more machines than people.

On its own, the easy accessibility of metals should not be a major problem. If more metals are needed than can be cheaply extracted from the ores then the price should rise accordingly. A high enough price will mean that society won't want to use that metal anymore. In many cases, substitute raw materials will be found. For example, we'll go and make our solar cells from silicon. By definition, we'll always have a supply of metals at the price we want to pay for them. They only become unavailable when the prices rise to where we don't want to use them. Advances in techniques are also allowing us to extract the metals from lower concentration ores better. For instance, the world uses significantly less of any specific metal to do a specific task. Now days we need less gold to make computers. The gold plating needed on computer connectors has gone from 200 nm to 2 nm in just 40 years.

This however, is not the case with all elements; particularly rare earth metals. These metals are not used for their structural value but rather for their unique electrical and magnetic properties (Davies, 2011). They are being consumed at an alarming rate and worst of all they aren't readily substitutable. For instance, each megawatt of power a wind turbine generates needs one tonne of rare earth permanent magnets. The elements used – neodymium, dysprosium and terbium are in short supply. Ninety-six percent of Rare Earth Elements are supplied by China. These have been deemed critical raw materials by the European Union.

2.3 Oil and Petroleum

As with minerals, petroleum is a non-renewable resource. Importantly, there is a strong correlation between energy use and gross domestic production. Use of energy depends on many factors including technology. Whereas industrial era steam trains ran on coal, modern cars and trucks depend on petroleum. Oil and gas extraction generally needs giant, high-technology drills, offshore platforms and vast systems of pipelines. All of this is operated by relatively small numbers of employees. These are large risk projects. When disaster strikes it can be catastrophic, as with the Deepwater Horizon oil platform which caught fire in the Gulf of Mexico in April 2010[22].

In the West, oil based fossil fuels, such as petroleum, were able to be extracted from domestic supplies during the 20th Century. After that a switch occurred to greater reliance on major overseas producers such as the Gulf States. There has been increasing concern about the ongoing ability to provide steady supplies globally. Two episodes featuring spikes in fuel prices include the 1973 Arab boycott of the West and the 2008 commodities boom. Higher prices can be offset by falling demand. Yet it's difficult to adapt land use to rapid price change due to its relative inflexibility. The significance of the correlation between land and energy use should not be underestimated. The average suburban household consumes 27% more electricity than the average urban household. The only response by the Government is initiatives to build less energy demanding houses. This includes smaller homes, which use less electricity.

Alternative energy supplies have been investigated including the use of renewables. In the UK the key source of renewables is wind energy. Unlike oil and coal however, which are compressed forms of energy, renewable energy can need large land areas. Biofuels for instance, compete directly with food production. This has encouraged development of both onshore and offshore wind farms. Offshore windfarms are more expensive than onshore but less contentious. This partly explains why so many have been developed in Scotland. Where windfarms are well located they may generate most of the time (85%). Yet transportation of electricity over long distances is dependent upon the grid infrastructure (including the use of special 'bootstrap' power cables). In the UK the age and capacity of the national grid, built in the 1950s and 1960s, is a major constraint. Recent Government scrapping of subsidies for renewables is seen as putting the UK at an economic disadvantage.

Replacing petroleum directly will be difficult and slow. Electric batteries rely upon energy produced elsewhere. Biofuels take land production away from food. Hydrogen is one such alternative but it's mainly produced using natural gas and oils. What is needed is to produce it from renewables which are currently expensive. New sources of oil continue to be investigated.

Constraints on global petroleum have focused on M. King Hubbert's (1903 – 1989) theory of peak oil. This is based on the famous bell-shaped graph depicting the rise and fall of American oil. A report by the oil executive,

---

[22] It's considered the largest accidental marine oil spill in the history of the petroleum industry with the discharge of 4.9million barrels.

Leonardo Maugeri (2012), gave compelling evidence that a new oil boom has begun. The constraints on oil supply over the last 10 years appear to have had more to do with money than geology. The low prices before 2003 had discouraged investors from developing difficult fields. The high prices around 2009 changed that. Maugeri's analysis of projects in 23 countries suggests that global oil supplies are likely to rise by a net 17m barrels per day (to 110m) by 2020. This is 'the largest potential addition to the world's oil supply capacity since the 1980s.' The investments needed to make this boom happen depend on a long-term price of $70 a barrel.

The country where production is likely to rise most is Iraq, into which multinational companies are now sinking their money. But the bigger surprise is that the other great boom is likely to happen in the United States. Peak oil theory has been revised. Investment has concentrated on unconventional oil, especially tar sands and fracking. Shale oil is high-quality crude, trapped in rocks through which it doesn't flow naturally. There are vast deposits in the United States. One estimate suggests that the Bakken shales in North Dakota contain almost as much oil as Saudi Arabia (though less of it is extractable). Yet extracting shale oil needs horizontal drilling and fracking which needs both high prices and technological refinements to be economically viable. Production of shale oil has a high energy input to output ratio. It has high ecological damage and investment risk. Despite a promising start, the North American sector has been hit by the recent slump in prices. This was caused by the ramping up of supply by mainstay oil producers such as Saudi Arabia.

2.4 Pollution

Industrialisation resulted in the use of a whole range of new products. From the outset, the use of new substances had unintended consequences. Knowledge about their effects on the environment took time to be understood. One such health hazard came from the use of arsenic. Known for its toxicity, it was used as a (green) pigment in the wallpaper of Victorian Homes. Manufactured most notably by the English textile designer William Morris, the use of arsenic continued until the 1870s and beyond. In the end the public at large realised the dangers and demanded safer, alternative products.

The 'by-products' of domestic and industrial processes were generally thought to be able to be easily absorbed within the local environment. When that optimism proved unfounded, they were typically controlled through sewerage and related infrastructure (as discussed earlier).

The grid was the means of conveying waste efficiently from urban centres to 'sinks'. The oceans in particular were thought to have enormous capacity for absorption. Yet over time, even this idea appears to be misplaced. There is growing recognition that some wastes already exceed the Earth's absorption capacity. Plastic waste items are commonly washed up on beaches around the world. Even in the world's largest ocean (the Pacific Ocean), huge, low density 'plastic islands' of waste products have congregated as a result of ocean currents. This is estimated as resulting from 4-12 million tonnes of plastic being dumped every year by 192 countries with significant coast lines (WWF, 2015). By 2050 it is predicted that there will be more plastic than fish in the oceans. Ocean acidification, lowering the water's pH level, is resulting from human emissions of greenhouse gases that are absorbed by the sea. The oceans have become thirty percent more acidic over the past 200 years. This will have disastrous consequences for coral reefs, creatures with shells and vulnerable fisheries. Furthermore, pollution is not only limited to physical or chemical contaminants. Noise pollution from international shipping is now understood to be having an impact on marine life in oceans.

The local impacts of atmospheric pollution in industrial towns and cities have been apparent for decades. The resulting health side effects have taken longer to become fully understood. Local sources of pollution were addressed through simple means such as making chimney stacks taller. This increased the dispersal of pollution.

The theory was that the absorption capacity of the greater atmosphere was enough to address any issues but this has been disproved. The first major concerns were based around the use of lead in petrol and CFC's in fridges. Both had been promoted by American Inventor, Thomas Midgley in the 1930s and early 1940s. There is a growing body of research that suggests that lead in petrol and paints may have resulted in increased levels of violent crimes in many Western cities before it was banned. Yet eliminating lead from petrol took decades longer than it needed to as oil companies, who owned the patent to leaded petrol, fought its regulation. In the case of CFCs it took an internationally co-ordinated effort to ban their use from production. Other less well known pollutants continue to travel globally. Their impacts have been popularised since Carson's 1962 book, 'Silent Spring.' The European Commission (Neslen, 2016) is now looking into what can be done to regulate endocrines. These hormone-altering chemicals are common in everyday substances from paint to pesticides and have been linked to an array of illnesses including cancer, infertility, obesity, diabetes, birth defects and reproductive problems. It's even suggested they modify male masculinity as with phthalates which are chemicals used in the manufacture of plastics. The effects of modern chemicals do not respect distance. Pesticides sprayed in China can end up condensing as far away as the Antarctic glaciers and Rocky Mountain tarns.

The most popularised issue is the impact of carbon emissions on climate change. The construction industry is a major contributor to this. Concrete, and more specifically, cement production, is a significant source of CO_2. The Keeling Curve which measures the amount of atmospheric CO_2 exceeded 400parts per million (ppm) for the first time in April 2014. Under natural cycles it is between 150 and 250ppm. There is a tipping point at around 450ppm where positive feedback starts and major issues arise. These could range from the defrosting of the Siberian tundra to the Amazon rainforest catching fire.

In terms of responsibilities for CO_2 production, China and the United States now shoulder much of the blame. As the world's second biggest producer, America's carbon emissions come mainly from the household sector (consumption). China's carbon emissions are largely industry or production related. The impacts on the global scene of climate change could be dire. A Should climate change fulfil the more severe projections then worldwide famine, anarchy and warfare are predicted within a generation (Pentagon report, Schwartz, P & Randall, D. 2004).

Global warming is thought to be responsible for the reduction in extent and depth of the Arctic ice cap, ocean acidification and extreme weather events. The potential for the collapse of the Western Antarctica ice sheet is particularly alarming for low lying cities. Not only underway, it is potentially unstoppable. The loss of the entire Western Antarctica ice sheet could eventually cause sea levels to increase by up to 4m. This is based on results from two scientific studies by NASA and the University of Washington. The rise in sea levels may be thus unavoidable in coming centuries, devastating low-lying and coastal (urban) areas around the world.

2.5 Resource Over-Use

Global increases in consumption since the industrial revolution mean that natural resources are consumed at a faster rate than they can be replenished. The timing for this is estimated to have been in the 1950s / 1960s (which coincides with the peak in productivity referred to earlier). Technology has improved the efficiency of resource use since that time. By the early 2000s a trend started for the real price of natural resources to rise. This has reversed last century's trend for real-price decline and also meant significantly greater fluctuations in the prices for natural resources (Ellen MacArthur Foundation, 2013).

The concerns around 'what happens from here' have been apparent for some decades. The implications for urbanisation are complex. A generation ago China and India were rural societies. They did little environmental damage because, as poor places, they used little energy. Now they are both economic powerhouses and highly urbanised, using a significant chunk of the world's natural resources. In essence, these countries have done well by substituting 'human capital' (cheap labour) for natural capital (resources).

Is the trend for continued substitution of natural capital for labour able to be sustained? This is a position put forward by those on both the political left and on the right. Some on the right consider that technological advances will find substitutes for depleted resources. On the left, some political movements still hold (utopian) beliefs originating from those in the past. Despite the ecological crises that occurred in Maoist China and Soviet Russia they believe that resource limits can be overcome by human endeavour.

Other more 'realistic' views hold that global urbanisation is an extension of the 'progress trap.' Its internal logic is that in the end it will lead civilisation to catastrophe. In the 1800s Thomas Malthus[23] predicted limits to growth based on the rising population of the industrial revolution set against stable food production. In hindsight, he didn't factor in declining birth rates and advances in production (for example, from the green revolution). Yet the concept still has great weight and has been applied at various times since, to describe what amounts to a 'progress trap' (Wright, 2006).

Malthus wrote an anti-welfare tract, 'An Essay on the Principle of Population.' He feared that continued population growth would lend itself to poverty. It chimed with the theory of Evolution (indeed, credited as a key influence on Darwin). This promotes a view that any human impacts are bad (despite being part of the environment). Malthus listed positive checks as hunger, disease and war. Preventive checks included abortion, birth control, prostitution, postponement of marriage and celibacy (which were preferred in terms of higher living standards).

The world's population is now odds-on to swell ever-higher for the rest of the century. This poses grave challenges for food supplies, healthcare and social cohesion. New analysis shows there is a 70% chance that the number of people on the planet will rise continuously from 7bn today to 11bn in 2100

---

[23] English cleric and scholar (1766 – 1834).

(Raftery, 2014). This overturns 20 years of consensus that global population, and the stresses it brings, will peak by 2050 at about 9bn people.

The role of increasing population growth on the environment is a matter of contention. Another perspective is that the demand for resources is coming more from the burgeoning middle classes of the East than from overall population demand. Our world is large and we could all adapt if we wanted to (note the discussion earlier on the anti-urban movement). The scale of the world is that all the 7 billion people could physically fit onto the island of South Georgia in the South Atlantic Ocean or Texas (where there are 7.3 trillion square feet of land). Based on around seven billion people on earth, we could fit every single person in the world into that one state, each of us living by ourselves, in our own townhouse.

In the end, the matter comes down to the very nature of material progress. The 'logic of capital' fails to adequately recognise the value of our natural resources including forests, agricultural land, mountains, moors and heaths. The 'hidden value' should be more explicitly taken into account when it comes to decision making. Rather than being a free resource to be exploited 'the commons' should be seen for the service they give (ecosystem services). Ecological costs of major infrastructural projects may exceed benefits. Yet rarely do we hear of plans to deconstruct such projects.

The Club of Rome[24] showed how major global problems are related. This includes poverty and hunger, environmental destruction, resource depletion, urban deterioration and unemployment. The solution they advocated was much slower economic growth, no growth or even negative growth. Neither this, nor anti-welfare tracts fit well with modern, western, statecraft and the expectation that these same problems are intended to be managed through increasing the national wealth. In Malthus's time it was essentially 'keeping the peace' but has moved onto general provision for societies' welfare. This raises fundamental questions around what society is for – to improve the position of the weak or to create a better, more 'advanced' humanity.

---

[24] The Club of Rome was a think tank known created in 1968.

Fuller (2007) set out four alternative visions for society:

	We = human bodies	We NOT human bodies
Increase population	Enlightenment progress - welfare or totalitarianism? (Marquis de Condorcet)	Cyborg utopia - hybroisation or purification (Donna Haraway)
Decrease population	Darwinian survival - liberalism or indifference (Malthus)	Karmic balance - cosmic benevolence or inhumanity (Peter Singer)

In making an assessment, Fuller's model usefully combines population, technology and outlooks. Earlier societies tried to avoid technological disruption. the West instead seeks technological fixes to its problems. The paradox to ending human suffering through technology is that it gives rise to unforeseen consequences that result in yet greater (albeit delayed) suffering. Technology has to be regulated to avoid this, either through direct controls (such as Genetic Experiment moratoriums) or indirect controls (including town planning controls). With this context we can start looking at the planning system itself in Part III.

PART III:
JUSTIFYING THE PLANNING SYSTEM

1.0 Pre-Industrial Origins

U rban planning was the exception for pre-industrial settlements rather than the norm. Land transport was often a primitive affair for communities that depended upon it. So much so, that it was often easier (and safer) to use water borne transport for long distance transportation. Lacking both funds and technology, most past communities were small scale. They built their settlements from locally sourced materials that used so called 'vernacular architecture.' There were notable historical exceptions. Organised 'labour' projects might be employed for monuments, civic or religious buildings where materials might be purposely imported over significant distances. Examples included Stonehenge and the Pyramids.

There are few pre-industrial peoples whose rulers needed to innovate or take a special focus in the design of urban form. This can be understood in the context of their relatively low population. Public planning was limited to defining the underlying structures of roads, canals, water supplies and defence works. Private initiative was left to fill in the rest. Governments were not concerned with standards for the use of land and housing unless actions were interfering with the interests of the rulers or other holders of power. Even today, planning laws are either non-existent or almost irrelevant, due to them not being implemented. This is especially the case for developing countries which constitute the majority of urban (and rural) areas in the world.

The democracy[25] of the Ancient Greeks was an important exception. They did think about how best to lay out their towns. Dinocrates[26] pioneered the grid style of street layout that has become familiar across the world, including modern American city dwellers.

They were also the first recorded society to debate the best size of a city. Aristotle (384 – 322BCE) insisted on the existence of a minimum population (from Politics, VII), as well as a maximum size. Aristotle did not give specific numbers. Instead, he emphasised the public function of cities. 'It is vital that the citizens know one another.' He was also worried about the

---

[25] Reforms introduced by Cleisthenes in 507 BC had given not only (rich) landowners but also non-landowners the vote.

[26] Dinocrates was an architect and technical advisor to Alexander the Great in the last quarter of the 4th century BC.

problems of security when cities became too large: 'Foreigners and half-breeds usurp without difficulty the rights of citizens because it is easy for them to escape notice owing to the size of the population.'

In Laws, V. 74, Plato (around 428 – 348 BCE) stated that the ideal republic would have 5,040 citizens. This was based on heads of households, suggesting an ideally sized population would be about 20,000 total people. As with Aristotle, he linked his ideal city size to the need for citizens to be able to communicate. He said: 'The city must remain sufficiently small to permit the holding of public meetings with all of the citizens present.'

The Roman Republic also made significant contributions to city design across its domain. This was particularly around the application of newly planned settlements that followed the pattern of a military camp. Uniquely, for an ancient settlement, its capital Rome, went above the one million mark. By its later stages Rome had in fact become a large welfare state. In the second century AD 175,000 people or about one third of the population received public assistance from the city. To cater for this swelling population a significant civil bureaucracy developed around various public projects. These included sourcing water via aqueducts.

In the Middle Ages Venice[27] proved another notable exception. On their tiny islands in the middle of the lagoon there were a number of spatial considerations. Its city plan was concomitant with the emergence of a strong city-state. The purpose of the baroque layout was to display power and strength. Strict zoning was present and land use was divided into several functions. For instance, industrial ship building activity was based within Arsenale on the main island. The main cemetery was located away from the settlement on an offshore island. With some parallel to the Ancient Greeks, Medieval Venice witnessed democratisation, at least for aristocratic families. They also displayed comparative tolerance to minorities. Yet they did instigate the world's first ghetto.[28] This was the burgeoning Jewish community which was restricted and segregated.

Elsewhere, ancient civilizations had developed sophisticated systems of urban planning. These included the Aztecs in modern Mexico, the Mayans in modern Mexico, Guatemala, and Belize and the Incas in modern Peru and the Andean regions on modern Ecuador, Bolivia, Colombia, Chile and Argentina. The 1573 Law of the Indies was an early attempt at design guidelines for the construction of newly colonized settlements. The 148 ordinances stipulated

---

27   By the late 13th Century Venice had come to dominate Mediterranean trade, making it the most prosperous city in Europe.

28   A ghetto is a part of a city in which members of a minority group live, especially because of social, legal, or economic pressure.

that towns should be built with a central plaza, or commons. This would then be surrounded by civic and important buildings along with arcades. The grid pattern begins in the plazas of cities throughout Latin America. Narrow streets branch out from this central space providing shade from buildings for pedestrians. There was also a mandated architectural consistency amongst newly erected buildings.

Finally, Amsterdam[29] also featured a strong planning model. The city council engaged in compulsory land purchase powers. They divided the resulting sites into plots of convenient sizes and sold them on the open market. This would be subject to covenants that bound their successors to stipulated uses. There were also controls on which types of bricks could be used for external walls. Although they were not a genuine democracy the Dutch did have modern elements. An example was a multi-national corporation (Dutch East India Company. This was financed by shares on the first modern stock exchange. Like the Venetians, they displayed tolerance – at least for wealthy minorities.

Amsterdam and Venice both represent urban settlements that 'evolved' over time rather than being planned settlements. Both were successful water-borne hubs for commerce. Both were set within unusual physical constraints that needed their authorities to step in with special provisions. Their terrain was so soggy that each house needed to be built on a solid foundation of piles driven into the mud. In the case of Ancient Greece and Venice, the democratic process gave a forum for the discussion on 'planning' matters which may not otherwise have occurred.

2.0 Industrial Pre-Cursor

In the late Middle Ages, London had no formal planning system – at least not in the modern sense of the word. This was despite an increasing bureaucracy to administer issues around an increasing population. Co-ordinated 'systems' of 'integrated community development' are children of urbanisation and the industrial revolution. This includes the Town and Country Planning Act.

Urbanisation was largely driven by market forces during much of the industrial era. Urban migrants, exploited by unscrupulous landlords in tenement housing, initially had to sort their own problems out for themselves. With unrestricted property rights, new industries and a rising population

---

[29] Amsterdam had by the 17th and 18th centuries become the centre of world trade, based on the sorting, processing, distribution then re-exportation of staples and luxuries around Europe and the world.

authorities were presented with a unique and complex set of problems (described earlier in Part II).

For urban authorities, however, the dilemma of who was in fact responsible for the problems became ever more pertinent. It was clear that the impact of living conditions could affect everyone. Plagues, fires and blocked roads were dangers to all social classes. The hidden deprivations of past communities had been scattered in the countryside. The conditions in Voltaire's Paris, Engel's Manchester and Reeces' New York were clear to all. Political pressure was in the end applied on both state and/or municipal authorities to respond. The absence of free market solutions gave rise to the first serious attempts by civic authorities to address poor living conditions in the industrial city.

Interventions, that would later form part of the overall planning system, evolved alongside the changing (deteriorating) social and environmental conditions. The planning system can be thought of as a response or action. It has come from 'political feedback.' In many countries, the precursors to planning laws were building or housing codes. These set minimum distances between buildings, minimum window space to enable sunlight penetration, minimum housing unit size, maximum building heights, fire escapes, and requirements for sewage-disposal facilities. Transporting people and goods on a daily basis required passable streets. This formed the basis for setback rules for buildings on public roads. Trained professionals working in administrative and enforcement agencies were needed to issue permits and enforce the rules.

As urban authorities around the globe encountered similar problems, they (unsurprisingly) adopted solutions seen to be effective elsewhere. This included clean water, safe neighbourhoods and fast moving streets. In the United States these came somewhat later than their European counterparts. Early city planners have always aspired to a certain kind of city – ordered, efficient, beautiful and socially just. Direct action came down to the politics of state spending. That is taxpayer funding of public provision and infrastructure.

An early and often cited example of a co-ordinated combination of 'control and funding' working together was the transformation of central Paris. This took place during the reign of Napoleon III (1852 – 70). Carrying out his vision needed vast collective organisation, bringing together a large number of specialists and co-ordinators. It was an all too rare case of direct involvement by the countries' ruler in city planning. With his far reaching powers, Napoleon passed some original legislation. This addressed the compulsory purchase of land and public health.

He also assembled a team of highly skilled technicians led by George Eugene Haussman (1809 – 1891). Haussman went on to produce the classic top down unified master plan in 19th Century Paris. Projects included the modern sewerage system and public latrines. Broad boulevards and new housing were enabled by the ability to remove slums and improve transport. These projects were decided upon and managed by the state, done by private entrepreneurs and financed with loans backed by the state. An underlying political rationale was that enlarged boulevards would prevent revolutionary crowds from barricading (incorrectly as it turned out). This formed the basis for an enlarged state role in urban planning to make improvements. Paris's centre became a magnet for consumption, tourism and pleasure.

Like today's modern state, there was a need to set up a public policy and regulatory framework for private-sector decision-making. The resulting set of incentives and sanctions meant some actions and outcomes became more likely than others. Momentum for such a large urban project also depended on the ability to resist (local) opposition. In this respect, Haussman was able to realise his ambition through greatly more authoritarian leadership than is available in most western democracies.

3.0 Justification of State Intervention

The allocation of scarce resources, such as land, between competing human wants is the subject of economics. Economists should therefore be natural allies of urban specialists by bringing analysis to bear on the problem of land use. Compared with its pre-industrial origins the greatest shift in town planning has been from privately run ventures to an inherently government controlled operation. Before planning legislation was passed, land use was allocated in any way the owner saw fit. The only limitations were those imposed by the grant under which they held land. An example is Manorial Rights. The only other obligation, was that placed upon them through evolving common law. Property rights had themselves evolved over time. This included the concept of justice for landowners against state imposition. This was embodied in the Magna Carta. These rights were intended to avoid the situation of a, potentially violent, seizure of a neighbour's property.

Market Failure

Protecting private property rights from 'random' expropriation was a principle supported by enlightenment thinking. It has become one of the foundations of the modern, rational state. Yet the initial promoters of the free market such as Locke, were writing before the industrial era. They could not have foreseen the modern day forces associated with the logic of capital and industrialisation. This includes the technological advances in construction methods, potential for industrial scale pollution or the overall urban pressures. Few economists today would argue that land 'markets' are perfect. This is based on history and current circumstance.

Private developers, generally speaking, will seek to maximise their private benefits. This can be at the expense of social and environmental costs. In chasing the 'bottom line,' companies may play it loose with health and safety standards. The case of industrial pollution is the clearest example to illustrate the point. Industries will 'over-produce' pollution, so to speak, if they don't have to end up paying for the costs of dealing with it. 'Optimal levels' of pollution for individual firms may result in sub-optimal outcomes from society's point of view.

In unregulated or unenforced situations, the results can be tragic. The Bhopal disaster[30] of 1984 is an infamous example. The leak resulted from a systematic failure to carry out a number of checks, any one of which could have prevented the disaster.

Market failure is not just something confined to pollution. House construction, prior to the credit crunch, was largely based on one or two bedroom apartments despite a need for bigger houses. After the credit crunch (2009), far fewer homes of any description were built. Allegedly, this was because of an absence of funds despite London being a world capital of finance! Elsewhere, the property boom and later credit crunch saw newly constructed towns left uninhabited. For instance, Castallon's 'international airport,'[31] was built at a substantial cost of £107m, opened in 2011 and then lay unused for years (Topham, 2015).

The allocation of land to its most desirable use without state intervention can only be true with both a perfect land market and entirely equitable income distribution. Whatever the ideological arguments, the practical reality is that

---

[30] Over 3500 people were killed when methyl isocynate leaked from a factory of the largely autonomous Indian subsidiary of Union Carbide.

[31] On the Costa del Azahar - Spain's east coast.

laissez-faire urban development does not produce satisfactory results. Some degree of intervention is necessary (Hallett, 1988).

Planning regulation that controls the rampant construction of modern buildings can be justified for the same reason other technology is regulated. That is, to address social or environmental costs. This is primarily for the sake of neighbours around the building site. It's also to make sure that the over accumulation of wealth doesn't have an effect on the wider community.

It is for this reason that few states have ever fully bought into the concept of a free market economy. Economists may still talk of the free market, but most countries have regulators to make sure private monopolisation is reduced to oligopolies. Think of the EU case for free competition against Microsoft - 2007. In the case of land use, common interference by the state prevents the destruction of land, its contamination and even landowners being able to place onerous restrictions on future generations.

Land is an interdependent asset and its value derives from activities beyond its boundaries. Land within an urban settlement benefits from its neighbours. Land in the same condition but located 100 miles away from an urban settlement is worth a lot less. Land therefore is a 'social good.' The potential use and value of it is directly constrained by neighbouring activity, which inevitably spills over. Denser urban development results in greater potential spillover.

The evidence shows that cities without any controls are governed by a combination of an unbridled market, cultural traditions, and brute power. These cities are unable to deal with insufficient public infrastructure, absence of public open space and poor environmental quality. Without planning laws, there is no mechanism that can mitigate 'negative externalities' emanating from land use. These are the many negative impacts on neighbours or the community at large. They include noise, obstruction of sunlight, parking needs, and unaesthetic construction. In the language of economics, private (or even public) land users have no incentive to 'internalise' these externalities. Regulations are needed to incentivise this. An unregulated market will likely produce the following conditions; substandard and dangerous housing, poor environmental quality and disparities in access to infrastructure, social services, and amenities (Alterman, 2014).

4.0 Land Use Controls

Building codes were the first form of urban regulation to emerge. Rules for fire resistant construction methods in England emerged after the Great Fire of London. Those associated with poor sanitation, damp conditions and lack of ventilation took until the late 19th Century to emerge. In the end, comprehensive codes emerged in the 20th Century. Their purpose was to make sure that a building was structurally sound and would serve its intended function during its lifetime. In themselves they signalled the end of 'vernacular architecture.' Yet they did not go as far as enabling governments to designate different tracts of land for different land use functions, differing densities, or design.

Instruments that dealt in 'spatial considerations' were at first ad hoc and weak. They were voluntary and advisory, much like the case of regulations in less developed, Third World countries today. In England, the Housing, Town Planning Act 1909 was the first attempt to deal with general land use problems. This included incompatible uses and lack of amenity land. The Act banned the infamously unhealthy, 'back-to-back' housing of Victorian developers. It was also the first time 'town planning' was used in a statute. Its principles were to make sure that there was greater open space and low-density housing. As its planning powers were discretionary, there was little take up.

Unlike building and heritage controls, the domain of most planning controls stops at the front door. Their focus is on external layouts and city form. Yet there are still 'grey areas.' Interior activities can socially affect the inhabitants (for example, overcrowding) and adjoining occupiers. The latter is where the impact on amenity is considered, such as the disturbance caused by unusually intensive use. What defines a residential or household unit can turn, not only on absolute numbers or whether occupants are related, but on whether the residents are all sharing communal living spaces (for example, kitchens).

Land use controls are called different things in different countries: land use planning, zoning plans, land management, local planning, spatial planning, town and country planning, urban and regional planning, city planning, environmental planning and development management. These terms all refer to different rule based approaches. They authorise government bodies to apply measures to steer or control urban and rural development, or conservation. In most countries these measures include statutory plans while in the United States and Canada they manifest as zoning bylaws. They also include the subdivision of sites or 'planning' controls, powers to secure land or financing for public services, and the control of development by permits, building and housing codes.

The planning system in the West operates as a separate (and generally secondary) tier to property rights. Being deemed secondary to property rights has far reaching implications for its ability to achieve the purpose for which it was originally set up.

The planning system doesn't usually control who occupies the land and their ability to exclude others. Instead it controls and manages the development process. As stated earlier, this represents the wealth generating part of land in the industrialised city. The State is in effect restricting the absolute right of landowners to do what they wish when it introduces a land use control in an otherwise free land market. At the least, it defines where landowners can do certain activities. This introduces the concept of 'distributional equity.' The major function of planning regulations is to allocate development rights for different land uses and densities. Some are lucrative to the landholders such as designating market housing or commercial sites. Others are undesirable such as designating for agricultural or other protected zones that prevent buildings or structures from being erected. As lucrative land in a particular region is limited, legally binding plans or zoning decisions are a matter of allocating financial gains or losses. This is what Hagman and Misczynski (1978) call 'windfalls and wipeouts.'

Planning regulations also set which land tracts have either good or poor access to public services. Planning regulations set out which areas benefit from positive externalities and those that will bear the brunt of negative ones. In other words, planning regulations have major implications for property values and thus for their owners.

Most civic laws relate to distinct spheres, such as governance, business, or child care. In contrast, planning laws relate to many spheres. As the entire range of human (and nature-based) activities need the use of space, and because space is often people's major property asset, the planning system affect many spheres of life. This includes the procedures, institutions, and rules for controlling urban and rural development.

The idea of zoning has also evolved. Separating civic functions has always been around in practice, such as the example of Chang'an (Part II). Early 19th Century examples include Singapore, founded in 1819. British swashbuckler, Stamford Raffles, commissioned Philip Jackson to draw up a plan. It separated civic functions, business and residential areas. Although rapid population growth meant that swaths of suburbs were soon needed, the basic zonal layout survives to this day.

The idea that rules would vary by district was a 1870s invention of a German engineer, Reinhard Baumeister. This included two sets of regulations. One was for the city and the other for the suburbs. These specified building height, setbacks and the amount of lot area that could be built upon. Baumeister's influence made its way into the British planning system of 1909. Yet it was more successful in Germany due to the municipal government owning one-half of the city's land area. This gave regulators the power to shape their city.

Zoning in New York, started with the comprehensive zoning code of 1916. At that time the main problem was individual site 'over development.' This concern is about a landowner being able to 'put up a building to any height, in any place, of any foot print, and use it for any purpose, regardless of how much this hurts his neighbours.' It quickly evolved into single-use, Euclidean zoning. This represented a strict separation of uses. Residential zones exclude commercial and industrial uses and vice versa. The success of its advocates[32] meant that its use expanded rapidly in the 1920s (Talen, 2012).

Planning laws have created a regulatory reality that is difficult to reverse in advanced economies (Alterman, 2014). Montgomery (2013) views planning regulations as 'code,' that is to the city what an operating system is to the computer. The pervasiveness of planning controls is perhaps the biggest concern for those seeking a return to free market ideologies.

There have been other attempts to address the issues arising from ownership more directly than a secondary set of planning controls. The philosopher and writer Rousseau (1712 – 1778) maintained that as long as property and laws exist, people can never be entirely free. Geolibertarians[33] considered that all natural resources are common assets. The most important resource of all being land. All individuals should have an equal right to access. As people did not make the earth itself, it is the value of improvements (buildings) only that should form individual property. Therefore, individuals should pay rent to the community if they claim land as their private property. Such rent need not be paid for the mere use of land. Rather, the rent is for the right to exclude others from that land and to protect one's title by government.

The ideologies behind Communism envisioned large-scale experiments to bring social equity without land ownership. This includes the Soviet Union,

[32] Particularly Edward Bassett (1863 – 1948) 'the father of American zoning.'
[33] Such as Thomas Paine (1736-1809).

most East European Communist countries and similar regimes in the East, such as China. They effectively nationalised most developable land extinguishing underlying private ownership. The state agencies thus came to control most land allocation. They had the authority to develop it directly or allow others to develop it.

Urban planning often led to the compulsory purchase of land and existing buildings. Extinguishing property rights isn't entirely without precedence, even in England. The Artisans and Labourer's Dwellings Improvement Act in 1875 aimed to remove slums of poorly maintained properties. These had been typically rented to the Victorian poor. The aim was to put new working class dwellings in their place. It was one of the key mechanisms to 'improve' the urban fabric of industrial cities. The agent was the local authority. It would designate the site, compensate the owners, clear the land and sell it to private developers. Yet the new buildings didn't have to cater for the persons displaced (Yelling, 1986).

It is worth noting that all modern countries have laws that empower the state, or its agencies, to take land or buildings for public purposes. These powers may be included in the planning law or be independent of it. They are known by different terms in different countries: eminent domain, compulsory purchase, compulsory acquisition and expropriation takings. Technically, they are an option in many western countries. Yet they are regarded as a last resort. This is despite their effectiveness in controlling property speculation. An example of this is under Singapore's Land Compensation Legislation. The circumstances in which such expropriations can occur are generally well defined and need justification. Obtaining a compulsory purchase order turns out to be a long, contested and expensive procedure. As such, the United Kingdom government is considering whether to give Councils greater powers. These would enable them to seize land and approve large-scale housebuilding to tackle the housing shortage. The aim would be to create a new generation of garden towns.

Numerous authors take the view that development rights (as opposed to ownership rights) were effectively 'nationalised' in Britain under the Town and Country Planning Act, 1947. This is hereafter referred to as the 1947 Act. The Act removed prospective development rights and statutory plans couldn't grant them. This started the need for requesting development permission by landowners and private interests. They are approved on a discretionary or case by case basis by planning authorities. Clearly, this took away a landowners' rights to develop. In return it gave certain reassurances to surrounding landowners and occupants that they and their property would be protected.

Communist countries never relied on the authority of planning laws to set the legitimacy of their own short- or long-range urban plans. There is a paradox in what is presented by the media linking planning controls to Big Government. Communist regimes, which granted few freedoms to individual initiative, did not need, or want, planning laws. Yes, planning laws restrain private actions until due process has been followed. Yet their very existence implies the need for careful consideration of actions in the urban environment by other parties. The Communist Party in China extinguished land ownership. By re-introducing planning law in 1990 it was actually a step forward in the democratisation of planning and land management (Alterman, 2014).

5.0 Evolution of Democratic Planning Systems

If planning legislation is going to be effectively applied there needs to be an understanding that restricting the use of land is for the common good. It also implies that the use to which land is put, be set by the long term interests of the community as a whole. This is seen as being preferable to the use of land being set because of the incidence and spread of individual land ownership.

The more comprehensive planning traditions that nations are familiar with have emerged over time. In western democracies the four main origins are:

- Britain (town planning),
- Germany (Stadtebau)
- France (urbanisme) and
- United States (city planning).

These all promoted 'second generation' controls or traditional measures for controlling land use and density of development. These included land use categories, lot sizes, permitted coverage of the lot, setback lines from the road or lot boundaries, floor area ratios relative to plot size, number of housing units, and so on. These types of measures are internationally the most prevalent planning regulations. Expressed quantitatively, they are perceived as helping planners rationalise the calculation of public service provision.

There are national differences despite the above similarities. No two societies create the same institutions. They will have distinct customs, different systems of property rights and the like. Different countries have their own legal systems and structures within which planning operates. In planning, there is no dominant format of planning legislation, nor is there a consensus about best practice. Regulatory measures vary not only from country to country, but also from city to city. Moreover, there is no internationally agreed-on classification of such regulations.

German Stadtebau, translated into English, means 'city building' rather than city planning. German planners had a much stronger orientation towards the physical placement of buildings within the urban environment. Process, in essence, is emphasised less than output. Germany was the model for city planning in the pre-First World War era. Yet association with a wartime enemy demanded a shift in approach by Allied countries (Slavitt, 1994). In French urbanisme, architecture plays a secondary role to the landscape. It provides for an ordered assembly of buildings subservient to the whole. The British system is about the wise use of land and particularly the split between 'town' and 'country.'

The rationale for adopting planning laws in Post-War Western Europe reflected more than the need to physically rebuild destroyed cities. It was also to create a 'welfare state' supplying housing, upgrading schools, and providing public services. The British 1947 Act aimed for the orderly development and reconstruction of bomb damaged cities. It included a 100% betterment levy and compulsory purchase powers. These were to substitute for the desperate lack of public finance that existed at the time. Despite the rebuild effort after the Second World War, planning laws didn't arrive in most West European countries until the 1960s.

The rationale for the US zoning model was based on thinly hidden exclusionary purposes, or effects. Planning law there emerged without any visible kinship to the other systems. Instead of resulting from a federal or state legislative initiative, planning law in the United States emerged from the bottom up. Local authorities used their 'police power' (an American term similar to regulatory authority) to enact rudimentary zoning ordinances. This was in order to protect the 'health, safety, and welfare' of residents.

The purpose of American town planning was a process by which society's resources can be distributed as equitably and efficiently as possible. The key words are efficiency, equity and process. Invariably, efficiency and equity appear as opposites. This contributes significantly to the social tension which often surrounds the town planning process. It is directly related to the frustratingly poor record of plan implementation.

Planning in the US is justified and supported when it serves to correct market failures. It is considered unjustified in interfering with the private market. Such political ideology results in a reactive rather than proactive planning focus which sits better with the neo-liberal agenda.

In the US, justifications for planning intervention often rely on economic efficiency arguments. They don't often appeal to 'the public interest' or 'social justice.' In practice, an American zoning plan acknowledges the inherent right to develop. It may limit but rarely bans development. In contrast, plans in other countries such as Germany, identify areas in which future development is not permitted (Klosterman, 2003).

The influence of these systems extends beyond the originating countries themselves. The tendency in developing countries has been to model the same planning laws enacted and practiced in advanced-economy countries (Alterman, 2014). The British belief in the merits of planning law was so strong that the government transported this innovation to its colonies. So at a time when some of the most industrialised countries did not have planning laws, some poor countries became the premature 'owners' of quite sophisticated (for that time) versions. Yet being born in disparate circumstances meant that the effect of such legislation was more limited, dysfunctional and discriminatory on the colonies than the British homeland.

The lessons learnt from Western planning experience in the Third World can be a distraction. Physical urban form remains important for countries experiencing urbanisation and democratisation. The IMF, World Bank report says many emerging urban centres are still taking shape. This provides policymakers with a unique but rapidly closing window of opportunity to get their cities 'right.' Developing and transition countries should ask a tough question before rushing to emulate the planning laws of advanced economies. Has the enactment and carrying out of planning laws enhanced social equity or exacerbated inequities?

6.0 Planning System Differences

Political systems and land ownership are inextricably linked. That is to say, the political philosophies on land use do not exist in a vacuum. Rather, they come about as a result of the governing class and, in particular, the relationship between Land Ownership and the Political System. They express what a society sees as the legitimate role of government vis-à-vis private interests.

Four different scenario's are set out below:

Political / Land Regime	Resulting Planning System
Liberal democratic nations with relatively many land owners e.g., US or Sweden.	A wide divergence of responses from relatively weaker controls in some US states to the best examples of European spatial planning.
Liberal democratic nation but relatively few land owners; for example England and Scotland.	Relatively stronger planning systems which can even tend towards land-reform.
Aristocratic nation with relatively few land owners; for example Latin America.	Generally, the elites are not going to look favourably on planning controls resulting in a minimal and/or non-functioning planning system. While there are exceptions, such cities often have a bad track record in proper land use and urban planning.
One party dictatorship and no private ownership	No planning controls as such, but can pursue urban development through centralised planning as discussed earlier.

Within each of these categories further distinctions can be drawn out:

Landowners

The wealth and capabilities of landowners may be as relevant as their numbers. Comfortable well off landowners, with a diversity of incomes from their land may tolerate planning controls more than smaller, more equitable free holders. The latter are dependent on the whims of commodity prices.

The pressure to intervene in land ownership is going to be most acute on the urban - rural fringes and the central core of cities. The urban fringe is where greenfield development can most easily take place but depends on whether large landowners are prepared to subdivide their estates into suburban plots. Central cities face fragmented private ownership and high previous investment in the public realm. The issue is the ability of the state to rationalise land into more conveniently sized parcels.

English cities, in the 18th and 19th Centuries, were largely built by a combination of landowners and developers. The organised building of long terrace houses was made possible by the landowners controlling large stretches of virgin land around the expanding cities. In contrast, fragmented land ownership on the Continent meant that mass urban housing couldn't occur in same way.

Political Integration

Politics sets the role of government in relation to private interests. It thus sets the level of detail over which planning controls extend. In England, development rights have been nationalised. The level of control at which state discretion is set comes through the general permitted development orders. This represents a centrally fixed position that has evolved along with both best practice and experimentation. Recent Government amendments have raised the controls to give greater flexibility in development. This includes allowing for new schools to be set up, converting offices into housing and for permission (in principle) to be granted for housing-led development. It has also been made easier to extend homes such as by building 'conservatories' (September 2012). This was intended to 'kick-start' construction expenditure at the height of the recession. Yet it was instigated without any basis having been shown as to the likely take up or regard to the impact on neighbouring land.

The degree of vertical integration within the political system also plays a role. Countries with a federal structure of Government (as in Canada and Australia) have legislation existing at both federal and sub-federal levels. In Britain it can only exist at a national level. A federal system can thus have more than one act addressing the same issue. One is to manage federal interests and the other to manage state or provincial interests.

Physical Context

Just as the best examples of pre-industrial planning occurred on densely packed land areas, so it remains the case today. Strong, comprehensive planning systems exist in areas of high population densities. Hong Kong, Singapore and Monaco are examples of highly populated coastal entities, constrained by shared boundaries with the mainland. They, like the Netherlands, may be able to create new land by reclamation, but this is a costly exercise. Their approach to urban expansion is dictated by lack of land availability. This explains why the Netherlands never adopted the United Kingdom 'garden city' approach. It did not have the option of creating towns an equidistant 64km from city centres. Any lesser distance would have simply created a metropolis, destroying any remaining countryside (Wagenaar 2011).

There are also differences between the levels of urbanisation. Parts of America and southern Europe are less urbanised than parts of Britain and North West Europe. The more heavily urbanised the area, the more amenable it is to planning intervention.

Development Pressure

A related reason is the rate of development pressure and change. Growing cities need stronger planning controls to those of shrinking cities. Mega-cities, like London, are distinguished by their wealth. Others in the Third World, are distinguished by their population growth. In contrast is the 'shrinking city,' typified by de-industrialised, rust belt, urban areas. A trend reinforcing this in the United States was for rich and middle class city dwellers to flee inner cities for outer suburbs. This was to escape having to pay the spiralling costs of addressing urban inequality. In shrinking cities, planning becomes reactive because it has little influence on the main forces at hand: deindustrialisation, demographics and even suburbanisation. The challenge in this situation is to retain sufficient population density to maintain a certain level of public service and quality of urban life. In these places urban space should be rationalised.

Culture

Culture has always had a significant bearing on architecture and building design (see Part V). Subsequently, it also has a bearing on what is considered worthy of protection. Controls on buildings can be strict indeed in certain places, depending on their special nature and qualities. For example, in English conservation areas permission is needed just to change the colour of a front door. Unlike the West, in Iran the focus of planning is not on economic, social or environmental objectives. Instead, it is focused on correct architectural style, such as reconstructing and maintaining Iranian-Islamic buildings. It is also about ensuring important plans have a cultural connection. There is no established 'development control' system as such. In a context of rapid urbanisation incompatible land uses are evident on the ground. The effects are congestion and conflict between vehicle and pedestrian traffic.

Institutional arrangements evolve over time, as do public attitudes towards government control. Culture plays a role in influencing politics. This in turn drives the legislative processes, just as political forces may seek to influence culture i.e., individualism and the free market. In the developed world, communities expect certain standards of living (i.e., welfare state). In the Third World, government intervention is not always expected or even desired. Countries also evolve differently due to historical circumstances. People may be more or less law abiding or anti-statist.

There may also be different focuses. For instance, the planning system in Britain has been built around its 'cult of property ownership.' Nordic countries have benefited from having been able to evolve over a long period of time in an insular environment. Their's is a cohesive, yet innovative orientated culture. For this reason they can feature a stronger vertical integration between national and local government (Nima Sanandaji, 2016).

Unexplained

Given the similarities in the issues around urbanisation, it may seem surprising that planning systems have not converged more over time (within western democracies at least). Political and ideological differences do give weight to different values, along with institutional arrangements, geography and culture. Yet not everything is able to be easily explained. A study[34] concluded that often there were no apparent explanations to explain differences based on the usual assumptions. This was despite considering legal frameworks, institutional structure, or transfer of knowledge among proximate or culturally similar countries. Often countries adopt planning solutions largely insulated from the experiences of other countries (Alterman et al, 2010).

7.0 The modern purpose of planning

The ideals of early planners to promote order, efficiency, beauty and social justice are still the moral basis for action in most countries. Such aspirations are fairly high level. If the basic purpose for urban planning is distilled, four main reasons emerge as follows (Klosterman, 1985):

---

[34] Addressing the question of whether state authorities should compensate property owners for the impact of land use regulation.

- Protecting the collective interests of the community;
- Improving the information base for individual and collective decision making. This is planning as a method. It's about integrating different information sources regarding future and current needs and pressures on resources;
- Protection of the needy in society (disadvantaged and marginalised groups);
- Addressing the external effects of individual and group action. Responding to the impacts and externalities of other groups.

Protecting collective interests can extend to 'spatial integration.' In China, it's linking the under-developed interior to the wealthier coastal regions and the water-short north with the well-watered south. In Western Europe, regional regeneration is a core goal. Planning can be part of a goal of homogenising the regions and ensuring territorial 'equality.' This is through subsidies for equivalent growth in all areas. The protection of the needy is also pragmatic. It equates with defusing the potential for social and political unrest in urban slums.

Since the 1990s, the idea of sustainable development has come to most fully represent the purpose of planning. This is defined as development that satisfies the needs of the present without compromising the ability of future generations to satisfy theirs.[35] Sustainable development is a change from planning's previously narrow emphasis. This was about capital and labour relationships and resolving the contradictions of capitalism in the industrial city. The case of sustainable development is about reconciling economic growth and conservation of natural resources. It's not altogether new. Patrick Geddes,[36] maxim set out in 1915 was 'Place-Work-Folk'. His terminology has thus been updated as place = environment, work = economic and folk = social. For Geddes, as with sustainable development, all three had to be in equilibrium.

Commentators have made a number of criticisms of the Brundtland version of sustainable development. Beckerman (1995) sees it as being totally useless since 'need' is a subjective concept. People at different points in time, or income levels, or cultural or national backgrounds will differ about the needs they see as important. It lacks clear guidance about what future generations may need to meet their needs, and what has to be preserved now.

---

[35] As set out in the Brundtland report of 1987 by the United Nations World Commission on Environment and Development.

[36] A pioneering town planner.

This has led to both 'strong' and 'weak' conceptualisations of sustainability. Strong sustainability seeks to preserve intact the environment in all its forms as we find it today. Weak sustainability, on the other hand, allows for some natural resources to be run down. Just so long as adequate compensation is given by increases in economic and social resources. To make the most efficient use of resources, sustainable development may need some measures associated with economic planning.

The meta-narrative of sustainability has not only mobilised planners and other stakeholders. It has become almost an obsession to take into account the most sustainable urban form. Planning controls are 'cross-cutting' across different sectors. Comprehensive (spatial) planning needs to give geographical expression to the economic, social, cultural and ecological policies of a society. The United Kingdom's National Planning Policy Framework (NPPF), gives some over-arching idea of how this might work:

- Economic – having enough land of the right type and in the right available to allow for growth and innovation, identification and co-ordination of development (infrastructure provision)
- Social – strong, vibrant and healthy communities, enough housing, accessible local services that reflect communities' needs, health and well-being.
- Environment – protect and enhance the natural, built and historic environments, use natural resources prudently and the like.

Due to the threat posed by climate change, national and local governments are adopting an increasing number of environmental rules. These are over and above the traditional amenities such as open space standards. Rules include a portion of each plot staying unpaved to allow water to seep away, or a portion of a plot to be set aside for wetlands or urban wildlife. In some countries and municipalities, green construction has been required for energy saving, water conservation, or recycling.

Sweden[37] has perhaps gone further than most. It introduced a new regulatory framework for the technical performance of buildings and physical structures. This includes renewable energy generation and other energy efficiency measures for buildings. In the United Kingdom, it relies on local policy drivers to support new technological waves. A notable example was the Merton rule from the London Borough of Merton. This measure, to

---

[37] Never a country afraid to pioneer planning controls.

require 10% of energy use to come from on site renewable sources, has turned photovoltaic panels and wind turbines from eccentric novelties into an aspiration for 'keeping up with the Jones.' In Wales, policy drivers support more impressive outcomes. For example, they have set a specific ecological footprint of no more than 2.4 global hectares per person in terms of consumption.

8.0 Planning for the Urban Form

It is contended that urban planning is nothing if it doesn't engage with the physical form of the city: a so called outcome based model. Yet even this stance can be disagreed with by those eager to promote a system dispensing 'procedural equity.'

The study of urban morphology covers the form of human settlements and the process of their formation and transformation. Despite massive differences in political and land ownership systems, there are remarkable similarities between modern cities around the world. Cities under both Western democracies and communism featured central, pedestrianised areas, skyscrapers and higher density inner cores. This shouldn't come as a surprise. Both economic systems used the same means of production, ideas of progress, application of technology and use of machinery. It is contended that despite attempts to put in place a comprehensive planning system, what took precedence was industrialisation. Urbanisation was just a consequence of industrialisation, as people migrated to the cities to seek employment and better services. The problem was that population growth outstripped housing and service provision.

Urban Physical Form

Informal (unplanned) settlements do not typically make specific provision for street layouts, rights of ways for utilities and urban services. Furthermore, they may have an inequitable distribution of land among inhabitants. Accessibility also emerges as a major problem as many residents of peripheral, unplanned settlements work in city centres.

When the state intervenes in urban form, the most basic decision made is where to build or where not to build, based on different land types. The allocation, zoning or designation of land promotes or differentiates particular

places or activities over others.   It creates a hierarchy of places and re-
territorialises space:

- Buildings you don't want located in certain areas.
- Buildings and sites you don't want modified.
- Buildings you don't want used in a certain way.
- Lot size, ownership and Subdivision.

The following framework sets out the approaches of how this can be carried
out. It depends upon whether it's the state regulating private ownership or the
State directing change to land in underlying public ownership.

State Intervention	Develop (Allow Buildings)	Protect (Keep Buildings Out)
Private land	Enterprise and residential zones, garden cities, end of pipe solutions.	Conservation areas, soft solutions and source protection, significant natural areas, flood zones, greenbelts.
Public owned land	Buying land on the urban periphery (Vallingsby 1950s), Total Place (UK), Regeneration, Infrastructure (need for ever more roads, constraints on future generations).	National Parks, environmental or landscape designations.

For development and protection areas to be effective they must be supported
by evidence. There has to be a realistic chance that industrial development
will be brought forward by the private sector in allocating enterprise zones.
Spatial categories (spatial order categories, area types) are areas defined by
specific criteria in which comparable structures exist and where similar goals
are pursued. The most important spatial categories include:

- conurbations/agglomerations;
- regulatory areas;
- structurally weak areas;
- rural areas.

Supra-local axes or communication axes serve the far-reaching exchange of goods, services and people. They connect agglomerations with peripheral areas and give locational advantages for the areas they traverse. They are also expected to stimulate development. Settlement axes provide for the linear concentration of settlements. They must also be co-ordinated with public transport systems. They contribute to settlement structure and the preservation of open spaces, especially in regulatory areas. For protection types, the land must not only have intrinsic values. It also needs some realistic future threat from development, bad practices and the like.

The focus of much planning is the desire for towns and cities to promote health, economic growth and beauty, within a functional, and aesthetically pleasing environment. Its purpose may only be to create an attractive physical environment. That is, managing development so that it is appropriate in its context. This can be difficult enough. Its concerns are primarily physical form and the interrelationships of function. The outputs are typically masterplans. Yet town planning has often aspired to setting a social agenda.

Optimal Urban Size

The most basic concern of social planning is around the appropriate size of a settlement. In the industrial age various ideas moved the debates of antiquity forward. The worst of urban slums has been removed from western cities. The focus of planning has shifted to a concern with traffic problems, human scale for the city and the nature of its physical and social environment. Howard's Garden City (1898) movement sought planned, self-contained communities. These comprise a mixture of employment and residential land surrounded by 'greenbelts' of up to 50,000 people. In contrast was the sense of modernism of French Architect Le Corbusier's (1887 – 1965). He proposed housing three million people in rows of identical apartment blocks, laid out in a rigidly symmetrical grid pattern (see Part V).

Assumptions about an idealised population size were of vital importance in conceptualising physical layouts that formed the basis of 'state led, 'blueprint' planning.' The 1947 Act required authorities to define a target population figure. This then made it possible to calculate overspill. It wasn't long before the practical difficulties of such an approach became clear. Birmingham's first Plan is an example of planning in the post-war era. It sought to give a level of spaciousness and avoid traffic congestion. The problem was that it assumed static population growth and an even balance of immigration - emigration and natural births over deaths (Chan, 2003). What eventuated was a major influx of immigrants from the British Commonwealth; particularly those from Southern Asia and the Caribbean.

Setting aside environmental constraints, optimal city size varies for cities with different industrial functions. There is a direct relationship between the economic and cultural wealth of a city on the one hand and the limitation of its population on the other. For Leon Krier, the architect, theorist and urban planner (born 1946), this was not a matter of mere hypothesis but historical fact. What is optimal is likely to vary over time, depending upon technological change. This is the case with transport and communications, the changing structure of employment and industry, rising real incomes and the greater availability of leisure time (Brown, 1972). This kind of structural change embodies the kind of economic development that modern societies depend upon for improvements in their living standards (Salter, 1963; Wragg and Robertson, 1978).

Neighbourhood Units

It's difficult to decide upon an ideal urban population size. What is easier is to think of the best way a city can be structured into residential sub-units. Housing is directly related to the community that results. This is by reason of shared residence. Even if residents don't live together in the same house, they still share a common space of some kind. It may be a boundary with a neighbour, a street or a common entrance in a block of flats. Blower (1973) listed five types of neighbourhood. These were arbitrary (where the only link is common territory), ecological (common environment), homogeneous (based on socio-economic status and ethnicity) and functional (based on geographical mapping of service provision). The final one has the best attributes of a community (close knit, socially homogeneous groups).

Clarence Percy[38] first conceptualised the aims for the 'neighbourhood unit' during the 1920s in the United States. These units were to have social aims; neighbourhood interaction and creation of a sense of community identity. They were also to be functional, self-contained and desirable neighbourhoods. Social, administrative and service facilities were all deemed important for an adequate urban existence. There needed to be a school centred in the neighbourhood of one quarter, to no more than a half mile, walking distance. Arterial streets were to go around the perimeter which contained a hierarchy of internal streets. Local shopping was restricted to the perimeter and at least 10% dedicated to open spaces.

---

[38] Planner and sociologist.

The idea of neighbourhood units caught on. Dutch and Swedish thinking of the 1940s considered the need for between 5- 20,000 inhabitants. Each unit would have their own schools and shops (both centrally located) within walking distance. The Dutch also conceived of larger centres within cycling distance that would serve two or perhaps more of those neighbourhoods. Each neighbourhood needed to be an area where individuals could live in safe and familiar surroundings. It also had to have all facilities for daily living.

Across the Iron Curtain, Soviet planning of the 1950s incorporated the logic of the mikroraion (micro-district). The intent was that its residents could readily and conveniently access the majority of their daily needs within that area. This included housing for approximately 5,000-15,000 people. The mikroraion was internally linked by pedestrian walkways. These gave access to services such as libraries, sports facilities, nurseries, health services and cultural amenities. A collection of mikroraions formed a larger district that had additional services, such as a polyclinic. The neighbourhood was linked to central place systems. The aim was to give the population with area-wide infrastructural amenities such as:

- basic centres; where low-order or small centres supply the basic daily needs of the population in the immediate area,
- middle-order centres; central places that meet more demanding needs of the population in the intermediate area;
- high-order centres; central places which are meeting demanding, specialised needs of the population in the extended catchment area.

The neighbourhood unit has always had its limitations and detractors. It quickly became clear that having residents of all the same generation or age band living together would make sure that there was a lifecycle of boom and bust in terms of communities' service provision (whether crèches, schools, employment, health or age car facilities). If the intention was to make sure that resources would be used efficiently to serve the local community, the Dutch neighbourhood experience was that ideological and religious differences interfered (post-war society). This resulted in many new neighbourhoods having to be provided with two or even three primary schools and churches.

Neighbourhood units also came under criticism from sociologists who challenged their foundation on a territorial basis. They saw that it was private developers who championed the neighbourhood unit. It was a bastion for the gentry and to keep undesirables as well as through-traffic, out. Their promoters pointed to the benefits that an appropriate density would bring.

This was both the healthy development of an area and to avoid over-crowding. Their detractors instead felt that this can readily be linked to eugenics, racism and functionalism. Reginald Issacs[39] noted the neighbourhood unit's potential for private developers to segregate racial, ethnic, religious and economic groups. They was done through physical design aspects that have similarities to those in gated-communities. Most vocal was sociologist, Van Doorn. He condemned the neighbourhood unit as reactionary and artificial (1955). In his opinion, social communities could not be shaped. People would find their own relations, inside and outside their own neighbourhood.

The promotion of the neighbourhood as a planning tool illustrates a tension between achieving the goals of planning to end social inequality and that of creating an authentic local community. Theorists often warn of the dangers in overstating the power of urban design to effect social change. The central place hierarchy functioned well in the 1950s and 1960s. Later on, somewhere in the 1970s and 1980s, the intricate structure came under pressure. Processes of scaling up and rationalisation led to fewer shops and facilities. These included libraries and childcare at the neighbourhood level. Demographic processes led to fewer people and people with different characteristics. Individualism and prosperity led to wider travel patterns and less dependency on local contacts. Technological progress made people less dependent on their daily environment. Car mobility replaced the need for proximity; the very embodiment of Zwischenstadten. Both De Vreeze (1993) and Esping-Andersen et al (2005), make the point that modern relationships are based on functional relations. These accord to occupation, personal interest and motivation, rather than on the local concentration of the direct environment.

Despite the apparent slipperiness of promoting neighbourhoods in the modern era, it is unlikely to be given up entirely. It is self-evident that direct physical proximity is the most authentic way humans can experience each other and their neighbours. In accepting that the mobility of people, money and information is much higher now than when physical planning originated, the aim of improving liveability remains.

So long as people go outside their houses and apartments by the original mode of transportation (walking) there will always be a place for good urbanism principles in neighbourhoods. These include connectivity, pedestrian orientation, compactness, land use diversity, enclosure and small blocks. Good urban design comes back to the ability to translate technicians' and architects' visions of desirable physical forms of urban development,

---

[39] Director of Planning for Michael Reese Hospital in Chicago, in the late 1940's.

whilst being mindful of different needs. Good design principles are well established but it is for whom they are designed that is important.

The modernist vision of cities was that the city and its inhabitants could be managed rationally by an enlightened administration. They could plan for the economic, social and cultural needs of all. The problem with this was that the local community did not always agree with the proposals being put forward. Perhaps the most famous confrontation in the history of urban planning was a David and Goliath affair in the 1960s between New York's Robert Moses[40] and Jane Jacobs[41] (Leo Hollis, 2014). Moses' plans were for modernisation and highway development. In particular, he had the Lower Manhattan Expressway scheme in mind. This scheme would have put a 10-lane straight line across Greenwich Village, Soho, Little Italy, Chinatown and the Lower East Side. Jane Jacobs became the advocate for Greenwich Village by claiming it would break up her community (refer to Part V).

Interestingly, Jacobs went on to argue her particular vision for urban form. In her mind, cities need at least a 100 homes per acre to produce enough street traffic to support exciting restaurants and shops. The height of six stories is ideal. Beyond that, they risked sterile standardisation. More recent research,[42] purports that neighbourhoods of 15,000 people within an area not exceeding 35ha is ideal. This would comprise dwellings, working and leisure facilities. It would give mixed use urban quarters and integrate all daily functions of life (Carmona et al, 2003).

9.0 Planning Tools: Funding, Regulation or Compulsory Purchase

'Shared visions' for communities are typically encapsulated through non-statutory documents. These include guidelines and community plans. Inevitably their agenda places pressure on short term corporate interests. Due to them lacking 'regulatory teeth,' some countries appear to have been more successful than others at producing them.

Society signals its attitudes by regulating against behaviour it thinks is harmful. In contrast, it regularises behaviour which it considers beneficial or where its attitude has softened. Planning regulations are designed not just to modify the behaviour of those building or undertaking activities. They also

---

[40] A city planner not unlike a modern day Baron Haussmann.

[41] Resident, journalist, author, and activist.

[42] Such as that of Leon Krier (1990).

function to influence societal well-being (including) behaviour through built form.

This harks back to the idea of physical determinism and the notion that a society is a product of its environment. Form and pattern zoning unquestionably exerts control. This is over things like social behaviour, daily patterns of movement, and access to public goods. As such, planning controls do influence how places perform – socially, environmentally and economically.

Even so, regulating 'where' something is or is not built does not come close to controlling whether something will be built. The grant of planning permission is not seen as state subsidisation, as there is no transfer of state resources. Regulations only result in desired change if those to whom they are applied have the capacity and willingness to change their behaviours. Compared to other control mechanisms, they are a powerful and appealing tool for policymakers.

Where reliance is placed upon the public sector to direct private sector development, it is referred to as regulatory planning (Brindley, Rydin & Stoker 1996). Generally, this benefits a few land and property owners from occasional planning permissions. The focus of such planning systems leads to the ability to be far more choosey or discriminatory about the type of development wanted. Often the aims of the system can be perceived as preventing certain types of development. For instance, those considered to contribute to 'market failure' rather than 'support' development.

In areas of rapid development, where lots of private capital is circulating, the regulatory framework can often achieve adequate investment in infrastructure. This can be without significant outlays of public money. The profits of the development are so high that it's possible to get the right level of servicing out of private developers to avoid public subsidisation. An example are the roads and sewers that private development seeks to use. This is most typically achieved through development contributions. A small part of that gain (profit) accrues to the council, via community infrastructure levies and ('Section 106') planning agreements. The bulk goes to the original landowner.

Where regulatory planning falls down is when growth levels are low – something that occurs both spatially and temporally. Urban policy is expected to create further urban growth out of shrinkage. Other than reducing or varying their burden to encourage private sector investment, regulatory measures are of limited use.

This highlights the difficulty to deliver societies' expectations through the planning system without recourse to subsidising development. Types of planning systems can be divided into whether the primary mechanism to achieve results on the ground is either regulatory or funding based.

The following table illustrates the differences between four different types of regimes:

Basic Planning System Typologies

Regulatory Planning	**Keynesian / Central Planning**
Controls	Controls
No Funding	Funding
Third World	**Private Management / Aid Operations**
No Controls	Few Regulatory Barriers
No Funding	Funding (often sporadic)

Regulation on its own can be burdensome. The above scenario on private management (Brindley, Rydin and Gerry, 1996) is about handing development over to the private sector. It largely sets its own rules. Under a neo-liberal discourse or perceived failures in Government intervention, this is often seen as a new option with interesting possibilities. Yet in many ways, it represents no more than a return to some pre-intervention state of affairs. Development is the prisoner to prevailing economic and social conditions. The ability to develop land is dependent on the availability of capital. A sufficient rate of return is needed for any type of development that depends on private capital. Returns made over the first few years of a building's life need to exceed the development costs sufficiently to make the desired profit. In Detroit, housing prices have been below the cost of building new homes. This situation makes sure there will continue to be almost no private development and continued population loss.

The evidence from de-industrialised Western cities suggests that private management achieves little through measured renewal of derelict areas, given the lack of enough of a rate of return. This is the position many newly industrialising countries find themselves in. They can't be too choosey, in terms of regulations, about what development they allow.

Alternatively, the funding for projects, or some part thereof, can be directly supplied by the state. This would be the case of central planning. It is worth noting that this was envisaged for the planning and construction of Britain's New Towns (under the 1947 Act). The means to do so were to be through separate development corporations appointed by the Minister. They had extensive powers to acquire and develop land, along with providing certain public services. The shift to modern 'urban entrepreneurialism'[43] in the West has been accompanied by reduced capabilities within the planning system. This not only reflects a shift from comprehensive land use regulations to a project-led approach. It also offers reduced powers to lever funding. Chinese municipal governments, in contrast, are regarded as prime examples of 'urban entrepreneurs.' They are actively involved in the development of urban projects and have ramped up the capabilities of the planning system. The direct state actions of these entrepreneurial municipal governments are diverse. They range from the provision of necessary infrastructure, cheap land and fiscal incentives, to the creation and promotion of grand development visions.

Based on the Federal Spatial Planning Law of 1965, Germany has a broad aim to make sure there are equal conditions regardless of geography. To minimise social disparities, a hierarchy of 'central place' cities have been defined and identified. These 'central places' give services and infrastructure for the surrounding regions. They accord with their importance, or rank, in the urban hierarchy. Both federal and state funding is then distributed according to a place's rank and tasks within the central place hierarchy. Cities with more service functions receive proportionally more funding.

Many (existing) urban authorities are going to lack the sorts of direct powers and resources held by national government. Their funding comes through rates or taxes, from the local landowners or population. Taxes are an indirect mechanism. They often need higher (and spatially less interested) levels of Government to instigate. They are seldom used, despite potentially having a huge bearing on the decisions of owners. Whether it's how an owner uses their land or how the public uses a public resource, such as a highway. Taxation, such as road charges, is an effective means of combating peak hour traffic. This is instead of land use, density control measures.

Leverage planning is another of Brindley et al's (1996) categories. It relies on planning authorities to stimulate the market from borrowing derived funding. A criteria to choose areas for urban development corporations to regenerate is the extent to which public sector funds would likely lever private sector investment. Clearly this benefits incoming developers.

---

[43] A proactive, economic role for urban governance in the context of globalisation; Harvey, 1989.

Taxpayers are increasingly reluctant to fund investment in the public realm or subsidise any activity that does not directly benefit them as individuals. Their motto is to minimise tax and self-interest and sits alongside increasing individualism (as discussed in Part I). Often, such income sources are not available or discouraged for ideological reasons. Tax (even more so than regulations) destroys the incentive to create wealth. This is the 'tax-funding' trap; higher taxes discourage capital flows. This means the state has less money to invest on infrastructure projects. It thus has to rely more and more on private funding (with all the strings that come from this. Yet how far can taxes and associated funding be cut before issues arise? Economic growth sounds tempting on its own but can ignore other hidden costs. This includes social instability, lower environmental quality of life, less equity and equality. Also, it is possible to do the opposite and improve situations by raising rates. This occurred in New York in the 1970s. Falling municipal revenues, high crime and social disorder had resulted in an historic low point for the city. Building fires[44] raged and abandonment began to categorise the period. Rather than reducing the tax burden as a response, the City raised property taxes on unused property. This forced owners to improve the condition of their buildings and had the desired effect of mobilising and revitalising the real estate market.

It was American economist Henry George who first suggested having a land value tax. This wouldn't discourage developers from constructing houses or factories. As the supply of land is fixed, such a tax becomes a cost of owning it. It could in principle bring about a decrease in prices. Owners of inefficiently used sites are either compelled to sell or lease them to more productive uses. Increasing the cost of owning land would drastically cut the incentives for speculation. This style of tax is being investigated by Governments around the world. Their intent is to discourage real estate investment over other forms of long term wealth accumulation (Smith and Dumienski, 2015).

Infrastructural funding is generally acceptable. It is seen as a part of government's delivery role and something which can support the wider economy. Most new development relies on existing infrastructural networks for example, supra-local or communication axes. The ability to connect to such networks and the cost of such connections is a key element in the profitability of any scheme. Building infrastructure has upfront costs but long term benefits. For instance, a greenfield housing extension needs an upfront connection to the highway network. This allows the housing it serves to be

---

[44] Many suspected to have been started by or for the owners to claim insurance.

built over time as supply is taken up. The installation of infrastructure is a key way to lead development and a means used in spatial planning to overcome the limitations of indicative planning.

Account is not always taken of the difference between outcomes and tangible benefits. The outcome of England's High Speed rail project (HS2)[45] is to cut travel times. What is harder to quantify is whether the passengers are more productive as a result from the few minutes they'd gain from arriving at their destination earlier. This is, given the significant investment needed and disbenefits from the loss of land. Net benefits often come down to financial vs. wider societal benefits. Conventional methods of development appraisal also tend to discount longer term benefits. A prime example is cost benefit ratios. They also don't tend to adequately capture indirect locational effects (Peckitties, 2013).

One modern variation in the United Kingdom's local government scene is tax increment financing. Infrastructure funds are borrowed in the local area in expectation of increased tax revenues. An example is the Earnback (tax increment finance-style) scheme model for infrastructure improvements. This has been used by Greater Manchester. The borrowings will be 'paid back' to the authority as real economic growth is seen. These 'earned back' funds will be reinvested in further infrastructure improvements to allow Greater Manchester to reach its economic potential. Depending on your ideological lens, this is either a perpetual cycle of regeneration funding or another scheme of 'fictitious capital'.

Another mechanism used in the United Kingdom and elsewhere, to avoid borrowing and get private funding, is the Public Funded Initiative. This typically involves large companies bidding for contracts. They not only build facilities and infrastructure but also maintain, clean and supply them for a period of decades. Government transfers the risk and responsibility to the private sector, while avoiding a huge capital programme on the public accounts. Payment can instead be made over 30 years.

Strong leadership is beneficial. It has shifted from the dictatorial style of Haussman's day to a more imaginative, place-based leadership. This is described by Hambleton's (2014) New Civic Leadership model. Following the collapse of Communism, growth of the city centre in Moscow was put down to what Ruble (1998) described as, 'imperial urban corporatism' rather than neoliberal market principles. Mayor Luzhkov (1992 – 2010) was in 1995 able to convince the then Russian President, Yeltsin that local authorities in

---

[45]   The second high-speed railway in the United Kingdom linking London, Birmingham, the East Midlands, Leeds, Sheffield and Manchester.

Moscow should control privatisation efforts; especially real estate development. This was unlike the case in the rest of Russia which was controlled by central government. Luzhkov encouraged city building using the public-private partnership strategy (see Fainstein, 2001; Kolossov and O'Loughlin, 2004). It allowed state and private agencies to 'act and make decisions together and pooled assets and risks to support development. The concept is similar to that of Brindley et al's (1996) partnership planning. Before Luzhkov fell from favour, Moscow had become the senior partner in all local economic activity (ibid, p. 84). Most of the city's income came from taxes (corporate, personal, and value-added). So city coffers encouraged and helped the boom in the development of office and retail space (Stanilov, 2007b).

Where private funding sources are unavailable for regeneration, the local authority has to look at 'ways within' their realm. They also have to be within the powers of competency available to it. This is clearly going to be problematic in those parts of the world where upfront capital is lacking. There is essentially a catch 22 where upfront private capital is lacking. It's simply not possible to get development without upfront (public) investment in infrastructure. The development of a connecting highway network is an example. Yet the state may simply not be in a position to give any measure of external financing. In the West, there are generally options available to fund urban projects yet urban decline from within can be difficult to resolve. The 'shrinking city' scenario in the US is worsened by property taxes being the main source of revenue. A fiscal crisis in the mid-1970s brought New York to the brink of municipal bankruptcy. More recently this occurred in Detroit which declared bankruptcy in July, 2013.

Selling assets is a mechanism to secure funding. For China, the benefit of shifting to a market economy was that they were able to free up the untapped value of land owned earlier by the state. According to the World Bank, local government delivers 80% of public services, but has just 28% of the revenues. Land sales to developers (land dispossessions) have been a lucrative means to finance local government. Research from Peking University suggests that the shortfall, more than 70% of local government revenues, is found through this means.

In the United Kingdom, the 'Total-Place' concept[46] came to popularise a more sophisticated way for joined up resourcing across the public sector. Rationalisation of existing public land was a key facet of Total Place. It recognised real world problems. Co-ordination across different agencies can

---

[46] Under the previous Labour Government.

be poor and issue complexity a big barrier to implementation. It sought to break down barriers both between and within organisations. In its approach to co-ordinate the delivery of public services it moved beyond distinctions of whether the private and public sector provides the services.

Tinkering with higher taxes and subsidisation is discouraged in western economies. None-the-less, governments do intervene using available macro-economic mechanisms. Following the 2008 financial crisis, the prices of loans (if you can qualify for one) became a lot lower in many countries. This was thanks to the continuous slashing of interest rates. This wasn't due to people suddenly not wanting loans and the banks needing to lower their prices to shift them. It was the result of political decisions to cut interest rates, thereby boosting demand.

Even in normal times, interest rates are set in most countries by the central bank. This means that political considerations creep in. In other words, interest rates are also set by politics. Some countries engage in this manipulation more than others. China's phenomenal urbanisation relies on the ability of its central government to intervene arbitrarily in the banking system if anything goes wrong. Its abundant foreign exchange reserves are used to re-capitalise the banks. Fixed asset spending has been equal to nearly 70% of the nation's GDP.

10.0 Central Planning

During China's socialist era, planning largely played a supplementary role. It provided technical drawings and solutions to the aims set out by the economic strategies of the government (Wu, 2015). The activities of planning were mostly restricted. Blueprints were produced and targets supported by a separate process of economic planning.

There's always been a temptation to move from purely physical land-use planning. This stems from the desire to control the economic and social processes that create demand for the land uses in the first place. In western cities, central government driven planning for the working class in 1940s - 1960s was done along these lines. Many industries and sectors around the world are still part funded by government. Governments may wish to develop specific markets or products. They may wish to take advantage of long-term shifts in the economy and changes in consumer trends. It is described as 'picking winners.' Without intervention, these markets and products may not exist. Low carbon technologies such as renewable energy are examples of this.

There are other reasons to engage in economic planning. It may be to make sure there is security of a particular supply chain considered essential for the functioning of the economy. Another may be to provide for the orderly restructuring of an industry. This can help firms survive, preserve jobs and prevent the loss of skills. The latter reason reduces the negative impacts of disturbances to the economy, economic downturns or changes in trends. One example is through government grants to delay the relocation of an industry in a single industry town. Another could be outright attempts to avoid general market led chaos, as occurred in the wake of the ending of communism in Russia.

The state may seek to co-ordinate the working of both the public sector and the private sector through structured mechanisms. One form of this is referred to as indicative planning. That is, the setting of (agreed) goals around production and supporting the private sector to achieve them through taxes, subsidies and grants. This is applied in many Eastern and Asian countries such as South Korea and China.

Indicative planning is contrasted with the more directive style of central or economic planning. The former is where the state sets quotas, mandatory output requirements and production targets. Both attempt to address ideals of efficiency and rationality in terms of how resources are used. This is based on long term plans for rational investment. The realisation of certain goals is viewed as needing the integration of economic, social and environmental systems. The quest for sustainability may lead intervention down the route of greater 'economic planning.' The 'circular' (rather than linear) economy is about this kind of integration. It's needed to design out waste and keep products, parts, and materials at their highest use and value at all times.

Economists have been quick to highlight the inefficiencies of the 'second world' and central planning in general, especially since the fall of communism (early 1990s). Yet it can't be denied that in its early decades the Soviet state was able to achieve rapid industrialisation (creation of new tools and factories). The state used its powers to move capital and labour resources from agriculture, where it was used inefficiently, to industry.

Redistributing a certain proportion of the productive surplus (the 'old' ceremonial fund) can mitigate or eliminate the worst effects of inequality. This involves intervention into the social relations of society. The Soviet central economic planning agency 'Gosplan,' trumpeted provision of full employment, price stability and even less selfish people. Today, the same principles can achieve seemingly astonishing results. North Korea gives an example of a super-centralised authority. With few resources, it has co-ordinated sophisticated high rise buildings[47] and advanced military technologies. The general principles of Communist nations were built around an organisational framework of successive (five year) plans. Targets vary from modest goals to calamitous mass mobilisation programmes. Perhaps best known of in neighbouring China during Chairman Mao's era.

These days the direct allocation of resources by Western States is, for the most part, discouraged. Directing the whole economy in the way that was done in the Second World War is even rarer. The state needs to know better than the market about what needs to be produced. The basic problem of direct resource allocation, or 'picking winners,' is that the government support may distort the allocation of resources across the wider economy. The economy may end up producing goods that are not in fact demanded by consumers. This was particularly true of the planned economies of the Soviet era. These of course represented the extreme of state micro-management. Products produced were often inferior. What was ordered might come in the wrong specifications. For example, steel might have been too thick or concrete the wrong constituency. Despite the use of subsidised materials, goods could end up worth less than the inputs that went into them. It was only when the regime collapsed that the organisational incompetence within many enterprises under communism was fully revealed (Beattie, 2010).

Technological change was also discouraged under centrally planned societies. Innovation took resources away from current production levels. This risked the wrath of the authorities should output targets not be achieved. Basing future targets on earlier targets also meant that there was no incentive to over perform. To do so would have invariably meant future targets would have been 'ramped up.' The overall effect was to consign the system to underachievement. The lack of private property meant individuals had little incentive to invest or exert effort to increase or even maintain productivity. The consequent deprivation under communism led to a shadow economy. This symbolically represents a rejection of the actions of authorities to manage the economy and a popular return to private enterprise. Despite this, the system still worked to a degree. It was fine when there was a problem to be solved but far less useful when you needed to compete against other, 'market led' industrial powers.

There was a spatial dimension to this. As discussed in Part I, a directive style of planning should be able to bring labour and industry together better

---

[47] Even if the standards of many building projects are far lower than Western counterparts.

than in a free market economy. Yet the reasons for doing so were often not for reasons of economic efficiency. An example, was the industrial town of Nova Huta, a satellite of nearby Krakow. This town was planned after the Second World War as a huge centre of heavy industry. Communist authorities wanted it to address what they saw as a class imbalance. It was to attract people from lower socio economic status to remedy resistance from middle-class Kracovians. Nova Huta had the largest steel mill (Vladimer Lenin Steelworks) in the country. Yet it was incredibly inefficient compared to similar operations elsewhere. Coal had to be transported from Silesia and iron ore from the Soviet Union. The outputs were shipped to other parts of Poland. This situation could only last for as long as Eastern Europe was protected from international competition due to the Cold War.

Examples of directive planning ending up being used for 'political' rather than 'economic' reasons are not confined to communist states. The Government of Kwame Nkrumah,[48] attempted to industrialise the country. The viability of many operations was undermined through poor siting (Acemoglu, Daron & Robinson James (2012). The endless stream of economically irrational developments was not caused by bad advice. Rather, it was his need to buy political support and sustain an undemocratic regime.

11.0 Politicisation of Planning

In the best sense, politics represents the extension of ethics into the public realm. Politics is how people should work out their own arrangements so they can live together. These are the processes and institutions through which whole communities are made and enforced. Ethics should guide politics, or if thought about in the reverse, then politics is ethics applied to groups of people. Urban planning addresses the following matters (Rydin, 2011):

(1) what society wants from urban change;

(2) the legitimate role of government vis-à-vis private interests; and

(3) the limits of governments ability to deliver societies expectations.

Politics helps decide the 'balance' between 'economic' and 'environmental' outcomes. If everyone agreed on the principles of planning, then outcomes would be judged by the efficiency of their delivery. Many early leading planners[49] conceived of an essentially apolitical society. The bureaucracy of

---

[48] President from 1957 to 1966 in Ghana.

[49] Including Le Corbusier in La Ville Radieuse.

economic administration would effectively replace the state. Le Corbusier saw the agreed discourse as one of modernism, economic rationality and political utility.

It has been clearly shown that the neutral and objective evidence of scientific knowledge does not, and cannot, drive policy in a democracy (Head, 2016). The 1947 English planning system was only able to be established because it formed part of a suite of post-war measures. This included the welfare state and the command and control economy. The welfare state was only achieved through high levels of consensus coinciding with the Cold War; where the 'nuclear genie' had to be held at bay. The post-war consensus didn't last. The shattering of the post-war national (Butskellite) consent in the United Kingdom started with events as far back as the Suez Crisis (1956). In the United States, it was the Vietnam War. Levels of consensus have continued to be sustained for longer in other Western-European countries (such as Sweden). In formerly communist countries, Stanilov (2007) equates the end of socialism with the collapse of the modernist project. It has seen the re-emergence of many voices that had been held suppressed by the communist meta-narrative in the spaces and patterns of post-Soviet cities.

The demise of societal consensus has gone much further than public opposition to foreign war campaigns. The State's ability to lead on urban projects depends on the relative power between state backed planning and opposition groups. Modern Western democracies' lack authoritarian backing. Their ability to instigate transformation is dependent on the level of societal consensus. It gives the concept of 'popular planning' its basis. This combines state intervention with an active popular base. It can revive the community and gain support from diverse groups and campaigners; particularly local and lower income groups.

The concept of the public interest[50] began to fall under attack in the light of social and cultural differences. Parties on the left focus on identity groups. Parties to the right of the spectrum focus on the individual. In the middle ground are community groups, professionals and families. They generally have significantly less vocalness. The basic problem is that the aims of individuals or identity groups, when in isolation from others, can seriously undermine what they need as fellow members of a community.

In Western Europe there is a consensus style culture where state intervention is accepted - even expected. The Anglo-American world lacks this culture which often results in loggerhead scenarios. Impacts of urban change fall variably on different people, groups and organisations. The core

---

[50] Which formed the basis of popular planning and much else.

dilemma is what happens when one group benefits from developing an area but at the cost of another group? How should society make the decision as to whether this development should go ahead? The example of Nkrumah's Ghana is one where political interference over who benefits from the resource outweighs what gets built or where activities take place. In the Anglo-American West, 'planning' is based on the use of land, rather than with the identity of the person who occupies or owns it. Such a stance deflects criticism that the planner, or more likely an authority, might be discriminating against certain types of companies or individuals.

This has not prevented societal dissatisfaction and opposition filtering down from the national to local (urban) level. Counter modernist movements, with relevance to politics at the local level have emerged. This includes the rise of 'green' parties with their challenge to the idea of material progress. Critiques of planning processes and outcomes have led to the concept of 'advocacy planning'. It was intended to assist disadvantaged groups in society (Davidoff, 1965). Since then Neo-Marxian urban sociology and free market neo-liberalism have combined to lead an anti-space phase (Castells, 1977). Serious mistakes have been perceived in the post war rebuilding of towns and cities. Most recently, deadlocks between rural landowners and urbanite controlled political organisations have dominated planning agendas in growth areas. In the last few decades planning has become very polarised. Polarised communities are going through a process termed 'affective partisan polarisation.' One group(s) imposes its views on others. Small, concentrated but relatively under-represented lobbies tend to outperform bigger ones (Olson, 2002). The erosion of place or locality as the main determinant of community makes the 'political community' one of the few remaining bridges between fragmented populations.

Given the above, it is not surprising that planning has witnessed a shift away from the positivist-empiricist 'technical' tradition[51] towards decisions driven by a political mandate. Having politicians make normative decisions is one thing. Typically, their agenda involves compromise through the balancing of competing political priorities. Short-term political cycles result in the swapping of ideological preferences and a short-term mentality. In many countries it's just about setting up frameworks for managing (dis)agreements between groups. The focus is on processes, not outcomes. This fits well with the post-modern ethic that there is no single solution. Politicians are always going to be interested in 'who' benefits from decisions. They may be

---

[51] Run by professional elites.

compelled to ignore planning criteria over local public opinion and ideology over empirical evidence.

Planning, by its nature, is best when the aims are clear, specific and well understood. It is harder to achieve if multi-objectives are set out trying to capture 'everything for everyone.' Ambiguity is another issue when used to avoid political controversy during its preparation. These issues work against long-term goals like sustainability. Such goals need the maintenance of a vision across the economic, social and environmental spectrum.

12.0 Politics and the Market

Democracy is demand led. The legitimacy of elected Governments depends upon having issues to address. This creates cycles of 'problem, reaction and solution.' There is a temptation to create or recognise something as a problem. A reaction from people is invoked who subsequently go on to demand something gets done about it. The Government then brings in a prepared solution to solve the problem created. More often than not, Government is called upon to intervene in any given situation it is called into.

A new mode of regulation has been applied in recent decades. It appeals to consumer culture, flexible capitalism (both consumption and production) and makes sure there is democratic social order. Countries such as Britain have seen a massive increase in general regulation by Governments. Statistics reveal that there has been a long term trend for each new Government to legislate more aggressively than its predecessors. This has been most marked in areas such as criminal and employment law. Forty Criminal Justice Acts have been introduced since 1997 (Sweetwell & Maxwell, 2015). The last thirty years has seen a massive growth in complexity of processes. No doubt this has contributed to the observed need for so many non-productive workers in the West.

Growth in the volume of regulations in the English planning system can be partly put down to responding to external policy drivers. This includes the European Union. Another reason is to prevent some mischief to the system. This latter point highlights the fall in trust in politicians and professionals alike. There is the need for transparency and accountability.

There may be more laws and regulations but paradoxically many have become increasingly declamatory. They are intended to 'send a message' rather than remedy a problem. Ministers for instance put faith in their 'media grids' which state when certain announcements will be made. Press officers have become more important than policy, and presentation more important than substance. Appearance is everything when political polarisation results in an absence of legitimacy and real power.

New processes, checks and balances have been instigated. They are to avoid inter-governmental conflict and make sure elected representatives are accountable. Power is being increasingly transferred to the judiciary whose anonymity means they can make unpopular decisions. A bewildering range of quangos and federal agencies, unelected and unaccountable now take control of many forms of government. New processes within the planning system have been set up. These include the input of semi-autonomous specialists in:

- Equality Impact Assessment;
- Habitats Regulation Assessment;
- Strategic Flood Risk Assessment; and
- Sustainability Appraisal.

These processes create further distance between urban decision makers and those taking action. As such, they also ameliorate against short term political decisions.

Consistent with the general malaise has been the rise of neo-liberal politics. These are based on faith in the free-market and minimal government intervention. They have sought to redefine the public interest with greater individual freedoms and service delivery efficiency. The market mechanism is the primary means to achieve that outcome. The agenda has been to restrict regulation. Initiatives include the Cutting Red Tape or the Red Tape Challenge. Even when market failure is well understood it can be a subject of large debate as to whether state intervention is the best solution.

No matter how well backed up by analysis, the neo-liberal agenda represents a distinct political perspective. Certainly, as much as any other group seeking additional regulation. Re-drawing of the boundaries of the market through political activism, electoral reform or saying a certain regulation should be or not be introduced is expressing a political opinion. Opposing a new regulation is saying that the status quo, however unjust, should not be changed. Saying that an existing regulation should be abolished, is saying that the domain of the market should be expanded. This means that those who have money should be given more power in that area.

When free-market economists say that a certain regulation should not be introduced because it restricts the 'freedom' of a certain market, they are merely expressing a political opinion. They are rejecting the rights that are to be defended by the proposed law. Their ideological cloak is to pretend that their politics is not political. It's an objective economic truth while other people's politics is political. Yet in reality they are just as politically motivated as their opponents.

Driving the neo-liberal cause is a belief that the need for development is paramount. Elections are won or lost on the state of the economy. Despite the massive generational rise in living standards in the West, politicians still believe people want more material possessions. It doesn't seem to matter who's in power. Almost every party demands that other concerns must give precedence to economic growth based on rising GDP.

Given their non-spatial agenda, silence on cities and support for the free market, it is no surprise that neo-liberals have been particularly critical of the 'planning system.' They also oppose anything else that might regulate the economic activity of the development industry. Their logic is that capital flows will be reduced where regulations and taxes eat into profits. With the planning system, it's construction costs that rise affecting which firms can enter the market. For neo-liberals the planning system is seen simplistically as a 'brake on the economy'. This is an oxymoron as 'planning' implies positive intervention. It is ironic that urban planning gets mislabelled or associated with central planning. The aim of central planning is just as geared towards production and economic growth as free market economics.

The shifting balance of decision making towards the private sector was noticed decades ago. Newman and Thornley (1996) identified this within different planning systems. Britain's focus is on a property led planning system. Sweden has gone for a negotiation planning style. The French have a more flexible approach to development plans.

It's only natural that there are those in a capitalist society anxious that national and local economies are not overly constrained by planning regulation. While the planning system can apply the brake in some locations it puts the accelerator down in others. The enthusiasm some governments have to reform the planning system can result in the blanket removal of rules. This is even when they are intended to protect resources from being exploited. An extreme example was Cincinnati in 2003. Politicians there 'switched off' the planning system altogether. In the United Kingdom, reform of the planning system has not been as extreme. It has none-the-less sought not to hinder development. The focus is to be light touch, fast and responsive, as highlighted by the independent, Killian Pretty Review of 2008 (for DCLG).

The return to the 'purity' of the primeval capitalist state is a re-run of the original market based approach of the industrial age. So neo-liberals soon find themselves caught in a Catch 22. 'Lessons learnt' from history between feudalism and the welfare state get forgotten or downplayed.

A lot of things that are outside the market today have been removed by political decision, rather than the market process itself. They include human beings, government jobs, electoral votes, legal decisions and uncertified medicines. There are still attempts to buy at least some of these things. In the case of bribing government officials, judges or voters this is illegal. When using expensive lawyers to win a lawsuit, donations to political parties, and the like, it is legal. The trend has been towards less marketisation. For goods that are traded, more stringent regulations have been introduced in the post Second World War era. This is on who can produce what (for example, fair-trade). How they can be produced (for example, carbon emissions). Finally, how they can be sold (for example, product labelling). Neo-liberalists may wish that the planning system be dissolved. Yet even when they do get their wish, the same industrial era, political demands for re-distribution are quick in re-surfacing, or those of the sustainability and diversity agendas.

The use of land stirs up the most primeval of human instincts and genuine conflicts of interest. As Adams and Watkins (2014) have pointed out, the benefits of regulations can make a substantial contribution in economic terms. Their benefit is to spot and resolve potential problems earlier thus lessoning the overall cost.

The planning system is still generally recognised as reducing tensions and allowing politicians to respond to demands to intervene. In the United Kingdom, this is the reason why there remains a continued acceptance across the political spectrum for restricting certain types of development. Also, unlike other countries, there is no significant pressure group advocating for compensation for the lost economic opportunities caused by restrictions imposed by the planning system. Despite this, there is a continued need to keep 'telling this story' as those that use the 'service' the planning system gives may only do so once or twice in a lifetime.

13.0 Alternatives to Planning

If planning systems have their place in Western societies, there is little doubt that traditional land use zoning can, at times, be inflexible. This exposes them to criticism. For Webber (1960), planners need to avoid seeking order in simple mappable patterns. Instead it's hiding in extremely complex social organisational arrangements (1963:54). Neo-liberals would go much further. They argue that government generally lacks the necessary information to correct market failures. The costs of government failure are usually greater than the costs of market failure that it is (allegedly) trying to fix. Economists have analysed the implications of the planning system on land and house prices. In England, the value of agricultural land is typically £15,000 or less a hectare. Residential land, in contrast, is worth £4m a hectare in a high demand spot such as Oxford. The price of housing has become a national issue.

In the essay 'New Society (1969)'; it was argued that in certain situations it was not worth trying to plan. The correct answer to market failures, according to neo-liberalists, is not regulatory control but greater use of market mechanisms. So for example, the solution to pollution is not regulation but tradable emission rights (see related discussion in Part IV).

Alternatives to planning fall into two basic categories. There are those that seek to modify or 'lighten' the burden of the system and others intended to remove government intervention altogether in favour of other mechanisms.

Allocating Land

Planning in the United Kingdom operates under a plan led system. A comprehensive and up-to-date hierarchy of national framework and local plans is necessary to make the work. The local planning authority needs to make provision for a certain number of houses based on agreed criteria (objectively assessed needs). There is often greater discretion as to 'where' such allocations go. The process is evidence based and adheres to the regulatory processes for example, sustainability appraisal, listed above. It is then up to the private sector to come forward with planning applications to seek approval.

There will always be exceptions where powerful interests get special treatment. These often represent the status quo and economies of scale. Take the logic of spot zoning exceptions which either allocate or zone an area for the benefit of a key employer. Such a practice can only be justified when a facility is of a strategic nature (why else should a special exemption be given). Interestingly, the United Kingdom Government has departed from locally derived land allocations. Most notably this was through setting up enterprise zones during the 1980s. More recently, a United States' zonal style has been proposed. This would give automatic permission on suitable brownfield sites (HM Treasury & Department for Business, Innovation & Skills, 2015).

A more comprehensive approach to allocating land would be community land auctions (Leunig, 2011). This system is akin to competitive tendering.

The local authority invites offers of land, and accepts those that are good value.   Good value is a combination of price and appropriateness for development.   The latter incorporates both sustainability criteria, as well as desirability for the final purchaser.   By making an offer, the landowner would grant the local authority the right to buy the land at that price, for a set period of time.   In effect the landowner is granting the local authority a call option[52] on the land in question.

The authority would auction the development rights to that land.   This would be based on a specified development envelope.   For example, it could be the ability to construct a certain number of buildings of specified scale.   It would set out the conditions under which planning permission would be granted automatically.   The authority may say that the land could only be used for residential use, with a maximum density, particular proportion of social housing, maximum heights, cycle lanes, environmental standards, community buildings, green space, and so on.   The council grants planning permission, and then re-auctions the land that it accepted for development.   It gets to keep the difference in value.   The developers could then get on and build the housing that they believe will sell well.   The theory is that the builders are best placed to know what sells – more so than the local authority.

Use of Private Agents to Aid the Public Sector

One common concern of the planning system is it being run by politicians and bureaucrats.   They will either promote their own interests rather than national interests, be incompetent or delay hard decisions.   The free market solution to public organisational monopoly is simple.   It gives applicants the right to choose whom they wish to submit their development plan for consideration. Applicants would have the option of going to their local council or if they prefer they could also go to a 'competing' council or a government approved, private sector 'accredited' agent.   This takes the role of the technical expert away from local planning authorities in much the same way as occurs with applications for building permits (s161 of the Housing & Planning Act 2016). The problem is that planning applications, unlike building permits, typically need a complex weighing up of values.   They aren't a straight forward assessment of whether certain (quantifiable) standards are met or not.   It also has implications for local democracy.   This inevitably blurs the lines between

---

[52] An option to buy the land at an agreed price on or before a particular date.

regulatory function and development interests, by removing independent oversight of public interest that Council's should follow.

Effects Based Controls

Effects based controls are intended to focus on the actual externalities produced by land uses, rather than the use itself. New Zealand's Resource Management Act (1991) is one such example.[53] Discretion over what rules to impose on land use sits almost entirely with the local authority. Where they are proposed they must conform to the overriding ideology on what can be controlled. This is set by high level legislative principles, and only latterly by some examples of national policy. Until recently, there has been curiously little explicit focus on the urban environment. This is a by-product of the competing ideological interests of the neo-liberal reformers and environmentalists who pushed the bill through. Neither group had any specific interest in the spatial differences of urban areas. In practice, it results in a pluralist process of implementation. Competing values are weighed in the absence of any clear normative direction. On the ground it has set up a loose, permissive and devolved style of zoning across different urban and rural communities. There are in fact 2272 different zones, management areas or policy overlays for a country with 4 million people!

Such a devolved approach is 'bottom up.' It lacks either direction or prescription. The adverse effects of developments are either discounted or mitigated through individual applications. This results in a technical fix mentality. Activities are allowed provided there is some way of mitigating the impact. It often entails the optimistic use of detailed, long term management procedures rather than a precautionary approach. A precautionary approach would see certain activities being stopped altogether. It also creates an unrealistic expectation that the intent of the legislation can be achieved at a fine-grained scale for every application. In reality, a broader view is needed taking into account the sum of these decisions. Predictably, cumulative impacts are not well addressed at the macro level. To control development, local policy often needs manual sized documents, full of rules for micro-management. The inherent limitations of this system are clearest when there are significant growth pressures (given physical constraints). Despite the inherent flexibility of the local authority to set their own rules, the national government has found it necessary to directly take over the urban planning for

---

[53] While intended to revamp the original, colonial era, Town and Country Planning Act, the former regime had not stopped suburban living on spacious 'quarter acre' plots.

both of the countries' largest cities. It was needed in Auckland due to housing unaffordability and relatively high traffic congestion. In Christchurch, it was the need to address the re-build after the 2011 earthquake.

Redefining Property Rights

It's possible to redesign property rights as a substitute for the existing system of land use regulation. This is a twist to a purely effects based, locally derived planning system. The maintenance of environmental quality could be redefined to restrict lawful externalities beyond the tolerances presently actionable in nuisance or trespass. One way to achieve this would be to apply the Pollution User Pays Principle in land use planning. That is the Government would define in law what makes an acceptable and unacceptable externality for land use planning purposes. Thus, the developer would need to conform to a set of minimum environmental quality standards. These might for example include restrictions on the height of buildings and/or the noise level at the perimeter of the development. There would be a presumption that the landowner had the right to develop their land, provided that they conform to the standards.

Reliance on the Courts

The most basic alternative is to have no planning system and simply rely on the existing institutional arrangements. People used to, and still do sort out their own issues. This can be through legal channels such as use of torts in the court system or non-legal (use of intimidation etc). In the absence of regulations, damages resulting from the use of a particular good or service can be addressed by the courts. As such, the planning system does duplicate other remedies available to settle neighbour disputes concerning adjoining activities and developments that might interfere with the enjoyment or use of land. These include civil actions and common law. While regulation is preventive and anticipatory, tort cases take place only after a complaint arises and are brought to court. In this sense, tort law is responsive, not preventative.

Private Controls

Given the prevalence of planning systems in Western countries, the absence of a state-level planning system attracts researchers seeking to discover how the market responds. This is the case with the State of Texas. That is not to say that in Texas there is complete private control and ownership of common resources. Houston retains some important powers that shape city structure. These include the siting and placing of public roads, utilities, other public services, taxation and environmental regulations.

In the absence of controls, developers and housing associations have instigated forms of self-regulation. These include private-law restrictive covenants. Such private controls serve mainly the middle and upper segments of the land and housing markets. They are largely absent from poorer areas (Siegan, 1970). The absence of state imposed planning regulations have benefitted better-off groups more than other groups. This has been criticised as leading to socially exclusive neighbourhoods and disparities in the quality of public services. The less controlled parts of the market retain more affordable housing than may have been available with planning regulations. Yet poorer environmental and service quality results (Alterman, 2014).

'Planning light' substitutes for comprehensive planning systems can address local amenity based issues successfully (from New Zealand to Texas). Where state regulation is significantly less than elsewhere (for example Texas) motivated, private sector interests make sure it takes place. When it comes to more complicated issues, such as a lack of affordable housing supply, the approach is simple. It is up to private, developer led initiatives to increase the supply of housing. This conveniently ignores the value of land and its economic potential, reflecting public expenditures on infrastructure in the vicinity. This includes spending on roads, schools or railway stations. Urban land ends up being used inefficiently in urban cores. The only places where development and expansion occurs is predominantly on the urban fringe.

PART IV:
IMPLEMENTING PLANNING

1.0 Agencies, Politics and Institutional Roles

Every planning law in the world contains both procedural and substantive parts. Planning law sets up institutions, ways of communicating with the public, access to information, and degrees of legal power granted to stakeholders. This is the procedural-justice approach. It focuses on the quality of communication between government and the concerned public, power relationships and the instruments of public participation. The substantive side are the various instruments that government bodies are empowered with to make a difference 'on the ground' (Alterman, 2014).

Modern systems of law are defined by territory. Geographical location is not generally intended to factor in the application of the law. The paradox of planning is that the law, or at least regulations flowing from the law, are intended to be spatially discriminating. This is at least in a generic sense across different land use types (for example, urban or rural). The outcomes being sought cannot apply equally across a territory, except at the highest and most abstract level.

Even if the broad, normative judgements for overarching planning legislation has been done well, implementation still needs to be considered. Policy analysis or the procedural-planning approach to carry out political aims using rationality and scientific theory are important. A systems approach is typically applied. This is concerned with the generation and checking of alternatives prior to making a choice. It also sees the aims, policies and programmes being devised in a fair, democratic way (Faludi, 1987, p.43 in Allmendinger, 2002).

2.0 Pan-National Government

The trend towards the increasing ascendency of pan-national authorities over time is noteworthy. The United Nations is the global umbrella organisation. It promotes international co-operation such as securing the peaceful settlement to a conflict. The United Nations also oversees the policies and certain projects of nation states. Affiliated institutions include the World Bank. This gives loans to developing countries for capital programmes. Neo-colonisation is associated with foreign aid being given through these agencies. It has perpetuated a one way flow of planning ideas and practice to the developing world. In September 2015, the 193-Member UN General Assembly formally adopted the 2030 Agenda for Sustainable Development. This set 17 bold new Global Goals and 169 targets. One included enhancing inclusive and sustainable urbanisation. This includes the capacity for participatory, integrated and sustainable human settlement planning and management in all countries.[54] Then in December, the UN Climate Change Conference (COP21) consented to the Paris Agreement. Its keystone commitment is to keep global warming 'well-below' two degrees Celsius compared to pre-industrial levels. How these goals are carried out will depend upon individual nation states.

Closer to home, the European Union has played a primary role in the integration of the national economies of Britain and the Continent (some would say undermining). EU membership has to date played an important role in producing convergence in the planning repertoires of its member states. With the Treaty of Lisbon, the European Union seeks to promote 'territorial cohesion' in addition to economic and social cohesion. That is to say, it seeks policies which avoid disadvantaging specific territories. The specific changes that the BREXIT referendum will have for Britain's planning system is too early to say. It would allow for divergence from the European systems in some way in the future.

The results of BREXIT point to a criticism that 'pan-national' (umbrella) organisations lack real democratic legitimacy. Yet they remain, in theory at least, a means to manage the 'spill over' effects of national policy. They can address strategic matters, including habitat loss or climate change, by getting around national inaction.

3.0 National Government

Nation states represent the most recognizable form of government. They are defined by territory and observable cultural traits. The nation state as we know it came about during the 19th Century as a result of European nationalist political movements. National governments had to secure a monopoly on law and enforcement before they could give effect to public services and manage

---

54   This 'non-binding international agreement' adopted at the Habitat III summit in Ecuador, 2016 has been described as the New Urban Agenda.

economic activities. The Netherlands is a good example. Its integrated national economy can be credited to the politician, Thorbecke. Following the 1848 constitution he removed the various class privileges of the urban elites that existed at the time. Of particular note was the abolition of local taxes which were collected at the city gates (which served as custom barriers). The control of finance results in the domination of policy making by the national government. There is a current agenda to re-consider this. Yet until recently 75-80 per cent of local government budgets in England were dependent on decisions made by Treasury and DCLG (CIPFA 2013).

Having come into being, the nation state has inevitably tried to reinforce its position. This is through the sense of communities 'coming together' through economic, social and cultural unity. Urbanisation plays a role. More important is the industrialised economy, universal education, mass media, uniform national culture and provision of transport infrastructure. England is an example of a state that is regarded as having a strong central government.

The defining characteristic of a nation is the degree to which its' public administration is centralised. Ironic as it may seem, given the history of his later movement, Marx was one such a proponent. For him, the state was to be used to transfer power. Society was intended to become ultimately stateless, wageless, moneyless and classless.

From one perspective decentralisation of local authorities from central government is seen to be desirable. The local communities are better served by government operating at their level. The converse view is that centralised control offers greater consistencies and economies of scale. In practice, a lack of political centralisation tends to be associated with regimes that are polarised. Somalia, at the current time, represents an extreme example where power is widely distributed. Its society is divided into antagonistic tribes that cannot dominate one another. Independence is more important for each tribe than being integrated as a national entity. The overall outcome though is chaos.

National Planning Administration

National government is where most property, building, planning and environmental legislation is mandated. Lobby groups, stakeholders and umbrella organisations will actively represent common interests. In particular, they serve or are influenced by business. There will typically be a Ministry appointed to deal with urban planning functions. Examples include:

- England – Urban planning is done by the Department of Communities and Local Government (DCLG). The Environment Agency is responsible for environmental permitting and regulation;
- Brazil – The Ministry for Environment administers national environmental policy. There is a specific Ministry of Cities (created in 2004);
- New Zealand – The Ministry for the Environment administers the full ambit of urban, rural and environmental management systems.

Urbanisation was important in the formation of the nation state. Planning related matters still make national headlines. Yet urban planning generally falls a long way down the pecking order of government priority. As with pre-industrial authorities of the past, many governments avoid addressing planning matters directly. In the United States, the Federal Government has little or no role in urban planning. This may present a weakness when for instance, an international agreement is supposed to be carried out by a nation state. What it does allow is for individual states and cities to have the relative freedom to develop their own responses.

When there is an appointed department the influence of other departments is typically greater. Treasury, for instance, will look to ensure that the sectorial, cross-cutting remit of future planning legislation avoids any impact on the wider economy. A countries' legislative architecture has important consequences. That means the degree to which the purposes of different statutes are consistent with each other and how clear the relationship is between different strategies and plans. Urban planning often gets subsumed amongst other related legislation. This includes water, climate, conservation/ biodiversity, special purpose, infrastructure and socio-economic planning.

Given the importance of 'the grid' to modern life, planning legislation should be aligned with that of infrastructure providers (e.g., transportation). Japan, for instance, has taken it further through its separate City Planning Act where urban outcomes dictate all other sectoral approaches. It is no coincidence that it employs a particularly strong interventionist approach in large centres like Tokyo, Osaka and Nagoya.

When embroiled in urban issues the national government will typically impose its will first and foremost upon capital cities. The straight, wide boulevards of Paris and Fascist Rome were imposed by over-arching planning authorities. Yet if capital cities are dominated by the state they are less likely to become 'growth machines' as a result of national considerations.

In contrast, England's DCLG sets out national policy and a framework for how development proposals across the country should be considered. Like other centralised regimes, it cascades policy aspirations downwards and across the country, using the subservient forms of government under the state apparatus. The system gives discretion and flexibility at the local level and does not have the mandate for direct interference with how London or other cities are planned at the micro-level. The result is that the system does not respond well to issues of scale such as the housing crisis in the south east. 'Place specific' communities administered by authorities surrounding London have a vested local political interest in resisting additional urban growth.

4.0 Local Government

The territorial form of local government is intended to bring people of common heritage or ancestry together as a political unit. This is to further their interest and increase their participation in government business. It is beneficial to do so as it is only when people feel a sense of belonging that deliberative communities can form. The motivation behind localism and nationalism are not dissimilar. They are only distinguishable by the scale to which they are applied.

With half the world's population now inhabiting cities, it makes sense to try to effect change 'locally' at city rather than national level. There is a trend towards devolution and decentralisation to the local level in the West. This reflects the fragmentation of government responsibility and breakup of the welfare state. It also increases the potential for spatial divergence in the level and quality of services that can be expected to result. England's Cities and Local Government Devolution Act 2016 allows for the transfer of national powers to cities. This is anticipated to provide an elected mayor for cities outside London (who already has one). It could also allow cities to address transport, housing, planning, policing and public health. Not unexpectedly, the keenest debate is around local financing. The key is whether cities should be responsible for themselves or are merely extensions of the nation state. If it's the former then this represents a reversal of the mindset that drove Thorbecke's reforms.

Defining what is local is important. The Victorian local government structure made the clear distinction between town and country. This reflected the prevailing social conditions and the scale where cultural differences were recognised. Cities, particularly metropolitan ones, are going to be too big to represent all local interests. The local unit could be a single town or a neighbourhood in a big city. Size and scale prevents a prescriptive approach being applied across the country. Yet local governments have varying degrees of autonomy.

England has spent much of the 20th Century searching for an idealised system of local government. That is one which achieves vertical and horizontal integration. The form of the state apparatus is subject to endless debate and tinkering. Harvey (2012) sees the focus of modern democratic societies on organisational form as a form of fetishism. Yet the outcomes of such discussions have real implications for how planning is conducted. This is because planning functions are done by local authorities. It explains the reason why in Scotland, with a population of 5.2 million, there are just 37 planning documents. New Zealand, with 78 authorities and over 4 million people, has a combined total of 170 resource management planning documents[55] (MfE, 2013).

Public decisions about land uses are strongly influenced by central government values under the centralised English system. The United States has a tradition of distrust in centralised power and long tradition of home rule. As such, decisions are made as close to home as possible. In the Third World the issue is often one of poor governance, with very weak forms of local government.

The most basic functional role is for a local authority to have jurisdiction over things that are local in nature. These include parks, recreation, and street maintenance. Municipality-related functions can be classified as main or subsidiary functions. They include:

- central place functions;
- commerce and industry;
- services;
- housing;
- agriculture;
- tourism and recreation.

National rulers have often struggled with local authorities who seek to usurp their authority. Politics at the local level is based on the local political interest. The wider national or even international goals may not prove popular with elected representatives. Decisions will be driven by local political

---

[55] Combined planning documents across the country would stack to a height of 10m or 80,000pages. There are also 50 different ways to determine building height and 200 versions of what can be done in a commercial zone (Minister Smith 10 Nov 2016).

interest. This applies even if it means the local politician is going against his or her own party policies. Decisions may ignore the government's own planning policies. They may give the go ahead to developments funded by wealthy elites or ignore slum development. Arguably, the potential for cronyism and corruption is worse. Local level relationships are more likely to be based on personal ties and friendships.

Devolution has also seen a shift of power from technocratic to local councillor politics. Localism gives people the means to resolve how communities should develop for themselves instead of adhering to a 'central interpretation.' They may run against the national or strategic needs argument put forward by Rousseau. Instead, they are based on the idea that policy works best when it is formed by those it serves. Deliberations on policies and operational matters have the benefit of local knowledge if they take place at the local level. Local planning needs to be context-sensitive. That is, tailoring it to specific political, cultural, economic and environmental conditions. Plans represent agreements between local government, public and landowners. A plan owned by a wide cross-section of the community has a strong chance of success.

Following the Second World War there has been a shift away from giving local government voluntary land use controls. This was the regime between 1932- 1947 in England. The national level took on a more guidance and supervisory role between 1947 and 1968. Recently, the government has re-awakened the idea of planning for neighbourhood units. This is generally led by Parish Council's. They may not cover all areas of the country but represent the lowest operational level of administration where decision making takes place.

In France, decentralisation laws were passed between 1980-86. They were long sought but previously held back by Jacobin fears of a break-up of the state. Each development proposal passes across the desk of one or more of its mayors. It is the mayor who, in conjunction with the technical services department, has the responsibility for preparing the commune's structure plan (Plan d'Occupation du Sol). The Mayor also grants a building licence (Permis de construire). The concern for decentralisation was whether the transfer of competence would go with the transfer of power. France is a large, sparsely populated country. Of the 36,532 French mayors, 11,000 preside over a population of less than 200 people and there is one mayor with only 3 people. How are Mayors to make satisfactory and efficient development and planning control? While some maintain that decentralisation has not been a success, a majority of people are committed to it. Moreover, they are seeking new and innovative methods of achieving it.

Competency is a key aspect to the success of local government and devolution. The welfare state in the United Kingdom was intended to give a universal service, no matter where you lived. This applied to everything. It ranged from the minimum time for the fire service to reach the site of an emergency through to the compulsory age which children must attend education. In practice, some localities have never been as well provided for as others (for example, rural areas). Local authorities end up managing two potentially competing aims; that of the provision of good, quality urban infrastructure and their management in a manner that is cost-effective for households and businesses. This is particularly apparent in the situation of local government in the United States. Due to the lack of any centralised distributive mechanisms, they generally rely, for the most part, on their own tax base for revenue. This is referred to as 'fiscal federalism.' Poor areas are thus always going to have poorer services. It inevitably sets in place a vicious cycle in which Local Governments can, in the end, 'go bust.'

Devolution in the West has not always been followed by increased funding to match the expected increase in the level of competencies. There has been a shift away from control towards efficiencies and the 'marketisation' of public services. Espoused by neo-liberal rhetoric this is reflected by financial limitations. Former 'service users' are symbolically being termed 'customers.' Local government has shifted from being producer driven (i.e., single provider). Instead, they are service delivery or customer driven. Besides, there is now less commitment to the view that different places must receive the same level of services. This is even amongst politicians on the left. They argue that communities across England are so complex that a one-size fits-all isn't appropriate. This is the case even for a large urban authority (Liz Kendall and Steve Reed, 2015). No longer desirable is a 'monolithic' and automatic one-size fits-all model. Instead, a more diversified range of providers of services is sought, tied to an outsourcing model.

With urban authorities seeking to mimic corporate boardrooms there are now commissioners of services. When it comes to new development, the state takes on the role of persuading, encouraging and incentivising the private sector. This is to provide the desired type of development in the preferred location. Customers get to exercise choice about public services rather a single authority acting as an automatic and monopolistic deliverer of them. The reality is about balancing the books, sticking to the bottom-line and maximising service provision at minimum cost. Often this extends to amalgamation of local authorities disregarding the commonalities of the people involved.

Changing circumstances are having profound effects on the City of Stockholm (see Part VI). It was a 20th Century exemplar of municipal planning and urban development. Yet by the mid-1990s it was no longer enjoying the exceptional conditions it had turned earlier to its advantage. Its former reputation had been achieved through efforts to build up an immense bank of properties. This allowed it to act as a real-estate promoter. Having exhausted the land reserve, it became too expensive to acquire new land for urban expansion. As such, it was necessary to shift from its traditional role as a planner and developer. The City of Stockholm now works with private promoters. It acts as a go-between for promoters and citizens, with the aim of defending the public interest.

5.0 Regional Government

There will often be tensions between national aspirations and local decision making. One mechanism to address the issues is through an intermediate form of agency. Another reason to set up such an agency is for the effective co-ordination of local actors in complex administrative areas. Often these links are across sectoral boundaries. They involve organisations with different motives and interests that don't tend to co-operate well together. Areas covered by regional authorities and specific administrative set ups vary widely. Creating such a tier of extra governance will only be relevant when the following apply. The administrative area of the authority must be less than the size of the state itself, but large enough to cover more than one local authorities. The benefit of such governance is to address mismatches between the scale of problems and that of local government to respond to them without the need for outright amalgamation.

The regional concept is closely connected to the garden city movement. It seeks to avoid 'urban strip development' by promoting satellite towns around existing cities. One of the first regional city plans was put together by the architect and urban designer Daniel Burnham[56] for Chicago (1909). This sought to create large-scale mass transit, including a highway system and freight and passenger rail improvements. It also envisaged an outer ring of parks, a more systemic pattern of streets, cultural institutions and the creation of a civic centre of government. Burnham envisaged Chicago as 'Paris on the prairie.'

---

[56] Burnham also worked on plans for Cleveland and Washington DC in the United States, and Manila in the Philippines.

Metropolitan strategic planning is a key tool for guiding the future shape of growing city-regions. Urban agglomerations are considered new engines of the world economy. Such polycentric urban structures have been referred to as 'urban diamonds' in places. Cities are represented as points, the infrastructure that connects them as lines or edges, and the large landscapes in between as the faces. The diamond concept goes onto developing synergies between cities and parts of the regional area. This includes major infrastructure, urban systems, rural landscapes, coastal spaces, ecological corridors and digital platforms (Vegara, 2015).

In China, the Yangtze River Delta Regional Plan drives economic growth, resolves intense inter-regional and inter-city competition and addresses growing administrative fragmentation. It includes a vision of the spatial structure which assigned specific functional roles to cities. The strategy also limited certain market actions such as expanding into ecologically fragile areas. The regional plan is comprehensive. It covers the local economy, social development, infrastructure schemes, urbanisation, public services and land use amongst others (Wu 2015:132). Furthermore, from a regional context, the plan also proposes a strategic plan for each city. The content differs greatly from the plans developed by the local municipalities. Although the plan itself does not have statutory status it imposed as a top-down requirement. Among other differences from earlier five-year plans local governments had the opportunity to contribute to the plan-making process.

Regional planning offers the potential to produce ecologically sustainable social, economic and political development. It is also a means to provide for the long-term needs of the population in a spatially-equitable way. In France, the founding in 1963 of DATAR[57] represented a shift away from a centralised planning system. The latter had a logic of urgency focused on massive home building. The former has a more global strategy for each town. This allowed for better reflection on how each territory should evolve. It heralded the launch of major development programmes in all economic and geographical sectors. The publishing of Regional development schemes in 1965 gave French urban structures most of their current form. The scheme for the Paris region resulted in the creation of nine new towns, five of which were around Paris. The British new towns contained some 25,000 homes, which were relatively small, dense and quickly built. The French designs placed more emphasis on planning for the future and long-term development. They contain a minimum of 10,000 homes. In the short term they were to be managed by a temporary authority for at least 25 years (some still are).

---

[57] The delegation for territorial development and regional action.

A region is a natural area for planning in a road based society. Goods are delivered nationally and people commute long distances. Travel to work, shopping or leisure patterns often won't coincide with local administrative boundaries set up in the past. Other issues in which regional authorities are potentially going to be successful in are:

- nature conservation and landscape management;
- agriculture and forestry;
- water management - Drawing up plans to manage water resources. Working out how to allocate them between farmers and urban dwellers. Deciding how much to take out of river systems without causing serious environmental damage;
- clean air and climate;
- tourism, leisure, and recreation;
- raw materials.

Regional tiers of Government are an amorphous level and so are unstable and liable to re-organisation. The average person can engage better with local authorities by influencing them politically. Comprehensive regional land use and transportation planning agencies are typically so remote and deal with such complex technical issues that they leave the average person helpless. Neither Wales, Scotland nor England has a formal, institutionalised and set up regional level of planning. This is unlike those found in other European countries, such as Germany or France. The rise and fall of regional planning in England is informative. Structure planning had been introduced under the 1968 Town and Country Planning Act at the County level. As is so often the case, the incoming Labour Government (1997) decided it preferred planning at the higher or regional level. This also better reflected practices on The Continent. Structure planning was replaced with new, geographically wider, regional planning authorities by the Labour Government in 2004. This situation lasted until after the 2010 election when the Coalition Government decided to abolish regional strategies and rely on local plans alone. These reforms were based on decentralisation and localism. They especially avoided what was described as the 'top-down' system of governance. This was where the regional imposition of targets was seen as creating resistance to economic growth. The scrapping of the regional spatial strategies meant planning was devolved to the local level. Only London retained the right to produce a 'regional' plan: 'The London Plan: Spatial Development Plan for Greater

London.' In the mega-city of London the argument for the need for a tier of non-local government is almost self-evident.

The removal of the regional tier in England says less about the best scale for 'planning'. It is more about the problem of reconciling the democratically elected wishes of an electorate. The public won't see the 'higher' or more strategic economic or social 'function' of their area in the same way as technocrats do at the national level. It's awkward for a local authority to impose aims that go against the wishes of their locally elected representatives. This can fundamentally challenge the basis of the Plan led system. Given the vacuum of the regional tier, the Government set a duty-to-cooperate for local authorities in England. Rather than a formal bureaucratic structure, it needs regular interagency meetings and co-ordination of engagement discussions. Yet the results are inconclusive. It isn't hard to appreciate that the more spatially extensive the issue, the larger is the number of agencies needed to join in. In the same way that 'too many cooks spoil the broth;' the English approach can turn into a bureaucratic nightmare. It would be more effective if government funding was linked to outcomes. Monitoring is needed by what amounts to a planning interagency broker as to whether there really is 'meta-participation' and 'meta-collaboration.'

Not surprisingly, sub-regional level organisations fill in the gap to some extent but in different ways. Regions, just like their Welsh equivalents, are spatially set by the national frameworks. The new approach of the English Local Economic Partnerships gives spatial discretion to those organisations in setting their boundaries. This may mean they are better able to react well to specific issues or challenges. Their focus is on promoting something almost everyone can agree with – economic growth. Yet they have shied away from tackling divisive planning issues in most areas.

6.0 Skills, Law and Process

Knowledge, Science and Evidence

The origins of Western style planning systems came out of the 18th Century's enlightenment. These had the universal values of science, reason, freedom, progress and logic. Most scientists and academics in the West have taken the view, until recently, that only civilizations that have descended from Hellenic Greece have possessed more than the most rudimentary science. The bulk of scientific knowledge is a product of Europe in the last four centuries. No other place and time has supported the special communities from which scientific productivity comes.

Compared to earlier versions, contemporary planning practice is more scientific. It balances competing social, economic and aesthetic concerns. The use of rationality in public health formed the origins of state urban intervention. The origins of defining landuses through modern zoning goes back to France. Industrialisation there had been strongly tied to government involvement. Napoleon I (1810 decree) divided industry into 3 classes and unhealthy industry had to be located outside towns.

In Britain, public health formed the rationale for Richard Cross's[58] Artisans' and Labourers' Dwellings Improvement Act 1875. This resulted in much of the early slum clearance in London. Plague hot spots were mapped out by the aid of scientific methods. The rationality of surveys and evidence gave the political legitimacy for state intervention.

Since then evidence-informed decision- making processes have got caught up in wider academic discussions around knowledge and science. Karl Popper[59] saw the need to distinguish between science that which could be proved, or disproved, through falsification. In his time this was a way in which Marx's dialectical materialism and other forms of 'bogus science' were discredited.

It wasn't long into the post-war era that the limits of scientific objectivity started to be acknowledged. This was even the case for positivists such as Kuhn (1962). Kuhn[60] continued to accept the consensus on the origins of scientific knowledge. Yet he challenged the prevailing view of progress by 'normal scientific enquiry.' It was also clear that Hegel's narrative had ground to a halt under the paradoxes of quantum mechanics. This narrative held that the 'unity of knowledge'[61] would be realised by the increasing understanding given by science. Research data may be quantifiable and statistical. Yet the evidence behind physical sciences is rarely conclusive. Nor could it be assumed that the connection between the sizes of events and the magnitude of their effects was linear and mechanical. This was especially the case within constantly changing economic and social systems.

There has been a decline in the belief of objective science and a societal shift from rationalism to emotion in society (as described in Part II). This has

---

[58] Richard Cross was the home secretary under Prime Minister Benjamin Disraeli's second Conservative Government.

[59] Austrian-British philosopher 1902- 1994.

[60] Kuhn had suffered trauma as a result of the Second World War.

[61] Where absolute consciousness would be reached.

meant science has left its mission as the sole pursuit of truth. Instead, it has become downgraded to achieving economic and social goals. The goal of science has shifted from truth and legitimacy. What matters most is performativity and the marketisation or commodification of scientific results. In other words, abstract knowledge is prized less than the kind that speeds up progress. With the devaluation of knowledge, all organisations are now said to be producing knowledge. Knowledge is being seen as a product of a technical process rather than a human intellectual work. As such, universities are de-privileged. The loss of confidence in science has seen the re-emergence in claims of bogus science. Notable debates have included the consumption of tobacco and municipal use of 'fluoride' in public water supplies. Climate change continues to be debated. For a time it was caught up between the likes of Lester Brown, founder and president of the Earth Policy Institute. He favoured urgent public action. Bjørn Lomborg in his 2001 book 'the Skeptical Environmentalist' did not. A more recent controversy was 'Climategate'[62] in 2009.

There has also been a shift away from knowledge being truth, regardless of time and space (universalism). Rather, the validity of knowledge is specific to time and space (relativism). Post-modernism tends to be anti-rationalist. All knowledge is socially constructed and so all 'knowledges' are equally valid. Truth depends upon the perspective adopted. The post-modern belief is that nothing can be proven in history, science or any other discipline. For all these reasons the social sciences, which underpin certainty in urban planning, have been in decline since the 1970s. Even goals such as the quest for 'epistemic justice' have been called into question. This makes up the strongest argument for state support of science and the welfare state.

The rise in methodological relativism is accompanied by the belief that those who live a particular experience are best capable of understanding it. This represents an exclusivist cultural view. Outsiders cannot bring anything useful to the table. Only Blacks have the right to write Black history. Women's history can only be written from a feminist standpoint. Western or male rationality or logic is denounced. Theorizing and knowing is equated with experiencing. Academic feminism has the most elaborated, particularistic epistemology of any discipline.

Anything coming from the old 'Hellenic age is treated with suspicion. So architecture courses won't teach classical orders. That would represent an impediment to freethinking originality. Ironically, the result has been the

---

[62] Involved the hacking of a server at the Climatic Research Unit at the University of East Anglia. Sceptics claimed that the leaked information showed climate data had been manipulated.

increasing numbers of geometrically shaped buildings being constructed across cities (refer to Part V). Where the beliefs of a non-local 'minority' are formerly incorporated in the planning system it will inevitability result in compromises on adherence to strictly 'rational' decision making. This is the case of the indigenous Maori peoples of New Zealand. Yet it has spurred interesting thinking, including an example[63] of a plan with a thousand year timeframe!

Decision makers often resort to (professional) judgement given the quantity of information associated with complex situations. Prevailing views (both professional and academic) shape the preparation of plans in practice. Such approaches are not confined to public practice. Business and political leaders also use rules of thumb and best guesses. Grand masters use skill and experience to make a reasonable choice and avoid obvious losses. People also make such decisions in real economies. These practices avoid a futile attempt to find the best move.

Such practices use existing social beliefs. They are a kind of collective certainty, the validity of which can't be questioned in public. Obscure authorities (opinion polls and the experts) promote floating propositions. Examples of such ideas include economic recovery to solve the problem of unemployment. Another is for technological progress to solve problems and give limitless human expansion.

Technocrats and professionals generally have better access and more time to explore relevant evidence than others. Disciplines which often claim unique understandings become perceived as 'high brow.' This includes landscape and heritage. Not even agencies which specialise in certain technical areas (for example, flood control) avoid accusations of being over-bearing. Knowledge gives its users power. Pierre Bourdieu (French philosopher, 1930 – 2002), noted that common sense is a mechanism of domination. From the outside, the use of evidence within the system is perceived differently. Expertise, scientific knowledge and reasoning allows for decision making to be kept and controlled within government institutions. The hegemony of planning processes furthers the grip on power for elected and appointed representatives. It gives them instruments for paternalist, clientelist and corporative relations within their constituencies. Further, it weakens citizen participation, along with direct democracy. The situation can be improved by making more of the information available. This includes the internet, cloud computing, real time data sourcing and increased speed of data/information flows. It means that traditional data gatherers and

---

[63] Ngati Rangi's Taiao Management Plan 2014

information providers are less in control of the information supply chain. This raises the expectations of users for participation.

In the Third World, many planners from the socio-economic elite, and those who identify with its values oppose calls for a new approach to planning policy. They do not want to disrupt their models of professional expertise such as demanding that planners learn from the people. Many professional planners in the Third World were trained within the rationalist paradigm. This is the case even if they identify with communicative planning approaches. Some planners have embraced the spirit of this new participatory approach. Yet they often they fail to bridge the gap between theory and practice. Many practitioners still support, consciously or unconsciously, the notion of the exclusive value of expertise. By doing so, the concern is that they do not validate the knowledge of residents or their right to self-determination.

Urban development professionals

Planning has taken on an independent professional and institutional identity. This represents a significant shift in planning practice from its pre-industrial origins to the modern era. How built environment professionals see themselves in the development process is important. This is both in the sense of how they interrelate with each other and also how the nature of the different professions has changed over time.

The Town Planning Institute was formed in 1914. Back then its membership consisted almost exclusively of architects, engineers and surveyors. This situation continued into the 1970s. There was a similar professional underpinning in Communist states. Professions there had to operate under the exclusive province of state-run design initiatives. In the Soviet Union, architects were a protected profession under Stalin. This all changed with the move to an imposed standardisation of production methods (refer to Part V). Consequently, the ability of architects to exhibit flair in undertaking individual projects was curtailed. Their role became one of merely adapting the system of manufacture to the peculiarities of the site. In contrast, modern Chinese architects remain prized as agents of both physical transformation and psychological uplift. Architecture and allied trades are described as tertiary services. They add value to manufacturing and construction enterprises and are distinct from other expressive forms of cultural production.

In the United Kingdom, the Report of the Committee on Qualifications of Planners changed the profession. The 'Schuster Report,' recommended university training. It also sought a shift away from the non-traditional disciplines to those having a special affinity to planning or humanities. Despite architects being much like planners, they tend to see themselves as part of the development process. Planners are seen, to quote Moore's *Utopia*, as the 'hangers on'. Part of this comes down to their focus on problem solving or design compared to a more process driven mentality. Architects will argue that codes and prescription are unnecessary. They impose conformity on development and inhibit creativity. That is often cited as the reason for problems getting attractive, new, one-off housing through government planning processes. It's hard for individuals to wade through 'petty bureaucracy' both in time and money. In the West, the average architect may only have 1 in 10 schemes ever come to fruition. This is blamed on the planners or decision making politicians.

There has been a positive trend in the rise of urban design professionals. This includes multi-disciplinary teams of planners, engineers, lawyers etc. The complexity of cities is why urban planning practice benefits from the support of a range of disciplines. Project based teams have to be able to analytically assess alternatives, using visioning and creative skills. This is applied in the making of masterplans or statutory plan production by private developers, co-operatives or local authorities. Yet, with the move to the humanities came a move away from Masterplanning towards greater guidance and control of change.

Urban design coined in North America in late 1950s. It replaced 'civic design.' This former discipline focused on the siting and design of major civic buildings. It encompassed city halls, opera houses, museums and their relationship to open space. Despite disruption, political and institutional change, 'internationalism' has remained a powerful theme in urban planning. There is also an increasing convergence between the virtual and the real world. This is through application of IT professionals. Machine learning and increasingly accurate simulations of development proposals are used (Ashton, 2009). Information sensors and monitoring devices, installed in the name of Smart Cities, have a role to play. They can collect data and allow Artificial Intelligence enabled data models to be run. Real-time data saves on service costs of managing cities. For instance, the content of rubbish bins can be monitored. Knowing which bin is not full can avoid the need for garbage trucks to be dispatched to every bin in the circuit.

The impact of the institutionalisation of professionals is part of their disciplinary success. Any discipline can succeed if its members are given adequate resources to solve their own problems. As such, there is an ebb and flow in disciplines like planning. It reflects the economic climate and being carried along with the prevailing ideologies and influence of the state (Fuller, 2007). Institutionalisation incorporates a variety of devices usually based on credit-laden modules (layer by layer). This includes lifelong learning, certificates of competence, training and development. The downside is that a planning professional's intellectual and cultural life becomes dependent upon institutional expectations. This results in a mood of conformism and passivity.

It's worth noting the role lawyers have in the planning system. For a start, increasing amounts of public policy are being placed in the hands of the judiciary. This is partly as a result of politicians inability to gain popular support and govern with leadership and conviction. Laws passed by Parliament or Congress may be reinterpreted according to the whim of activist judges.

Under some (more adversarial) rule bound planning systems it's the common lawyer, rather than planners, that holds sway. They act upon the wishes of clients at different stages of the planning system. In these settings, every person wishes to put his or her case forward in the most persuasive way possible to win. There are no prizes for coming second. Those blessed with confidence, gifts of oratory and clear writing will be able to make a good job presenting their own point of view. We see it daily in Parliament. Not everyone has those gifts. The directors of projects and promoters do not need them every day and nor do they know their way around the arguments, policy and law. The same goes for objectors. So it is important that promoters and objectors can call on someone to do that for them. These advocates are lawyers in the main. In theory, anyone can have a friend to help them put their case and even in the Law Courts an ordinary person can assist. The freedom to bring in a helper or to appoint someone to act on one's behalf is an important one.

Decision Making Organisations and Process

Planning systems are created and maintained, for the most part, by state run organisations. The 'traditional' bureau-professional organisation was characteristic of the post-war welfare state (Clarke and Newman 1997). Those found at the top mainly concern themselves with principles (policy). Generally, those at the bottom deal with cases. As with other frontline workers in bureaucratic organisations, supervision is hierarchical. Co-ordination takes the form of standardisation of work processes (Mintzberg,

1983). Between which there may also be a series of layers. Each inherits principles from above and transmits procedures down below.

In bureaucracies, the distance between those who deal in principles and those who deal in cases is supposed to be as great as possible. These principles aim to make sure that public service organisations safeguard public values. These include impartiality, neutrality and objectivity in dealing with citizens, equal treatment of equal cases, and predictability of outcomes (Du Gay 2005, Clarke and Newman 1997, Terpstra and Havinga 2001).

Lipsky M. (1983) observed that in a bureaucracy, what happens at the street level can be disconnected from what policymakers thought would happen. Even if carried out in the manner prescribed, hierarchical and authoritarian institutions, are inherently artificial and top-down and find it difficult to change or act quickly to new situations. They are bound by internal rules to make sure that due process happens. There are parallels with Bennis's findings on democracy. Many have also noted that such agencies do not have consciences and moral compasses in and of themselves. Bauman notes (1989; 163 in Du Gay 40) how these agencies have instruments to obliterate responsibility. This is achieved through the detailed division of labour and ends from means. This has implications. Each individual fails to embrace responsibility for the final end of state machinery and social control. They are incapable of participating in the debate and consensus of civil society that drives social change. Institutions are conservative and inegalitarian in their nature. They can't accommodate cases where society organically and spontaneously evolves new norms. They maintain their integrity through disciplining the people working within them. This is through policies, charters, directives, codes and rules. Needing to co-ordinate personal actions as a whole, they cannot allow people to act on their conscience. It is about people at the top commanding those at the bottom. This has implications for planning in areas of high growth. It creates a dilemma between the need for fast and efficient action and the process of legitimisation of consent. The latter needs a bureaucracy like system to make sure of due process. Both are necessary but each constrains the other.

Like any professional work, planning consists of the direct application of principles to cases. Professionalism is based on the use of professional skills, expertise and knowledge. These are acquired through professional training and experience, in analysing and solving problems (Duyvendak et al. 2006, Freidson 2001). As such, there is a tension with professionals (planners among others) working in bureaucratic organisations. Professionalism needs autonomy at the frontline level to enable professional judgment. Supervision takes place by peers and colleagues rather than by officials higher up in the organisational hierarchy. In this case, standardisation of skills is the dominant form of co-ordination (Mintzberg 1983).

Public professionals act within a legal framework. Yet as Terpstra and Havinga (2001) argued, they deal with rules and regulations in a different way compared to workers in a bureaucracy. This formal application of rules is not their main focus but the achievement of goals. What is important is whether the system is geared towards certainty or discretion at the front line. Professionalism serves a system of discretion better than a more legalistic approach to planning. In bureaucracies, where the central discipline is procedures, not persons, the opposite is the case. It's more than just coincidence that the English system allows its civil service to 'muddle' through difficult issues by planning discretion. This is in contrast to Continental approaches. These seek the maximum degree of certainty both for those who administer and those under administration. An example is the German system and the traditional French, legalistic approach. As such, Continental approaches are orientated towards planning implementation being a technical exercise.

There has been a significant shift towards managerialism in the West (often referred to as New Public Management). The bureau-professional organisations of the past have been changed. This is due to the introduction of private sector management techniques into the public sector and the re-orientation towards business values (Denhardt and Denhardt, 2000). It has also cut professionals' autonomy. Their positions have been weakened vis-à-vis managers and service users and through the setting of goals and methods of professional practice (Kirkpatrick et al. 2005). Accountability procedures have increased bureaucratisation. Also, performance management has narrowed the focus of professional work to quantifiable and measurable outcomes (Diefenbach 2009).

In parallel with managerialism, there has been a trend for planners to orientate themselves strongly towards adherence to correct procedure. Due process, rather than the actual building of structures or delivery of programmes, often appears to be the focus of effort and time. This affects the effectiveness of implementation on the ground.

7.0 Plan Making

Land use plans come in all shapes and sizes. Typically, the best examples are produced at the local level and address what should occur on a site specific basis. There are three key aspects to plan making; enforceability, detail and comprehensiveness (width and breath).

On enforceability, there are plans that are merely indicative and lack formal power. Germany makes great use of informal planning processes. These allow consent and co-operation to be reached amongst concerned stakeholders. In contrast, such mechanisms are considered light weight under more adversarial circumstances. In the Anglo-American context, design guidelines are unlikely to dissuade developers bent on some particular project. This is especially if they are advisory and feature 'vagueness, obscurity and lack of teeth'.

Other plans are more regulatory orientated. In the United States, land use zoning carries the ability to grant development rights. This combines plan making and permission giving. This was the case in the United Kingdom with the 1932-1947 zoning plans at local level. Since the 1947 Act, the United Kingdom has shifted to a discretionary-based system. Land use plans have a guiding role for the development management process (described below).

Modernist planning has been characterised by aspirations to a comprehensive approach. That is, taking all reasons into account in the development of the plan. The original 1947 Act Plans set up a process sequence of survey, analysis and plan. The duty to survey reflects a rational-comprehensive approach to planning. Starting with a survey of existing conditions, it leads to an analysis upon which to base policies to achieve aims. Part of its failing (such as with the Birmingham Plan example) came down to the assumption that the population would stay stable. Also, there would be little growth in the volume of motor traffic. The legacy has been ongoing. This is based on analysing the present conditions and finding problems rather than considering other possible scenarios.

One of Brindley's identified planning types to emerge in the post-war era has been that of trend planning based on 'predict and provide.' The aim is simple enough. It's to produce what people want. It benefits incoming developers and potentially more landowners than regulatory planning. Yet capital gains are more thinly spread. It is favoured by those without established land banks or close enough relationships with planners. Ambition has tended to outstrip its reach. In terms of the depth or detail of plan typology, there is a continuum between flexibility and certainty. The 1947 Act plans were more towards the latter end of the spectrum. They concentrated on land use at the expense of many other factors. This includes national investment programmes and social and economic aims.

Where two tier planning authorities exist, such as in England, there is an ability of the 'higher' level authority to give the overview. The remedy of the Town and Country Planning Act, 1968 was for a single development plan, but one done at two tiers. The 'upper tier' structure plan consisted of a broad framework of policies looking forward up to 20 years ahead. This was supported by a 'key diagram' showing land use, transport and environmental proposals diagrammatically. Rather than a locationally specific map base, it would sketch general lines of development over an area with a broad brush. In a sense, it gives the link between national economic and social planning and land use. Local Plans (the 'lower tier') were prepared by district rather than county councils. They had to accord with the overall strategy set out in the structure plan. Local Plans were to contain much more detail on land uses and densities. They would deal with local issues but within the context of the policies set out in the structure plan.

Under the current administration, it's now up to the role of Local Plans to give an upfront overview (or spatial element). This is followed by more detailed policy considerations. The Local Plan process can ensure a consistent approach to site suitability. This is where alternatives can be best considered. Such processes take time. Unsurprisingly, from a political perspective, there has been a temptation to produce a raft of ad-hoc style 'permission giving' mechanisms to 'stream-line' the process for approval. These include Simplified Planning Zones, Enterprise Zones and Local Development Orders.

The divergence between certainty and flexibility can be seen in the traditional French approach compared to England's. The traditional French approach of prescription had regulations. These spelt out precisely the nature and content of development control decisions. They set up a system of plans. These legally binding documents provided the regulations for given areas that were all-embracing in their content and their coverage. In contrast, public sector planning bodies in England have been discouraged from positive plan making from the Thatcher era onwards. This includes master plans. Rather the preference is with indefinite and unspecific policy-based statements or aspirations. Into this interpretative void, developers have leapt with their consultants. They are followed by public pressure groups, residents' associations and the like. They all have their own private interests and axes to grind.

One means to make sure of successful outcomes is the application of design codes. Design codes are precise and provide technical instructions on how to construct buildings in a certain area. They may set out each buildings' required size, proportions and design detail, as appropriate to their location. They were common in the 18th Century. Indeed, Georgian terraces owe much of their uniformity to statute. This fell out of use in the mid-19th Century evidenced by the far greater variety of late Victorian buildings. They have played almost no role in 20th Century British planning. Yet they are used extensively in Germany, Netherlands, Scandinavia and the United States.

Their advantage is they ensure all buildings complement the existing character of a neighbourhood. This boosts a sense of place, creates local buy-in, reduces opposition and, not surprisingly, allow for quicker and thus more profitable development. Everyone wins in theory. For the United Kingdom they are tailor made for neighbourhood planning. They give a means for local people to direct issues that matter to them. The need for legitimacy and working through democratic cycles leads to problems in keeping pace with economic cycles. This includes keeping in sync with the plans of higher authorities. They may be able to be changed without the same intensity of democratic scrutiny. The plan making cycle (plan, implement, monitor and review) incorporates the latter (as plans never quite go to plan). Yet when plan making is seen as slow, expensive and controversial (or all three) often the review aspect of plan making gets ignored.

8.0 Development Management

Development projects are about achieving a certain goal. There are many motives: land ownership means little if there is no potential to modify or improve the environment. It may appear simple enough to regulate 'development.' A building is a building. Yet simplicity disguises a raft of problems about definitions of specific activities. Most people think they can recognise a new building and also a structure. Yet if it happens for example, to be a construction crane then should it still be classed as development? Many challenging definitions have been the subject of case law in the UK. Development depends on the factors of its size, permanence and physical attachment to land. Scenarios are as diverse as the height of fences or hardware associated with new technologies. Control is related to new development. A concept of existing use rights makes sure that owners of existing structures do not have to meet changing standards. In many situations, even the demolition of a building is also deemed to be development.

There is normally a threshold set by the planning authority at which development needs consideration. In Britain, it's set at national level and termed the General Permitted Development Order (GPDO). This grants permission for specified minor works which otherwise would count as development. It also contains the use class orders which remove the need to obtain planning permission for changes of use within defined categories. New Zealand's system is a contrast. Everything on land is permitted by default unless a district authority chooses to place a rule in a District Plan that says otherwise.

In effect, the United Kingdom order defines and separates different uses. They are seen to have varying incompatibilities and impacts when juxtapositioned with other uses and users. In other countries, it's zoning ordinances which specify the mix of uses and other development characteristics. These are set out in a detailed land use zoning plan of some kind. While agriculture is generally left out from planning control the scope of what is allowed is not unlimited. Forestry is often regulated and likewise in the United Kingdom is equestrian use. About the latter, the difference between grazing and keeping animals was held to be whether extra food was being brought in (Sykes vs. SOS 1981 JPL 285).

There are also some basic questions about what homeowners are allowed to do in and around their homes. They are allowed uses incidental to the enjoyment of a dwelling house. Yet understandably this does not always provide for every eccentric hobby. In the case of Wallington v SOS, Wales [1991] JPL 942, the Court disagreed with the owner's desire to have 44 dogs on a residential site. There are cases which have addressed the nature of a house itself. For instance, the case of multiple occupations and what makes up a self-contained unit. Whether a change of use is 'material' relates to a case-by-case judgment of significance. The case of Bendles Motors Ltd v. Bristol Corp, 1963 1 WLR 247, illustrated this point. A free standing, gravity fed, egg-vending machine of only 9 square feet was deemed to have become a 'creeping retail use' inside an existing petrol station.

These types of order are secondary legislation made by Governments under the Planning Acts. They are the subject of regular amendment. The general fall in construction output following the credit crunch was followed by a number of significant changes. The Government lent heavily towards liberalising Use Class orders and Permitted Development Orders.

In the United Kingdom, development management is the permission giving process for land use development and activities. As such, it marks the front line or interface between public administrators of the planning system. It's between those who manage the cases for the planning authority and the private sector proposing the development. In many other countries, permissions are conceived of as an exception to the rule. The general proposition is that a Plan will tell a developer whether a proposal can or cannot go ahead in an area.

Once there is agreement with the planning authority that permission is needed, and the promoter wishes to pursue a development proposal, then they submit a planning application. In the planning world of the 1980s an application was basic. It may have just shown a red line around the site in comparison to today's photo simulations and lengthy analysis.

In England, all applications have to include a design and access statement. This is not just a description of the development. It explains how the design was arrived at. It may also cover what local planning policies have been observed or any public engagement that has been reflected in the design. Finally, it many detail how relevant principles of good design have contributed to the proposal.

Certain types of major development are additionally subject to an Environmental Impact Assessment (EIA). The EIA carries out a European Council Directive. As with plan making, EIA's are about evidence gathering, forecasting and predicting the impacts both on and off site. Contrastingly, in New Zealand, every application has to include what is termed an assessment of environmental effects.

Planning applications are recorded in a register available for public inspection. It is generally publicised in the local press, on site and notified to neighbours. The public administrators in turn assess the suitability of a proposal. They weight it against policy and different aspects such as landscape, traffic, amenity, historic environment, biodiversity and others. The Government can call in planning applications for their own decision. This power applies to cases which raise issues of national significance. It's used very selectively. Only a tiny portion of the total number of applications submitted to local authorities ever get 'called in.'

A local planning authority can make a decision to allow out right, allow with conditions, or refuse a planning application. Decisions should be made in line with the provisions of the development plan for the area, unless material considerations indicate otherwise. Granted planning permissions will normally be accompanied by conditions. These can cover a range of matters including the detailed appearance of a development, access requirements and landscaping. Yet conditions must meet prescribed tests and be necessary. A condition shouldn't be imposed on a planning permission that wouldn't otherwise be refused on the basis of adverse effects.

The promoter wishes a 'smooth ride' through the system. Inevitably, there is negotiation between them, the decision maker and sometimes other stakeholders. Deals are done. When an issue can't be settled through a condition, the site promoter may instigate measures which sit outside the permission. These form a separate contract, termed a planning obligation. Such obligations may take the form of a planning agreement or a unilateral undertaking. As with conditions, they must meet certain tests.

The ability to negotiate with developers over contributions is a key skill for those involved in development management. Negotiation is commonly needed. Matters include securing agreement on policy aims, achieving smoother resource allocation and more effective implementation. Healey and Forester describe how the role of the planner acts as a mediator to secure a voluntary agreement. The purpose of the planning agent is to redress power imbalances between players. No single party can become so powerful they do not need to negotiate (Bounds, 2004).

Any person or organisation can object to a planning application. There may also be a need for consultation with government agencies, neighbouring authorities and other bodies. The planning officer responsible will then compile a report to the council's planning committee with a recommendation. This will be based upon any consultations, the extent of compliance with relevant development plan policies, regard to earlier planning decisions and their thoughts, having visited the site. In practice, most minor applications will be decided at officer level under delegated powers. Where elected members make the decision, they are not bound to the Officer's recommendation. They are entitled to make their own decisions but need to be mindful of the consequences to defend, should the decision be appealed. Meetings of local planning committees are generally open to the public.

An unsuccessful applicant has a right of appeal to the Secretary of State. Most of these appeals are against the refusal of planning permission. It is also possible to appeal against the conditions that are attached to a permission. Finally, an appeal can be made where the planning authority has failed to give a decision within the prescribed period (usually 8 weeks).

In England, practically all appeal decisions are made by independent planning inspectors. They are employed by the executive agency, the Planning Inspectorate. Yet where a proposed development is deemed to be of major importance, it may be 'recovered' for determination by the Secretary of State. They then consider a recommendation from an Inspector. There are three procedures for the consideration of evidence. Most appeals are considered through written representations. There is also provision for evidence to be heard. This can be through a full inquiry which involves cross examination by advocates. Another means is through a hearing where the inspector is responsible for conducting a structured discussion on issues that are likely to stem from the Council's decision. All planning decisions can be challenged in the courts. This can be either on procedural grounds or by judicial review of the reasonableness of the decision.

Once development has started, it's the role of enforcement teams to make sure that what has been agreed is adhered to. Enforcement has been described as 'protecting the gormless but coming down heavily on the greedy.[64]' Being akin to policing, it earned a disproportionately high amount of airtime in the BBC Programme – 'The Planners;' compared to other planning activities. Yet enforcement of planning decisions and rules is essential to maintain the integrity of the decision-making process. It helps to uphold the public acceptance of the decision-making process even if it has been described as the 'Cinderella of planning.' The mechanisms that can be applied by an authority have grown in scope and complexity.

Enforcement is not inexpensive and without risk to the authority. Some cases have the potential to sap significant resources of the authority in question to 'address the issue.' A recent example was the cost involved in the mass eviction at Dale Farm, Basildon of the Traveller community. Unless penalties can give a revenue stream they are generally reactive and complaint driven. There is also a right of appeal against an enforcement notice. Certain activities may have strict monitoring schedules imposed. If people do not complain or enforcement is not given due resources, then all the policies, rules and regulation of the planning system amount to very little.

9.0 Property Values and Compensation

Typically, the private sector, characterised by profit motives, does most development. By virtue of its control over development, the planning system influences but does not control land values. This distinction is important. Planning control affects property values for better or worse. From its beginning, betterment and compensation have been major considerations of natural justice. Compensation is for those whose land has decreased in value. For example, those whose land is being adversely affected by nearby development. Betterment by a planning decision is where there is the possibility of a more profitable use of land. This might be residential as opposed to cropping. The amount gained by a potential purchaser in obtaining planning permission for a more valuable use of land is termed 'hope value.' It is achieved through a possibility of profit and not any works that the landholder has carried out. In gaining permission, the seller (former owner)

---

[64] By the former secretary of state for DCLG, Eric Pickles.

profits at no outlay. This could be described as fictitious capital. Generally, this arrangement is achieved through options. A site promoter would buy the land off the owner once permission is secured.

In England, the 1909 Act allowed local authorities to recover 50% of any increase in land value and owners could recover any fall in value. This was soon changed so that owners were able to delay paying local authorities until the actual value had been realised through sale. In practice, the collection of betterment proved impossible.   Also, authorities wishing to control development got lumbered with hefty payouts to affected landowners. The Uthwatt Committee Report[65] introduced the two important concepts of shifting value and floating value.   These concepts influenced much of the later discussions on the relationship between land use regulation and property values. The concept of shifting value is based on the idea that the demand for any given type of land use in a particular region is finite. Land use restrictions in one municipality may cause downward value changes there, but at the same time may increase the value of land in another municipality where the regulations do permit development. Floating value refers to the speculative nature of potential land values. Landowners assume that if planning regulations didn't stand in their way a lucrative land use could 'land' on their own plot or site. This is often wishful thinking. These concepts challenged the traditional rationale that plans should grant development rights. They also undermined the compensation entitlement argument for a reduction in development rights.

The 1947 Act not only nationalised development rights, but also nationalised betterment gains by introducing a 100% betterment levy. This was the development charge. It may appear outrageously high in current times.   Yet it was, at the time, predicated on the vast majority of new development taking place on public land.   Needless to say, it was soon deemed to be ideologically incompatible and removed by later Governments.

If the United Kingdom adopts a more zonal planning approach, it should revisit the potential for betterment. To not do so would result in a missed opportunity for authorities to redistribute some of the hope value back into community funding.   Typically, benefits are gained through planning obligations. They are used to secure facilities that are a consequence of a development. This includes schools, health services and public transport. A particularly common use is with affordable housing. A certain number of units in an otherwise private development are made available for social rent housing or 'key workers.' These include teachers and nurses, who would not

---

[65] This was a famous war time named after the committee's chairperson.

otherwise be able to afford the high costs of housing in the areas where they work. Recoupment through the s106 mechanism has suffered as a result of the recent boom and bust cycle of the property market in the United Kingdom. This is because the viability of proposals granted under fairer conditions has changed for the worse.

The financial implications of decision making and the potential for planning authorities to be swayed by development obligations into allowing 'inappropriate' development are significant. It is an established principle that local planning authorities cannot be guided by any consideration of the effects of their decision on the value of the land. Nor can planning permission be bought or sold through the developer paying monies to gain the grant of permission. Planning obligations must be deemed necessary to make the development acceptable in planning terms. It must be fairly and reasonably related in scale and kind.

10.0 Environmental Management

The origin of environmental management emerged from the nuisance laws first instituted in Victorian times. Such nuisance laws were the primary means of land-use control up until the 20th Century. Despite the planning system becoming dominant, they are still influential. In England, the Public Health Act (1948) set up a Local Board of Health. New quasi-governmental organisations were subsequently created. These administered the poor law, public health and sanitation. 'Health' remains a strong reason to justify intervention. It is necessary in many developed countries to address hazardous levels of air pollution caused by industrial production.

In the United States, campaigners on environmental issues began from conservationist origins in the 1960s and 1970s. Often they were from hunting and fishing clubs. Over time they evolved to become a powerful political force. In the end they forged landmark environmental legislation enforced with aggressive litigation (Dowie, 1996).

The resulting system has been described as command and control, prescriptive and detailed. It came under criticism for imposing unnecessary costs on business and constraining innovative approaches. In the field of environmental regulation, policymakers have increasingly moved from prescribing technologies to setting performance goals. This allows developers to propose their Best Practical Option. There were initial ethical concerns around legitimising pollution. Yet there have been inroads into a more market-based approach (buying and selling) of controlling pollution (Kamarck, 2007). This includes American pollution permits and United Kingdom Landfill Tax.

The theory is that these approaches lend themselves to addressing problems where coercion is simply too expensive to monitor / enforce. Yet the success of performance-based standard approaches is often limited. The culture of the Environmental Protection Agency caused problems when they were initiated during President Bill Clinton's administration of the 1990s. In this instance, the administrator was intent on ensuring projects wouldn't fail to meet their aims. In so doing it worked against 'innovative, but risky' approaches (US GOA, 2002).

Recognition that the environment has value does not reduce the need for resource use. Decisions are still needed around natural resource allocation as in pre-industrial communities (refer above to Section 1.4). The Californian drought, 2011 – 2015, highlighted tensions surrounding resource allocation for environmental, agriculture and municipal water supply sectors. Farmers wanted the water for agriculture. City authorities were reluctant to ban water use. Environmentalists sought to hold back water to make sure river temperatures were adequate for salmon. These sorts of severe weather conditions present authorities with difficult decisions. This is where compromises between competing aims need to be made.

Most environmental protection legislation is a 'one stop shop'. It's possible to conceive of it being split up and incorporated within sector-specific pieces of legislation. An example of this would be an Act for how new airports are planned, balancing economic and environmental aims. It may aim for more flight capacity, but also require that environmental impacts are addressed during the design and location of new runways.

There are often strong planning policies in autocratic states, both capitalist and communist. This is where the role of the state becomes all dominant and the pursuit of industrialisation all enticing. Controls on other forms of regulation are typically weaker. This ranges from health and safety to environmental pollution. In China, pollution continues to defy and indeed defeat the outcomes sought through the planning system. The Tianjin port warehouse explosion (August 2015) is indicative of the greater risks authorities there are willing to take compared to those in the West. In this event, 85 people were killed and hundreds hospitalised from the storage of 'dangerous chemical goods'.

With its democratic tendencies, planning tends to put the economy and people at the centre. Environmental planning has been interpreted as a regulatory process running parallel to, and distinct from, spatial planning. Notable exceptions are the Netherlands and New Zealand. This separation of planning and environmental functions is less integrated. Yet it is seen to be administratively efficient. Environmental management is more technical in nature than value laden planning. It can be argued that if it was handed over to local decision it would increase the variability of environmental outcomes. In Sweden decision making is devolved but avoids this potential problem. The aims of national environmental policy are supported by targets and are also binding on lower levels of government.

A relationship between planning and environmental authorities plays an important role in outcomes. After all, the origins of both came out of similar issues associated with the industrial revolution. The inter-relationship of both systems is perhaps strongest over the issues of contaminated land and hazardous substance use and storage. Granting permission to remediate contaminated land should not be seen as a privilege. Instead, it should be openly incentivised. In contrast, a hazardous substance should be controlled. This is where it could potentially enter either a sensitive receiving environment (river) or if it is near to a sensitive use (residential).

It's common for a proposal to need permissions both through planning and environmental regulation to start. Often both sets of regulation have competing demands that need to be balanced. The provision of environmental management measures may result in changes to aspects of a proposal. This in turn can undermine other planning considerations. Proposals that turn conventional wisdom on its head typically suffer under conventional regulatory processes. An example is cogeneration and district heating schemes. This is where residential units are powered by energy from waste. 'Incinerating' waste would typically be located well away from residential areas.

There is a debate over which process should take precedence. Should a development obtain planning permission first and then an environmental permit - or vice versa? Parallel tracking makes sure environmental permits are dealt with in conjunction with the planning permission. Developers are encouraged to discuss proposals with the environmental regulating agency before submitting an application. Yet both systems can overlap successfully. The scope of the planning regime for protecting the environment can be wider than that of the pollution control regime. In effect, pollution control is unlikely to have regard for the effect of noxious emissions on the development potential of an area. Neither will it consider whether the location of a particular process would make the area less attractive for securing its regeneration.

Some developments illustrate how the planning system and environmental management come together more than others. Municipal waste 'incinerators' and nuclear power stations, perhaps more than any other developments, have captured the public's imagination. Often this has been in a negative way that has inspired highly organised local campaigns and legal challenges. Failure of earlier technologies due to a lack of understanding is partly to blame. The worst of these plants were quickly shut down and others were forced to close once legislation was put in place to limit emissions. The association lingers, despite the fact that technology and regulation have improved. In England, the Environment Agency regulates about 100 large, complex, high-risk Energy from Waste facilities. Some of them deal with hazardous waste. These need bespoke environmental permits. Challenges to environmental permits are few and far between. The process is considered less political and more objective than the planning process. But it is also highly technical. This can make it difficult for non-experts, including consultees, to understand. It's harder to find grounds to challenge environmental decisions than planning ones. The purpose of environmental decisions is much narrower and their subject matter more technical. Most recent objections from local communities to new plants are during the planning stage. Once planning permission is granted the principle is set. The planning process has not only served a democratic function. The project, if successful, has passed an important psychological barrier to wider acceptance.

11.0 Public Participation

In democracies, 'dissent as a virtue' is in theory widely supported. If opposition is not protected, then there is no door through which reasoned debate can enter the affairs of government. It's not only valid to consider the views of local residents in decisions. It's also important to consider the role that urban design can play as an intentional and active part in shaping the democratic character of the city. Yet public participation doesn't guarantee rational debates. In increasingly polarised communities, it is harder to have restrained, post-modern discussion.

The level of public involvement between different planning systems is a key means to distinguish them. Post-Second World War planning had little direct input from the public. From the start of the 1947 Act, 'bureaucratic' planners did their homework behind closed doors. Some commentators have cynically suggested they gave Councillors a number of equally unpalatable options from which to make a decision. The system was based on a 'decide, announce and defend' mentality. The original level of public involvement may have appeared poor by modern, Western standards. Yet the introduction of the system itself represented a significant 'democratic correction' to the unfettered rights of land owners to develop their land. If planning decisions were unfavourable, the recourse was through the Court systems. The trouble was, not unlike today, that planning raised its fair share of disputed decisions. The Court system was expensive and time-consuming for the average citizen to pursue.

The range of groups and sectional interests mushroomed in the post-Second World War era. These included group based interests of diverse identities, beliefs and needs. They also developed in terms of their sophistication. These third parties[66] fought hardest for greater levels of participation. Henri Lefebvre, the French Marxist philosopher and sociologist, argued for a 'right to the city.' That is the right to join in the process of producing 'urban space' as well as accessing the advantages of city life. This is more a call for direct action rather than working through institutionalised processes.

In the end, the legal system of appeal proved too simplistic. The idea of 'community' has been eroded. Yet it has become an organising label for planning to make connections for public engagement and bottom-up processes. These include evidence gathering, mediation and governance relations. There remains a popular view that professionals shouldn't impose plans and proposals on communities. It is not just the New Left that seeks greater community involvement. Neo-liberals take the view that local government, funded by public money, should seek more public accountability. So to better represent the views of stakeholders they should also seek greater community involvement.

Response

There is a recognised continuum of public engagement. This is often referred to as the 'ladder of participation' (Sherry Arnstein, 1969). It ranges (unsurprisingly) from virtual non-participation through to citizen control. The latter involves mass participation or direct democratic models. Sitting in a half-way house in the middle of the participatory ladder is public consultation. It has become seen as something of a shibboleth. The advantages and disadvantages of public consultation are set out as follows:

---

[66] Neither applicant nor decision maker.

Advantages

- Educates all participants about needs of communities;
- Key element in vibrant, open and participatory democracy;
- Reduces conflict;
- Increases quality and efficiency of decisions by drawing on local knowledge;
- Social cohesion – real connections with communities;
- Re-discover 'place-based' norms;
- Brings out local 'knowledge;'
- Accomplishes a transparent look at the facts and opinions surrounding an issue and places it in the public domain.

Disadvantages

- Militates against bold and imaginative actions. Results in adoption of the 'lowest common denominator' position;
- Slowness of weighing up evidence;
- Costs of participation and consumption of resources;
- Complexity of issues. In a sense, government preoccupation with growth makes planning a lot simpler than balancing a myriad of competing aims;
- Never going to resolve fundamental conflicts of interest;
- Where there are two sides to an argument and everyone understands that. For example, if one part wants something and another party the opposite then other forms of conflict resolution are more appropriate. These include negotiation or mediation;
- Each person's opinion differs based on their background, personal experiences, values and culture.

Consultation has never been a one-stop solution to taking the 'pain' out of planning decisions. It needs extra resources and delays decision-making. Above all, it represents a balance. A decision maker is not necessarily bound to abide by the results. Yet consultees are unlikely to accept the outcomes if there's no evidence that views have been listened to, through meaningful dialogue.

Yet not all countries have embraced consultation within planning systems. France has only recently embraced it. In Russia there is still no real culture of citizens' participation, except for a few all-too-rare experiments. In the United States, concerned people are encouraged to seek justice (or simply democracy) in an indirect fashion. That is by working through non-profit organisations. These act as a moderating buffer between the citizenry and the government. The most powerful and influential non-profit organisations ironically tend not to be run or organised around democratic principles.

Development management in the United Kingdom has for a long time been based on consultative principles. Before planning permission is considered, those most likely to be affected are given the details and opportunity to object. The results from consultation aren't always predictable. If they were, then there wouldn't be any need for them.

This in itself creates a tension between representative and consultative democracy. Politicians are there to make decisions on behalf of their constituents. Most are elected on a mandate. This can run counter to having to consult before making a decision. The 'consultation culture' even feeds back into the structure and nature of the organisations which carry out the planning system. They may need to review their services as a result of customers' feedback on the authority itself.

In an attempt to overcome legal deadlock, associated with expense and tortuous back end processes, the UK Government introduced upfront consensus building stages into Plan preparation (Jones and Gammell, 2009). That was in 2004. Consultation with communities is now focused on engaging on the needs, concerns and problems of proposals from early on. Consultation results have also been elevated in status and are given the same weight as more conventional evidence. What this means is that the perceptions of stakeholders can pass as evidence.

The rise of utilitarian managerialism as a model for public organisations is worth mentioning. It is based on settling disputes between affected 'human' parties through process driven agendas. One source of difficulty is the relationship with 'out of town' stakeholders. Planning processes take years to unfold and the resulting plans can take even more years to be carried out. Officials aren't going to know if a small company intends to move to a new site in an industrial estate earmarked for housing. The community that joins in a planning process may not be the one there when the plans are realised. Sometimes the characteristics of communities in a place are changed to an entirely different demographic. This includes variations in socio-economic status, race, ethnicity, age, household composition, legal status, educational attainment, job capabilities, religious affiliation and sexual orientation. It poses a great challenge for participation in planning. There are efficiencies from engaging 'expertise.' Public consultation attempts to do the same but using a wide spectrum of ordinary people across all imagined local communities. Unsurprisingly, it can be a complex and often fruitless exercise.

Planners are also called to represent the community of the future. Otherwise it won't have a voice in the 'present' planning processes. Equally important is the ability to recognise the intrinsic value of the environment. Again, this is regardless of whether human parties have sought its protection.

There is an art around undertaking consultation exercises. This includes the nature of the message being consulted upon and how it is expressed. Consultation skills represent a core competence for urban specialists. The aim is to avoid positions between parties becoming too entrenched. There are visualization techniques available. These include computer modelling and technical wizardry to show the outcomes of particular projects. Online portal systems have undoubtedly enhanced consultation. Yet when unaccompanied by printed material it can disadvantage those without easy online access to relevant documents. Examples are the elderly and rural communities.

Clear thinking in policies should result in better outcomes. The early 1947 Act Plans were typically free from the sort of jargon that makes current plans incomprehensible to the public today. The earlier 'command and control' style documents was littered with obligation-inducing language such as:

- should;
- ought;
- must;
- have to;
- need to;
- supposed to.

More in-line with neo-liberal ideology than best practice psychology, obligation-inducing words have been replaced with positive statements of intent. That is where to build, rather than where not to build. Other buzz words have been introduced. They underlie subtle differences between stakeholders, users and other groups. Jargon and abbreviations have crept into professional language and carry particular assumptions. The diversity of opinions in society, consequent potential for opposition and the requirement for consultative exercises have changed the game. There is a strategy of 'constructive ambiguity.' This maintains vagueness around contested issues to achieve agreement. The result for end users of planning documents is the power of language to describe reality has been replaced. The purpose of language is instead to avoid readers engaging with reality.

This practice also assists those making difficult decisions from staying out of the media eye. The media and digital outlets have become increasingly omnipresent. They have shifted from providing steady streams of consistent information from credible sources to being unashamedly partisan with what evidence they present[67]. New technologies and the growth of alternative forms of media, so called social media, have given a new platform to engage. Social media make it extraordinarily easy to join debates, in contrast to the passivity of the TV generation. Yet it also encourages a certain 'mob mentality' that divides as much as it connects. Algorithms feed people what they want to hear. It directs and often distorts people towards an expression of solidarity, outrage and shunning those we don't like. This isn't helpful for the built environment to be determined by emotional reasoning, or accepting perception as reality. Much of it will stay in place, after all, for generations to come.

12.0 Beyond Consultation

The success of increasing levels of public consultation for decision making is variable. Increasing levels of public participation and localism do not always improve the rationality of decision making. Participation generally delays government responses. It can even weaken the ability of urban professionals to carry out the sustainability agenda. A decision can be decided on the weight and feeling of popular opposition. It can be made without reference to how the nature of the proposal stacks up against agreed planning criteria.

Opportunities for debate and engagement may be sub-optimal for pragmatic reasons. These include costs and time. Worryingly, another reason is because of the pressures exerted on planners from powerful interests. Those with money are better able to exploit the opportunities for participation. Developers lobby and engage local government to get favourable controls to do what they want on their own land. If taken too far this defeats the purpose for which the system was set up to begin with.

---

[67] The fallout of the US Election 2016 has spurred some reflection: http://www.nytimes.com/2016/11/13/us/elections/to-our-readers-from-the-publisher-and-executive-editor.html?_r=0

Authorities' need to motivate the public by explaining why they should get behind plans and proposals. The public aren't going to be interested in some abstract policy in a local plan. Instead, they focus on impacts on society, whether proposals build the community or personal consequences. Property prices is an example of the latter.

Local community backing or citizen mobilisation is less likely if methods aren't simple enough for the public to grasp. Education could be an important part of the tool-box. Educationists in the UK, as in many other countries, have been turning their attention to social cohesion for decades. Approaches within planning are far less known about. A German example is soziale stadt (social cities). This is where social work becomes a means of intervention in conflict ridden districts rather than more formal consultation tools. There is greater use of 'soft tools' based on behavioural science approaches to policy. An example is 'nudge theory.' This can improve the uptake of policy initiatives. It shifts the focus away from buildings to the people behind them or the psychology of urban change. It supports behavioural change in communities but it doesn't address the technological availability of infrastructural systems. Awareness of the problems isn't enough to affect the change. Often it's only through the persuasion of neighbours that people change the way they do things. The controversy of impacts is often just about making the change (development). Once in place, people do adjust to it over time. This was the case with the Eiffel Tower, which despite initial public criticism went on to become an icon of a nation.

It may be that much of the benefit of consultation is 'therapy.' The urban legibility of many places has suffered in the face of rapid physical change and development (Lynch, 1960). For Jameson, cognitive mapping[68] had an important role in allowing society to find its way back to rediscover normalcy and historical consciousness.

In allowing urban evolution, the planning system can be likened to change management. Accompanying this idea is the need to extol the virtues of creating a compelling 'change' story. Discussing change helps address the forces that lie beneath peoples declared views or opinions. Often it is deeply hidden. It lies beneath layers of prejudice, misinformation, confused expectations or earlier unsatisfactory experiences. Shedding conditioned thinking takes years of self-assessment and re-appraisal from what people previously accepted without question. This is the case of new technologies, such as the Energy from Waste facilities discussed earlier.

---

[68] Producing of mental maps by inhabitants to represent their environment.

Education in general has shifted to 'self-management' and various forms of cognitive behavioural application (Hartley 1997). It no longer teaches conformity to a standardized order (as during the early modern age). Instead, it focuses on the uncertainties of life (particularly the workplace). It demands flexibility and adaptation to change. Mentoring, self-appraisal and guidance are set out. These allow the individual to choose the appropriate courses of action from a range set by the state.

Normative behaviour and compliance with change are seen as the consequences of free choice. They are not seen as having been imposed. There is a new 'pastoral' power of education accompanied by a vindictive protectiveness in certain sections. It accords with the freedom of liberation, the diversity of a post-modernist culture, the imperatives of production (flexibility) and of consumption (choosing).

As discussed in Part I, the results of such conformity include de-socialisation and a lack of collective rituals. This is the so called absence of a 'social centre.' People need to identify themselves with the area they live in to achieve consensus. That is to identify with its territory and cultural inheritance in something like the way people identify with a family. Otherwise the politics of compromise will not emerge. This necessitates some kind of pre-political commitment. It isn't always easy in areas of high migration and change. Encouraging trust is not something just for government – in fact one could go further and argue it's not its place.

Society has come to expect more inclusive models of decision-making than consultation. Often this is due to the perceived inadequacy of traditional policy processes and bureaucratic models to deal effectively with diversity. A new form of policy-making has come to be known as 'co-design' or 'co-creation' of policy. Relevant stakeholders and citizens are brought together and engaged with early on in the policy-making process. This is intended to encourage trust and make policy more user-oriented, targeted and efficient. This can be mixed with formal, creative techniques such as design thinking with willing stakeholders. Design thinking originated from techniques that architects and planners have traditionally employed for the resolution of problems. Involving solution-focused thinking it starts with a goal or a better future situation before tackling the problem. The City of Bologna in Italy is a leader in getting local communities to co-create and co-manage its urban commons. There are three categories: living together (collaborative services), growing together (co-ventures) and working together (co-production).

An alternative approach is to surrender decision-making power to the 'community.' There has been much discussion in the United Kingdom over the last 5 years about spatial autonomy and localism. One mechanism is the use of local veto's for proposals such as town extensions and inshore wind farms. This is a move away from 'experts' who are seen as being based in some 'distant' local authority to more direct democracy. This is where the local community is given a right to override the 'planners' when what is being proposed is not supported by local people. Should an authority try to impose something that is not supported by local people, then there would be a right to create a new plan within a set period of time. This would depend on a majority of people in an area voting against what is proposed.

13.0 Success, Failure and Realism

The built environment gets shaped by countless human choices. Each of these choices is guided by a range of values and visions, but many have unintended consequences. Much comes down to the external manifestation of the logic of capitalism as discussed in Part II. This includes three factors. First, the predatory nature of business (its winners, losers and monopolisation). Second, an unbalanced economy (due to the forces associated with comparative advantage). Last, excessive urbanisation (with associated environmental degradation).

State intervention is intended to improve the 'spatial outcomes.' This would not otherwise be achieved in the urban environment. The mindset of planning in China is based on visionary city planning for the future. In particular, it's about how to do the right things at the right time' (Wu 2015). Within democratic regimes it is often easier to interpolate 'present conditions into the future' (i.e., trend planning). Planning for 'startling' new scenarios doesn't come easy.

Even when it is compulsory to produce a plan they may not get prepared. This may be due to costs and economic constraints as cited in the case of cities in Uzbekistan (Ryser, 2008). Cost is often cited as the limiting factor in the United Kingdom for not keeping plans up to date. Yet the reason generally comes down to political paralysis caused by competing special interest groups.

In the UK, over the last 30 years, there has been a shift away from master planning. This gives the greatest certainty about desired land use outcomes. The focus is now on the abstract nature of modern policy formulation. This has placed a much greater emphasis on implementation. The over emphasis on development management creates a situation described as 'planning by appeal' (Parker & Doak, 2012). This is where both developers and decision making authorities contest over proposals about what each wants to achieve.

Systems of discretion and lack of plan made guidance mean that decisions at the local level are readily carried into expensive and time consuming appeal proceedings. The outcomes are uncertain.

The value of planning departments depends on whether they improve the value of the urban products being created. That is over and above their own costs of administration and lost development opportunities. Where planning has been found wanting, it's described as an economic burden. Certainly, there is a direct cost in the administration of the system in central, local and private sectors. Besides urban specialists, there is a need for support workers to do consultation and dialogue exercises. When this fails, there is a need for legal departments. This is not to mention more administrative roles such as management and Human Resources.

There are many processes that planning authorities are obliged to do to 'promote good planning.' These are systematic of the failings of managerial and performance indictor cultures (for example, New Labour administration). Measures such as equality impact assessments or strategic environmental assessments end up as 'tick box' exercises. They don't add value to the process.

The system costs alone are now in the order of £1 billion per annum for the UK. Systems such as England's, which prides itself on discretion and flexibility, inevitably cost more to administer. It also needs a high skill base from its professionals to make sure that the best decisions are made. A system which is definitive on what is acceptable development is a lot easier to base a course of action around. Discretionary systems are ones in which there is a need to balance numerous matters of material consideration.

Public Sector Projects and Regulation

By one estimation ninety percent of masterplans remain unbuilt (Cowan, 2012). The question the planning and design professions have spent a lot of time reflecting upon is why. In the past, government authorities imposed their top down visions. These often went against the wishes of communities or even appropriateness of the site itself. For instance, Baldwin Street in Dunedin (New Zealand) is arguably the steepest street in the world with an average 35% gradient. It came about as a result of following the grid plan prepared by colonial planners in England. The planners had no knowledge or consideration of the terrain on which Dunedin was being laid out.

Some design plans go even more disastrously wrong. An extreme example was Stalin's Palace of the Soviets project. Intended as a symbolic replacement for a much-loved building, the Cathedral of Christ the Saviour, it had to be abandoned. The Cathedral was knocked down and its clerical occupants who protested were dragged off and shot. Only then was it discovered that the land could not hold such a massive building anyway. Water seepage into the foundations could not be stopped.

Public state developers in the modern Western World generally need to follow the same planning controls faced by the private sector for reasons of accountability. This is a situation that would never be conceived of under a centrally planned system. Having state agencies subject to state controls may avoid the above examples of inappropriate development. Yet it also raises a dilemma. Is it possible to have a neutral decision making process? Also, is it efficient to have state sector projects go through potentially conflicting public processes.

Politics is short term and populist but a long-term view is needed to plan for infrastructure. The two don't mix well. Infrastructural projects desperately needed in the United Kingdom get repeatedly delayed or shelved altogether. These include new power stations and transmission lines. Good infrastructure is a great enabler of economic growth but poor infrastructure inhibits it. This entire muddle is not just an inconvenience. It carries a real economic cost that is perpetuated through the planning system. Yet it really just reflects the wider democratic schisms within society.

There was no better illustration of the tensions between democratic accountability and technical rationality than the fate of the Infrastructure Planning Commission (IPC). It was the decision making body for nationally significant infrastructure projects set up by the former (Labour) Government in 2009. Its purpose was to produce a long-term infrastructure plan. As an organisation it was to be one free from political interference and changing priorities. Thus it could thereby deliver certainty for investors and the people who have to build infrastructure. Yet the new Coalition Government considered this unelected commission unaccountable as it didn't report directly to the Minister. Its powers were thereby transferred back to the Minister's control in 2012.

Critics of planning are not short of many wonderfully descriptive examples of 'waste.' The inquiry over Heathrow Terminal 5 cost £80m. Seven hundred witnesses were heard. It produced 100,000 pages of transcripts and sat for 524 days. It took eight years from first application to government approval. The reasons for this are still controversial. The decision-making may have been lengthened by both the lack of, and then changes to, Government policy. There was also the changing position of the Highways Agency/Department of Transport. It also took the Government, who called in the application within three weeks of submission, two years to arrange for the inquiry to start. Yet it's also clear that the adversarial nature of the process gave highly paid lawyers the potential to profit out of the situation.

When Methods Fail

Having had access to good evidence and expert knowledge is a start. The chance for 'glitches' to result occur where institutional capacity is lacking and the regulation is technical. In practice, the plan maker has to deal with information gaps and make decisions under conditions of uncertainty. The approach used and the consequential result can fall short of the target. If not falling short it might over-shoot the target or have unintentional consequences.

Even if good evidence is available there's no guarantee that public officials will boldly 'follow the evidence.' They may conform to the political signals of Members or the cultural and organisational practices of their own organisation. The planning process is inescapably anchored in political values, persuasion, and negotiation (Majone 1989).

A common issue is having many, and sometimes conflicting, aims. The resulting difficulty is setting priorities and the ability to focus on feasible targets. It may not be possible to optimise strategies due to time or political pressures. There are many plans and programmes that need to be grouped together to give a complete overview.

Inevitably, there are issues ensuring horizontal and vertical co-ordination across all departments of government needed to carry them out. Agencies may have different priorities and funding arrangements to deliver on aspirations. They are also subject to constant 'jostling' by stakeholders to amend policies and strategies. Planning frameworks and hierarchies are open to challenge during their preparation. This can change their trajectories.

Planning authorities need to keep up with complex demographics, population changes and trends of technological use. Patterns of land use, expectations about mix of housing types and reliance on public transit may change. They may in fact have been very different at the time the rules were first put into place. Often rules in force may have been formulated under an entirely different set of urban conditions. A fundamental re-boot of them was considered too difficult.

Rolling back existing regulations is often difficult. This is due to property values, public finance considerations, and political concerns. The earlier layers of regulations too easily become uncontested norms of 'good planning.' Mandatory plan making may be done. Yet rather than leading future change it may only amount to catching up with development patterns that have already changed.

Evolving public goals are often grafted onto old regulatory methods. These create strange hybrids, when in fact new ways of thinking are needed. Rules guide what gets built but often the aim (physical outcome) is unclear. Layers of convoluted rules produce a city form that might never have been intended.

For instance, it is asserted that over-regulation is preventing people in England building the houses they want. Over the years, a host of detailed building and planning regulations have been interpreted. These make it impossible to build tight terraced housing. They include demands that 100% of parking be off street, housing without steps up to the front door and minimum space given between each unit. The result is perverse and antithetic to the functioning of the community. Almost uniform, on-street parking does not make Chelsea a slum. Having almost entirely all terraced housing in Pimlico does not blight its residents' life chances. Steps up to many Notting Hill houses do not prevent the elderly living there happily. In themselves, these requirements are individually hard to object to. Houses should be liveable for as wide a section of the community as possible. Cycling should of course be encouraged. Yet the net impact of regulations operating in isolation is to prevent developers building terraces of houses and low-rise flats.

Inability to keep pace with change is an argument that neo-liberal commentators will typically use against state intervention. Yet a large part of the difficulty is the time consuming processes of democratic consultation that the authorities must work within.

Planning authorities are often left to deal with the (spatial) effects of an issue not the cause. The economist would use taxation as the tool to change behaviour before regulation. Increasing taxes on fuel reduces the use of cars, congestion and fossil fuel dependence. It is more effective than planning authorities requiring developers to 'build up' in the hope that higher densities will encourage cycling and walking. Another tool is the road pricing scheme. In the West the ability of local government to issue new taxation may be limited. This goes right back to the reason that central government has sought to limit the ability of local authorities to issue taxes within its local area (as in Thorbecke's day). The Government in Shanghai, in contrast, has been limiting the number of new private car registrations (50,000 per year since 1998). When such economic tinkering is politically unacceptable, it falls back onto the 'planning system.' Planning can direct the impact of regulation onto a relatively small segment of the community i.e., developers. Yet it has limited ability to influence the use of cars directly or make sure trips between different employment and residential land uses are of short duration.

More typically, compromise sets in while carrying out the original design plans. A curious example is how the development of Tel Aviv veered erratically from the simple, garden city plan intended. The main thoroughfare of Allenby Street was intended to run north-south, parallel to the seafront. Yet it got diverted in order to reach a coffee house built on stilts over the beach.

Even basic principles of urban design can become the subject of unintentional results. Take the cul-de-sac. This road design was a favourite of post-Second World War developers. They promoted small and ad hoc urban extensions off through flow roads. Cul-de-sacs were originally promoted for safety concerns. That is to restrict cars in streets where children could play. While they achieved what they set out to do, their extensive use cut neighbourhood connectivity. Changing the goal of the system to 'breaking down barriers to interaction' or increasing efficiency meant that the idea of a road that leads nowhere was flawed. Cul-de-sacs were later re-discovered for a period in the 1980s as a means of lengthening car journeys and thus changing behaviours around car use. Walkways or cycle routes were in contrast fully integrated into residential environments. Even if the cul de sac was built, people would still drive regardless of its length. The evidence is that when it comes to congestion people will prefer to change route, then change job, then change transport. Overall, people would rather change their job than get on a bus!

There is also what Odum (1982) described as the 'tyranny of small decisions.' Failed outcomes come about as a result of a large number of small, individual (planning) decisions. These produce a complex, unanticipated behaviour of the system as a whole. No one plans, or even desires, the overall outcome.

Environmental Impact Assessments are just an information gathering exercise. They don't identify the most desirable site for the activity or the impact if it's denied and construction goes elsewhere. Nor are they necessarily 'scientific' in the same way as would be the case if the assessment was of an actual intervention. Decision makers will be attuned to potentially significant adverse events coming about as a result of large causes (Ormerod, 2005). When a river becomes polluted a single source is the easiest to remedy. Natural systems are governed by power laws and large catastrophic events can occur at any time for no reason at all. They're characteristic of the system itself. This means that sometimes only a small shock to the system can have a large effect, while a big shock can be absorbed without much change.

Finally, the system relies on individuals and organisations to promote the betterment of the community. That includes bringing forward proposals aligned with planning expectations. Despite Brazil having public participation embedded in their planning system, its building and urban standards are often based on international norms. They are thus beyond the economic capacity of many of its people. This has given rise to the widespread informal settlements on the edge of large cities.

Where agreed goals are chosen, such as new housing in an area, it does not necessarily motivate developers or landowners to bring about their implementation. This partly explains the vast difference in price between agriculture and urban land parcels. Property development is a long term game, with the triggers being profit rather than common goals. Having purchased a piece of land a site promoter may sit for years. Conditions need to be considered right for development to occur. This includes planning regime/market condition etc. At any given time, sites may not be viable for their intended use particularly given the cyclical nature of the market. Site owners may alternatively choose to hold out in times of land price rises to get the greatest profit. Such is the story with the recent housing crisis. This was a finding[69] of the Government's investigation into stalled housing projects with planning permission.

Finally, adherence to regulatory systems depends upon societies' adherence to the rule of law. It's assumed that far more people are willing to comply than those for whom stronger intervention is needed. Where persuasion is not enough, progressively stronger approaches are needed (Ayres and Braithwaite, 1992). An intervention feedback loop is created under a discretion based planning system. There's an ever expanding number of permissions. Each is granted on the need for compliance with many conditions in perpetuity.

In England, there is discretion on the part of the local authority as to whether to take action. For instance, there needs to be a clear public interest in enforcing planning law and planning regulation in a proportionate way. Taking action must be balanced against the provisions of the Human Rights Act. This is with regard to the potential impact on the health, housing needs and welfare of both those affected by the proposed action, and those who are affected by a breach of planning control. Yet faith in the planning system depends upon enforcement. An authority must not only be given the mandate, but have the capability and competency. To consistently ignore breaches of planning control will undermine the whole system.

---

[69] Including that by former DCLG Minister, Eric Pickles.

Unintended Results

Even when planning controls achieve their goal there can be a price to success through 'system feedback.' Explicit targeting of assistance to deprived areas can increase problems for their inhabitants related to stigma and poor place image (Hall 2006). 'Issue transference' is another unintended result or 'spatial' problem.' Civic authorities, for instance, took action against the homeless camped in Grand Central station on the pretext of them disturbing passengers (New York, 1980s). Moving such individuals elsewhere may have solved the immediate issue but it transferred the problem. They continued to camp out but perhaps not in such a high profile location. This 'out of sight, out of mind' mentality is a common approach adopted to improve specific environs.

Removal of informal housing structures (slum clearance) is a classic conundrum for Third World authorities hoping to remove 'blight.' The removal of gypsy pitches in the English greenbelt is an ongoing planning saga between local government, the court system and travellers.

Another common feedback situation relates to the risk of urban flooding. Hard solutions (stopbanks etc) would have been traditionally proposed. They allow development within a community to continue. An unintended result is for such measures to increase the overall risk to the community as a whole. This is because further development adds to the overall risk, should the defences fail to protect the community. A more holistic response might be to relocate the whole affected community. Yet it is likely to be politically challenging. Depending on the compensatory mechanisms available it might also be prohibitive.

A more realistic approach is to simply 'block' future development in flood prone areas. This would prevent additional risk to life and property. An unintended consequence is to drive investment away. This leads to socio-economic decline for existing residents. This was the case for Jaywick residents, in Essex, in what is now one of the most deprived neighbourhoods in England.

Another mechanism would be to allow further development provided there's 'flood proofing.' This is where the habitable part of new buildings must be above the height of expected floodwaters. Garages would be typically accommodated below. Yet this creates a new risk to life for inhabitants. They may not want to sit it out without amenities until floodwaters subside in the habitable part of the building. By attempting to traverse the surrounding flood waters they expose themselves to risk.

'Jurisdictional reach' of an authority is a common issue affecting the ability to manage an issue. Real issues do not respect administrative boundaries and occur beyond where control can be exerted. This occurs at any number of scales. One of the most commonly cited is the 'leapfrogging' of greenbelt controls. Developers may not accept compromised viability resulting from more expensive brown field development. They will search out greenfield land beyond the greenbelt boundary

Development capital can move over the border to less restrictive, administrative regimes even within a city area. Popular urban areas that demand effective controls to manage the look of new housing, or how public services ought to be located, become victims of their own success. Planning laws and development control can deeply impact the existing sociocultural and economic order. This can include personal health and safety, housing prices, employment opportunities, family life, personal time (spent on travel), and accessibility to public services.

Planning regulation can force the supply of adequate and affordable housing. Yet it may also pile on the costs to develop land, thus raising housing prices (whether intentionally or not). By impairing the distribution of urban benefits among social groups, planning laws may exacerbate social differentiation and social exclusion.

The worst category is so-called 'wicked problems,' which are highly resistant to resolution. The term was originally coined by Rittel and Webber (1973) about problems of social policy. Climate change would now be regarded as the most challenging. A purely scientific-rational approach cannot be applied to wicked problems because of the lack of a clear problem definition and differing perspectives of stakeholders. The solution depends on how the problem is framed and vice versa (i.e., the problem definition depends on the solution). Stakeholders may have radically different world views and different frames for understanding the problem. The constraints that the problem is subject to and the resources needed to solve it change over time. So the problem is unlikely to be solved definitively.

Circumventing the System

There will inevitably be tension, conflict and compromise between developer and the regulator. That is, unless their 'cultural' aspirations are aligned. The development industry is never going to be able to always 'second guess' how a proposal may fare through a highly discretionary system. It draws different balances between competing values from one day to the next.

Developers are faced with a system of regulatory complexity and pressures. They generally take the shortest route or line of least resistance, to get a development proposal through the planning system. Only big building companies can afford to fight a planning battle. So this is the reason why large scale, unoriginal, edge of town development wins the day.

The so called 'players' of the free market, which may most actively promote free market values, are also the greatest users of it. It is no surprise that incumbent businesses are often the greatest users of the planning system. Under the logic of capitalism local producers do not like being forced into competition with new producer. The competition between different companies for survival forces them to defend themselves against rivals.

Naturally, favouritism and manipulation can also come into the equation. When that doesn't work there are 'tricks of the trade,' given that the planning system is 'blind' to ownership. A personal history of enforcement action applied against the developer is not something that can be taken into consideration.

There are certain strategies that assist in getting approval. Often an issue for gaining permission relates to a site constraint. That is something recognised by the planning system as being of value (but not necessarily financially). This could be a protected building, tree, potential newt colony or wildlife site. Rather than submitting the details for how this might be resolved on site, a savy developer may seek legal or illegal means to demolish, destroy or remove the impediment. This means it's no longer a consideration in the granting of planning permission. There have been several examples in 2015 of London site developers destroying historic pubs[70] on sites they own. The local authorities concerned have ordered that they are re-built again brick by brick.

One strategy is seeking permission for a proposal that just avoids triggering the need for extra scrutiny. This applies to the processing thresholds in a screening opinion which generate the need for an EIA). Another, is to divide a project into two separate planning applications. Generally speaking, it's easier to secure part of the proposal before expanding upon it. Then the impacts of the permitted part of the proposal are not counted against the second part. As mentioned earlier, it often comes down to negotiation. If developers need a building with at least five storeys to break even, then they may begin with an opening position of 15 storeys. Through

---

[70] For instance, the Calton Tavern in Maida Vale and the Alchemist in Battersea.

dialogue with the planning authority and compromise they may end up with seven storeys, thereby looking like a win / win.

The final circumvention is to ignore the planning system, deliberately hide urban activities and/ or build anyway. There are one quarter of a million people living in illegal additions on rooftops or filled-in airwells in the centre of buildings in Hong Kong (Smart, 1992). In the UK, newsworthy cases include whole houses secretly constructed in the countryside. In one such case of deliberate concealment, Mr Fidler constructed a large house inside straw bales (discovered in 2006). A similar case was that of a barn exterior containing a five bedroom house, built by Mr Beasley in 2002. They evaded discovery for the time in which enforcement action is needed to start their removal. Retrospective applications to legitimise these structures were then made. It took 'judge made' law at the Supreme Court to turn them down.

Naturally enough no one likes to lose. The planning system can take a personal toll on owners and site promoters. One case involved a site owner who failed to have his greenfield site at a key arterial entrance to the city rezoned for a business park in the 2000s in Christchurch, New Zealand. He responded by constructing an unsightly tarpaulin fence around the property perimeter as a public display of what was possible as of right. More disturbing is a recent example of a fire at the South Oxfordshire DC council offices (Jan 2015). It was believed to have been started as a culmination to a long running planning dispute. The fire was started on the first floor of the planning department by an arsonist who drove a car into the Council building.

Public Participation Failure

It's a truism that the greater the community buy in to a plan the more likely success is. At the 'local' level the incorporation of citizen participation into conventional planning has had persistently paradoxical results.

Delays in preparing the 1968 structure plans resulted from the addition of policies sought by groups that had little or nothing to do with land use planning or the physical environment. The proliferation of public interest and environmental groups since the 1960s has been empowered by new mandates for public participation. It has given citizens a significant role in land use and planning decisions. Groups now come and go with the issues of the hour. Examples included the location of picnic sites, nuclear free zones, racial or sexual disadvantage. Modern examples might be the banning of fracking or Genetically Modified crops.

The public distrust of Government has permeated politics since the latter part of the 20th Century. It may be explained as citizens having perceived a disconnect between the aspirations of policymakers and the realities of policy implementation (Kamarck E., 2007). Planning is synonymous with sustainability but many systems in the West still deliver large, land-greedy, energy wasting, retail, leisure and recreational facilities. There remains an assumption that economic growth is necessary to overcome poverty and produce wealth for environmental clean-up. It may be no coincidence that 'messianic' statements, about what can be achieved from secular policy makers, have come at a time of organised religious decline.

Environmental rhetoric has a totalizing character. It turns land use decisions into moral battles between irreconcilable opposites. The modern planning system almost needs public-spirited citizens to mobilise. In doing so they become that much decried, 'narrow-minded, single-issue' creature - the NIMBY.[71] The term may be recent but NIMBYists are not necessarily a new phenomenon. Their roots can be traced back to those opposing Christopher Wren's (1632 – 1723) City of London grid. In the modern world, it has become synonymous with the hypocrisy of residents living in attractive and prosperous areas. Having benefited from free market policies they espouse conservation values in order to protect their property values and environments.

As mentioned earlier, there's a difference between the motivation of urban authorities, tasked with strategic goals, and those of the 'average person on the street.' Embattled planning staff often have limited personnel, resources and narrowly defined technical expertise. They often find themselves caught between the moral passions of citizens, the arguments of land use attorneys, and the testimony of duelling experts. Inevitably, politicians, not being able to live in a separate world from those who elect them, join in.

The current regulatory regime blends technical expertise, procedural requirements, and citizen input. As such, the public process can reinforce some of the most socially and environmentally damaging tendencies of current development patterns. In doing so it simultaneously undermines faith in government—and more generally, in the democratic process.

In a perverse sense, community opposition to a development increases its coherence. A common outcome of 'places over the market' and the fear of change. Perhaps this is rightly. A lack of resistance may be interpreted carte blanche by developers as the 'green light' for their particular form of development. When villages are transformed into towns, and towns into cities it represents a preference for housing needs over existing 'culture.' Yet

---

[71] Not in my back yard.

existing residents who have bought into consumerism can't argue that their existing culture is unique and worth protecting.

In some cases, democracy may be holding the wider community to ransom. There has been a demonstrable need for additional runways around London for years. Yet Barnes and Richmond have higher numbers of top lawyers and bosses per head of population than anywhere else. A proposal for the expansion at Heathrow airport faces formidable hurdles.

NIMBYism is at times a selfish response of responding less to others needs compared to those of the local community. Yet it chimes with the emotion laden values of post-modernism. Such groups represent social units. They may have the economic and political wherewithal to challenge the placeless logic of corporate development at the local level. Take home county opposition to accepting spill over populations. This results in inner city overcrowding in areas of high change and turn-over (poorer, ethnic and renter populations). People who fight development don't get to choose the amount of new construction throughout the country. They only get to make sure it doesn't occur in their backyard. It has the effect of driving intensive resource use further away. No doubt strongly held beliefs presented as a moral crusade defy rationality. Yet so what? NIMBY values encapsulate belonging.

Saying no to NIMBYism is akin to saying no to democracy. Yet public participation can be curtailed through legislative change to processes. First is the assessment of strategic proposals by an authority at a higher tier of government. More direct mechanisms include removing third party appeals by community or environmental groups. Another means is limiting consultation to those who are deemed directly affected. This is typically defined in terms of physical proximity. The difficulty with the latter is deciding who is affected. Is it only adjoining neighbours, landowners or tenants? People may have strong emotional ties to a place even though they do not live there. Certain groups or cultures do appear to have greater attachment to places than others. These include indigenous peoples, among others, whose cultures are worth protecting even though they may be strongly anti-industrial.

Finally Corruption

Those administering the planning system control a lot of development capital. As such, there is always going to be the potential for the illegitimate use of public power to benefit private interest. 'Legal corruption' is where power is abused within the confines of the law. Those with power often have the ability to make laws for their own protection. The concentration of power at the top of large-scale societies gives the elite[72] a vested interest in the status quo. They are able to set the agenda for everyone from a privileged bargaining position. And they will continue to prosper in times long after the environment and general populace begin to suffer.

The powerful can make substantial private 'donations' to those in government. They can also distort public opinion by buying the control of the media. Finally, they may subdue those dependent on the employment, investment or purchases they offer, by threatening to withdraw them. Subaltern classes have territorial interests. They are often the ones over-ridden, in part, by the planning system. The quotation of an Argentine planner highlighted the severity of the issue: 'We are the anti-planners. If someone has a parcel and wants to invest there, he just comes here and asks us to change the zoning code. So we change the code and everybody is happy, there are more construction jobs, ten more blocks are paved and he has done his business.'

Democratic states typically maintain checks and balances. These separate the legislature and judiciary from the executive. Yet even in democratic countries endemic corruption can make the unbiased execution of planning authority questionable. Italy is a case in point. Decentralisation of powers for planning decisions creates problems for professional planners in South Korea, as local culture relies on nepotism.

Non-democratic countries tend to be based on extractive regimes. They often claim the right to appropriate assets as needed. This is of course anathema to a market economy. Businesses want secure property rights and confidence not to be interrupted by an unaccountable, arbitrary government. Inevitably, practices of corruption are more prevalent in these countries than others (Corruptions Perceptions Index by Transparency International).

One-party states show the malaise of corruption more than any other. Stories of endemic corruption within the ruling party of China (and therefore the state) illustrate the point. This involves senior CCP officials in thievery and lawlessness. The source of regime decay originates from the success with which China achieved its two central aims: economic growth and repression of pro-democracy forces.

The enormous wealth produced in the 25 years of high economic growth have encouraged so called 'looting' by ruling elites. These are especially applicable to wealth generating sectors. They include property, energy, telecommunications and natural resources. While nominally owned by the Chinese people they are understood to be able to be 'acquired' through

---

[72] The elite comprise those in control of more economic resources than others.

patronage networks. Being free from the checks and balances of a free society creates the right environment in which those profiteering can get away with it. This situation not only harms the Chinese people. In the end, it undermines the party's authority, legitimacy and integrity. Its elites are considered to be motivated more by private gain than the party's corporate interests or long-term well-being.

Despite President Hu Jintao's '8 Do and 8 Don'ts,' corruption is difficult to root out of such a party culture. Analogies have been drawn to the 'tragedy of the commons.' Those who enter the party and move up the hierarchy inevitably come to expect a share of the spoils. While some confine themselves to petty theft, they quickly notice everyone around them busy stealing. To delay before cashing in may mean they miss out on the spoils (Minxin, 2014.). The system itself is intrinsically linked to the problem. There's a contrast with the situation in neighbouring Hong Kong. There the complicated set of land use mechanisms assists in preventing corruption (Ryser & Franchini, 2015).

PART V:
FROM VILLAGES TO VANITY SPACES

1.0 The Role of Ethics and Morality in Planning

Procedural Planning

Every planning law in the world impacts upon the concept of justice for better or worse. Planning is a quasi-judicial process. It's concerned about how matters are addressed procedurally between parties in conflict. Unsurprisingly, it can be summed up as administering the 'golden rule.' That is, the weighing up of the (unrestricted) right to develop ones' own land against the right of adjoining occupiers to the peaceful enjoyment of theirs.

Freedom as a concept has become less associated with politics in the West. It is instead consigned to production, particularly consumption 'choices.' Property (land) ownership, and other natural rights, were originally thought of as being bestowed by God, another theological source or a particular understanding of the nature of humanity. It has now morphed into an inalienable human right, but one that potentially conflicts with other human needs. Ethics invokes the 'right to the city' which has been incorporated into Habitat III. Yet space cannot be equally available to all possible uses and people. Space is invested with meaning, particularly in the context of power relations. It will always belong to some more than to others (Hillier, 2008). Unfettered capitalism led to the (democratic) solution of urban planning. Yet in creating realities (or rearranging existing reality) and imposing those on space, urban planning obliterates others' realities and needs. This particularly impacts upon the economic freedom to produce and develop (1972a D.o.E).

Moral judgements that an activity is bad per se are different to spatial judgements. Building codes protect people from dangerous designs. These apply uniformly across all parts of a city based on the nature of the building. Buildings represent consumption. So some environmental thinkers and campaigners see urbanisation as bad by definition. The city is the place in which society produces most waste and uses the most energy, water and food.

Urbanisation clearly has ethical implications. To use the term 'urban sprawl' is to pass judgement on it. Growth and progress are similar words but their acceptance depends more on the context. Locating a village on fertile land beside a river is a good idea. Yet when the village grows into a city and residents pave over the good quality, low lying, agricultural land it becomes a bad idea. Most people are happy enough to be prevented from driving on the wrong side of the highway. Yet they're less impressed with being taxed for driving on over congested stretches of the highway. Individual freedoms give collective consequences. Human inability or unwillingness to foresee such long term consequences may be inherent to our nature.

Planning systems address the negative side of development. They aren't anti-development. Even so, they go against the belief of 'spatial relativists.' Those who see ownership and markets, for instance, as the only mechanism to decide the location of things. Planners tend to making judgements on what's right or wrong based on where an activity occurs. They are seen as 'zoners,' in that they assign and divide space to reflect certain beliefs. For instance, dirt in the garden is fine but on the street it's bad. Transgressions occur when actions are deemed out of place - as might be considered if one eats food in the bathroom. These are more correctly considered 'inappropriate' or wrong in the context in which they're located. Most land uses fall into this category. Zoning sets up dichotomies. An example, is between desirable activities and the sorts of undesirable activities that Orwell talked about (Part I). Another dichotomy is between public and private. Most important for the UK is the difference between town and country. Boundaries such as these take on a symbolic significance. They allow communities to gain insights into themselves and the meaning of their existence. Yet such thinking on borders is challenged not just by neo-liberals but by post-modernist theorists. The French philosopher Gilles Deleuze, for instance, believes that borders are indeterminate and artificial constructions (Furedi, 2016).

The way the Human Rights Act, (HRA) 1998 is applied in the UK is detached from environmental concerns.[73]   Sometimes the search for justice leads back to the cornerstone of the modern legal system. There have been a number of high profile cases[74] about 'unfair planning laws' since the Human Rights Act (HRA) 1998. These concern the right to stay on land without planning permission where it can be shown that the form of occupation reflects ethnic identity[75]. The rights under Article 8 (the 'right to family life') appear to override planning law and policy. It is unlawful for a local planning authority to act in breach of the convention rights without statutory authority. This is determined in the context of whether it's in the interest of the

---

[73]   This contrasts with countries, such as Chile, which provide for environmental human rights in their constitution; i.e., the right to a healthy environment.

[74]   Buckley v UK, Chapman v UK and Connors v UK

[75]   Chapman v UK: while being a member of a minority with a traditional lifestyle different from that of the majority of a society does not confer immunity from the general laws, it may have an incidence on the manner such laws were to be implemented.

economic well-being of the country and the rights and freedoms of others. The proportionality test revolves around weighing up the rights of one party against another. Another category of recourse to the HRA has been about impacts caused by a neighbouring development on the lives of residents. This includes whether there is a right to build a turbine that spoils the view from a neighbour's house. These have been less successful. The decision maker has had to strike a balance between private and public interests. This is much in the same manner as applied under the planning system. The right of the landowner to develop their land won the day. There has been a long established principle in English Law[76] that land owners cannot protect their views. The rationale is that it would unduly limit the freedom to build on one's own land and thereby hinder beneficial development.

Often the root cause of planning issues comes back to neighbourhood disputes, bickering and petty dislikes. These stem from the form of tenure being private ownership and the perceived threat to property values. The planning system becomes a low cost dispute resolution service. It's necessary to develop some 'quasi-objective' means to define what is acceptable on any given piece of land.

A primary motivator for planning was to make sure that desirable and undesirable development were kept separate. This was discussed in Part III. The general principle is that capital flows to good investment opportunities for desirable development. Examples include amenities, houses or retail. Hence wealth becomes concentrated including spatially. Planning can give a means to secure better outcomes (public space, community facilities and the like).

Undesirable development includes for example, certain infrastructures and unfriendly uses such as heavy industry. It becomes directed to cheaper land that is often associated with being closer to poorer people, if not distant from everyone. Planning constraints have typically elevated the significance of certain natural and cultural resources. An example is landscape, which doesn't in itself have high monetary value. Undesirable development is thus forced to circumvent between these constraints and high value land uses.

Planning laws may give no more than a framework within which freedom may be realised and enjoyed. Such a framework is necessary in a complex, civilised (and particularly Western) free society. This makes sure that conditions for all people can stay tolerable or be capable of improvement. It can go from being a reactive system, to one which positively promotes certain values. This is based on an understanding that the whole can be greater than the sum of the parts. The role of planning can be extended further on the self-

---

[76] First recorded in 1610.

evident moral position of equitable principles. These include promoting social inequality and democracy. This represents a shift from physical planning into more social and economic spheres.

For the issues outlined by Walzer (Part I) this is always going to be difficult. In the Anglo-West the debate covers the benefits or problems around high rises vs suburban housing. Le Corbusier's solution of tower blocks was to create a greater sense of order and equality when compared to other housing solutions (Hollis, 2014). Yet the mentality of architects, such as Le Corbusier, displays a disinterest in how people live. Despite this, UNESCO[77] has listed 17 of his projects as world heritage sites. They are said to reflect 'a new architectural language that made a break with the past' (BBC, 17 July 2016).

Conversely, moving planning back into a more market orientated approach raises ethical questions. This includes having private agents making decisions, setting of pollution markets and even the 'right' to home ownership. About the latter, the state has a housing obligation for those who need help. Home ownership itself has become a form of capital accumulation, for example, saving for old age or to endow offspring. As it promotes inequality, it cannot be termed a right. The UK Government suggests there is a national need for 250,000 more homes each year. Morally, it should be more concerned with the 60,000 people now in temporary accommodation. These people ought to be the chief focus of policy attention. The rest it can be argued make up 'demand' rather than 'need.'

Planning law consciously strives for long-term (and often uncertain) aspirations. It typically stands for a collective desire for fulfilment nearer the apex of the hierarchy of human needs. Yet every building project has some positive motive. As such, ethics within the built environment is often not straight forward. Relevant questions to assist in drawing a conclusion include (Kirkman, 2010):

- Are the goals of the project worth reaching?
- Are the means used to reach the goals of the project appropriate?
- Does the project conflict with projects other individuals or groups are pursuing?
- What is the character of the person pursuing the project?
- What consequences follow from the project?

---

[77] The UN Educational, Scientific and Cultural Organisation – the UN's Cultural Organisation.

The answers to such questions allow us to understand the values and normative principles for the communities being served. Most commentators reject there ever being a single right way of deciding what trade-offs are acceptable or how resources should be used. The Ancient Egyptians prioritised the veneration of the dead over the needs of the living in building the Pyramids which sounds quite alien. The climate change agenda proposes a 'right' course of action. In doing so it faces an uphill challenge by potentially placing the needs of future generations over the needs of the living. That is by diverting resources away from material progress.

The statutory underpinning for most of planning is set out in state and local statutes. Yet the development management process does not capture all Kirkman's considerations. Principles are also included in professional planning codes of ethics (if those codes exist). Often codes of ethics exist for longer-established, filial professions, such as architecture and engineering.

With respect to ethical mandates, urban specialists are increasingly drawn into the Declaration of Human Rights, the Millennium Development Goals, and International Treaties for Sustainability (for example, The Paris Agreement). Many cities are paying explicit attention to these treaties. That includes those in the Third World. They have adopted some as official benchmarks for their planning agendas.

Forward-looking perspectives, such as Agenda 21, focus on future generations. Climate change comes as a blow to modernism as it invokes a new form of morality, showed by Pope Francis and his encyclical (2015). With climate change, all (humanity) are affected, although certain groups will be worse off than others. Low carbon technologies may not only be seen as a beneficial but moral as well.

In recent times, morality has been redefined by some to be more than just about behaviour between humans. It can also encompass relationships between humans and the environment (i.e., animal rights and intrinsic worth). A planning system has to take into consideration the role of those who now don't have rights. This includes future generations and biodiversity. If it doesn't then the system is arguably not fit for purpose.

The shift in the West, from a tradition of the monotheistic privileging of human beings over other life forms to a more pantheist perspective (where everything is spiritual) could further complicate planning. In some Eastern religions, there is considered to be a life force common to all life forms, regardless of surface differences in appearance and emotional attachment. In Ancient Rome, everything ended up being tied back to some 'spiritual function.' Even the Roman sewer had a spiritual function in purging the city [6BC].

Discouraging Immorality

Illicit land use activities, though rarely extinguished, can be readily banished from sight. More often than not, such activities are able to locate in specific, defined locations. For secular authorities, this is about making the best of both worlds. They may try to retain cultural integrity while cashing in on the financial rewards. Activities such as theatres, brothels and taverns were built outside London's walls in Stuart times. Yet they were located close enough to the city in what amounted to a regulation free zone.

Dubai, a Muslim country, has its own 'lucrative niches with their own special rules.' These include financial enclaves and media areas. State censorship and bans on alcohol and skimpy clothing are suspended. Singapore is also happy to profit from foreign gamblers in casino complexes. Yet it doesn't encourage its own citizens to bet. They must pay just to enter.

These are examples of an intended decision of an authority to decide where certain activities might 'not' go. The rise of Las Vegas as a gambling capital came about through a devolved system. This allowed an authority, situated in a 'harsh and difficult environment,' to devise its own rules to take advantage of revenue generating activities which were banned elsewhere.

In most Western countries, drinking was seen by religious groups as a vice and therefore pubs were discouraged. Secularisation since the Second World War has seen the British pub become a community hub. It should apparently be protected against higher value developments (for example, housing). Into this 'moral confusion' came motorway pubs; the first being opened off the M40.

Consistent with relativity in moral matters, there are increasingly few land use activities that are banned in the West. In New Zealand, legalising prostitution has led to some rather perverse situations through the planning system. For example, residents may object to a brothel being located next door. Yet this can only be on the grounds that the sign advertising the establishment doesn't have adverse effects on the local amenity. The issue is not only everything being accessible. It's also difficult to resist the 'hidden persuaders' promoting consumption in the advertising industry along with commercial TV (Packard, 1981). These days we could also add social media. It may be seen to be more about changing consumer behaviour where features of consumers' behaviour may have adverse effects on society. Examples include alcohol misuse and obesity. Post-War Sweden took the approach of taxing its people to the point that they cannot afford the consumption of alcohol. At the same time it re-distributed the wealth back to community projects (among other things). The state also used tight spatial controls requiring alcohol stores to be located in 'out of way' locations. An example, closer to home, was the town of Blackpool. It considered (2014) outlawing provocatively-dressed hen and stag parties from its town centre through a Public Space Protection Order (PSPO). In the end, only street drinking was banned. Another example in the UK and Ireland are 'no fry zones.' This is where fast food outlets are banned near schools to keep children from temptation.

Divisions and Segregation

Social and economic segregation (discrimination) is one of the most actively discouraged vices in the West. There are strong links to human rights legislation. Physical space has the power to separate through social control or by excluding one group or function from another. Formal means of 'carceral' architecture' include barriers or edges (linear features). Railroad cuttings, walls, gates and space (distance) can be used to close one area off from another. Water bodies can also form an important edge to many cities i.e., shoreline or rivers.

Post modernism is ideologically obsessed with inclusion (in theory but not always in practice). For instance, architect Norman Foster gave a nod to the growing importance of transparency in decision making through the design of London's City Hall and Berlin's Reichstag. This was achieved through the use of glass. By permitting the passage of light, glass may be symbolic in showing transparency. Yet it is also impermeable to everything else. It is, after all, a popular material for security barriers and the outside of banks. So it divides as much as it opens up (Moore, 2012).

Segregation can be a neutral concept in response to the needs of both strangers and inhabitants alike. Rather than strangers being excluded they are in a subtle sense controlled. From the street markets of the Middle Ages to older neighbourhoods in the New World, the throughput of strangers was controlled and directed by an interface with inhabitants that created urban safety. Space was policed by controlling the presence of passing strangers. This creates both a sense of urban safety and liveliness (Jane Jacobs). In contrast, modern systems of 'defensible space' aren't as successful. They are based on stranger exclusion and the surveillance of spaces by inhabitants.

There is a trend towards ever-greater forms of societal protectiveness. This is provided by a raft of new technologies for protection, surveillance and exclusion (Soja, 1995). Deliberate attempts may be made to reduce the habitation of a space by 'undesirables' (for example, squatters). These include installing uncomfortable benches, closing access to public toilets, or making surfaces skateboard-proof, which then render the spaces uninviting to all citizens. Although it affects all citizens, it has a proportionally greater impact on those seen to be undesirables. In Western cities there is increasing recourse to the use of regulation against ambiguously defined undesirables. This includes the broad powers for Councils in England to make Public Space Protection Orders. These serve as much as a means to move the homeless on or prevent street politics, as they do for what they were originally intended. That was to address dangerous or anti-social elements.

For the control of space, the most basic consideration is the 'right to move.' Many scholars promote a universal 'right to move' (Sandel, 2016). This is based on several philosophical grounds, including:

- The idea of a common ownership of the earth;
- A natural right of movement existing before the advent of nation states;
- An ethics of cosmopolitanism;
- Utilitarian notions of the benefits of immigration to both receiving countries and immigrants.

According to international law, everyone has a right to seek asylum from persecution or war. Yet there is no automatic right to move elsewhere for economic reasons. This poses an ethical question. Is there is any morally relevant difference between people dying from bombs and others dying from extreme poverty? National borders pose the greatest barrier to free movement. They're based on concerns about the effect an influx of immigrants might have on the housing market and social cohesion. Yet it should not be forgotten how internal controls on movement can and have operated, even in modern times. Authorities used the Propiska system under Communism. This is where people got stamps in their internal passports indicating which city or town they could get housing and find employment. This both gave the permanent right to dwell in a particular house and restricted the ability to move on. It was used to curb migration for example, from rural to urban areas. This 'passportisation' of the citizenry of the Soviet Union began in the 1930s and reached its all-encompassing scope in the 1970s.

Throughout history, the main means of spatial segregation has been through informal means such as class, gender and race. There are many cases in which distinct zones of interaction have been set to manage these encounters. It is noted that the primary issue, in a practical sense, comes down to whether the distribution (for example, share of resources) was or is fair.

Cultural examples include the Islamic separation of a private household into male and female parts. Then there is the public allowances (sections) for Jewish men and women along Jerusalem's Wailing Wall. While wholesale racial separation is rare, South Africa's Apartheid system illustrated an extreme example. In theory, this was based on South Africa being one country but four racial groups. In practice, it gave enfranchised whites complete political control. Blacks were given services greatly inferior to those of whites, and to a lesser extent those of Indian and coloured people. Blacks represented the labouring class. Apartheid centred on compelling people to live in separate places, defined by race. The overarching aim was 'racial harmony.' Segregation in more subtle forms is still used in certain circumstances. It has a similar aim to prevent 'cultural' (racial) clashes. In modern Dubai there is little of what might be termed public space. In itself this is a deliberate act to prevent protests. Segregation works on the principle that different social groups are allowed different rights, privileges and restrictions. This arrangement is made possible by division into 'zones.'

Exclusionary zoning involves certain residential communities continuing to be able to exclude other groups from their areas by using planning policy designations. Planning controls set up to impose racial segregation often went alongside direct exclusionary principles. Zoning impositions were once the mechanism of colonisation imposed on non-Western cultures. British colonial planning had its separatist concept of the 'dual mandate.' The French had what is termed 'associationism.' An example of the former included Singapore. Its plan of 1819 had racial segregation as a fundamental organisational concept. Even where it was skilfully done, as in French Algeria, it was often without concession to indigenous society or culture. Associationism was intended to instil in indigenous populations the notion of the superiority of newly built settlements over their own. It was thought they would increasingly use and occupy these new spaces themselves. Colonisation was often associated with purer expressions of planning. Conquering powers are far less compromised in overriding democratic, indigenous or property rights than in the imperial homeland. For instance, land readjustment in 1930s Japanese colonies was done in a far more draconian fashion than would have been tolerated in Japan itself. Often it would be without compensation.

The German approach to zoning was more about controlling the intensity of use than keeping functions separate. Mixed uses had existed there for centuries. In contrast, early proponents[78] of planning in the United States, defended class segregation. The New York zoning resolution of 1916 decried that bankers and leading men should live in one part of town. Shopkeepers, clerks and technicians would live in another. Working class in another. The 'noble' intention was that they could all enjoy the association with people of their own kind. In North America, zoning rules changed in the mid-20th Century from a flexible hierarchical model to a flat model. Mixed uses were allowed in the former, while in the latter land uses became exclusive. This shift meant that the density and house types were controlled creating a socially divisive pattern. This prevented the construction of apartments and exclusion of multi-family homes in single family house areas. The findings of research show that local governments do not favour approving even a small number of two or three-floor apartment buildings. They found that 30 percent of municipalities within metropolitan areas would not even approve such minimal multifamily housing which is often used by minority groups. Instead, single-family (or double-family) homes are preferred. This can be rationalised as protecting existing home owners and 'thinning cities.' The aim was to neutralise the evils of the slums (Pendall, Puentes, & Martin,2006). Allowing too many people to spatially aggregate is viewed as threatening the system and carries political fall out.

The powerful will seek to use space to fragment those dominated into as many small groups as possible, while maximising the spatial scope of their own network. The system is based on avoiding large-scale symmetric solidarity at the lower levels (H&H, 266). Social order is achieved where the benefits of capitalism can be retained through the creation of a quiescent working class. Design (deliberate or unconscious) will physically prevent too high and dense a rate of encounters. This is the reason for the design of peaceful industrial relations through the spatial form of Le Corbusier and Howard's new urban genotypes. The aims of zoning and prioritising home ownership were tied to social morality. In advocating for this, social conservatives in the United States, such as Hoover, are now seen darkly by the New Left. They concern themselves with divisions created between working and managing classes, as well as feminized home and masculinized work place environments.

In a free society, people can choose where they live within a country. This above situation is less apparent under planning systems where allocations or

---

[78] Such as Robert Winton.

zones are not rigid. This includes the United Kingdom and New Zealand. There is always the ability to seek planning permission for uses not envisaged in the original plan. Yet as was noted earlier, participation in a consumer society depends on the financial ability to consume. Price remains a key means of segregation. It continues to be acceptable for exclusionary zoning practices to exclude groups from areas. This includes gated communities and using market processes around planning designations to price out those who cannot afford to live there. For the poor or marginalised in the Third World, their only option may be the ghetto.

The Ghetto

Traditionally, people built the homes they inhabited and in the Third World many still do. In Latin America, these slum areas[79] are constructed out of makeshift materials, such as tin and wood, and are usually not serviced by basic necessities such as water and electricity. If the authorities do become involved it's typically limited to basic sanitary infrastructure.

The term ghetto is often synonymous with slums. These have come about as a result of a lack of financial capacity rather than legal restrictions. Cities aren't full of poor people because cities make people poor. Rather cities attract poor people with the prospect of improving their lives. Turner's model (based on 1960's Peru) had rural migrants moving from the province to the city centre on the basis of location at any price. With security, they shift to the periphery where ownership is obtainable. Cities are not always, as some might assert, better places to be poor. Slum dwellers may be forced into worse conditions than where they came from originally. In theory they might be able to improve themselves. Yet often they find themselves disconnected from the economic heart of the metropolis. If there is a benefit in having people of the same class together, it is the strong system of social ties that tend to develop in informal urban settlements. Their social networks are important to their wellbeing. Community members recognise that if they were to be relocated by the authorities their links may be severed and their quality of life would deteriorate. In 2009, the Centre on Housing Rights and Evictions produced a report on the global analysis of forced eviction. It concluded that it 'ranks amongst the most widespread human rights violations in the world.' Attention should surely be directed at the inability of people to stay put in

---

[79] Densely populated and distinctively named barriadas, barrios marginales, colonias, favelas, inquilinatos, and rancherías depending on the country of location.

cities. That comes down to the potential ground rent being extracted from the land they occupy.

The lower socio-economic classes of many Western societies previously lived in similar slum environments. Since then, the building stock in these areas has been upgraded. It gives increasingly higher standards of accommodation. This was possible because the cost of building standards kept pace with improving wealth and capacity for urban renewal. It involved the removal of poor quality housing, most recently in the 1950s and 1960s. This came from the introduction of wholesale urban renewal programmes. Jane Jacobs (1965), famously documented the negative social effects of razing. Instead of renovating run-down tenements they got replaced by functionally adequate, but characterless low-income housing blocks. By shifting communities into new housing it destroyed long standing social capital and the intangible resources built up in community networks. Authorities improved physical conditions but at the same time broke ties and social relations. Political authorities need to consider the existing character of the local community when considering plans for development (Bell and de-Shalit 2011). Parallels between ghettos and institutionalisation have been extended beyond economically marginalised people. For instance, the biological-medical model of disability has been criticised. In a similar fashion to ghettos, people who cannot function in society become confined to their homes or institutions.

Gated developments

The rich make sure they can insulate themselves physically and socially from the pressures of the city. They do not need to walk in public areas or take the subway. Rich enclaves have often formed within chosen urban, political boundaries. Most of the many squares of London are available only to the occupants of the buildings owned by the estates. Russell and Leicester are notable exceptions. It's a trend that parallels the increasing numbers of immigrants moving from the Third World into Western countries. Of particular concern is the phenomenon of gated communities. They are constructed for a small portion of the cities' populace. It's possible to argue that such communities don't directly affect the wider community. Yet in occupying proportionally greater areas of land they become disconnected from the regular urban street grids. They often have their own schools, universities, shopping malls, golf courses and sport clubs to cater to the middle and upper class inhabitants. In Argentina and Chile there are cases of private developers building private highways to link gated communities, and of exclusive transit passages for dwellers to access the cities' business districts. Significant fragmentation and social polarization can arise as a result of these growth patterns. Gated communities are rare in Continental Europe and Japan. Unsurprisingly, given their past fondness for such zoning practices, they are far more common in the United States and many parts of the Third World.

They can also be grouped by ethnicity, religion, and other characteristics. Some gated communities do provide for lessor income brackets. These include a favela in Rio de Janeiro. More often they are usually (urban) 'islands' oriented to those with good incomes and who quickly leave behind the values and knowledge of those living in urban bad-lands. These residential enclaves disengage from the problems of the wider communities. As such, those involved tend only to think about getting the best bargain for their own association. Their actions need to be at least compatible with the good of the wider community. If every group only presses for what it wants, the total demands either contradict each other, or are likely to be too great to be met.

Inclusionary Planning

Most of us live in a relatively free property market and desire to live with our socio-economic equivalents. Attempting to create 'balanced' neighbourhoods and communities in this context appears problematic. Thomas Schelling suggests that it is impossible to predict or influence the distribution of segregation in society. Only its general features can be known. There is an irony in proponents of marginalised groups criticising planning per se for 'sub-optimal' outcomes. The system itself is a response by the state to market failure. The issue may have arisen because along the way social justice was dispensed with as part of the mandate.

The perceived value of government is based on delivering economic benefits for its citizens. It lacks strong ideologies or absolute principles around the public good. 'Urban justice' is a concept about public policies promoting social equity and fairness. More so at least than the market, or pre-existing social forces, would have given rise to, without public regulation or intervention (Fainstein, 2010). Carrying out Lefebvre's 'right to the city,' San Paulo[80] guarantees each citizen the right to sustainable cities. This is understood as the right to urban land, to housing, to sanitation, urban infrastructure, public transit and public services, to work and leisure, for

---

[80] One of the most unequal cities in the world.

present and future generations. Bogota has extensive slum settlement issues. Its Territorial Ordering Plan (2000) sought to increase equality, maximise integration and construct democracy by generating a participatory element in the construction of the city. There is encouragement for an urban culture among the citizens, consisting of a shared vision.

Visible symbols that are deemed 'offensive and objectionable' can sometimes fall foul of planning rules. An example was a swastika visible on a house as in Zdrahal v WCC; NZ, 1993. Such assessments are inherently subjective. What is deemed unacceptable can change over time.

The UK planning system, as in other government areas, is subject to an Equality Impact Assessment. This attempts to combat what is seen as an androgynous people based approach to planning. This serves to limit the disproportionate impact that certain policies might have on protected 'characteristic groups.' Economic affluence is not one. The sorts of minorities that the legislation is aimed at are groups without strong spatial identities. Often there's an indirect link between them and areas of lower socio economic status. Yet if this is the case then it duplicates efforts that lie at the foundation of planning practice. That is to ensure that cities are as accessible, safe and convenient as possible to those of limited means and capability.

'Upward mobility' is much higher in cities where poorer families are integrated into mixed-income neighbourhoods (RTPI Spatial Publication). Mixing people on different incomes and classes helps drive social progress. Not surprisingly, the cure for exclusionary zoning is inclusionary zoning. There is no uniform approach, instead zoning and planning regulations vary from place to place. These instruments are intended to combat exclusion. They enable or mandate neighbourhoods with some degree or format of mixed housing types, densities, or types of eligible households. The US[81] is now regulating to diversify wealthy neighbourhoods through affordable housing provisions.

As might be expected, the Soviet Union was at the forefront of pursuing equality. Milutin's linear city, first promoted in the 1920s, sought an elongated urban formation. It consisted of a series of functionally specialised, parallel sectors. Generally, the city would run parallel to a river. It was to be built so that the prevailing wind would blow from the residential areas to the industrial strip. The sectors of a linear city would be:

1. a purely segregated zone for railway lines;

---

[81] United States Department of Housing and Urban Development.

2. a zone of production and communal enterprises, with related scientific, technical and educational institutions;
3. a green belt or buffer zone with major highway;
4. a residential zone, including a band of social institutions, a band of residential buildings and a 'children's band;'
5. a park zone; and
6. an agricultural zone with gardens and state-run farms (Sovkhoz).

The concept allowed for more effective growth than concentric cities. The latter set up the basis for an inevitable need for displacement as expanding activities seek additional space. Expansion could be accommodated through adding additional sectors to the end of each band. The city could become ever longer, without growing wider. Residents would all live at similar distances from the various functional zones. They would all be equally exposed to the negative phenomena of industry and traffic and would also have equal access to the recreational areas, water and woods. This was preferable to concentric settlements. Green zones around such cities, exemplified by Moscow, meant only those on the city outskirts were within quick reach of the woods. It would also appear superior to capitalist cities where only the privileged have a view (for example, parklands or water). Linear settlement structure would be conducive to creating a city without preferential residential locations. So they also avoid social segregation.

Promoting Morality

It was Benjamin Franklin that said that only a virtuous people are capable of freedom. 'Improving individual character' and enhancing community morality is often regarded as the business of religion. In traditional societies, Places of Worship were the 'locus of communities.' They gave order by 'policing' the space around them. It is often the case that places of worship influence the local character. This may be visually through distinctive architecture or audibly, from the 'call to prayer' in a Mosque or Cathedral Bells. They also provide a spatial anchor and community through the different services, festivals and music.

The idea that beautiful buildings may have power to improve us morally and spiritually is not a new one. There is a role of the environment in determining identity (the idea that where we have been brought up influences what we believe). Typically, planning rules have come into being since many places of worship have been built. Any new facilities get entangled in expensive consultation processes in the effort of getting planning permission.

Some faith groups may use converted theatres and industrial warehouses rather than erect new structures. In the end, churches in employment or industrial estates subverts the role of that area.

Changes in cultural-religious dynamics are always going to challenge the presumption that morality can be encouraged. The 2009 Swiss minuet debate was where demographic and cultural change manifested itself into a national debate on a particular form in the built environment. Back in the UK there have been cases as to whether non-traditional religious symbols can be used in prominent locations within conservation areas. These challenge rules set up to protect the character of the traditional housing stock.

Prominent industrialists (and landowners) in the late 19th and 20th Centuries promoted 'model villages.' The most famous examples are William Lever's Port Sunlight, George Cadbury's Bournville and Joseph Rowntree's New Earwick. They were social experiments where the physical and spiritual improvement of residents was sought. They made use of consistent and reforming architecture. Quaker Cadbury banned pubs, while paying for sport and wholesome recreation. The legacy of such villages continued into the Garden City movement.

2.0 Culture

Culture and Place

Culture arguably has significantly more influence on built form than ethics. Society has always invested heavily in culture; that is the whole of its knowledge, beliefs and practices. For traditional societies, this is through the ceremonial fund. Modern society has a much greater potential for cultural pursuits (for example, recreation).

Culture and different spatial levels can be distinguished in the following sequence. Space → area → region → territory → place (Randviir 2002). We take on board space through our senses. Vision is the dominant sense but the urban environment is also perceived through others: acoustic, smell and feel. Places take on cultural and social significance that together produce meaning. It is strongly linked to emotions and memories (Jacob, 1961).

Place is socially constructed. As such it develops over time as a result of habitation, (re)development, incident and memory. People become attached not only to real places but imaginary ones. An example, is Tolkien's Middle Earth. We even publicly debate abstract representations of places. An example, was the opposition to Transport for London's proposed removal of any reference to the Thames River from its London tube map. In the digital age, certain places and geographic icons have taken on new (global) understandings and significance. Local places have even less significance than before. New possibilities for local interaction have been created by the augmented reality game, Pokemon Go (released in July 2016). This involves players of the virtual game needing to enter real world locations near their smartphone's location to do virtual activities.

Place remains an important container and stimulus for community and effective local relations. Government (spatial) intervention has the potential to influence culture (both positively and negatively). This is through physical design, spatial regulations and potentially, virtual interaction.

Nature of Households

Living arrangements depend upon the nature of those living together. A core concern of planning has always been about providing enough space (or spaces) for a household or family unit to prevent over-crowding. Corbusier and F. Wright had alternative visions for desirable urban living. Yet both believed in the importance of providing for individual households (families).

An ordinary family home is quite different from a drop-in centre for the homeless and so the nature of the accommodation reflects this. It is harder to define when a home becomes something else if living arrangements are blurred. This can be through extended families, catering for elderly relatives and other sub-units. A kitchen is often used as the physical expression of self-containment of a household unit. It becomes a measure planning authorities use to define physical living arrangements.

Newham Council in East London has, in recent years, undertaken a huge enforcement programme against 'unacceptable Dickensian style conditions. These have been created by unscrupulous, rogue landlords' (Council leader, Sir Robin Wales). One such reported case (Daily Mail - 26 June 2015) was that of a three-bed house which was home to 26 Romanians, including a toddler. Seven people were sleeping cheaply in a windowless basement that had air vents blocked up. The others slept in three 'overcrowded' (but more expensive) bedrooms. The fact the living arrangements could not be described as a household was the mechanism to trigger planning enforcement powers. An Enforcement Notice was served requiring the unauthorised use to cease.

It is possible to apply for a change of use in England to have a house in Multiple Occupation (Sui Generis). This is where several different households are living or sharing facilities, such as a kitchen or bathroom. The Chartered Institute of Environmental Health Planning have issued national guidance on what they expect in terms of amenity for houses in multiple occupation. This includes the need to take into account the unique size and occupancy levels of shared houses. This is to be balanced against the need to make sure tenants are given rooms that are functional in size, shape and layout.

Private and Communal Houses

In Victorian times, the open space provision of inner city houses often included nothing more than the outside street. Occupants of such cramped and overcrowded houses emerged to take refuge in pubs that served as extended drawing rooms. Replacement housing for Victorian slums at least made sure there was height and spacing. This allowed good access of light and air and to control densities. A maximum height of four stories was generally recommended. Provision of interior courtyards, eventually introduced by regulation, came as a big improvement to tenements. Again, this increased light and air. Single-room flats were not favoured. It was considered that while existence in a single room for a single man or women may be possible, this should not be the case for families. Children who were to become future citizens were not to suffer such degradation (Yelling, 1986).

Minimum room sizes were insisted upon and still are in many cases (there are various specifications around the UK). In some areas they may be a hindrance to bringing younger, more entrepreneurial residents into a city. In overpriced cities like London, apartments may be so small they're barely functional. For instance, there is a debate between authorities and developers over the acceptability of a standard double bedroom. The latter may built rooms that give only enough space to physically squeeze a double bed into. Kitchens can be also small and often there are no dining rooms. Just as in Victorian times, the justification is that eating or drinking out is an acceptable way to share common space. So, in theory, the inhabitant isn't being unreasonably confined by a compact flat. Tiny apartments force people out of private spaces and into public areas. These latter areas act as centres for socialisation and consumption.

The profit motive encourages developers to provide residents with tiny inner city apartments. Yet there is something wasteful about the super-sized suburban American and Australian houses of the late 20th and early twenty-first century. They can be hundreds of square meters in floor area. These homes give storage for the increasingly high levels of material goods owned by their inhabitants. Internally, suburban houses have reflected spatial forms of class society. Domestic space organisation has to deal with relations within and between classes. Buildings, individually and collectively, allow us to recognise society. The structure of house space for new middle class households is described as ringy. That is, they are squarish rather than elongated, rectangular and low on asymmetry. The space is for that of a single class, protected by a highly selected boundary and a single solidarity.

It can be difficult to tease culture apart from general health and well-being. Such is the case for access to sunlight. It was worshiped in ancient times (for example, Stonehenge) but almost forgotten in the Victorian house. In the modern home 'solar access' or the right to sunlight has become a key quality of life. Environmental psychologists point to the body's circadian rhythm or nature's alarm clock. It also helps prevent the North European phenomena of Seasonal Affective Disorder. New houses are also more integrated with gardens than in earlier times. Conservatory extensions are common place. These give greater solar access, warmth and extra indoor living space.

Government house construction in the post-war west attempted to promote family life. The household was intended to reside in a self-contained unit. In contrast, the Communist system sought to develop a more equal community through Communal houses[82]. Social engineers in Soviet Russia sought to replace individual or family orientated 'bourgeois' living. The supposed benefit was for the sake of creating a society based on equality and co-operation. The 'virtues' of communal living were short lived having been imposed on communities. They were unpopular from the start due to their lack of privacy and the resulting nervous exhaustion they induced upon their inhabitants.

There have been attempts in the West for voluntary, experiments in communal living. Given their generally short run, the 'hippy movement' experiments were less successful than the Israeli Kibbutzim communities. The latter were communal settlements and farming co-operative movements set after the Second World War. They featured large communal dining halls that double for community activities. There are small, often one-room units for couples. Children lived together with their year group in special children's houses. They shared schooling and extra-curricular activities. Yet observers noted trends in the changing physical structure of such communities over the years. For instance, family housing grew in size as children's houses were

---

[82]   The Karl Marx Hof housing superblock in Vienna is a legacy of this ambition. It combines communal gardens and equally communal bathrooms.

abandoned. Communal dining rooms shrunk in size while sports halls, auditoria and guest houses were developed. In terms of employment, there was a shift from agriculture into other enterprises. New kibbutzim are opening as social and economic entities in the cities. They attempt to maintain the basic ideology in a different environment. The 270, or so, kibbutzim in Israel play a significant role in the economy, while comprising only a small percentage of the population.

Given the pressures on housing and lack of affordability in high growth areas, the potential for a (modest?) return to communal housing is being thought about (Ridge, P. 2016). Self-governing communities still survive in parts of London. They each consist of about 70 persons. While avoiding any formal ideology these communities' member's pay their food and bills collectively.

Privacy and the Culture of Place

The normative landscape, or way in which people do things, depends on the social arena. Even within 'civilised space' (oikoumene) different behaviours are exhibited. People behave differently in modern cities depending upon whether they are in banks, cathedrals and libraries.

In Part I the cultural character of villages, with their Dunbar style relationships, was discussed. There is a progression of cultural change from villages through to towns and finally cities. This was observed in the post-war new town programmes of Cumbernauld (1956), Skelmersdale (1961) and Milton Keynes (1967). Smaller plot sizes in the end give less individual privacy from neighbours. Ralph Waldotmerson[83] (1857) observed in 19th Century London that as urban densities increase, more hedges, fences and garden walls go up. Modern day 'gentrifiers' defend their territory in the same way, through a focus on private property. Despite smaller lot size, large cities are well known for providing anonymity. The larger the settlement, the easier it is for individuals to bypass difficult relationships. This is particularly if there is recourse to authorities. Such lack of grounding provides the basis for the formation of sub-cultures and the basis of all 'artificial living.'

There is a sense of tension between accommodating communities within close distance of employment and providing for the existing character of a place. 'Cultural change' embodies cultural preferences. It is often discounted under a pro-development focus. Sometimes decisions can go either way.

---

[83] American essayist, lecturer, and poet.

Housing extensions have been rejected[84] if they impinge on the existing separation between a larger city and an outlying village. This reflects the importance of having 'areas of separation' to prevent coalescence.

Community goes when its identity gets swallowed up into a greater whole. The West is characterised by intense possessive individualism and a resulting tendency towards isolation, anxiety and neurosis (refer to Part I). The lack of knowledge of ones' own neighbours promotes further dependence on government. Examples range from neighbour disputes to local emergency responses. To break this cycle, the UK Coalition promoted a national programme of localism (in 2010). It encouraged people to 'help themselves.' Commentators note that its success was muted. It was felt that British society may have passed a threshold beyond which it can't return. There's too great a dependency on Government, too much urbanisation and individuals have become too specialised and unable to be practical.

There is another issue when urban densities build and section plot sizes decrease. The potential to 'grow your own' on your own block of land disappears. This imposes complete reliance on transportation to retail and employment locations. Frank Wright's Broadacre City tried to counter this by 'building out, not up.' This was the same as the earlier Garden City models set in England. They championed the belief that each family should own their own house, surrounded by an acre or more of land. It gave the basis for protecting suburban values of community, convenience and privacy.

In contrast, wilderness or border regions allow people to better work out their own identities. The continuing need for such places has been long held. Individuals like naturalist George Grinell (1849 – 1938) held this view in the 1900s United States. They had been influenced by the romanticism movement and believed urban living was making people soft and was destroying the American culture. Their legacy for wilderness experiences was finally borne out in the establishment of Yellowstone National Park.

Architectural Styles

The Roman architect, Vitruvius (80–70 BC to c. 15 BC) described good design as firmness, commodity and delight. The third aspect relates to the link between art and architecture and how it can spark the imagination and move the spirit. It goes beyond architectural fondness. Rather, it implies an attraction to a particular way of life the structure is promoting and the values we want to live by. When seen in this way, the role of architecture is about

---

[84] This occurred, for example, in a decision over housing on the edge of Preston (Planning Resource, 2013).

conveying messages. In past times, it has conveyed moral messages. In more recent times, it's been used for the purposes of propaganda and conveying political messages. Architecture can suggest but doesn't have any power to enforce. There is no absolute correlation between the powers that shape a space and the relationships of power that the space shapes. Fixed forms of power i.e., straight lines = tyranny, wiggles = freedom, don't exist. There is also a marked difference between the intended messages sent by 'producers' and the received message of the rest of us (environmental consumers).

Classical architecture has proven to be the definer of beautiful buildings. It uses frontal columns, repeated ratios and symmetrical facades. The Parthenon in Rome is considered perfect on the basis of its superior mathematical order. Even Le Corbusier liked it for its brutality, intensity, delicacy and strength. The Ancient Greeks, Romans and Educated classes of the renaissance achieved stylistic unity through this style. It stretched from squares and avenues to whole cities.

Gothic architecture, which emerged across Europe during the Middle Ages, is another hugely influential style. It gave expression to many distinctive churches, cathedrals and a number of civic buildings in Europe. It has been noted for its ability to appeal to the emotions, whether springing from faith or from civic pride. Originating from Romanesque architecture, it combines features of ancient buildings from Roman, Byzantine and the other local traditions. With characteristics including the pointed arch, the ribbed vault and the flying buttress it has been described as the epitome of German architecture. Many of the larger churches built in this style are considered priceless works of art and are listed with UNESCO as World Heritage Sites (De Botton, 2007).

Baroque architecture was the building style that began in late 16th-century Italy. It took Renaissance architecture and used it in a new rhetorical and theatrical fashion. Often it expressed the triumph of the Catholic Church and the absolutist state. It was characterized by new explorations of form, light, shadow and dramatic intensity. Venice, an essentially baroque city, was described by Byron[85] as the finest urban tapestry in the world.

Architecture has become increasingly subject to fads in modern times associated with 'cultural change.' During the 19th Century there was an increasing emphasis on originality rather than classical or gothic architectural styles. This was associated with a loss of visual harmony. Unfortunately, this trend has continued. For most schools of architecture in the Anglo-West, a

---

[85]   Lord Byron (1788 – 1824): the Anglo-Scottish poet and leading figure of the Romantic movement. He
       was a self-described 'refuge from change.'

modernist agenda has dominated for over 60 years that employs concrete, steel and glass construction method.

Culture Wars

Modern art is considered to have peaked between 1910 to the 1930s. About this time the central symbols, institutions and beliefs of western culture came into being. It was also when German architectural modernism or Bauhaus style started to become influential on modernist architecture. It had begun before the First World War. Yet it was the absence of censorship in the resulting post war context, alongside an upsurge in the radical experimentation in all the arts that catapulted it into the mainstream. In a world without a centre, aesthetics and art became central. The cry 'make it new[86],' resounded over the subsequent decades. Modernists were creators of the new rather than preservers of the old. German architect, Buno Taut, typified this movement. He had been deeply affected by the First World War. He sought society to abandon cities and start living, once again, amid nature, using primarily glass architecture in buildings. He started out in the Swiss Alps, finally developing a style referred to as Alpine Architecture. He sought for renewal that might raise western culture to a higher level. In doing so he went beyond politics, nationhood and petty concerns.

With its mission to transform society, modernism had something of a religious character. It strived towards nothingness and nihilism. In doing so it valued straight lines, minimalism, abhorrence of wild nature, the dislike of beauty and the past. Ornamentation was seen to be heretical. Modernism rejected paintings, sculpture and mere decoration, in favour of pure space. There was little that was soothing about it, in its quest for pure, absolute forms. These include cubes, cones, spheres, cylinders, pyramids and squares. It took on a Platonic attitude that knowledge properly resides in pure, eternal, absolute 'ideal forms.' Modernist buildings would come to symbolize nothing but ideal geometrical forms.

Unlike past styles, the message conveyed merely symbolised a brave, new world of science and technology. As an international style, it sought to unite architecture and fine arts with mass-production technology. Value depended on functionality. Le Corbusier described it as 'form following function.' This significant idea set function as beauty and mass-production as reconcilable with the individual, artistic spirit. Modernist architecture was reduced to merely the decoration of construction (what is functionally necessary).

---

[86] Originally espoused by poet and critic, Ezra Pound's (1885 – 1972), in the post First War World era.

BUILD OVER THERE

Buildings, it was thus concluded, should look like their contents. For the American architect, Venturi, some buildings are what they are, while others are only what they appear to be. Proponents of modernism considered this to have introduced 'correctness' and 'honesty' into design. So for instance, museums should look arty. Ports should look like boats. Architecture for deprived areas should reach for the sky.

New construction methods linked the universality of concrete as a medium, to the universalism of architectural style. This was expressed as 'In Los Angeles one builds the same as in Amsterdam; in Tokyo as in Paris[87].' The needs are the same. The customs are the same. The materials, thanks to reinforced concrete, are also the same.

In pursuing a break from the past, modernists sought that their work be poured out on both new and old cities. For instance, Brasilia[88], the new capital of Brazil, was intended to be a model of this new reality. It showcased a new modern bureaucratic efficiency and an ideal for the rest of the sprawling, struggling country to emulate. It applied broad avenues, undulating steel and concrete building. This was intended to erase the legacy of colonialism and the chaos of poverty found in Brazil's coastal cities (de Botton; 2007).

Interestingly, the modernist movement only prospered briefly inside the Soviet Union. This happened whilst Soviet era planners were borrowing from European architecture[89] to show the progress of socialism. That ended when Stalin came to power. His approach was to build everything on a much grander scale than elsewhere. He had neoclassical design incorporated into the aesthetics of apartment buildings, roads, and institutional buildings. The aesthetics of the central city were made ornate and interesting. This contrasted to the drab apartment buildings that were outside of the city centre (Alden and Crow, 1998).

Some modernists in the West were advocating, during this time, that the cities of Europe be torn down and reconstructed in the image of American cities. These ideas inevitably ran up against more traditional outlooks. Jane Jacobs sought to counter the brutal modernism of Moses's large-scale projects with a different kind of urban aesthetic. It was one which focused on local neighbourhood development, and on historical preservation. This led to a battle of normative principles about the physical form of her neighbourhood in Greenwich village. Jane Jacobs' reactionary approach didn't escape being

---

[87] Attributed to architect Robert Mallet-Stevens (cited by Forty, 2012; pg 103).

[88] Located deep and high in the interior of the country by its president Kubitschek in 1960.

[89] Chinese architects have been doing much the same in recent years.

subject to criticism. She was accused as advocating for her own tastes (being a NIMBY).

Jacobs was successful in preventing the severance of her community. Yet her success encouraged rising land prices within these older (vibrant), inner city areas. In the end the predatory practices of gentrification became too great. The 'character' of the area became marketed to the wealthy as multi-cultural, street-lively and diverse. This now occurs elsewhere through the actions of real estate agents, financiers and upper class consumers following their private profit-maximising interests. This process drives working class people out and gradually allows the creep of an artificial culture that Jacobs would probably have abhorred. It is an issue for any well-meaning urban programme of regeneration. They can inadvertently push poorer people to the urban outskirts, forcing them to travel further to employment.

The sorts of 'clashes' between advocates and detractors of modernism led to a new style of post-modernism. Post-modern architecture expresses many things simultaneously[90]. What characterises the post-modernist architectural movement is fragmentation and an opposition to rationality. For post-modernists, spatial 'fragments' are designed for aesthetic ends (Hall, 2006 p 100). The result is an 'eclectic' style of different periods. This includes reinterpreting heritage features, creating parody, ambiguity, contradiction and paradox. A building is viewed as a medium to celebrate differences and languages. Charles Jencks viewed postmodernism as 'double coding' through eclecticism. That is, it combines modern technology with something else (an example would be a traditional building). It's supposed to communicate with the public and concerned minorities (but usually just other architects). It was these sorts of mixed style proposals that HRH Prince Charles has attacked over the years. His most high profile 'judgement' came during a speech to the Royal Institute of British Architects (RIBA) in 1984. In it he compared an extension to the facade of the National Gallery in London, to that of a 'monstrous carbuncle on the face of a much-loved and elegant friend.'

When called upon to design non-authoritarian qualities for a pluralistic society, the mix of symbols is more important than pure form. Post-modernism revels in manufactured differences and facades placed over standardised substructures (Crang, 1998pg 116-117). It's cheap, disposable architecture; palaces of kitsch and so forth. Yet Las Vegas Strip architecture has been rebranded. Now it's a grab bag, eclectic, allusive, paradoxical and comes with a complex inclusive order without a dominant theme. Postmodernist buildings do reflect and refer to their environment (Venturi, R.,

---

[90] For example, Bonaventure Hotel in Los Angles.

Brown D.S. and Izenour, S., 1977). Yet any attention post-modernism does pay to 'place,' undermines the real, unique identity of places (Dovey, 199, p44; Huxtable 1997, p3). Jameson criticised post-modernist architecture for cannibalising past styles and for its superficiality and depth. Within a placeless and anonymous environment, individualistic or specific group opportunity can be given. Yet it must fit within the prevailing cosmopolitan world view. Philip Johnson's (1984) AT&T building (now Sony Tower), in New York, perhaps best symbolises the internal problems of post-modernism. Post-modernism yearns to return to the absent centre, a central communal space. Yet there is nothing left in common to fill it with. So the architects gave up and designed the top of the building to resemble a Chippendale clock.

There are different strands to post-modernism. Some strands embrace the historical references that modernism had shunned (possibly ironically). Deconstructivism took a far more confrontational stance to architectural history. In 'disassembling' architecture, it rejected the post-modern acceptance of such references. For de-constructionists, geometry was to deconstructivists what ornament was to postmodernists. Deconstructionists take a particular interest in manipulating the surface of a structure. They will use non-rectilinear shapes which appear to distort and dislocate elements of architecture, such as structure and envelope. The finished visual appearance of buildings is characterised by unpredictability and controlled chaos. If architecture is defined as enclosing space, then post-modernism sought a counter movement to change internal spaces. This has been the subject of criticism. Architects should design for people rather than some utopian, abstract conception of humanity.

Is there a way to reconcile different architectural styles? Can government intervention over aesthetics ever be justified? The answer depends on where you are based. In Iran, national performance specifications make sure there is a national style of architecture, buildings and open spaces across the country. Specifications of conformity set uniform, Islamic, indigenous architecture. This includes historic buildings and urban environments. The mandate for this state imposed style lies with the coherence and authoritarianism of Iranian society.

In the West, the difficulty for imposing a style is finding out what it should be from the diverse range of views in society. Augustus Pugin[91], writing back in the 19th Century, concluded that architecture was either good or bad. As the medieval was the last 'moral' style, he declared gothic to be morally superior. As might be expected there is little support these days for such a view.

---

[91] Pugin was co-architect of the British Houses of Parliament.

Weber, for instance, flatly rejected the contention that there is an overriding spatial or physical aesthetic of urban form. The idea of beauty is shaped by the culture around it: a force that helps identify which sensations we should focus on and apportion value to. It is true that a modern city can function perfectly well without a slavish adherence to any architectural style. That said, unrestricted choice tends to result in outright aesthetic chaos.

Signs are the best example of architectural 'symbols' that result in clashes between dominant values and that of local distinctiveness. Unlike all other structures their purpose is not to be an object or entity in their own right. Rather it's to point the way to something else. Examples include a political agenda, product or service. Billboards are restricted through the planning system for reasons of aesthetics, amenity and to avoid sensory overload. For example, they may distract drivers. It may be argued that advertising customer goods can inject colour into grey street life. Certainly, they are often bright to attract attention and give instant identity and branding. An example, is the Coca-Cola billboard above Red Square, Moscow. More commonly, corporate signage, clashes with local amenity standards[92]. In other places a fight back has been started. Some city administrators are seeking to 'turn the tables' by replacing advertising signs with community billboards or Art (as noted by Landry, 2016 in the cases of Paris and Tehran).

The final design of building proposals can also reflect the clash between dominant values and that of local distinctiveness. The problem is often in the desire for them to all be distinctive. This is through being physically separated, taller or architecturally distinctive. Sometimes uncompromising, contemporary architecture can be justified. This may be on the basis of excellence of design and sustainable construction, despite being a departure from local vernacular architecture. Seeking to prevent new architectural expression inevitably draws parallels with 'freedom of speech' issues. Yet such freedom is self-defeating. It merely produces an architectural and design process culture that puts itself under pressure to 'manufacture' originality.

Successful integration of new buildings into an established historical context are rare. This was a point picked up upon in Heinrich Hubsch's book endorsing regionalism – In What Style Shall We Build (1828)! The application of separation and physical distance is necessary with bespoke designs to insulate the building from their spill over effects on the local context. If applied widely across a city it results in a loss of overall spatial coherence. A form is produced. It is one of unrelated and competing or

---

[92] An example, of this was when the orange Sainsbury supermarket logo was ditched for a local convenience store in the pristine seaside town of Frinton-on-Sea, Essex (2014).

isolated monuments surrounded by roads, parking and (often disparate) landscaping. There may be no consensus on a universally correct style of architecture in the West. Yet architectural incoherence remains a key justification of planning.

There is also the undesirable cumulative effect of repetition and standardisation. This results in a 'placeless' environment - one that is detached from historical context. Brutalist architecture may be forgivable, if cheap and functional. There is a difference between finding concrete a useful medium and wanting everything to be made out of it. In Russia the 'fad' began after a thorough and detailed speech by Soviet leader, Khrushchev, in 1954 about concrete construction practices. The speech incidentally lasted almost two hours. The post-Second World War, Soviet authorities' enthusiasm for concrete manufacture went too far. It reinforced a culture in which almost all structures were made out of it. This was the case even when natural, locally sourced materials could have sufficed.

The standardised, New Urbanist approach rolls out Poundbury-inspired urban villages in the UK and the Mid American small town vernacular in the US. Each are preferable to an eclectic mix of modernist, traditional, deconstructivist, high tech or green designed buildings all competing for visual dominance.

Allowance for new forms of functional architecture is enhanced when it takes on board aspects of the local culture. For instance, Japanese designs after the Second World War gave concrete buildings a wood like appearance and character (Forty, 2012; pg 138). Modern Sino-Architecture borrows far more from Western architecture, than it does from the courtyards of the Quing Dynasty. Yet it's being encouraged to explore Chinese culture, for the sake of national identity. Other attempts to give concrete a regional character are through the choice of aggregates. What is needed is architecture which respects the location of place. This includes both the surrounding styles (space) and time (style of construction). This supports communities of place. As such, there is some justification for local councils to be given veto power over building projects that fail to respect existent architectural styles.

Historic Buildings

The survival of an aesthetic expression is played out in the preservation of the historic environment. Historic preservation is more than just preserving an architectural style. In the United Kingdom and Europe we are accustomed to towns becoming a gradual, organic juxtaposition of new and old. Any other town thrown up in a single, brief period feels contrived.

Basic intervention theories of historic preservation are framed in the dualism. Either the status quo is retained or 'restoration' creates something that may never have existed in the past. John Ruskin (1819-1900) was a strong proponent of the former. Emmanuel Viollet-le-Duc (1814-79) argued for the latter. William Morris (1894-1936) was particularly concerned about the practice of attempting to return buildings to an idealised state from the distant past (i.e. Viollet-le-Duc's approach). This practice involved the removal of elements added to a building's later development. Morris saw such elements as contributing to its interest as a document of the past. He thought such practices were lying. Instead, he proposed that ancient buildings should be repaired, not restored. Their entire history should be protected as cultural heritage. This took Ruskin's approach one step further. That is to accept work done to the building since its origins as equally valid to the continuing story of the building.

Since the 19th Century, the debate over restoration verses anti-restoration has dominated conservation theory. This is particularly around the symbolic nature of key buildings. Historic preservation is tied to specific sociocultural narratives, often shared by parts of the population. Familiar features of a landscape are often fiercely defended once they become linked with cultural or personal identity. This was demonstrated when the Campanile in St Mark's Square Venice collapsed in 1902. The dilemma for the authorities was whether to replace it with a replica or a more modernist interpretation. The mantra, 'where it was; as it was' eventually won the day.

Tastes change and in a pluralist society there are different meanings for objects and structures. Some historical monuments can make the transition between one era and the next. The spire of Berlin's Wilhelm Memorial Church was destroyed in the Second World War. The Church was almost demolished. Yet following pressure from the public it was incorporated into a new design. In doing so a broad spectrum of meaning was achieved across generations. When an icon is intensely significant to a city, the public debate can end up in paralysis. This in a sense is symbolic of the fragmented sense of community underpinning it. After New Zealand's Christchurch Cathedral was severely damaged by an earthquake in 2011, the Church has found itself in a very lengthy, public debate. It could restore the original design or replace it entirely with a modernist inspired design. The modernist case was that, compared to Europe, New Zealand hasn't got the same sense of historical value and depth of tradition. Therefore it's appropriate to just build something new (van der Lingen,2013).

The perceived meaning that historic features have can present ideological challenges. This can result in their removal or destruction. It need not go to the extremes of the Taliban,[93] ISIS[94] or the removal[95] of the 37m high gold painted statue of Mao Zedong. There is a tendency within the New Left to question the continued existence of statues in the UK public realm. Many of them reflect the historical dominance of some particular group. Campus groups around the UK are reported to be demanding features they disapprove of to be removed.

Interestingly, the story of historical protection under Communism was not what one might imagine. Despite their authoritarianism and desire to 'leave history behind, they didn't start with a knee jerk attempt to remove all remnants of the past. In its first 8 years, over 10,000 buildings were protected by the Soviet State because of their special interest. Just under one third were restored. Even Lenin was against the indiscriminate destruction of Tsarist monuments. He believed that socialist culture needed a base from which to grow (States, 1985). This attitude wasn't about connecting with the Tsarist past, or glorifying history. Rather it was to portray a time of decadence, oppression and exploitation. Starting from the 1920s, authorities depoliticised monuments and neutralised their former symbolic power. In 1928, the emphasis changed again and numerous historic buildings were torn down (as the example Palace of the Soviets project showed). Stalin's view had some parallel to what was happening in American cities. It was all about transforming Moscow into a beacon of modernisation. This focused on three key projects: subway, canal and the Palace of Soviets. Nothing was sacred but the grand historical mission as Stalin defined it. From the 1930s, there was a shift away from internationalism towards the pragmatic use of Tsarist era imagery (myths and heros). This is used to encourage patriotism and promote loyalty to the regime. Its ultimate expression was reached during the siege of Leningrad in the Second World War. The cities' Department for the Protection of Monuments extolled workers to risk their lives and resources for preservationism (including objects from the Tsarist past). Labourers and resources were even diverted from defence needs. This shows how an ideologically driven regime, having abandoned its past, was then forced to re-connect back into it.

---

[93] Destruction of the Buddhas of Bamiyan (Afghanistan) (2001)

[94] Unesco Heritage Site in Palymra (2015) and Nimrod (2016)

[95] BBC (2016)

Modern Planning for Historic Buildings

Few Western nations are faced with a similar need as the USSR had to mobilise their population through nationalist support. Yet there is still a need for us to reconnect to our past. For the post-modernist generation the ongoing loss of heritage is resulting in the long term outcome of 'non-places' (placelessness and uniformity). This is a lack of shared connection to history and use. Jameson has described a need to give an anchor for memories and spiritual roots. We need an awareness of history to piece together our fragmented lives.

Even with conservation controls, old buildings only survive if they can adapt to new or changing uses. New modern designs and the sameness of cities (i.e., age of building stock) reflect capital investment over time. Some argue, for instance, that the industrial revolution preserved England's villages. Industry moved from village to town with the workers leaving behind their Tudor or Georgian villages intact. If it wasn't for planning protection, then historic buildings are only going to survive if the cities they're located in miss out on earlier capitalist cycles of (re)development.

For many areas, there's an inevitable conflict between the need to conserve the older, historic parts of cities and house an increasing population. This sort of issue is as common in the UK as it is in Uzbekistan. It results from the economic logic of redevelopment. There's too often a preference for comprehensive redevelopment schemes as opposed to incremental development. Demand for increasing revenues in the property and capital market can lead to unsuitable, out-of-scale buildings in historic centres. The pressure to introduce large scale floor space for commerce, retail and services challenges existing small scale structures. The need to keep building in the post Second World War era has coincided with the artistic style of modernism. Its emphasis is on 'differences from' rather than 'continuities with,' the past. Preservation is the antithesis of progress.

There is a strong contrast with how earlier civilisations treated their history. Past generations felt that they belonged to a stream that flowed through past time. In contrast, modern generations have a consciousness filled and absorbed by the present. Jameson's view is that this signals the end of societies 'awareness of history.' Historical legacy is often seen as a hindrance to the future by the development industry. This includes past architectural styles.

The first instance of state intervention in the protection of heritage came in the UK during the latter 19th Century. This was Gladstone's Ancient

Monuments Protection Act (1882). At this time even Stonehenge was being chipped away by souvenir hunting tourists. Intervention was limited to what was defined as monuments, rather than buildings. The broader heritage protection laws that we are familiar with weren't introduced in the UK until the Town and Country Planning Act, 1947.

Some historical buildings are preserved for their architectural statements. Others are preserved for association with past events and people. In the United States, the Supreme Court had originally approved of zoning only as a way of enhancing property value. Protecting historic buildings was seen to go against this principle on account of the potential devaluation and failure to give compensation. So it took until 1965 before a decision of the NYC historic preservation ordinance finally led to the protection of the Grand Central Station.

Despite its tendency to roll out regulation, the EU does not have a historic places directive. As such, it's up to individual countries to decide how they go about protecting their heritage. The proportion of monuments forming part of the building stock varies throughout Europe. In England it's two percent. In Switzerland it's ten percent. Germany is ranked in the middle, with an estimated proportion of between three and five percent (2000). Unlike other European and overseas countries, the conservation of monuments in Germany is not centrally organised. It also has to grapple with the complexity of whether protection is about being 'proud of the past' or *Vergangenheitsbewaltigung*. The former includes monuments which make an impression through their beauty and distinctiveness. The second category include the need for the nation to come to terms with its past. This includes a category of monuments or objects that are witnesses to history. It includes characteristic building and monuments of the Nazi and German Democratic Republic period.

Historic preservation regulations form part of the third generation of planning controls. They set what should be protected from new development because of its historic value. Preservation regulations are making inroads in developing countries. In developed countries, they are being extended to address not just the importance of the building itself, but also its setting. Conservation areas (1967 Civil Amenities Act) are a good example. They are designated by local authorities and English Heritage. Controls are placed on the modification or demolition of buildings, including protection of trees. Restrictions alone doesn't make protection a surety. UNESCO designated Westminster in London as a world heritage site (including the famous, 'Big Ben'). It has now placed it on the 'endangered list'. This is because of the number of modern skyscraper proposals in close proximity (as reported in 2013).

The motivation on owners of historic buildings to comply with preservation controls differ from controls on 'new builds'. Rules on new builds restrict what can be built on a site without permission. Conversely, controls on historic buildings attempt to restrict entropy. It's inevitably hard to make owners of buildings maintain them against their will. It's much easier to make sure that what gets built on a vacant site follows a specific design. Preventing the historic building being demolished or dismantled, forces the owners to seek another use, or sell to someone else who will. Controls to protect historic buildings ensure that letting the building sit idle and deteriorate involves the opportunity cost of lost rent.

Flexibility of use

Buildings tend to last longer than activities within them. Modest, practical structures are capable of extension or alteration. They are most readily able to be adopted to uses unforeseen when they were built. Architect, Richard Roger noted this when he compared the history of use for Building 20 and Media Lab, at the Massachusett's Institute of Technology[96]. The first was a sprawling 250,000sq foot, three storey, wooden structure. Built in 1943 for radar development, it went on to become an incubator for many technological developments. Its design allowed for chance meetings and impromptu collaborations. The second building cost a lot at the time it was built in 1985 ($45m at the time). Yet it developed a reputation for ill-functionality and non-adaptability, which fostered academic turf battles from the start.

Some historic buildings are clearly more resilient and adaptable than others. Their ongoing life depends upon finding a continued stream of human uses. This in turn depends on their adaptability. For instance, whether room size and shape can be altered and circulation and servicing systems changed. A school building that's adaptable might become flats, a power station, an art gallery, even a church or mosque. Less interchangeable are large, free standing buildings surrounded by an open space barrier. These include Churches or major public buildings.

---

[96] MIT is considered one of the most prestigious universities in the world. It has a history of breakthroughs in disciplines such as engineering, physics, mathematics and computer science.

From protection to straightjacketing

Preservation regulations have achieved a 'politically correct' status. Yet they can also 'flip' the prevailing economic cost argument on its head by adding value. This is despite restrictions applying to what you can do to your historic building, so long as your neighbours are in the same position. The aristocracy with their castles and stately homes have benefited from opening them to visitors. At a larger scale, whole areas can achieve differentiation through tourism. The (cultural) tourism sector relies on attractive, historic urban areas. This includes concentrations of historic buildings, museums, galleries and charming residential quarters. It makes it attractive to well-heeled cosmopolitan residents and tourists alike.

Controls can confer a collective identity to residents and stronger identification with a place. Maintaining the historic architecture and urban design of cities is important. It allows them to continue the distinct, individual identity and culture that they have. As discussed in Part I, identity is a significant part of what motivates each one of us[97].

Jane Jacobs argued that protecting older, shorter buildings would keep prices affordable. At least more so than providing brand new (and expensive) rebuilds. Recent research has shown that historic regulations are often the focus of conflict and legal challenges. Historic regulations can lead to higher property values, loss of affordable housing, and gentrification. They are often counter to 'building up' city centres and re-development which can feedback into encouraging greenfield expansion. It's not all gloom though. Cities like Paris have managed this dilemma through having different functions and identities within areas. For example, there is a dual historic and outer core (La Defense) thus creating efficiency.

Sometimes history does become a straight jacket. When tourism alone becomes the economic lifeblood, productive uses are squeezed out. The preservation of historic buildings can become the only reason for the continued existence of the city itself. This extreme situation overwhelms and empties the culture. It's becomes a different city if the indigenous culture has left and only the building facades remain. Venice, in particular, went from an economic powerhouse to museum. Its economy is now based on tourism: pizza, gelato and glass blowing. It depends upon foreigners who make their income elsewhere choosing to spend it there, admiring the glory of its past. So it has become the city with the oldest population in Europe. The main

---

[97] For example, refer to Edward Hall's 'behavioural iceberg'

difference between Venice and an American theme park, that Europeans so abhor, is the age of its buildings.

Cultural Institutions and Festivalisation

Pre-industrial cities were designed around event spaces, such as the Greek Agora or Roman Forum. Medieval cities revolved around a festive calendar with a spectrum of feasts, Saints days and carnivals. Festivals were a means of distracting people from the harsh realities of everyday life and occasionally the existing social order.

As inhabitants of industrial cities moved away from rural traditions, new traditions had to be invented. This gave meaning to urban life. Civic culture replaced the Church and royalty. It became the main creator of cultural events which celebrated history and culture. To give a substitute, authorities in industrial cities have felt the need to have a set of institutions of high culture. Their architectural materialisations were considered major tasks of city building. In the same way, at a national level, identity was promoted through shared national heritage. The recognition of the working classes as a market group also started to cause wealthy manufacturers to sponsor culture. This was in the form of opera, museums and public festivities. This gave a platform to showcase their goods and services and commodify public spaces. The ultimate expression is 'invented' 'fantasy' places where culture is commodified for financial gain. Disneyland remains the quintessential invented place.

Theatre, operas and museums involve large fixed costs. Cities give the platform for these institutions and the larger the city, the bigger they can be. Drama can be affordable in larger cities because the fixed costs can be spread across thousands of viewers. Cultural institutions can be successful urban renewal strategies. They bring in a stream of artsy visitors to make a place fashionable and 'cool.' Iconic buildings are built to attract tourism and investment to a city. In America, major cultural projects have become centrepieces of downtown revitalisation efforts. The best example of such large institutions is Frank Gehry's iconic Guggenheim Museum (New York). Successful, new pieces of townscape are those that are integrated with existing areas. They add quality to them and secure their futures. While some achieve this, there have also been plenty of 'white elephant' projects.

Artists and intellectuals used to produce works because they were convinced that what they were doing was valuable in its own right. The guardians of these included their benefactors and state apparatus. Museums and universities set out which segment of the population benefited most from the collective symbolic and cultural capital. This was something that everyone had contributed to, both now and in the past. Often it went to multi nationals and local bourgeoisie.

Now, the cultural elite are reluctant to uphold and clearly define standards. There are no fundamental principles to uphold and accept. Nor is there responsibility for forging consensus around what ought to make up the achievement of excellence. Any claim that privileges a particular art form, way of speaking or educational achievement is dismissed. The grounds are that it doesn't possess any special merit over and above any other. Cultural experience is reduced to an instant, emotional connection. The problem is that anything not deemed directly relevant or accessible to ordinary people is out. A standard, with a capital S, is inconsistent with the mood of contemporary culture.

'Participation' in the arts links into the celebration of culture. Yet such cultural popularists aren't responding from any rallying call from the masses below. They have become involved merely because it gives them a role to play and lever by which to control society. This partly explains the more pronounced role of Government in culture. It's no longer arts for arts' sake. Rather the current approach is to transform Britain's cultural institutions into centres of therapeutic engagement for excluded people. In a deeply divided society, art and culture becomes a substitute form of cohesion, participation and self-esteem.

Culture has now come of age within the planning system, with its inclusion in the National Planning Policy Framework. Planning obligations have become a useful tool for ensuring cultural venues get provided. Yet in itself, this is a narrow definition of how planning can promote culture. This is evidenced by the earlier discussion in Part V on places of worship and model villages.

Urban strategies now seek to focus on the innate resources of cities – their histories, spaces, creative energy and talents. This is about using 'cultural' assets and resources in an attempt to be distinctive. That is to regenerate urban fabric and prosperity. Cultural production has become a major element in urban economies. Since the 1980s, the image of 'central city' has been re-imagined, with an associated combination of physical enhancement and cultural animation.

The soft infrastructure of events, programmes and activities is as important as the hard infrastructure of buildings, spaces and street design. Events are described as 'time-based resources'. They add dynamism to previously stagnant cities and help polish up jaded images. Events may be ephemeral but they fit into consumer culture. In particular, they generate the most precious of modern commodities – symbolic capital. Unlike the fixed world of hard infrastructure, they allow us to provide for choice and changes to identity (if we can afford them).

Where available, they have drawn on existing historical roots. This has seen the taking over of the existing festive calendars of others, such as the Mardi Gras in New Orleans. Much has also been made of the fringe events of the 1960s to 1980s. These were originally put together in reaction to the staid nature of many official programmes. No longer just cultural matters, events have become part of the wider task of revitalization. They are linked to a series of externalities. This includes the need to stimulate economic growth, bolster social inclusion and develop new identities appropriate to a changing urban landscape. Cultural events and festivals have mushroomed across the West. Every sleepy town seems to have a museum or heritage centre. Entire cities have transformed themselves into major stages for a continual stream of events. This is described as the 'festivalisation' of the city.

Cities are competing for a 'sense of place' – the Latin concept of 'genius loci' that goes beyond the physical or sensory properties of a place. What is sought is to create an attachment to the spirit of a place. A place has, in certain cases, become a brand. A brand can survive significant social, cultural and technological change. There is a clear image of what a place such as Paris, Edinburgh and New York looks like, feels like and the story or history it conveys. A sense of place may be enhanced, reconstructed, portrayed or otherwise invented by novelists, musicians, artists, designers and imaginers. Personal memories of places are the setting of experiences. They are associated with events, people and interaction. So there has been a shift from cultural events as the creators of meaning to that of their preservers. Culture by the symbolic economy or experience economy has become a means of consuming the city (Zukin 1995; Ritzer, 1999 and Pine & Gilmore, 1999).

3.0 Public Space

Different cultures have different arrangements about the social usage of space. This is the way in which people use and colonise space. Waldotmerson's (1857) observation was that greater care is given to private spaces than public ones in England. Paris represents a contrast in this regard. It has urban garden squares with terraced houses on all sides which shade public squares in summer and shelter them in winter.

The public realm is defined as the public face of buildings, the spaces between frontages, the activities taking place in and between these spaces, and the managing of these spaces. Everything in the built environment has design and purpose behind it – even if the cognitive processes are now redundant. Buildings are seen together. They contribute to the art of relationship. Each building is seen as a contribution to a greater whole (Cullen, 1961 p 10).

Urban form is traditionally based around two (public) spatial parts. The first part is the space of major public buildings and functions, which is typically a sparse system. Space surrounds buildings with few entrances. This stands for a global-to-local arrangement on urban form. This is where a distinct global structure is imposed over and above the level of everyday interaction. It is the ordering of space that is as much the purpose of the buildings rather than the physical object itself. Such development essentially transforms space through objects.

The second part is the space of the street system. This is the theatre of everyday life and transactions (where people need to negotiate). This is a dense system, in which public street spaces are surrounded by buildings and their entrances. In London, dwellings relate more to the system of streets, but in Paris, dwellings relate more to courtyards.

The orientation and frontages of plots are important. It's better to have narrower lots on narrow streets to give a more compact, walkable arrangement of houses. Houses appear to be associated in a neighbourly way, instead of isolated and cocooned from the neighborhood. Larger lots are more acceptable on thoroughfares. Wider frontages are best on east-west streets. Narrower ones are preferable elsewhere. These give the best orientation to sunlight. Intersections are where fine-grained diversity is needed most.

Uniform frontage has been required in Europe for centuries, to make sure there is harmony. Some activities should have more claim to key street frontage and public space. These include street markets, cafes and small scale shops. At the other extreme is car parking, warehouses, large scale industry, large scale offices and supermarkets. Large buildings using a single entrance can have a particularly deadening impact on streets.

Modernist ideas have resulted in many tensions with the above arrangements. An example is where the exterior of buildings has to be seen to reflect the interior. The relationship to public space becomes merely a by-product of their internal planning. Also, on private lots, the garage that was formally a small structure at the back end of the plot has usurped the porch. This highlights the primacy of the car in residential environmental design. There has also been a shift away from buildings having distinct fronts and backs. In commercial areas there are few or no windows and little sign of human presence. This means there is less opportunity for interaction. It mirrors the physical outcome in the morphological structure of modern urban areas. Outward-facing urban blocks have been replaced with inward-focused complexes of buildings referred to as 'pods' (Ford, 2000).

Blank walls are an end in themselves. They intimidate, they deaden the street and break the continuity of experience for passer's by. Whyte (1988) felt that blank walls were becoming the dominant townscape feature of United States cities. They declared the destruction of the city, its streets and the undesirables who might be on them. As opposed to featurelessness, variance gives meaning. Fronts should face public spaces and be active. They need to include entrances, social displays or public activities. Backs are for more private activities (facing private space). With thought it's possible for repetitive, boring façade elevations to be avoided and be prefabricated for speedy erection.

Modern society has also moved away from a continuous open and distributed street system. It is now discontinuous. There are more closed local domains such as 'estates' (for example, cul-de-sacs). The modern housing estate typically includes the following aspects that reinforce this pattern. That is outer boundaries, open space barriers that create buffers, few entrances with separate tower blocks and separate staircases (which avoid random encounters).

One of Jacob's key principles was that the type of urban form found in older neighbourhoods was more conducive to community life. This is by giving residents plenty of opportunity to meet causally on the street, in shops, and in public spaces. Such encounters give some of the glue that holds society together. It does so without intruding into private spaces and private lives. Many of Jacobs' views have been taken up into 'New urbanism.' This is a vision of urban planning that is about recreating 'traditional' streets and pedestrian-friendly 'mixed-income' communities. This reality of New Urbanist principles do not always live up to the hype. They have been criticised as creating affluent, suburban, self-absorbed areas. Handpicked social housing tenants (a minority) are hidden behind a sterile vernacular of quality, neo-Georgian facades.

The aspects of positive and liked urban environments have been well researched. Jack Naser (2003), lists five attributes: naturalness, unkeep/ civilities, openness and defined spaces, historical significance and order (coherence, legibility, clarity). Kaplan and Kaplan (1982) noted coherence (easy to recognise), complexity (keep people occupied), legibility (can be explored) and mystery (new information if explored). On the Continent, the street system supports a café society. In Britain there has generally been significantly less piazza style life produced. This is despite the first pedestrianised street being Pantiles in Tunbridge Wells back in 1638. It may say more about climate than anything else. Warmer nights in the Mediterranean can support a chattier, more outdoors existence.

It's easy to rally opposition to defend against an immediate threat to a neighbourhood as Jacobs found in the case of Moses's new motorway. Rapid or wholesale change can 'rupture' continuities of place. They justify planners intervening to attempt to 'freeze' place identity, through policy and (top-down) master-planning techniques. Most change occurs gradually, from incompatible uses or loss of local businesses to higher value uses over time.

As discussed earlier, retaining the physical neighbourhood is only one aspect. The lure of a 'locally distinctive place' draws more and more homogenising, multinational, commodification in its wake. The result is the ubiquitous chain stores which like to be everywhere. They maintain uniform standards through their corporate policies, such as McDonalds and Costa's. Through advertising and symbols, they exert a cultural hegemony associated more with 'western freedoms,' than tastier burgers.

It's difficult for the planning system to single out the ubiquitous chain stores on the High Street from the traditional independent 'mum and pop' stores. As stated in Part III, there is an absence of a specific focus on ownership. So multinational retailers get an easy ride. In many cases Tesco are able to set up chain stores even on streets described as the cultural heart of a city. The planning authority[98] is unable to take into account who the end user is. Their response to local concerns is simply that the occupier of the retail space isn't a valid planning consideration.

The ability for such (older style) urban form to produce culture has to be weighed against other variables. It is often difficult to evidence that a part of the city is essential and therefore should be retained. The significance of 'loss of place' can always be debated. Crang (1998) downplays it by suggesting that few cultures in the end stay 'place bound.' What local culture often amounts to speaks more about their limitations of communications and transport. It's not apparently about any fundamental interaction or connection. Yet in reality, those territories that come with a specific local culture are often sought out and in demand. Travellers to somewhere exotic generally don't wish to find it has been taken over by the same western, global, cosmopolitan culture that exist back home.

---

[98] Application reference 11/01502/FUL Chelmsford City Council for Moulsham Street.

An inclusive city should make its citizens feel like real owners of its public spaces. It is the poor, in particular, who have a focus on defending their sense of territory. If highly inclusive environments are desired then they must allow a range of people and activities to come together in a way that is cumulative and mutually reinforcing. Provision in this regard would mean greater accessibility and inclusive spaces to join in. These inclusive spaces include clubs, libraries, parks, and community gardens.

The increased need for gathering spaces raises the relevance of public space in the digital age. The fight becomes over how public space functions, looks and feels (who owns it seemingly a secondary matter). At another level, coffee houses, bookshops and pubs etc are supposed to provide the realm where citizens can debate, resolve issues and thereby give social cohesion. This realm exists between the state and private domain. In other words, they set a neutral ground where individuals can come and go as they wish. Yet such 'public spaces' are geared towards 'extracting cash.' They aren't about allowing citizens to just enjoy their time. Social capital in a developed world is supposed to involve the integrated lifestyle of higher profits from deeper socialising. Adding to the social capital and environmental quality of a place provides for an increase in economic value. A region can (apparently) make its own wealth. Inhabitants only have to see each other as potential customers or business partners.

These areas are increasingly important for the economic life of cities. The more competition cities confront from the outside, the smoother they must operate on the inside. Now cities have to compete to develop cultural and creative resources to attract the creative classes.

The more traditional means used to attract companies include offering cheap land, labour, energy and good communications. They may combine this with strict but supportive zoning regimes (such as those found in the United States). Yet these same zoning policies have often prevented a dynamic and meaningful urban environment. So the down town in many cities, such as Chicago, Detroit and Atlanta, consist of commuters and tourists by day and are deserted at night. Similar modernist zoning in Soviet era cities resulted in mono-functional zones that were only vibrant when they were used fully. For example, during parades. Outside these times the same squares and boulevards were empty.

Provision for a 24 hour society of apartments and night life may counter 'dead periods' in city centres. Yet some authorities, like the City of London, consider such a goal is akin to attempting to 'have your cake and eat it too.' Their strategy has been to focus on office redevelopment and evening entertainment. They don't want residents who would in the end complain about the noise.

Planning can't force people back into living in shrinking cities when their powers are limited to the physical environment. The best authorities can seek to do is to design activity and vitality back into public spaces that are well maintained and vibrant. Authorities may need to convince commercial landowners of the benefit of it. City authorities are after an elusive buzz, fizz and special kind of energy. It's that quality which proves magnetic for the production of products and performance of services (Professor Michael Storper). This has to be something that can't be copied by cyberspace, where many people are retreating to spend more of their lives in. The virtual world is generally regarded as threatening the vitality of public spaces.

Creative Cities

Creative cities reflect the increasing centrality of culture in urban policy. There is a transformation from industrial to more creative spaces in Western cities. The previously industrial Ruhr Valley has been experiencing a symbolic 'creative re-boot,' This was described as moving from the hammer to the guitar. Industry has gone. There's now a new creative community making and exchanging ideas in art, architecture and music.

Fashion and design industries attract international clientele. Cities such as London, Paris and Milan have linked them with museums and historic quarters. Legner (2009) argued that 'cultural quarters' are one of the distinguishing signs of the post-industrial city. New York responded to de-industrialisation by giving up the dream of ending social injustice at the local level. Instead it elected centralist, workman type Mayors like Koch, Dinkins, Giuliani and Bloomberg[99]. They strove to make New York as attractive as possible to employers and middle class citizens (Glaeser, 2012).

The creative cities concept is about nurturing creativity through an inclusive culture. This embraces open mindedness and experimentation. City downtowns emphasise the arts, toleration for alternative lifestyles and fun happenings. This is supposed to manifest itself in creative clusters which accept the bohemian aspects of the recipe (Ooi, 2007). Such formulaic approaches to encourage the springing up of brilliant, Bloomsbury style groupings should be regarded with scepticism. The historical evidence is that high creativity can co-exist equally with wretchedness and brutishness. Think of the Harlem jazz scene or Parisian Bohemianism. More recently new

---

[99] Until the more popularist Mr. de Blasio was elected in 2013.

directions of music have emerged from shrinking cities. These include techno Detroit, Brit punk and house music in Manchester and Sheffield. This form of activity thrives in places with little commercial value. This is what attracts creative artists in search of free space or low rent.

What is inadvertently happening, via satellite TV and the internet, is the spread of pseudo overseas prosperity to third world youth. Just as the media encourages consumerism within western countries, its imagery instils a chronic, collective case of 'Fear of Missing Out.' This includes social, religious and sexual freedoms, along with livelier nightlife and better job prospects (Ash 2015).

The reality is that expensive cities may in fact be killing creativity (Kendizor, 2013). New York City, a traditional incubator for artists, has now become a 'gated citadel' for creativity. Cities, where the cost of living has skyrocketed, are no longer places where you just go to be someone. This includes New York, San Francisco, London, Paris and others. They are places you only live in provided you have the right connections. Journalist, Simon Kuper, described them as vast gated communities. They are where the 'one percent' reproduces itself. The notion of a 'creative class' has become a frozen archetype. It doesn't boost the economy of global cities. Rather, as urban studies theorist Richard Florida argues, it is a product of their takeover by elites. The creative class plays by the rules of the rich, because those are the only rules left. Adaptation is a form of survival, but also a form of abandonment as well.

Over the past two decades barriers to professional entry have tightened and geographical proximity has become valued. This coincides with digital media making it possible for anyone, anywhere, to share their ideas and works. In fields where advanced degrees were once a rarity, art and creative writing schools, now view them as a must.

While some people will succeed, those that fail pay a high price. Failure in an expensive city, for risk gone wrong, is more than the average person can endure. As a result, innovation is stifled and conformity encouraged. The creative class becomes the leisure class. Either they work to serve their needs or they abandon their fields entirely (Heathcote, 2014). Creative cities need to get beyond a slogan, a tradeable abstraction or a mere asset class. To do so they counterintuitively need to pursue the kind of policies that will restrain its success. The key to a successful metropolis is, paradoxically, a degree of failure that allows for experimentation. Musicians, artists, the punks and graphic designers of the past slept in cheap studios and lived off government grants. If those are gone, the creative life won't happen. The idea should be to ring-fence some land to allow for spontaneous, unplanned activities. This would be to prevent property value increasing to the point they just get sold off to the highest bidder.

Knowledge cities

Relying on culture to provide the economic clout of a city may be too simple. Florida (2003), emphasises the need to offer starting places for creative entrepreneurs. This extends to the former neighbourhood centres which give ideal locations. The focus is on the provision of core public services: safe streets, fast commutes and good schools. Scare resources can't go everywhere and aesthetic interventions can never substitute for urban basics. The starting point is fiscal policy and creating a liberal tax climate for those areas to help starting entrepreneurs.

The secret used to be to embrace new technologies that have come before in regular patterns over decades. These were referred to as Kondrieff wave cycles. The latest 'wave' have produced a new bountiful medium of ownership. It includes the advent of the personal computer and the world wide web. The barriers to documenting ideas are significantly lifted through the use of open sourcing and networking. Computing has in theory unleashed limitless capital within the world.

The knowledge society represents a re-branding of classic free market capitalism. Its endorsers claim it has resulted in a so- called 'revolutionary change in the history of social relations.' Yet the reality is less rosy. The web, like other (physical) markets, has become dominated by a relatively few players. These include Google, Facebook, Amazon and start-ups like Uber and AirBnB. Their business plan is based on exploiting the collaboration of others to capture and extract value. It's not about returning value to those that contribute. The shift has also paralleled structural economic changes of deindustrialisation meaning a shift to service economy. It includes employment deconcentration which means there are less jobs in the inner city. Finally, there is occupational bifurcation meaning there is polarisation into high and low income earners (Jargowsky, 1997).

Advanced technologies are now particularly sought after. According to the Brookings Institution, advanced industries including hi-tech manufacturing and skilled services[100] have led the recent United States recovery (Yueh, 2015). IT firms have tended to be more successful outside inner cities, for example, Silicon Valley and the M4 corridor.

---

[100] Defined as having one fifth of employees with STEM - science, technology, engineering and maths skills.

Every sign is that new industries and new businesses of the future are only going to be digital. Learning routines, acquiring skills, providing communication links between organisational layers are routes to paid work. These can be wiped out instantaneously by an innovative computer programme. The difficulty is that not everyone can become a web designer, despite an idealised free market. United States steelworkers or UK ship builders had their industries wiped out by Japanese and Korean competition. Few managed to turn themselves into London investment bankers or Silicon Valley computer engineers (Chang (2010, 219).

As noted within Part I, this business cycle may be different. Society can no longer count on awaiting a fourth Kondratiev wave cycle of innovation. Even if it does arrive, don't count on it resulting in additional employment. Talent, energy and resourcefulness need to be directed towards constructive ends. Some, like Jeremy Rifkin,[101] are deeply concerned. They believe that if there aren't enough jobs then civilisation will probably disintegrate into lawlessness. From that point there would be no easy return.

4.0 Employment, Poverty and Economic Planning

The welfare-state assumed that full employment was needed for efficient economic growth. Neo-liberalism has broken this assumption. Unemployment or low paid employment spells inequality. A society may prosper even if many of its members lag behind market leaders. The consequences for marginalising full employment as a policy aim are widespread. They include a de-moralised middle class and a myriad of inefficiencies that result in a loss of 'productivity.'

Impoverished, insecure and excluded workers now make up a majoritarian. They have become a putatively dominant power block and a major political problem for the establishment. This is both in Britain, following the Brexit referendum result and in the US after Trump's successful election campaign. Social services had previously benefited the middle class. Their inclusion and support was important in sustaining the political appeal of these services. There also remains a large minority underclass in the modern UK. These people include those who have never experienced the general rise in living standards during the 1950s- 1980s. Or they could be casualties of social breakdown, the unskilled, elderly, disabled and the chronically sick.

---

[101] American writer and economic and social theorist.

In Britain, the poor used to be differentiated into the 'deserving working poor' and the 'useless poor' during the 19th Century. That was on the basis of their dependence on the state (Atkinson and Moon, 1994a). Explaining continued poverty in the West is an ongoing academic debate. That is, whether people are poor through no fault of their own or whether they are in some way responsible. The former poor are seen to be there because the system is unfair. The latter due to some form of 'original sin.' Attempts to explain the persistence of poverty and social inequality cover many aspects. They include social-science arguments for class interests, bad geographic luck, hobbling cultural patterns, ignorant leaders and technocrats.

Poverty has been largely eradicated in the West. It's given a degree of latitude to think of the issue in terms that it's (absolute) poverty not (relative) inequality. For 'egalitarians', the resulting wealth of the wealthiest is bad in itself, as it disfigures society. Marxists would go further, in their belief that one cannot have freedom in a world with inequality. Freedom and equality are interchangeable. If some cannot afford something another can, then they are not free to take advantage of their 'legal' freedom to pursue happiness.

There is a need for some means of social mobility in modern societies. This is to make sure those living at the bottom in polarised cities don't get too frustrated. The redistribution of wealth, in favour of the least well off, is to avoid socially unacceptable consequences. Where community members have little prospect of securing work opportunities, they become increasingly left out from community life. There are also linkages between family breakdown, poverty, poor educational achievement and criminality. Also, a disproportionate amount of crime is committed by men.

Egalitarians might want to eradicate offending wealth by repealing low tax rates on capital gains. They may wish to roll back the gains of the super-rich by enacting a wealth tax. Yet there is little evidence that any of these approaches has so far been successful in being taken up. Those who stand to benefit most from the present global economic structure are concentrating on protecting their own interests. This is irrespective of what is happening to other people. They include the producing class which is that group of individuals who create products and services and create wealth. In particular, they seek to obtain a tax system that favours them. Tax exemptions for rich landowners in Ancient Rome mirror tax havens in the West. They have successfully argued that low tax rates motivate the starting up of companies and help them to grow. This guarantees them freedom to trade their resources with as little interference as possible from others.

The fashionable 'relativist mindset' poses a problem in resolving the situation. It is difficult to argue that attempts to deliver distributional justice are anything other than an act of coercion of one group over another. Fairness is just one group's idea; largely it is self-interest hidden within common sense decisions. The solution is simply the 'market' to deliver outcomes that no one willed.

The political left is thus seen as shifting power away from local communities and democratic institutions towards centralised, bureaucratic structures. The latter are supposed to be better equipped to administer the fair and equal distribution of benefits. Yet benefits paid to recipients go straight to landlords, rather than providing people with their own units. This leads to a growing sense of powerlessness and alienation from the political process.

Besides, the universalizing logic of rights and entitlements of the modern welfare state has undermined parts of society. This includes family and social ties in civil society. The charity and non-profit based sector is largely funded through Government grants. All of this has resulted in ever-greater state dependency. Some things that government cannot and should not bring about would be better left to non-government agencies.

Just as with Communism, the welfare state may simply not be economically sustainable in an era of slow growth and ageing populations. To build an alternative basis for stability, the welfare state needs a larger and larger share for those most disadvantaged (H&H, pg265). This then competes with the system of production, which needs to maximise its share of the surplus to re-invest.

For these reasons, there has been a shift in terms of what to plan for from the politics of 'red' to 'green' by the New Left. Old time Marxists suggested that high productivity need not be linked with worker exploitation. Rather, if it's necessary, the natural environment could be used. Alleviation of human misery has now shifted to care for the environment at large. At a superficial level, this shift marks an increase in ambition, while at the deeper level, an admission of defeat. Policy goals are defined primarily with human self-restraint, birth control and pollution reduction. The goal in the end appears not to be welfare maximisation, but suffering minimisation. Setting a certain carbon emissions standard, for instance, isn't that politically controversial. Setting a certain level of minimum income that requires economic redistribution is controversial. Corporate environmentalism is acceptable whereby labour exploitation is compatible with clean environments.

Uneven Development

The economic and social environments of high poverty areas may have an ongoing, independent influence in terms of personal insecurity and tension. This is linked to:

•   the signaling effect that vandalism and anti-social behaviour has on generating more crime (for example, 'broken window theory');
•   family structure (and particularly one parent families);
•   a culture of poverty (generating a system of ruthless and exploitative relationships).

When the norm for a community is welfare and worklessness the result is alienation, conflict and failure. The global underclass, in the fragmented periphery, lives in a virtual 'techno-apartheid.' For instance, there are many cities (for example, Sao Paulo) which do not seem to need the country's poor, either as producers or consumers. Fifty percent of that population are economically irrelevant. The Government there takes a basic approach of ensuring little more than maintaining civil order.

Poor people have to live somewhere. For Trotsky, uneven development reflected the exploitation of people in one place by those in another. This includes peripheries by centres and rural areas by cities. Again, this is a consequence of the pursuit of progress. Uneven development results in nationalism and ethnic differences. It doesn't matter whether it's peripheral regions or even global. The simmering Scottish independence debate is a good example.

At a city scale it also drives fiscal conflict between the inner city and rich and defensive suburbs. The central city is where most past investment has taken place. Suburbanisation caused the hollowing out of many American cities leaving them bereft of a sustainable economic basis. This produced the so called 'urban crises' of the 1960s. It was defined by revolts of impacted minorities, chiefly African-Americans in the inner cities, who were denied access to the new prosperity. Riots are seen as a tipping point in terms of a community. For instance, following the 1967 riots in Detroit, the white population of 55% in 1970 declined to 11% by 2008. Coleman Young, Detroit's mayor (1974 to 1994) also contributed with his black-power style advocacy rather than more integrationist goals. He polarised the city, affecting it both fiscally and socially. The real question to consider is whether a suburban ring can prosper around a dying urban core (Adams & others 1994; Voith 1994).

Society needs to provide something for people to do with their lives i.e., constructive work. A balance between human skill bases and the location of jobs is assumed to come out naturally through market mechanisms. Jay Forrester[102] showed how subsidised low income households, without equal effort at job creation, were disruptive to a city. It increases overall unemployment, welfare costs and despair (Forrester, 1969).

Regional planning can be a means to re-distribute economic activities to under-performing areas. There does need to be an 'agreed understanding' of the economic function of the area. For 'Diamond projects' in Latin America, it's about achieving competitiveness. Every city is seen to have a unique economy, demographic and geography. So the strategy for achieving competitiveness must be flexible and responsive to diverse demands. Each territory in the region must identify its role and its development strategy through dialogue. Furthermore, it must synchronise efforts to become a more diverse and attractive place.

In practice, striving for regional income equality is often a thankless task in a market economy. The post-War 'new towns' in England never attracted a supporting level of jobs to their residential areas. Thus, Garden Cities ended up as dormitories. It's beyond regulatory planning to resolve. This contrasts with the more organic way in which residential areas are set around employers.

Alternatively, regional planning can link jobs to populations through transport. This is the case with High Speed rail (HS2) linking the South and North of England. It's costly and the benefits of reduced travel time are not convincing. A better alternative to improve connectivity might be rolling out free wifi across the city and public transport. Getting to work can, in theory, be as productive as being at work. The functional role for the north of England might be better rebranded from the provider of cheaper housing and labour. Rather, it should focus on simpler, more sustainable, but no less educated, living practices.

Only under Communism can capital be, in theory, directed to make sure there is full employment. Yet Szelenyi (1996) suggests that socialist cities were under-urbanised. This contrasts with the over-urbanisation which is occurring in Third World countries. Under-urbanisation meant the growth of jobs outstripped the growth of population. This was partly because of how the

---

[102] Forrester was the system's scientist who undertook the Club of Rome's assessment of global over-growth.

propiska system was played out between different areas. Yet in theory, it could have enabled a balanced work and housing arrangement.

Local Solutions for Regeneration

From a policy makers' perspective, there's a moral imperative to continue to invest in the inner city. Not only that but in a practical sense as well it's the area where it's most readily achievable. Central Business District's represent places of economic potential due to their centrality. Appropriate levels of city service should be retained at the very least to avoid further decline. Improving service levels may need new forms of delivery that overcome political fragmentation and fiscal imbalances between city and suburb.

In the West, urban shrinkage is an indirect result of political and economic decisions discussed in Part I. They lie beyond the sphere of architecture and urban planning. The solution may not be to try and recreate a 'high tech' something. We should also consider going back to concentrate on the primary and secondary (manufacturing) sectors. There is also a need to build an energy efficient infrastructure between them. With fewer jobs available, in the future there may need to be alternatives to formal work in the marketplace. This has parallels to Engels' view on Victorian Manchester.

If the private sector isn't investing and the state simply can't provide, then all that's left is to take matters into one's own hands. In the workplace, workers can make relationships with themselves rather than vertical relations with the business owner who employs them. Market leaders in deprived areas may find it convenient to pool their resources with people outside their own societies.

In the end, job creation depends on capital investment. Regeneration has to begin with businesses and the city is a great place to start. The sheer variety of jobs in cities allows people to figure out what they can and can't do well. This is something that's denied in an agricultural based society. One benefit of high density living and having so many people together is that it should better allow people to resolve their issues by their own efforts. That is without government and external private enterprises taking over. Social capital offers the poor economic self-determination. They can pool their resources with family or friends in an otherwise 'desert' of deregulation or lawlessness. The greatest power of the poor lies in their ability for cumulative purchasing. The Brixton Pound in London is a good example. It's a means to increase the circulation of goods and services within local communities and improve relationships.

There are measures the state can use to reduce economic impacts. These were addressed in the UN Conference on Trade and Development's Annual Report (UNCTD, 2016) for the current global economic stagnation. It argued for a return to more co-ordinated investment by Government on strategic sectors, a drive to industrialise and the control of capital flows. The latter form of economic protectionism might see laws to regulate plant closures. This would be to protect local communities from the effects of rapid capital mobility and sudden industrial change. It could see fund managers needing to hold onto their assets for longer. This approach is starting to be voiced again by some in the West. US President Trump, for instance, sought to rally support in the Detroit area during his 2016 presidential campaign by this means. He suggested punishing motor car makers that were shifting their capital out of the US to plants in Mexico.

The UNCTD (2016) also seeks to promote the local-ownership of corporations and restrict large-scale discount outlets. The latter examples are focused on operators like Wal-Mart. These operators have a business plan based on displacing small and diverse family or locally owned stores (Shuman 1999, Ehrenhalt 1999).

The government can also respond by creating 'work for the disposed.' The goal in a market economy is to improve what Storper (1997) termed place competitiveness. It's the ability of the urban economy to attract and maintain firms with stable or rising market share. The aim is to maintain or increase standards of living for consumers.

A key policy of the neo-liberal agenda to promote growth 'spatially' has been the application of 'enterprise or empowerment zones.' These are based around manufacturing and industrial activities. Firstly, it's a response at a regional or local level. Secondly, it's anti-planning in a sense. The basic premise is that government policies have kept the free market from exploiting economic opportunities of an area. These include land use zoning, property taxes, pollution regulations, labour laws and other 'red-tape.' Its fulfilment is the idea of fully privatised cities.[103] Three have been proposed in Honduras (Rodríguez, 2015). They have been criticised as being unconstitutional and benefiting the wealthy. Promoters, however, see them as an important means of economic transformation. They claim such cities will allow local and foreign investment to end poverty for thousands by creating new jobs.

---

[103] Referred to as an Employment and Economic Development Zone.

The issue, for enterprise zones or private cities, is that rarely do business owners want to put money up front into risky schemes. In practice, it's largely up to public sector investment to achieve results for urban renewal. The key to achieving change in specific locations is for the state to do regeneration led master planning. Implementation is then by special, organisational delivery vehicles.

The success of the delivery side of planning was seen during the 1980s. Lord Heseltine championed the regeneration of Britain's inner cities, the best example being London's Docklands. It was instigated through a mix of enterprise zones and urban development corporations. The latter were government, quango style agencies. These UDCs had powers to acquire, hold, manage, reclaim and dispose of land and other property. They could carry out building and other operations, enhance the environment, provide utility services and transport infrastructure. In addition, they could also provide financial incentives for the private sector. Funding came not just from central government, but also from the proceeds from the disposal of development land (Tallon A, 2010).

The application goes far further than the neo-liberal west. Its most successful outcomes have been seen in China. The country there inaugurated four Special Economic Zones (coastal towns) in 1979. Factory imported experts, container ships, shopping malls and skyscrapers soon followed. Such was their success, that these 'instant cities' multiplied at astounding rates. Indeed, it has been a case of GDP on an ever-upward trajectory, largely backed by a transfer of technology from foreign firms.

An issue is that new jobs don't always go to nearby 'ghetto residents.' There is also a diversion of resources (subsidies) away from educating residents to police protection (and any others needed to administer these zones). Firms that do locate may be financially marginal and provide a weak base for long-term development. Lastly, where they do help one neighbourhood, it may only serve to shift 'the problem' elsewhere.

It is foolish to think that building a business park and a good road to the airport is enough to inspire economic revolution (Leo Hollis; 114). Rather, it takes talent, education and creativity to achieve a driving force for urban productivity and transformation.

Regenerating places is easy compared to regenerating people themselves. Inner city communities are rarely homogenous. If the poor are members of minority groups, then they can be further restricted in terms of opportunities. The means to improve the poor are wide ranging. They extend from providing public schools to mass transport. The paradox is that if a city succeeds then that will attract more poor people.

The most politically acceptable remedy for 'the underclass' is to provide education, training and social reforms. This is fine in principle, only to the point of deciding what gets taught and how it should be done. The traditional ideal was that 'education was valued for its own sake.' The current approach is of progressive education. This is based on Rousseau's romanticism, mixed with the commodification of the senses and the passions. The former is about choosing, playing and freedom. The latter is about fostering production rather than consumption. The main purpose of education thus focuses on 'production' and being an engine of economic growth.

The role of the state in local regeneration is to encourage integrated, bottom-up approaches, for:

- **building community capacity and stimulating innovation** This includes social innovation, entrepreneurship and changing capacity. The latter is by encouraging the development and discovery of untapped potential from within communities and territories;
- **new business models that improve control over scarce resources** by converting local 'waste' streams into by-products;
- **promoting community ownership** by increasing participation within communities. Also, it involves building the sense of involvement and ownership that can increase the effectiveness of government policies; and
- **assisting multi-level governance** by providing a route for local communities to fully take part in carrying out the government aims for all areas.

5.0 Accommodation and Living Arrangements

A key policy for the recovery from recessions, and the promotion of growth is building more homes and filling them with 'stuff.' Such consumption style economics follows the advice of British economist John Keynes, 1883 – 1946. The Government, led by former Prime Minister, David Cameron applied it following the credit crunch and later recession. This was by pursuing a house building programme to boost the economy. Construction may be useful. It represents one of the few (secondary) sector activities left in the country. Yet making it the means of economic success rather than the outcome is flawed. It depends upon a flow of fictitious capital. It can also result in the decline of fixed capital. This is for example, when industries are converted into condominiums.

Extending or enlarging homes inevitably triggers amenity based standards of the planning system. It is claimed that stopping such projects puts a 'brake on the economy,' yet this is a false logic. No doubt construction for its own sake produces work. Yet who is going to invest their time and money in a property when it can be devalued at their neighbour's whim. Putting a stately country house onto a suburban plot may appear appealing in times of over-inflated property prices. Yet it's questionable whether such 'over-development' is a sound investment to begin with. This applies equally to the landowner as it does the wider economy.

Permanence of Settlement

It's assumed that everyone wishes to have a home or at least a permanent structure. Traditional society was predominately mobile. Some 'distinct' cultural groups retain this preference for mobile occupation of land, even while living amongst their more static brethren. These include Bedouin communities in the Middle East, gypsies in Europe and various indigenous peoples around the world.

Most economic and institutional systems actively promote permanent settlements. In fact, it is difficult to integrate mobile living practices in the face of fixed private property, dwindling commons and planning controls. Planning legislation tends to have a disproportionate impact on mobile communities. The 2012 eviction of residents from the green belt at Dale Farm, Basildon (England), is a reminder of how planning controls still interfere with a 'way of life.' This was a case where the residents owned the land they were evicted from.

Since society achieved a steady agricultural surplus, most communities have sought to define permanent space to call their own. Those groups which failed to secure land ownership have always been at a disadvantage. In the case of the Scottish highland clearances,[104] a significant number of people were removed from their traditional land tenancies where they and their ancestors had farmed for centuries. This was because they did not have the right of ownership. Other marginalised groups were retained in the towns for specific economic reasons, but again denied the right of property ownership. An example was the Jews living in the Venetian Republic. From 1516 they

---

[104] Forced displacement during the 18th and 19th Centuries.

were forced to live in the ghetto, from which they could have been removed if the authorities had deemed it necessary.

Land tenure and the titling of property rights gives people security against eviction. It also provides them with a source of capital, and allows them to qualify for formal loans, using their house or land as collateral. As noted in Part I, there is a link between the spread of land ownership and democracy. Tenure security gives people a chance to develop a greater sense of belonging. It also gives them the willingness to invest in resources and efforts to improve their communities.

In modern England, private land, even disused land, is guarded as fiercely as the rest of the economy. Through ancient powers, the Government continues to sustain a system of ancient injustices. These curtail alternatives and lock the poor into rent and debt. In 2012, the Government dropped a late clause into an unrelated bill[105] criminalising the squatting of abandoned residential buildings. Its lateness meant that it could not be properly scrutinised by the House of Commons,

The irony was that land and property stayed empty during the recession of 2010 (there were under 1,000,000 empty properties). What happens if neither the owner or the state is interested in a beneficial use? Surely there comes a point at which it may be preferable for those in need to be allowed some form of occupation rights, given no damage results. Even squatters in the Third World are now better off than the homeless in western urban centres in this one respect. Such an approach would have the extra benefit of incentivising self-reliance. It would be similar to that currently found in rural areas where assistance isn't always around.

The relative number of people living in mobile homes in the United States is worthy of attention. It's estimated as 20 million according to Census figures. Although mobile home parks are found in Canada and there are sites for static caravans in the UK, they are not found in the same number. This trend began in the Great Depression of the 1930s. It was when people started living in trailers, which had been designed for travelling and vacationing, for reasons of necessity. Eventually these people started to make these tiny mobile units their homes (Hurley, 2002). Now, not everyone who lives in a trailer park is poor and homes may not necessarily look like trailers in the conventional sense. Inside they're potentially spacious. They may include 2-3 bedrooms, a fitted washer and dryer, two bathrooms and also include an island breakfast bar in the kitchen.

---

[105] Under Section 144 of the Legal Aid, Sentencing and Punishment of Offenders Act (LASPO).

Explaining the impetus for some in the US to live in mobile homes comes down to some basic reasons (Geoghegan, 2013). Housing and land in the United States is cheap. So it's relatively easy to provide some form of electricity, sewage and water supplies. Some even add a clubhouse and a swimming pool. In comparison, it's too expensive to do all this in Europe. Public transportation is better in Europe. So there's a comparative advantage to the poor living in a central urban area there. In the US manufacturing is located up and down major highways. It's much easier for people with these jobs to not want to be in central city areas. There's also the ingrained American ethos of private home ownership, so the alternative of a rented city apartment is not always attractive. Another cultural factor is the American love for freedom and mobility. Even though in reality mobile homes are never very mobile, it's the attraction that you can pick up and leave any time if you didn't like your circumstances, in a way you can't with a house. Finally, there are policy issues of limited housing options in the United States for low income people. The threshold at which they're eligible for subsidised housing is much higher than in European countries. So people that might live in a council house in the UK don't have that same opportunity in the United States. Back in the 1930s, people started parking trailers on the outskirts of towns and cities. That's when they became associated with working class and impoverished people. The location of many trailer parks resulted from a combination of 'institutionalised discrimination.' This stemmed from federal-backed mortgages being denied to owners of mobile homes. It was also about zoning laws that forced these communities to the outskirts of towns and cities.

More flexible work and life patterns, could extend the desire for mobile homes in the future. Advances in technology will also make this aspiration more achievable. Advances in super-light weight materials allow for homes to be created as modular 'pods.' They can be moved from place to place with far greater ease. For instance, polymer sheets have been produced for lightweight, flat-pack homes. These turn into perfect alignment after being removed from a backpack (Harvard Universities' Johannes Overvelde - 11/03/2016).

In the Third World, the reliance on mobile or transitionary urban accommodation is far more significant than in the West. The lives of such people are based on fraught trade-offs. This is in order to optimise their housing cost, tenure security, quality of shelter, journey to work and often personal safety (Davis, 2006). They are often neglected by local governments and plagued by poverty, crime, poor hygiene, and lack of access to economic opportunities. Even where population growth has slowed, informal housing remains prevalent. This is the case in Latin American countries due to the economic crises of the 1980s. Many local governments have devoted their attention solely to more lucrative, higher-end development. This only perpetuates the plight of poor city dwellers.

That isn't to say attempts by authorities to discourage informal settlements, per se, are not ill- founded. In the Third World, they increasingly have to develop on vacant land which is not suitable for living. This includes, forest or flood-prone areas, areas close to drains, foothills or downwind of pollution. These slums are a negative part of a city. They stand for failed governance, regulations, dysfunctional land markets, and unresponsive economic systems. As slums densify, whether horizontally or vertically, it places further pressure on existing infrastructure and services. This includes roads, transit, water, sewage, gas, telephone, waste collection, security and others. They also produce all the more familiar first world concerns of sprawl. Productive agricultural farmland is sterilised and vulnerable ecosystems damaged. If slum growth overwhelms city growth then this makes the situation worse. Urban poverty is exacerbated, development goals derailed, and the cities' comparative advantage, on attainment of economic goals, eliminated (Verbeek, 2014).

The UK has, in the past, taken a 'hard nosed' approach to slum housing. The likes of the Housing Act 1930 required all slum housing to be cleared in designated improvement areas. The Third World though, represents a significantly greater challenge. The capacity for the authorities to create improvement areas is so much more limited. As policies to halt slum expansion have typically failed, the approach of removing residents has become far less common. Whether this is a significantly more enlightened approach can be debated. Slums represent a major section of population that are too often exploited by the politicians for their aspirations.

Government and community collaboration to increase infrastructure provision has raised living conditions in some self-help communities. Yet neglect remains prevalent in many others. Since the 1960s, many land use programmes in the Third World have focused on the legalisation of land tenure. When established communities are not threatened with eviction or demolition they have in effect achieved de facto tenure. Formal land tenure is then not necessarily as attractive as might be thought. Residents may be opposed to seek the regularisation of their land titles. This is contrary to a common shared belief among analysts and international organisations (for example, the World Bank). Many informal settlement residents do not want to pay property taxes or submit to building codes. They have little desire to use formal credit systems for loans because they do not have a steady income to repay debts.

The Right to Housing

Housing has always been a basic human need, but many have sought that it become a human right. This is the intention that everyone has access to a safe, secure, habitable, and affordable home. In pre-industrial society, the majority were excluded from the resources (including housing) they needed. A minority lived on in affluence. This still holds true in the Third World. The latest generation of programmes to address informal settlements, such as the Favela-Bairro (Slum to Neighbourhood) in Rio de Janeiro, have taken a new approach. This is aimed at urbanising hundreds of informal settlement communities. Beginning in 1995 it is a cross-sectoral partnership between the Inter-American Development Bank and the Municipal Departments of Urban Planning and Housing.

Physical upgrading of favelas includes improvements to water and sewage systems, street lighting, and garbage collection, opening up of streets, creation of public spaces like parks and playgrounds and building of amenities such as community or health centres. The program differs from many earlier state-led efforts because it focuses just as much on upgrading social infrastructure. Social services are administered by civil society organisations. They include the provision of day care facilities, drug and alcohol prevention, education and job training, and youth leadership activities. The success of the program comes from its integrated approach. It considers physical and social elements of planning as necessarily related and potentially complementary efforts.

Modern Western Countries find themselves in a position where there is 'enough to go around' but in practice it doesn't. There has been a strong link between planning, the welfare state and housing provision (linked to the replacement of slums). For William Thompson[106] (1900), overcrowding was the product of the failure of private enterprise to supply enough housing. The approach was for the organised dispersion of population by municipal action. This was deemed the only practical and satisfactory remedy for such evils. The key to success was to get land close to agricultural prices. This made sure that the unearned increment arising from urbanisation was not privately appropriated.

Anglo-American nations have not gone as far as defining a 'right to housing.' In Sweden, it came in after the Second World War in recognition that its stock of housing had been built over two preceding centuries. Most

---

[106] Peoples' champion and London councillor.

neighbourhoods consisted of four- to six-floor multifamily dwellings. They were densely packed together. The city's working population lived in homes that were often just one- or two-room flats. Often overcrowded, they lacked basic sanitary facilities.

In the 1940s, the Swedish Parliament adopted a national housing policy that would become one of the pillars of the Swedish social system. This policy recognized that every citizen was entitled to adequate housing at a reasonable price. Not only did housing become a legal right, but the policy went onto eliminate overcrowding and cap rents at 20% of household income. By law, every one-person household was entitled to at least 30m². That is a one-room flat along with a kitchen and bathroom. They also had to meet strict national standards. For each extra person in the household, there was to be another room measuring at least 10m².

Across the 'Iron Curtain,' Soviet citizens were also given housing as a right. Rent costs were fixed at 1928 levels throughout the Soviet era, even up to the collapse of the empire. Yet in the latter decades of the 20th Century, the iniquitous outcomes of Soviet planning became clear. It revealed a chronic story of housing shortages. There were decades-long waiting lists, except for those close to the seat of power who still obtained central locations (Alden and Crow, 1998; Gentile and Sjoberg, 2006).

Providers of Housing

The State may provide housing. This was the case in the Soviet Union style design and build solutions. Construction is the West is generally done by a professional builder or construction company. These are accredited with having the necessary skills and expertise to meet demanding building regulations. Such firms operate under the uncertainties of economic cycles. Their number and responsiveness can act as a brake on construction capacity. It is a case of people needing to wait for the developers to show up, even if theoretically there should be enough suppliers in a free market.

Financing may not be an entirely private sector affair. Often there is state funded, financial help, through subsidies, and a need for affordable housing. Contributions are obtained through the planning system. These lessen the burden of demand on public amenities and services that would result from future developments on the existing community. Minimalist tax regimes are often not capable of funding the social infrastructure!

In the West, the Government has recently encouraged some self-builds. A good example of this was in Vauban, Freiburg, Germany. It didn't rely on volume house builders for the development of the new homes. Rather, the incoming residents were encouraged to form building co-operatives or 'construction communities.' They would design and manage the building of their own properties.

The residents came together in groups that shared the financial risk and cut the typical cost of a home (by 25%). The use of an architect and a contractor (and a council funded project manager) gave certainty over the eventual cost of each apartment in the blocks that were built. Many of the owners chose to 'self finish' their homes to keep the costs down still further. This is simple to do if you already have had a contractor build a watertight envelope for you.

Occasionally employers give accommodation for their workers. Such corporate style provision for design and build is rare. Examples are: remote mining settlements, clergy and some forms of rural accommodation. Where workers have to move into an existing area with insufficient housing there is a strong argument for employer support. Either they should provide housing or at least subsidise their transport costs.

In the Third World, it's necessary for future inhabitants to resolve their own housing problems. Despite the low building standards, 'self-help housing' gives a means of accommodation for new immigrants and the poor. It also costs little to governments strapped by limited financial capabilities. In fact, in Latin America, it has been politically expedient for Governments to allow builders to ignore their regulations. Although there are many self-help programmes, they are usually 'credit based.' This means that those who use the funds must first qualify. Qualifying for such funds usually needs a stable income to repay the credit, which applicants are often unable to show.

Construction of Housing

The archetypical cave man resolved his housing problems by use of the shelter already available. The communities of ancient Petra (in Jordon) extended this principle further. They created caves by carving into red desert cliffs. Vernacular architecture relies on the ability to source local materials and use local traditions in construction. The difficulty of transportation, limits stylistic choice. It is sobering to think that even in the future, slum cities will continue to be built using basic materials. These include crude brick, straw, recycled plastic, cement blocks and scrap wood. Even this maybe preferable to Cairo's City of the Dead. This is where around a million people use Mameluke tombs as prefabricated housing parts. It's one of the strangest examples of what is referred to as, 'inherited housing supply' (Nedoroscik, 1997).

With wealth comes an understandable desire for better and more permanent materials. Venice is a good example. It's original form used temporary wooden structures. The medieval city changed to use new construction materials of stones and glass windows. Sourcing stones relies upon local geology and Venice had to import theirs from the mainland.

In the UK, the variety of stones gives individual counties a distinctive look. They range from Scottish sandstone to Essex flint stones. Owing to its absence in the South-East, much building construction relied upon wood. After the Great Fire of London, new regulations, were introduced to avoid any repeat of the tragedy. Wood was replaced by bricks for construction. New ideas in construction resulted in different styles and so different materials. Books[107] allowed self-made builders to construct houses from any style found in the world. This ended regional types of architecture. It also encouraged the gathering of materials from much further afield, which were by then more accessible.

Modern thinking on architecture has its focus on 'making it new.' This has resulted in mass-produced houses of uniform standards. For Corbusier this was seen to be both healthy and moral. Yet in Alpine Architecture it wasn't the intention, although few knew it at the time. The pre-occupation on glass materials was known to be prone to freezing or overheating. The result, originating from ideas associated with the trauma of WWI, was actually to make sure that inhabitants wouldn't get too comfortable (Moore, pg 300).

Modern planning systems may still require the continued use of regional construction materials for aesthetic and amenity reasons. Jerusalem, for instance, continues with certain pre-Independence British regulations. These mandate the use of local building stones in construction. More recently, sustainable construction principles have extended to the re-use of on-site material. Typically architects and developers would have overlooked existing on site material. It is now increasingly common practice to use former construction material in new buildings. Countries that use an integrated approach to spatial planning and building standards would be well placed to effectively incorporate these principles. These include Norway and Sweden.

Industrialised Housing

The construction sector in the UK is now expected to give a mixture of housing. This means either bungalows, terraced houses or apartments. Homes have become mass produced commodities. This is the same as with

---

[107] Such as John Loudon's, The Encyclopedia of Cottage, Farm & Villa Architecture (1933).

other sectors of the economy, for example cars, fridges and TVs. In theory, developers should pay attention to the potential needs or desires of potential buyers and tenants. It reflects the profit motive. This is the case of upper socio-economic housing where the 'image' being sold becomes more important than the commodity itself. Rather than selling houses, developers sell images of desirable lifestyles. 'Place' is important because that's what drives their returns.

In contrast, in catering to economies of scale, mass produced homes will always be in some way imperfect. Building companies won't fully predict the future inhabitant's ways of living or give much thought to the local community. We live in cities, streets and buildings constructed for us by people we don't know. We also share them with other people, most of whom we also don't know. The desires of both the builders and fellow residents will never fit together perfectly. A relatively, high standard of building quality imposes a manufactured, industrialised (artificial) living environment on most of us.

Most house builders are not interested in commissioning architects and designers, let alone notably good ones. Also, the standards of development depend on wider issues than just architecture. In fact, an advantage of pre-fabricated buildings is that they don't need to divert skilled labour away from other industries and into building production. As such, speculative housing is often seen as being negative from a place-identity perspective. This is where units are built before being on-sold. The profit incentive squeezes out the unique qualities that underlie monopoly rent – hence the need for regulations! The result is sameness, as identikit, standardised designs are rolled out by large firms across the country.

Functional buildings should be suited to their physical environment. Regional architecture is attuned to both the use of local materials and also its ability to resist adverse weather conditions. Universal (modern) architectural fashions will not necessarily work as well under different climates. The Art Deco craze preferred flat roofs over pitched ones. They were promoted by the likes of Le Corbusier as being superior on technical and economic grounds. He considered them cheaper to construct, easier to maintain and cooler in summer. Yet unless construction and maintenance was exceptional, they suffered in wetter climates. Ponded water leaked into the internal structure resulting in what was described in many Anglo countries as the 'leaky building' syndrome.

The uniform, even drab, appearance of housing estates has often provoked criticism. In Kista,[108] Stockholm, architects focussed on the quality of the dwellings. They gave little attention to creating the sort of attractive atmosphere that would make for a vibrant neighbourhood. Yet for the policy makers with their focus on equality, this wasn't necessarily a disadvantage. Uniformity was another way to make sure that no one would be better off than another.

In France, the logic of standardisation epitomised the grand ensemble (housing estate). In the 1980s this was referred to in the administrative jargon as a priority development zone or ZUP.[109] These developments were mostly built in areas known as operational development zones,[110] which were developed and serviced quickly on the edges of towns. The 'ideal' ZUP was considered to represent 8,000 to 10,000 homes on average. It would house a relatively diversified population. The principle of the ZUP was technocratic. The land was acquired directly by the state which would decide upon site plans. Construction was entrusted to major public works contractors. They were able to offer low construction costs in exchange for framework contracts. These contracts lasted several years and covered thousands of homes. In a single decade, the edges of French towns were covered with ZUPs.

No country embraced the drive towards the use of mass production in apartment building more fully than the Soviet Union. This was particularly the use of standardised, factory produced materials or pre-fabrication. The Soviet Union might have been expected to embrace Le Corbusier's view that houses can be considered 'machines for living.' Yet their focus on pre-fabrication was a practical not ideological move. It emphasised the need to address the problem of overcrowding and housing shortages (Forty, 2012).

The result was that Soviet planning delivered thousands of tiny, poorly built housing units in huge blocks. Don't forget that they didn't have planning law. The units were typically five stories high and rectangular-block buildings. Only during the final couple of decades of the Soviet era, were 'system buildings' erected. These represented bigger and taller apartment blocks than were the apartment building norm (Alden and Crow, 1998; Smith, 1996). Yet in the absence of regulation, local environmental degradation associated with construction practices was a problem (Weclzwowicz; 2002).

The best means to address problems of standardised housing is through the use of regulatory instruments, especially design review. Design review sets

---

[108] Built from the 1970s, comprising working and middle class residents, it adjoins a significant ICT hub.

[109] Zone d'urbanisation prioritaire

[110] Zones opérationnelles d'aménagement

out rules and discretionary decision bodies. They assess architectural design proposals in terms of what is 'good architecture.' Design rules may control the shape, style, materials, and colour of buildings, roof types, and the design of retaining walls. By design rules, governments may be able to require that multifamily residential buildings add large (and expensive) lobby spaces or recreation facilities. Some design controls restrict the design of private gardens. Others impose restrictions on the shapes, materials, or heights of fences. Many of these rules cost money and delay the permit approval process. They thus get criticised for raising housing and other costs (sometimes intentionally).

Developers prefer greenfield sites. There's less start-up costs associated with dealing with what may already be on site. Greenfield sites also give greater flexibility to create the right shaped and sized parcels of land. It was recognised early on that decentralisation, in suburban extensions, also needed cheap and rapid transport. In Thompson's day this was by the electric tram. To achieve this necessitated more municipal housing (for higher density), transport and more control of land.

Adequate transport has been a common oversight, even by the central planners. Too many estates in both the East and West may have looked fine on plans. In reality they turn out to be dismal, distant from employment or city centres and lacking in public transportation or services. Ideally, compact city features are designed in from the start with integration of residential and industrial areas. This is especially where high growth is expected such as expanding Third World cities.

5.0 Suburbs or High Rises

There has been a debate over for a long time over whether it's better to aim for high or low rise living. The question is, what best provides for the resident's needs? In the West, dense cities attract younger, single people. They are good places to work and get knowledge, but also to meet each other. Suburbs, attract young parents because of better schools and larger homes.

Suburban living is assumed to be explainable by technology/functional reasons, particularly, the private motor car. Yet such explanations fail to illustrate suburbia's beginnings, 50 years before the invention of the motor car. The best explanation is that suburban processes are essentially sociological. Suburbs provided freedom and individuality never before available to millions of people. This was the freedom surrounding house ownership, which carries with it an ability to modify, decorate and customise as desired.

There was also a political rationale that suburbs eliminate industrial conflict. Debt-encumbered homeowners would not go on strike (Boddy, 1980). They gave the (typically) male worker the ability to return from his day at the factory or office to a private domestic environment. There he would be secluded from the tense world of work in an industrial city characterised by pollution, social degradation and personal alienation. His wages were to pay the mortgage. The physical and emotional maintenance of the dwelling would be the duty of the wife. Capitalism and antifeminism fused in campaigns for home ownership and mass consumption.

Suburban living is also driven by culture and those ideas of earlier societies. The suburban ideal has the dwelling as the primary symbolic entity. There was a strong focus on housing forms characteristic of immediately previous societies. People in England went for cottages that followed the mock-Tudor style. This was a symbol of the 16th Century triumph of Protestantism. In the US it was the ranch, while in Spain the hacienda. These past environments were 'small community, few encounters' type places. Meetings which did occur were non-random and even strongly controlled. There's less chance for causal interaction. This was because of the different structure of commercial development and lack of public spaces. So suburbanites either stay isolated from one another or seek social capital elsewhere. The only other option was to invite neighbours into their private spaces. This was a form of community Jacob's called 'togetherness.' Suburbs have become associated with the language of emptiness and the geography of 'nowhere.' This is symbolised by whether to have cul-de-sacs or more urbanist crossings such as the junctions of two streets. The soulless qualities of suburban living played a critical role in the dramatic movements of 1968 in the United States. At that time, discontented white middle class students went into a phase of revolt, seeking alliances with other marginalised groups.

Suburban land use controls in the West made sure that high standards of privacy were achieved for residents. This was through over-rigid rules requiring 'space between dwellings.' Privacy is complex. It is thought of in terms of solitude, intimacy, anonymity and reserve, seclusion, distance and isolation (Westin 1967; Mazumbar, 2000). In Anglo-American countries, privacy is based on physical distance. Others base it on the control of interaction. Both types need their own design responses. Other cultures do value the importance and have respect for privacy but often express it differently. In eastern cultures, concern for privacy has been a major structuring element of urban areas. In the Islamic tradition, enclosures in small open spaces give a sense of security. Private users should be able to choose how much privacy they need through adjustable filters. Designers typically use permanent, physical and visual barriers.

Suburban outdoor spaces induce strongly conformist spatial behaviours. A good example is the front garden. They were only possible due to the invention of the push lawnmower. This allowed one person, working alone, to realise the ideal picturesque tradition of close cut green grass. Apartment housing has open space but it's often the communal space around flats. It's private open space in the suburbs. If people in apartment blocks don't work together, their communal open space quickly deteriorates. That is, unless there is a competent central 'management' set up.

Outdoor layout, space and other measures of residential amenity are key concerns in planning. Outdoor space is generally viewed as positive. Its functionality may be restricted if it is merely the amorphous left over around detached buildings. Detached houses and large plots have always been the norm in land, abundant societies such as the United States and Australia. Yet the use of space in these societies has been a disaster from the standpoint of the rational use of land and space. This is possibly topped only by the trend for rural lifestyle blocks, which are even worse by this criterion.

Suburban cities have 'frittered away' space. Yet most of the spaces around individual suburban houses and commercial uses are not accidental but planned and demanded (i.e., setbacks). Suburban houses have at least four times as much infrastructure per dwelling unit than walkable neighbourhoods (Condon, 2010). In Houston, prices are only held down by abundant construction. Fifty six percent of jobs are more than ten miles from the city centre. Although California pioneered sprawl, changed approaches have increased densities, especially in Los Angeles (L.A.). The density of new housing developments is at an historic high. Having once become a leader in transit use, L.A. now ranks far behind other states in fuel use and vehicle travel (Sperling & Gordon, 2010).

Planning's original purpose was to make sure densities didn't get out of hand so as to control unhealthy conditions. They were backed by various regulations that prevented high density development. Yet they quickly became an aim in their own right. Now almost the reverse approach is needed for the mature cities of the West. Regulations are supposed to promote 're-densification.' This is through regeneration of existing city cores and supporting hubs, brownfield re-development and urban retrofitting.

Londoners know there are thousands of acres of unused and underused land within the M25. It awaits the high-density, low-rise building preferred by the property market. Another massive reservoir of vacant residential property in Britain is under-occupied property and underdeveloped city land. London is awash with small houses and empty rooms. Its residential density is the lowest of any big city in Europe. Detached houses, spare rooms and gardens are the nation's luxury. Britons had 1.5 rooms per person in 1981 and have 2.5 today, even as new house building is declining. Freeing up this capacity should be the overwhelming goal of policy. Planning controls in high growth areas of Britain may be too strict. Attempts to build over private open space for housing was known as 'garden grabbing.' The practice was restricted by the Coalition Government through amending the definition of brown field land to no longer include gardens. Brownfield development has taken priority over greenfield since Tudor times. Back then the first rules were introduced for buildings to be re-built in place of earlier building footprints. This is an old origin of the 'brownfield first' policy in UK planning. Permitting an extra storey, apartment or back extension on every existing property would drastically increase density and capacity. It is thus possible for London to 'grow higher without growing high' (Jenkins, 2015).

If the land market is finite, and there is significant pressure to expand, the only way is to build higher. Essentially, extra stories create more 'space' on a fixed piece of land, so high rises are a means of multiplying space. The premise of 'pile 'em high' is needed. This is when surrounding private property can't be secured through market mechanisms or when planning restrictions restrict tall buildings.

Tel Aviv started as an English Garden city: a Bauhaus white, self-contained, structured community surrounded by greenbelt land. Early on there were stringent restrictions on building height. Growth pressures soon reached the point where it was realised that the only realistic option was to build up. The rules had to be amended. For the authorities, another driver was the concern that if Tel Aviv didn't get skyscrapers neighbouring Ramat Gan would.

Over restriction on the part of planners leads to stagnation and higher prices. In Brasilia, the government devised Plano Piloto. It was a plan that posed extensive growth restrictions in and around the government administrative area. The initiative played an important role in the preservation of Brasilia's modern architecture. But it also led to dire spatial and social consequences in later stages. While most Brazilian cities maintain fairly high densities, building restrictions in Plano Piloto have encouraged growth to occur in a sprawling manner. According to studies conducted by Dawall and Monkkonen (2007), only 15 per cent of Brasilia's population resides in the city centre. Comparable metropolitan areas, like Curitiba and Recife, have 70 per cent for the same category. Besides, less than 10 per cent of the city's urban area is found at the core. Understandably, this pattern of development has imposed immense traveling costs for workers from the lower, middle and working classes. They live in favelas and satellite cities located as far as 76 km from the city centre. Congestion has emerged as one of Brasilia's prime concerns. Commuting times reach twice that of Curitiba and Recife for equivalent lengths. Brasilia serves as an example for where a master plan, 'ignored the social and economic realities of Brazil' (Dowall and Monkkonen, 2007).

For Le Corbusier, 'building out' had never been the way to solve housing shortages. He was also seeking something else. That was, to redesign the home as the key to re-forming society. The narrow mental outlook of suburbanites would be addressed. This was by having families living in high-rise complexes known as a 'Unit T.' Apartments would be assigned according to the size of a family and its needs. There would be no class distinctions. Rational design, coupled with mass production, stood for environmental social engineering. It provided calm, order and neatness that would inevitably impose discipline on their inhabitants. This was very much Le Corbusier's 'home as machine' mentality.

It represented a radical departure from the norms of the time. Yet it came at a time when French officials had been unsuccessful in dealing with the squalor of the growing Parisian slums built in 16th Century layouts (Clapson, 2003). Le Corbusier's approach was seen as an efficient way to house large numbers of people in response to the urban housing crisis. After individual projects, such as Immeubles Villas (1922), he soon moved into studies for entire cities. He sought that the over-cramped and chocked conditions of Paris, be resolved by building upwards to densities of 1,000 persons per hectare. In 1922 he presented his scheme for a 'Contemporary City' for three million inhabitants (City of Tomorrow). He believed that his new, modern architectural forms would give an organisational solution that would raise the quality of life for the lower classes. The centerpiece of this plan was a group of sixty-story cruciform skyscrapers and steel-framed office buildings. Each was encased in huge, curtain walls of glass. These skyscrapers would be set within large, rectangular, park-like green spaces. At the centre was a huge transportation hub. It included depots for buses and trains, as well as highway intersections on different levels. A guiding principle was to keep pedestrians separate from cars.

One the first English examples was Sheffield's Park Hill (built 1957-1961). It was based on the concept of having 'streets in the sky' such that milk bottle floats might drive right up to the top floor of a block of flats. It had something like the 'streets in the sky' concept. The aim was to keep the 'solidarity of the street and face-to-face interaction.' (Prof Michael Hebbert, Professor of Town Planning at UCL). Yet such towers were far from the intended vertical streets. Streets offer shops, open spaces and places for meeting, walking and relaxing. They are places of meeting and exchange. This is in contrast to the resulting high rise buildings with no connection to their environment.

The tower blocks arising in the inner-cities were big, bold expressions of 20th Century modernism. They were certainly popular with an architectural elite and politicians on the left. Indeed, concrete constructions in general have been identified with by the politics of the left (Forty, 2012). In Britain at any rate, left wing politicians were fuelled by attempts to maintain their electoral advantage. This was by keeping the urban scenery shifting, even if life otherwise stayed still.

The rise and fall of such developments has fitted a common pattern in the West. Bijlmermeer (on the outskirts of Amsterdam) is one such example of this new style development. Constructed in the late 1960s, it housed 100,000 inhabitants in almost identical ten-storey concrete blocks. The walls of each were mass produced in factories. Landscaping features (parks and lakes) separated the housing blocks. Roads built on viaducts separated them from pedestrians. Walkways were covered. Originally, it incorporated planned collective facilities – bars, daycare centres, and hobby rooms to stimulate communal life. It was also intended to be linked to employment uses by a metro line. Yet, as is so often the case with urban infrastructure, the planned metro line never eventuated. From the mid-1970s Surinamese immigrants, originating from different cultural conditions of the rural Third World, started moving in. The new residents had little idea of how to maintain the blocks and the physical conditions within Bijlmermeer declined. There was also associated increases in vandalism and crime. In the end, its reputation became highly undesirable. Action to redress the problems took time to eventuate. It was only through the formation of a community group, which gained enough influence with the authorities, that it became possible (Moore, 2012).

Other similar developments have been less fortunate. Thamesmead, a brutalist housing development in London, was billed as a 'twenty-first century town' when it was built in the 1960s. By 1971 its reputation had taken a nose dive. It served as the backdrop for the dystopian violence of Stanley Kubrick's, 'A Clockwork Orange.' Trinity Square in Gateshead, also known as the Get Carter Car Park (from the 1971 film 'Get Carter'), was demolished in 2010. The Brunswick Centre in London also seemed destined for the bulldozer after it became a 'rain-streaked, litter strewn, concrete monstrosity.

Yet, in the end, it was redeveloped (Tom Heyden, 2014). These examples of tower block failure couldn't be blamed on the unfamiliarity of former Third World inhabitants to apartment living. They were more to do with high turnover rates. This was associated with people who felt they didn't belong and so no longer cared for their environment. These buildings also suffered from technical issues, such as lifts being slow or unreliable. Predicted by critics, concrete construction materials in damper climates suffered more than their dryer counterparts. They quickly develop stains, streaks and mould growths (Royal Institute of British Architects, 1946).

Utopian, modernist housing projects in the end alienated their inhabitants. Yet it probably goes deeper. English culture and lifestyle does not fit well with high rise living. Tower blocks are generally not built for inhabitants who are wanting to put their own money into the projects. Also, people simply didn't like their lives being re-organised in this way (Professor Hebbert at UCL as reported by Heyden, 2014). They were seen as paternalistic. 'The top-down maneuvering of people's lives. In Britain, by any account, the free citizen became increasingly unhappy with them.'

By far the most significant event to influence public opinion was the Ronan Point disaster in Newham. This was a tower block collapse which killed four people. For London and the 1960s, the tower block collapse was as influential in city design as the fire of London. Architects and planners will defend their 1960s and 1970s predecessors as having made genuine attempts to alleviate real problems. Tower blocks certainly helped relieve pressures of overcrowding. There were also attempts to architecturally reconcile some of the elements of suburban and high density living. One such development was Habitat 67, a cluster of modular buildings in Montreal, designed by architect Moshe Safdie. It included 354 prefabricated, precast concrete modules. This made up the 158 apartments which were up to 11 stories in height. Importantly, each with at least one roof terrace for its private garden. Each unit was intended to be an identical size but this had to give way to demands for varying shapes and layouts. Loadings became complicated. Together with the need to meet fire codes, this made the design far more expensive than intended.

Failing to design these tower blocks around the values and culture of the inhabitants was one major issue. Another reason urban designers got it wrong was traffic. As with Greenwich Village, N.Y., the rise of the motorcar was seen as so inevitable that dual carriageways were controversially constructed through traditional neighbourhoods. Most planners favoured building outwards. This included JR Jimmy James, the chief planner at the Ministry of Housing and Local Government from 1961-1967. The high-rise developments were, as in Tel Aviv, an architectural solution that reflected the political decision not to lose population to the surrounding counties. Had some of these areas got an administrative boundary extension to allow greenfield development, the high-rise blocks would probably not have been built.

'Issue transference,' as a result of well-intentioned state action, is still alive and well. The focus of European planners, in well managed, central city areas has resulted in 'saucer' cities. This has immigrants and the unemployed marooned in high rise housing on urban outskirts. In contrast, the 'donut' shaped American cities were shaped by rampant market forces. At least this had poorer people concentrated in derelict cores and inner suburbs. This meant they were, at least, closer to employment areas.

6.0 Third Dimension

High rise living is a relatively recent phenomenon, compared to the role of tall buildings used in the civic and commercial sectors. In pre-Industrial societies, tall buildings were exceptions and usually of some civic significance. The tallest structures in medieval cities and towns were usually Church spires. Their towers were narrow and few people, other than the bell ringers, had to climb them.

The authorities liked their castles and towers. The fact they were artificially higher than their surrounds conferred important advantages. They were useful places to observe from, allowing an early warning for defence and fires. The small, walled, medieval hill town of San Gimignano in Italy produced an amazing range of towers that survive to this day, each no more than 51m. These weren't constructed for civic pride. Rather, they were for the needs of rival business groups, reflecting a local community at war with itself.

Economics started to play a part in terms of the need or desire for scale. The wool making centre of Bruges was one of first places to tower over its surrounding religious structures. Finally, office work which originally had been done in coffee houses and people's homes moved into purpose built offices.

The scale of buildings, at the time, was still reined in by the structural limitations of early building materials. Traditional buildings using load-bearing masonry are no more than 6 stories high. Significantly taller buildings need further technological innovation. This is to allow people to safely move up and down in them and also to avoid the need for enormously thick, lower walls.   William Le Baron Jenney's 138 ft Home Insurance Building in Chicago was seen as the world's first true skyscraper in 1885.   It had a revolutionary weight bearing skeletal-frame.   Later, Taut's idea of glass monuments were adopted by Miles van der Rohe in his skyscraper designs of the 1920s.   This was soon copied by other modernist architects and became the origins of the modern city skylines of 'crystalline' steel and glass office buildings.   No one these days builds skyscrapers without windows.   They serve as much to see out of, as to be seen within (quite unlike Cathedrals).

More than any other developer, Manhattan developer, A.E. Lefcourt, sought to transform urban blocks within New York City from tenements into skyscrapers.   New York suited skyscrapers.   Its natural advantage was a bedrock base which is cheaper to build upon than other, more difficult geology.   Skyscraper development acted as a magnet for speculative investment.   This reinforced the extreme volatility of the office-building cycle. Each building boom saw city centre sites redeveloped at progressively higher densities.   Re-development every 25-30 years was the norm in Chicago (Hoyt, 1933:335).

The skyline is the most distinctive aspect or image of each city.   The skyline in New York that was emerging had aesthetic appeal (Barras R. 2009) but it also carried symbolic power.   Skyscrapers became a powerful culture symbol for the optimism and energy of American capitalism (Domosh, 1988). Comparing the number and height of skyscrapers between cities is akin to the relative scale and economic power base. It didn't go unnoticed on the other side of the Iron Curtain and it was Stalin who gave backing to various projects of prominence.   In 1931 he insisted that the Palace of the Soviets had to be a 'little taller' than the Empire State building.   A statue of Lenin to adorn it had to be triple the size of the Statue of Liberty.   Even authorities in modern North Korea want to build more skyscrapers.

For a skyscraper to be labelled supertall, it needs to be over 985ft. Some of the world's tallest buildings bolster their height simply by constructing unused space.   This is a practice referred to by the Council on Tall Building and Urban Habitat's (CTBUH) as, 'Vanity Height.' Vanity Height is classed as the distance between a skyscraper's highest living space and its architectural top. CTBUH lists the 10 worst offenders, with unused space ranging from 27 up to 39 per cent, with five of them in Dubai.   The skyscraper with the greatest Vanity Height was found to be the iconic Burj Al Arab in Dubai.   It is architecturally 1,055 feet tall.   Yet the top 405 feet are 'useless' and without this unused space, the skyscraper wouldn't qualify as supertall.   The ratio of the living space in this luxury hotel, compared to the useless space, is 39 per cent. By mid 2011, there were 54 buildings that were taller than CTBUH's 980ft cut off. There are now 72 supertall buildings occupied worldwide.

Elsewhere, the New York Times Tower and the Emirates Tower in Dubai have 31 per cent unused space. None of the skyscrapers listed in CTBUH's top ten are outside of Dubai, China or New York. According to CTBUH, 61 percent of the world's tallest buildings - 44 out of 72 - would not be classed as supertall if the unused space was removed.

At these heights, the economic logic of multiplying space breaks down. Their space ratios make them costly and inefficient to service. As San Gimignano shows, there have always been reasons to build tall, other than just financial gain. The developer's rationale can differ from that of the architects in support of these projects. London's Shard is now Britain's tallest constructed building. In arguing it's planning merits, architect, Renzo Piano, claimed that his creation, 'is not about arrogance and power' but intended 'to celebrate community ... surprise and joy.' Besides, its height will mean 'it will disappear into the sky.' The tower's developer, Irvine Sellar, put the case differently. He said, 'this is London, this is The Shard, we can kick sand in the face of the Eiffel Tower.' This suggests the building is more about arrogance and power, than its architect might have suggested.

These contests of the 'exhausted typology' of American style skyscrapers continue. However, OMAs design of the Central China Television building in Shanghai was supposed to come as a high-tech alternative. Rather than a single shaft, it's served by a core of lifts, a big loop 51 storeys and 234m high. These special lifts travel both up and sideways. The theory of the design is to engineer intercommunication and break down barriers between company departments. This occurs from buildings being stacked up floor on floor which occur elsewhere.

Sometimes developers (or the future occupants) need to be protected for their own sake. This can be due to the increase in natural hazard risk from the potential for earthquakes. There is also a case to limit the size of skyscrapers on the basis of the economic resources they tie up, the extravagance they represent and the impact is can have on the wider economy. After the 1893 Chicago slump, the city council capped the height of future buildings, an ordinance not rescinded until 1923. Yet the consequence of this would restrict office development during the second construction boom of the early 1910s. In contrast, laissez faire development was allowed to continue in New York.

The height of buildings is the most common reason for intervention; particularly for amenity. It is thus no surprise that tall buildings like The

Shard are divisive, and not just with the French. There is vision behind them, but not necessarily a collective one.

The reason we can enjoy the great historic monuments in Paris, such as the Eifel Tower, are because they're not obscured by nearby buildings. A 1974 regulation imposed a height limit of 83ft in central Paris, and this stays in effect. Skyscrapers were essentially banished from the historic core. The majority of Paris's skyscrapers are now located further afield in the dense, La Defence area.

New York may allow for skyscrapers but it also regulates them. From the late 19th Century there were community protests over the loss of air and light. Antigrowth supporters sought height restrictions (125ft) to streets like Fifth Avenue. That was to prevent them becoming a 'canyon with impacts on congestion, property values and the city as a whole.' It was the resulting outcry over the construction of the 42 storey Equitable Building in lower Manhattan in 1915 that finally tipped the argument for authorities to take action. The outcry came from neighbouring building owners over its seven-acre shadow that was cast.

A simple comprehensive zoning resolution was introduced to address the effects of height. Yet it wasn't long before it was deemed to need amending. Between 1916 and 1960 the original zoning code was amended more than 25 times. In 1960 a new 420 page code of zoning ordinances was produced from the earlier simple classification of space. This included business, residential and unrestricted to 13 types of residential, 12 types of manufacturing and 41 types of commercial districts. It introduced a complex system of floor area ratios (or FAR). While the standard building in 1916 was a wedding cake; the 1961 code was for a glass-and-steel slab with an open plaza in front (ref: Talen, 2012).

London also has its fair share of controls. Sir Christopher Wren's, St Pauls was the tallest building in its vicinity at the time. It has become the symbolic view shed and rationale for maintaining views that modern development would otherwise seek to dwarf. The Shard was furiously opposed by local people as it progressed through the planning system for good reason. This was by Southwark council and by historic buildings and conservation authorities. It gives little or no architectural focus or end-point. No civic forum or function is offered except luxury flats and hotels. It stands apart from the City cluster and pays no heed to its surrounding context in scale, materials or ground presence. The tower seems to be better placed either in Dubai or at least Canary Wharf. It is the destruction of one set of values for the other's gain. Yet in the planning decision The Shard wasn't deemed to affect the St Paul's view shed. In terms of the other impacts, the planning discretion offered by the UK planning system in the end meant decision makers could say 'yes.'

Every recent skyscraper in London has become a landmark at best. A reference point external to the observer. At worst, they are merely 'post-modern signature or trophy buildings.' They exploit the post-modern phenomenon which links the cultural value of architecture with its economic value. As stand alone, geometric objects each individual skyscraper has come to stand for product differentiation. The Shard and Gherkin are current examples but larger buildings are being planned. Admittedly the same can also be said for the OMA design in China even though it lacks the degree of height of conventional skyscrapers. Collectively, a group of individual objects doesn't contribute towards a whole. As objects, they take something away from the rest of the unity of the city. They gain traction among the wider public as 'new' things which are an end in themselves and also by shifting the urban scenery. Their interest fades over time as people wish to move onto the next new thing. They are celebrated by some as providing architectural diversity and choice, rather than being identikit designs. In the end, the only choices available are to those with enough wealth.

It's always going to be difficult to say that skyscrapers, the symbol of the modern and post-modern city, have no place. Yet deciding their general acceptability is one of the most critical debates around urban form. It's associated with the trade-off between the promotion of density and efficiency (a good thing) and the social issues resulting from their lack of human scale. High buildings still represent the best means to resolve the progress / sustainability paradox. It's a question of degree, but high density living can have a lower environmental footprint. Yet the use of steel and concrete in skyscrapers is resource and energy expensive. Less material is now used than when the original skyscrapers were built. This was to compensate for the original's hand calculated designs. It does mean that our modern equivalents are less robust. Their lifespan is only around a maximum of 25 years before their materials need replacement. They are also incredibly maintenance and service intensive.

Skyscrapers can complement the city and be compensated for by open space outcomes. This was the case with Le Corbusier's design of repetitive skyscrapers in a park style environment. England's high rise apartment buildings tried to emulate this by surrounding their tower blocks and linked slabs with large, open, communal spaces. In the end, by seeking surrounding shared open space it meant overall local density gained was reduced.

A report by RIBA (Neale, 2009) noted that Georgian and early Victorian houses achieved densities of 80 units/hectare. This was due to such houses being built in straight lines and often in terraces, which maximises plot coverage. Roads were narrower and houses were built alongside each. In contrast, many newer schemes used the 'distributor-and-cul-de-sac' model. This results in a lot of unused space within the road layout. Clearly, a town composed entirely of tower blocks of 40 storeys standing next to each other is going to be hard to beat. Kowloon in Hong Kong reaches 1,250 units per hectare, which equates to 5,000 people per hectare. Elsewhere, commentators are left to wonder why the modernist inspired revisions to the urban fabric have been so extensively carried out. Their benefits have offered so little improvement over earlier forms.

PART VI:
FROM STREETS TO THE SEA

1.0 Transportation and Efficiency

In having all modern conveniences in the one place, cities resolve the tyranny of distance. We choose to live together for social interaction and also because it's an efficient way to access all our daily needs. These fall into the three main categories of 'home, work and shopping.' Cities give the next best means for people to access goods and each other efficiently. This is both between cities and their hinterland, but also within the city itself. There would not be any real need for cities if we could transport ourselves anywhere, instantaneously. This is, of course, the possibility science fiction gives us to consider.

Transport links have always formed the cornerstone of all urban public space. The contiguity of the transportation network sets it apart from all other land uses. Defining the corridor width represents a tension between achieving public efficiency of movement whilst maximising adjoining productive space. The latter is typically in private land ownership. More often than not, transport space is best administered as part of the public realm. This is the case even when it has been developed by private interests. Transport modes are not productive in their own right and must be maintained. As with other utilities, they are essential for the functioning of the urban environment.

Modern towns formed in the 19th and early 20th Century were based on the grid-iron pattern. This approach was criticised by the Austrian Camillo Sitte. He perceived that the grid-iron pattern led to monotony and sterility. Throughout his major text[111] he argued for a renewed emphasis on aesthetics in urban design. So, streets that wind or have irregular frontages are better because they give a constantly changing prospect for the moving observer. Le Corbusier attacked such thoughts of 'deviation' (1929, p5). In contrast to Sitte, he considered straight roads to be the 'way of man.' This was because man had a purpose and therefore sought the shortest route. These philosophies influenced pre-war German and post-war American engineers. In the end, it resulted in intercity motorways being constructed in different ways. The American practice adopted Le Corbusier's principles of efficiency. Their German counterparts choose Camillo Sitte's approach of offering the best scenery to create 'culture' (Forty, 2012).

---

[111] City Planning According to Artistic Principles (1889).

Railways

Nineteenth and early 20th Century suburbanisation depended upon the opening of new rail lines. As with highways, increased usage over time is stretching their capacity. For instance, London's tube carries almost 4 million people per day. There are warnings that by 2030, parts of London's tube within Zone 1 could be almost inoperable. That is despite extensive upgrade projects, such as CrossRail. The railways of Mumbai are in an even worse state than those of London. They carry 6 million persons per day and their long term expansion is hemmed in by slums. Their inhabitants took advantage at the time of what was deemed to be surplus vacant railway land. Expanding the network is sensitive. The tenants' only right to be re-housed is if they have managed to survive in-situ for over 10 years in their dwelling.

Many ambitious railway schemes have been proposed over time. Joseph Paxton,[112] proposed what was called the Great Victorian Way. It was to have consisted of a ten-mile covered loop around much of central and west London. It integrated glass-roofed streets with railways, shops and houses. Essentially it would have created a 'Year round street'. This would have linked up the railway stations around the city and resulted in a time of only 15min to get across London. An Act of Parliament was even passed before the project was shelved.

Sometimes whole cities have been planned around railway schemes. Nikolay Alexandrovich Milyutin's linear city concept of the late 1920s is one such example. It is based around a rapid transport system for moving people and goods along a single major arterial railway route. The concept did end up being partly applied in Volvograd (then Stalingrad) among other places.

Future railways are intended to cut travel times between cities. In England, the High Speed 2 project is to link London with England's northern industrial cities. More advanced options for high speed travel continue to be proposed. For instance, a hyperloop proposal has been suggested by futurists to give the ultimate speeds for commuters. Pods running along magnetic tracks would use a propulsion system, that could carry people through vacuum tubes at up to 500mph.

---

[112] English gardener, architect and Member of Parliament. He designed the Victorian Crystal Palace in London in 1855

Motor Cars

For all the 'think big' railway schemes of the past (or future), none have come close to the influence that the private motorcar has had on the city. Cars are a spatially more diffuse form of transportation and difficult to control. With the increasing dominance of the motorcar has been the need to manage traffic flows and circulation. It is logical for wider corridors to give greater capacity. This is particularly between main areas of public congregation, for example town centres, and outlying urban areas of residence. Such was the case of the layout of 'medieval' Sienna, Italy. Its main roads progressively widen the closer they get to the Town Hall, which is located in the centre of a large piazza, closed to wheeled traffic.

Between the 1920-1940s a new philosophy sought for the separation of modes of travel. There was an intention to distribute traffic through a hierarchy of routes matched to traffic flows. The interests of efficiency reigned supreme. Certain routes were designated for higher traffic loads. The number of pedestrian crossings was cut. Limitations were also placed on the number of other roads connecting into them and private driveways stopped from opening into them (Alker, 1942).

Soviet Cities were also intended to accommodate private motor vehicles. Yet unlike their counterparts in America, Soviet citizens were not supposed to be dependent upon their own cars. They could thus consider themselves more truly free (Siegelbaum, 2011).

It was in the West, in particular, that cars became seen as a symbol of the future, money and post-war progress (refer Part I, Section 3.1). The highway programmes to give a means of realising this dream led to many planning 'battles.' This included the one between Moses and Jacobs in Greenwich Village. Typically, these highway projects attempted to impose unnatural order, uniformity and symmetry on an organically developed, but pleasingly chaotic street pattern. Often this organic pattern had been built up over centuries. In the end, it changes the fabric of streets from an open and ringy distributed system, to one which has lots of stops and ends. Wider roads created barriers to movement across them. This created severance and fragmented urban areas into local domains.

Worse, other parts of the urban environment were seen by authorities as needing to be re-designed around car needs. The Bressey Report of 1937 is worth recalling. It went so far as to propose turning Regent Street into a motorway (with pedestrians confined to elevated walkways). Trafalgar Square was to be turned into a car park!

There has been an associated exponential growth in street furniture and parking, intended to accommodate driver's needs. Yet it is often scattered, with little concern for the overall effect for anyone other than drivers. The result is visually and functionally cluttered urban scenes. Of all features needed to support the private car, parking lots are the most expansive for their use of space. Often car parks are required through the planning system. Ironically this is the case even in the otherwise minimal Houston planning code. They are associated with land uses in order to internalise the impacts of car use on a dispersed land use form.

The ultimate extension of a car-dominated community was perhaps Architect, Geoffrey Jellicoe's 'Motopia.' It proposed a 30,000 person commuter town in Staines, Middlesex. Like Paxton's Great Victorian Way proposal it remains unbuilt. Based on a rigid grid system of buildings, it was to feature an expanse of rooftop motorways separating people from cars. It would have achieved a high population density. Yet this would have been at the expense of needing many rules and regulations underlain by rigid ideas for how people would have to live.

Motorways

Motorways between cities and towns evolved during the first half of the 20th Century. Germany was the first 'off the block.' It rapidly constructed a nationwide system of motorways in anticipation of their use in the Second World War. Britain, heavily influenced by its railways, did not build the first motorway, the Preston By-pass (M6), until 1958.

Just as in urban environments, motorways needed changes to adjoining land uses. This was to take into account the visual perspective for vehicle drivers. It was clear that car-based observers had only a limited time to read signs compared to the more discerning and prolonged attention of pedestrians. Starting in the post-war era, landscape architects[113] argued for a focus on simplicity and flow in the surrounding countryside. Such functional modernism saw conflict with local authorities and organisations. This included the Roads Beautifying Association which sought to plant ornamental trees and shrubs. These planting were seen as interrupting the flow of the landscape and distracting drivers travelling at speed.

---

[113] For example, Brenda Colvin, Sylvia Crowe and Geoffrey Jellicoe.

By the 1960s, motorways were being specifically designed to by-pass central urban areas around the country. This was for reasons of motorway efficiency. The policy again had its detractors. These were particularly those existing land uses, such as high street retailers, who benefited from the through flow of traffic.

Transport planners have tended to define the need for more highways by a supply-led logic. This is treating the city as a system: a set of inter-related impersonal, aims and component land uses which produce traffic. Predict-and-provide models are used to work out how much development may be needed for social and economic reasons. This allows them to then analyse the implications for the road network.

Road networks have to be expanded again and again to maintain efficient routes to escape the city and get to the country. This is needed in response to ever increasing levels of car ownership and road travel. The greater capacity for car travel and enhanced accessibility that highway engineers gave only encouraged new urban development on the periphery or outside established areas. The greater efficiencies given by better roads only resulted in greater car use. Thus a vicious cycle of more highway building was started which resulted in more wastage.

The Future of Roads and Highways

The presence of the private motor vehicle within our cities is dependent on the availability of cheap oil reserves. As discussed earlier, this is unlikely to change significantly in the near future (see Part II). The traditional logic has been to locate cities near natural resources. The importance of urban infrastructure is such that it has reversed this logic so that it shapes urban development. The traditional method is to decide on the next urban area and then worry about where the infrastructure should go. It is now seen as desirable to locate new urban centres where the existing infrastructural patterns give best support.

Mature cities benefit from increased densities and development within existing urban areas. This is more so than low density urban sprawl or rural developments. In Paris, the ambitious, 'Métropole du Grand Paris' is proposed. It combines land use with an ambitious transportation network, including driverless subways, across a new metropolitan region. This includes improved orbital links, routes between suburbs and the historic core, as well as promoting massive housing schemes to address affordable housing.

In the end, infrastructural change has been 'driven' by exploiting technological development. Autonomous forms of private transport are emerging in the West. They are capable of navigating roads with limited or no action from the driver. Such technologies offer the hope of improving safety by removing driver error. This includes eliminating reliance on tired or intoxicated drivers. They are also considered to be able to cut congestion and improve fuel economy. This is through the efficient operation of acceleration and braking controls. If this can be rolled out for road bound transport, it is not inconceivable that it might be extended into self-flying, people carrying drones. It is impossible to fly legally in this manner under current regulations in the United Kingdom. It would need years of testing to get anywhere near a public rollout and would result in the need for new infrastructure. If these hurdles could be overcome then its extensive use could circumvent highway gridlock and encourage much greater patterns of urban dispersal.

In emerging megacities, such as Mumbai in India, commuters lie on train roofs and hang off doors. Within this context it's desirable to focus on expanding existing public transport systems and increase the share of public and non-motorised travel (Global Commission, 2014). Surface-based public transport and rapid rail can give the best solutions. For instance, Curitiba[114] adopted a cost-effective integrated land use and transit system. Its integrated transportation system[115] includes bi-articulated buses, single fare and efficient bus stops. This acclaimed and emulated rapid-transit bus system allows for users to pay one flat rate to travel throughout the city. Collector buses work throughout a hierarchical system. They bring passengers from outlying areas to main city arteries. Curitiba's bus system is credited with saving approximately 27 million automobile trips and now serves 1.3 million passengers a year. This is approximately 85 per cent of Curitiba residents depend on the bus system as their main source of transportation. Multiuse 'Citizenship Streets' located in the city outskirts give their communities a centre. This centre includes retail, sport facilities, transit connection, and government offices.

---

[114] This was one of many unorthodox ideas adopted by former Mayor Jaime Lerner (1971 to early 1990). He described his approach as 'learning-by doing'.

[115] Rede integrada de transporte.

Walking and Cycling

Car based movement is pure circulation and basing cities around cars is not conducive to social interaction. In fact, driving is the antithesis of social activity. By their need for dedicated 'movement space', cars take away any role highways may have had before for social space. Health experts have also noticed the correlation between car-dominated environments and the secondary impacts on health. Industrial cities were associated with obvious health problems of disease and pollution. Inhabitants of post-industrial cities suffer from cancer and obesity due to reduced exercise, resulting from car dependency. So there is now encouragement for 'healthy towns' to embody the benefits of walking, physical exercise and socialisation. Options include, fast food-free zones near schools, designing safe and appealing green spaces and creating dementia-friendly streets (NHS, 2016).

The principles behind Soviet era micro-districts were for all services to be accessible on foot. As such, they were closed to through traffic. Only emergency vehicles, delivery vehicles and residents with cars could travel in them. In the Modern West, it has been campaigners and local initiatives that have sought to re-establish alternative modes of transport. An example, is Danish architect, Jan Gegl's Stroget Car Free Zone in Copenhagen. Urban design seeks to maximise social interaction, no matter how old fashioned this may appear in the *Zwischenstadten* age. People will walk if there is something to walk to. The most important walking destinations are the corner store and transit stop. Pedestrian journeys are rarely single purpose. Optional activities are the by-product of movement.

Given the changes to urban density and current planning outcomes being sought, it's not always easy to set up the micro-district. Generally, it's pedestrian orientated cities that are easiest to return to pre-industrial city centre walking patterns. With careful design, it's possible to ensure that origin destination trips take place past outward facing buildings blocks. This maximises by-product effects and provides a mechanism for generating contact (Jones, P., Hillier, D., & Comfort, D. (2004).

Since the 1970s, new approaches have resulted in refocusing on where development should go to reduce the need to travel and the demand for road transport. The more recent climate change agenda reinforces this trend. Where walking significant distances is impractical, cycling can take up the shortfall. Cycling is often viewed as a second-class form of transportation in England and America, in contrast to The Continent. Whereas cars isolate people, bicycles integrate people socially. Cycle way paths are embedded in Third World cities such as Bogota.

In the UK, there has been greater flexibility set in highway standards.[116] The key urban design principles of permeability, legibility, vitality, variety and adaptability are now firmly embedded in planning and design theory. The emphasis is shifting towards more connected places favouring walking, cycling and public transport. Government policy now favours mixed use, rather than single use areas. Making cycling more attractive is a sound policy but in itself it won't necessarily change the behaviours of drivers. There is also a need to combine such an approach with another that cuts the numbers of vehicles entering a city. London has done this by carrying out its congestion charging zone policy.

2.0 Landuse Control: Past, Present and Future

The success of advocates, such as Edward Bassett, meant that the setting of Euclidean style, single-use zoning, expanded rapidly in the 1920s (Talen, 2012). This represented the substitution of zoning for planning, meaning that United States municipalities could ignore future planning needs. They did not have to consider future residents, just undesirable land uses (Cullingworth and Caves, 2003).

So long as there was access between different business and residential areas, no further thought was given to co-ordinate land use and transportation. The interrelationship between 'work, home and market' was not a key concern. This resulted in 'friction' between people getting from one zone to the next. That is to work, shop, visit family, friends or colleagues. As such, the efficiency that was otherwise achieved was not as great. Worse still, the hardships were imposed on the poor, as there was no need to locate good jobs close to affordable housing.

In theory, the sub-optimal outcome of poor transport linkages between different uses need not arise. Japanese architect, Kurokawa's Wall City proposal of the late 1950s both strictly separated land use and minimised transport. This concept was for the erection of a sinuous wall across the countryside. Living space would be accommodated on one side and working space directly across on the other (Graham, 2016).

---

[116] First with DB32, then with People, Places and Movement and more recently with the Manual for Streets.

Zoning protected the amenity of residents. A key measure was minimum lot size. Yet it resulted in more land being taken up by city urbanisation than was necessary. In fact, if restrictions were strong enough then places lost population, as wealthier, smaller families replaced poorer, larger ones. For neo-liberals this of course appeared deeply ironic. It was zoning itself that causes urban sprawl and the loss of agricultural land which started the debate on urban size and limits that goes on to this day. It is worth noting that zoning served a need at the time. The 'lack of the regulation was creating disinvestment and waste on a large scale' in the city centre. Zoning encouraged residents who might otherwise have moved out to the city outskirts to stay.

This modernist paradigm of separating land uses was also copied in Soviet era city planning (Engel, 2007). In the case of the linear city, it was to consist of a series of functionally specialised parallel sectors discussed earlier. Some of the idiosyncrasies can be explained by the ideology of the time. Milyutin put enterprises of production and schools in the same band. The was justified from his reading of Engels' statement that 'education and labour must be united.'

The mindset of having uses neatly separated continued until quite recently in Western planning schools. Even with the shift in academia, functional zoning will probably stay entrenched in practice. This is for a multitude of factors. They include the preference for zoning by social institutions, financial and political conservatism, market segmentation, product differentiation, discrimination, industry specialisation, (management) incompatibility or security (costs of multiple users), different leasing periods reducing liquidity (investment) and protection of property prices.

Areas of Production

The amount of land needed for production in any given location comes down to the nature of the economy. In a centrally planned economy, all land conceived of as necessary for economic functions would be allocated or zoned for that purpose. In other words, central planning strives for national self-sufficiency in production.

Economists in the West follow the theory of comparative advantage. This suggests that it's better for a country or locality to specialise (David Ricardo). The forces of globalisation drive this anyway. As a result, the areas of production 'wax and wane' due to business competition and the whims of the financial markets. The original need – to separate noxious industries from housing – has largely gone in the West. It is as much to do with the demise of many forms of hidden work, as a result of labour legislation. Today's business parks are instead as much a home to hotels, gyms and warehousing as they are to industry. I have previously noted the importance of the secondary sector to a country. As such, I feel there is still a need for plots of land in the UK both to accommodate factories and also to allow for the owner to 'grow the facilities.' That is if the opportunities arise.

I accept that change is not going to happen overnight. Much of the challenge for the planning system is in protecting the ongoing functioning of industry and 'noxious uses.' They are threatened by authorities who are acting on behalf of the complaints of nearby residents. This is the issue of 'reverse sensitivity.' It's where separate sensitive uses encroach upon primary and secondary land uses. Political pressure is exerted for tougher environmental standards that curtail or shut industry down. It is again an issue resulting from increased transport options and ownership flexibility. In the past, factory workers would live next to their place of work. Now 'out of towners' move in without any loyalty to the factory in their midst.

Planning for office buildings is far easier than factories. Factories are based around their machinery. Offices are about creating large enough floor spaces dedicated to people working at desks. Commercial letting is about finding the right sized building to allow the efficient running of organisational structures.

In the age of large, hierarchical companies it made sense to provide for corporate offices. The need for such large-scale offices has declined in the 'internet age,' with the 'virtual office' and outsourcing. There has been a shift from structured office working patterns to flexi-working, dressing down and other related changes. The distinction between work and the home has blurred. So too has the distinction between separate office environments and residential uses. Office work used to be done in homes and coffee shops. Today these same places serve the same purpose. That is alongside book shops, libraries, publicly accessible lobbies and shared bookable offices.

The trend may have its limits. Modern firms believe the unrestricted communication of open plan offices cannot be achieved by workers based in their homes. Offices give social cohesion. Clients and suppliers still need to come together at times. People are said to buy the messenger before they buy the product. Ironically, leading technology firms, such as 'Google' have cracked down on their 'working from home' policies. They are promoting more home like environments in the office instead. As such, the commute and the need for integrated transport networks seems set to stay.

The UK Government's recent switch to a more permissive regime, for allowing office space to be converted to housing was one of the measures to address the housing crisis. Overnight this created a significant windfall for office block owners, who readily switched to building new homes due to their better resale value. England lost more than six million square feet of office space in 2014. This was a result of a government policy intended to boost the supply of new housing. Research for the British Council for Offices found that relaxed planning rules were making it easier for developers to convert empty offices into homes. This was leading to a shortage of offices. The changes to these rules were intended to be temporary and 'kick-start' the housing sector. However, the Government have indicated they may make the rules permanent (FT p4 9/9/2015).

Retail

The amount of land needed for production is difficult to estimate. For a sector where there is no value and surplus value being produced it is even harder. In many traditional communities and slums there is no separation of retail from other uses. In Naples, Italy, for instance, some shop owners serving their neighbourhood continue to live in their (tiny) shop. Owner occupation has great potential to bring with it better management.

There is still some latitude to separate retail from other uses. This applies even in the modern context of promoting mixed land uses. A shop for the sale of hot food in a residential area might be controlled through the planning system for amenity reasons. This can allow the potential for odours and other amenity impacts to be considered irrespective of other processes. These include statutory nuisance controls (Moore & Purdue, 2012).

The main rationale for separating retail from other uses is perhaps not their use but their scale. The coming of age of large modern supermarkets has a large amount to do with the relative freedom of market mechanisms. In contrast, under French law nothing can be sold for less than it cost the farmer to make it. This means that small shops can't be undercut by supermarkets running loss-lender products.

Shops enjoy locations with the maximum probability of random visitors passing by. This is typically at street level along busy thoroughfares in town centres. Town centres are the one location where the greatest variety of different services are to be found together. These include professionals, retail, banking and others. Town centres are for efficiency and the convenience of walking. In the UK they evolved organically through the decades without necessarily adapting to the changing consumer. Now there is a shift from retail to leisure style activities. There remains a need for diversity of choice on our high streets. When a High Street has too much of one retail use, it tips the balance of the location and inevitably puts off potential retailers and investors. Unlike malls, high street competitors often suffer from little or no management. Those town centre managers typically have varying powers and responsibilities. Often they lack retail and consumer knowledge. Into this vacuum, local authorities must respond. The early 2000s was the golden age of consumption and 'out of town' roofed malls. UK examples included Bluewater (Kent), Lakeside (Thurrock) and the Trafford Centre, Manchester. These were located on dictated new greenfield locations. Able to achieve economies of scale, they became magnets in their own right.

Out-of-town centres provided clean and attractive destinations, cheap parking, a healthy retail mix, things to do and the right marketing to get them there in the first place. Created by large corporations to serve our pleasure and use, they are also intended to manipulate us for profit. In this, they are highly managed, with any form of distraction being kept outside. All the rules are set by a single set of owners and the internal uses are in effect zoned, creating distinctive social and functional worlds. These 'pod' developments have each use conceived of as a separate element. They include shopping mall, fast-food outlet, office park, apartments, hotel and housing clusters. These are surrounded by associated parking and usually their own access onto a collector or main distributor road. They also create a new social space. Even in Houston, people can discover the benefits of people in density at the 'edge of town' mall of Galleria.

Of concern is whether they are private takeovers of parts of the city for entertainment and shopping. They neglect the use of public space for the needs of citizenship. Shopping centres deliver what the customer wants. That is safe, clean and orderly places imposed through agreements, contracts and private surveillance. This is in contrast to the frustrations associated with management of High Street shopping areas contributed to by the declining public sector (Minton 2012).

Large stores continue to represent a threat to the High Street. A planning system that favours high streets and restricts larger store formats also gives greater equality. It favours small business over large units. There are new signs of how far the scale of shopping centres will increase. The increasing attraction of on-line shopping is affecting retailers generally. One trend is for shops to become entertainment centres and concept stores. These attempt to add something over and above online shopping, without needing the stock levels held before. For out of town malls, the scale produced earlier this century may never be repeated. The function of town centres may also change. The Danish architect and professor, Jan Gehl, has seen a trend for people to travel into Copenhagen. Their focus is to stroll around and meet up with friends. Perhaps if they feel like it they may undertake some shopping.

Mixed Uses

Traditional neighbourhoods provide for an array of lifestyles. Suburbia only has one choice and that is to own a car and use it for all travel (Duany et al 2000 pg 25). In modern cities, advocates for mixed uses contend that traditional forms offer more choice. Residents are more likely to be within walking distance of stores or can even live above the store they own.

New urbanists have gone for what Montgomery (2013) describes as form code. This is a set of rules that prescribes the shape of spaces and buildings without necessarily dictating what can happen there. It's more a recognition that the form of work in the West has changed. Under the past philosophy certain uses were excluded. The logic is now inverted to the advantages accrued from mixed, integrated uses. There are synergies, or opportunities, to be gained with the clustering of businesses together, such as education and research facilities. Locating public buildings and institutions in key locations can amount to a form of state sector subsidisation. This potential benefit from public sector planning allows for the allocation of scarce resources in a rational and profitable manner. It thus increases the productivity of the 'private sector' (Pahl, 1977).

There are still situations when its best for businesses to be located away from residences based on the potential for conflict. These include hours of operation, parking, deliveries and impact on residential cohesion if no one is residing there. Another amenity issue is the need to manage signage.

The biggest issue remains that of noise. Noise generating activities include cafes, bars, night-clubs and amplified music. Often it's the social and cognitive context in which noise occurs that decides whether it's intrusive, rather than the physical environment. Such psychic costs are the major source of noise-induced problems. Continued exposure to background noise can lead to raised blood pressure, heart rates and stress in children (Evans et al, 2001). Noise generating activities need to be kept separate, or at least on strict operational hours, to protect noise sensitive uses like housing. Often the solution is to have buffer areas, even if it is only separation of streets, highways or sound-proof fencing. When land is set aside to achieve adequate separation distances, it may be mixed with landscaping, mounding.

Planning for utilities

Modern utility networks go hand in hand with technical progress. Western cities are usually associated with consistently high standards of infrastructural provision and management around all basic services. In the Third World, even where modern goods and products are consumed, provision is often unsatisfactory. Solid waste management has proven difficult in the favelas and informal settlements of Latin American and Caribbean countries. Infrastructural and topographic irregularities usually impede, or make efficient refuse collection difficult. This inefficiency begets improper and unhealthy waste disposal, but it also creates opportunities for unskilled labourers.

In the West, the philosophy around the provision of basic infrastructure is often changing to meet higher environmental standards or sustainability considerations. This can be led by the planning system through both national and local impetus. In the case of solid waste, there is a shift from facility provision to improved resource efficiency. This includes the phasing out of traditional landfills. The goal is to keep products and resources in use for as long as possible. It can be achieved through recovery, reuse, repair, remanufacturing and recycling. What is sought is to match the higher levels for reuse and recycling of waste materials seen in Third World countries, without the unhealthy side effects of intensive labour scavenging. Developing a more circular economy in the UK could create 200,000 jobs. It would also contribute to improving Britain's labour market situation. Research shows that improving resource efficiency can make a 'valuable contribution' to improving Britain's labour market situation (Morgan & Mitchell, 2015).

As with transport management, a 'supply on demand' approach has been introduced to meet the demand for energy and water. A shift is sought from centralised schemes to decentralised energy and localised water supply and treatment. Urban street cables, power lines, heat pumps, telecommunication utilities (mobile towers) and power boxes have traditionally been permitted in most cases, as of right. The standards have been set by national utility providers. In some cases, they have a perceived impact on health, but more often it is their impact on amenity that is the concern. It isn't efficient for network providers to have to address such concerns on a case by case basis across the whole country. Some form of national policy is desirable.

The most common, large structures to be erected within the rural landscape are those of pylons and latterly wind turbines. Both sets of structures can compromise not only landscape values but also spiritual qualities. These include the views that empty horizons can evoke such as knowing one's own insignificance and the like. It was Amercian naturalist writers of the late 19th Century who described the 'unspoiled natural world as a way to spiritual truth.' In the UK, planners insisted that new 150ft tall pylons be more attractive than Russian or American designs. Sir Reginald Blomfield was brought into design the 1927 pylons. His gradually narrowing, steel lattice pylons were narrower at top than the bottom. They were supposed to evoke the shape of the Egyptian gateway to the sun.

With infrastructure it is most efficient to have structures using the lightest possible frames. For bridges, this implies that the design should stretch over the widest span, at the lowest cost. In prime locations, the design of major bridges has caused fierce aesthetical debates. Examples include Sydney Harbour and San Francisco. Recently there has been significant public discussion about the symbolic pedestrian Garden Bridge project for the Thames River in London. Any bridge is intrinsically set against nature to begin with. The Garden Bridge is deliberately intended to represent this contradiction, at considerable expense. Its promoters see it as showcasing the ability of London to maintain natural features, trees and the like, in an entirely unnatural setting. See also the section: 'Greening the City'.

Ideally, energy and water planning should become integrated into urban design and planning. Too often it is the context within which such development fits. It is recognised that a low energy, urban society is concentrated with higher densities. In contrast a high-energy urban society is dispersed. Full integration of the energy sector in the UK would mean planning for the National Grid would be integrated into the planning process. This would mean that energy planning would happen in parallel with new housing, employment and retail development.

Ports, Airports and Energy Generation

There are many planning issues for utilities that are a necessity for national and regional economic development. Port and airport companies have a vested interest in seeking the ongoing efficient operation of the physical resource they operate. That is, to retain competitiveness by providing for the choices sought by consumers.

The rural land around airports has become popular for country living. The waterfront location of ports has made the land around them popular for coastal living (see below). These areas are prone to gentrification and issues about reverse sensitivity. Port facilities in many Western cities have fallen victim to higher value uses, for example, housing. It's not so much that the level, intensity or 'environmental' impact has worsened over time. Rather, it is a changed relationship between the past residents and the new residents that drive these new tensions. The former was associated with port labour. The latter have no association with the port activities.

There may be significant benefits from locating power generation facilities, such as coal and nuclear, in sparsely populated areas. This depends upon the level of technological risk. Yet unlike in the recent past, there are now new constraints to be considered in these places such as wildlife and scenery. Urban containment helps to maintain low population densities outside of urban centres. This plays a role in containing the threats posed by hazards. The Lake District National Park, famous for its tourism, came into being before the Sellafield nuclear power plant. It may in the future become the national site for the long term disposal of high-level radioactive wastes. There is a certain perversity if this was to happen. If there was a major event at the power station, it would degrade the values and reason for the national park's existence.

There are no easy answers, in the post-modern paradigm. The best that can be achieved is to minimise the numbers of residents living near such facilities. Where this is not possible, it is up to the local authority to thrash out some political or technical 'agreement' with local community groups. This would minimise tensions between their amenity and the national interest. It is difficult to be prescriptive as each situation is unique. There may be different operational rules to consider. Also, the potential for adaptation may vary. Examples could include quieter technologies, noise standards and hours of operation.

3.0 Managing Open Space

The means to separate different and incompatible land uses is a reason to have open spaces. The work of Stiibben and Baumeister, in 19th Century Germany, looked at how the health needs of urban residents could be maintained. Their conclusions were to lower urban densities, increase air flow, lay sewer and water lines and provide park land (my emphasis added). The net effect of the work of these 'regularists' would substantially change the organically-derived romantic character of the mediaeval city. It became the rational, orthogonal layout, typical of modern cities. There is a balance to be struck between efficiency, convenience and space. The challenge is in finding ways of organising activities which are functionally efficient, convenient to all involved and aesthetically pleasing as well (Healey 2006).

It wasn't long after, that rising wealth inspired advocates for civic amenity to demand change. This was in the form of the beautification movement. Trees give a contrast (a foil) with hard urban landscapes. The soft form, built up through the imagery of trees and other natural phenomena, might serve the cause of social stability (E. Howard). How they should be planted within formal open spaces is more of a cultural debate. The siting of trees can be as regimented as physical structures as in classical French design. Alternatively, it can be grouped in parks as in the English design. Naturalised settlement implies an absence of geometrical neatness in layout and architecture, whilst a row of trees represents geometry.

Open spaces can be used for many urban activities. Yet by definition they are less versatile and dependent upon the weather and season. In the modern world, one might expect less 'open space' in urban environments as the capacity to enclose space increases. Yet the trend has gone from buildings that define and enclose space (pre-industrial), to buildings as objects in space (industrial). In traditional urban environments, large buildings with little to contribute by way of interaction with surrounding uses were embedded in the urban fabric. These include law courts, churches and theatres. Now they often stand alone. Open space wastage has increased, in the sense that open spaces created are less useful than they were in the past.

Cities have always had the city square or piazza as outdoor living rooms. Parks and gardens have different qualities. They can both give welcome relief from the sensual overload of city streets and act as a backdrop for recreation and relaxation. Many are iconic, such as Olmsted's Central Park in New York. Cities can be compared by how much parkland they possess. The rebuilding of Shanghai has come about with no substantial parks having been built. Based on land area, Shanghai has 4% parkland while in contrast, London has 40%.

As a public resource, the use of parks and the segregation of activities within, is inevitably a matter of contention. The UK National Playing Fields Association thrived in the inter-war period. It recommended 6 acres of playing fields per thousand people. This has been widely used by local authorities as a basis when stipulating play area provision for new housing development, and in local plan policies. Needless to say, the use of such space, as with other public spaces, has not escaped the cultural debates inherent in the West. For instance, feminist groups have criticised the sports field as standing for a sort of sacred male space and sought reform.

The interface of urban uses with parks is generally seen as something to be actively allocated for. Jane Jacobs noted that what matters most about parks is what surrounds them. Provided the areas are well maintained, those residing close to them gain from higher property values. Higher residential density was preferable for Jacobs. Apartments could be sited without outdoor living space alongside parks. There is a need to make sure there is enough development density around parks so that the resource gets well used at different times of day.

Greening the City

The modern city symbolises the triumph and transformation of the built environment over the natural environment (Creswell, 2004). The inhabitants of Ancient Greece saw the natural world as dangerous. Their small settlements were surrounded by forests in contrast to the modern English equivalent. That is artificial countryside, without genuine wilderness. It was only when nature began to vanish from modern human life as direct experience that its rarity was appreciated. It first re-emerged as an idea in the arts, before in the end it returned to our cities.

The relationship of urban communities to the surrounding countryside is an important consideration even in advanced nations. The attractive qualities of Charles Perry's neighbourhood unit 'reflected nostalgia for rural living' (Allaire, 1960). In England, there is a propensity to talk about 'garden suburbs.' Depending upon your view there is a need to build many new garden cities to meet housing needs. There is a significant degree of irreversibility in the conversion of rural countryside to urban development. It's different with redevelopment within an existing urban environment on brown field land. David Rudlin[117] notes that greenfield development 'takes an area of virgin soil, covers it in concrete, builds a house or five hundred, and then, inch by inch, tries to recreate the beauty (gardens, apple trees, roses and birdlife) that was smothered.' Leafy suburbia is intended to make it hard to tell where the countryside ends and the town begins.

The ideal Dutch city of the 1920s makes a contrast to the garden city. It was thought best to create spacious green arteries within the urban fabric and not transfer residential areas into the green countryside (Wagenaar, 2011). The help of British town planners was sought in rebuilding cities in Belgium on garden city lines after the devastation of the First World War. Popular

---

[117] Winner of the Wolfson economic prize.

resistance put a stop to it.   The only exception was development on the outskirts of Ypres (Uyttenhove, 1990).

Stockholm County Council made sure that the most was made of its privileged geographic situation.   This was rarely found in the world's great capitals.   It allowed the adaptation of development to the geological and topological character of the region.   In geological terms, the city and the region are characterised by long troughs in the hollows of rock formations. The urban areas have been concentrated mostly in these depressions.   These form   long   axes   stretching   along   the   public   transit   infrastructure. Neighbourhoods are organised around train and metro stations, where services and homes are most densely concentrated.

The regional green network became an extension of the city.   The principles were set in the 1930s and adopted by neighbouring Swedish municipalities.   This form of urban organisation has left many open spaces, both natural and developed.   It is these spaces that make up the regional green network.   None of this huge network belongs to the Stockholm County Council.   It is made up of State and Crown lands, including the gardens surrounding the castles.   There is also municipal and private lands, mainly farms and forests (Ducas, 2000).

Elsewhere after the Second World War, a new consciousness about protecting   naturalness   emerged   from   the   environmental   movement. Advocates, such as Ian McHarg, sought to 'Design with Nature' (as titled in his book).   This placed an emphasis on designing to maintain the integrity of natural ecology.   It improves amenity.   Unlike parks though, green space is more about tranquillity, inspiration and allowing room for natural processes to operate.   It does not rely on hard infrastructure.   There are health benefits associated with green spaces.   These include quicker recovery times for patients in a hospital having a green space full of trees compared to those with a view of a brick wall.

Reducing impermeable surfaces reduces the 'heat island effect' associated with an overuse of asphalt.   Working within natural thresholds can protect the natural hydrology if no more than 30% of a catchment is urbanised.   By doing so it avoids higher and unnatural runoff levels.   It also allows natural watercourses to be maintained.   These principles are being integrated into some planning systems, including the UK, in the form of sustainable urban drainage systems.

No one builds cities for environmental reasons alone.   There is a tension in replacing the grid's pipes with more expansive natural systems.   McHarg's writings were a precursor to the wider sustainability agenda.   At the time his style led to confrontation with advocates of 'progress.' Commentators have noted that the outcomes from environmental legislative needs for designations and buffers around 'protected areas' can seriously impact developable land and thus urban pattern. These include the United States Clean Water Act and Endangered Species Act. The protection of 'insignificant' pieces of wetland can have significant consequences for built form. Developers criticise current wetland rules by noting that if they had been in place from the beginning, they would have prevented cities from ever having been built (Slone & Goldstein, 2008). Greening the city or bringing the countryside (or at least an idyllic version of it) to an urban population results in an associated cost. This generally includes reduced urban densities and space taken away from development. One can argue that it's not essential for additional green space to be created. Vertical walls and roof top gardens can achieve 'green' gain without displacing urban use. Yet they are relatively more expensive to build and maintain.

McHarg's legacy lives on in experimental projects such as the Iporanga 'tree house' in Sao Paulo. This three storey tall structure is tightly nestled into the forest, with the trees all but scraping the windows. Though much of the home is made of steel, glass and concrete, it never feels out of place. This is thanks to the way in which outside foliage plays a central role in the design scheme.

In the era of sustainability, various writers have sought to resolve the dilemma between cities and the environment. They have argued that cities based 'on the grid' can better absorb the affects of more people. As a city doubles in size there is the scaling of efficiencies. The secret of creating an environmentally sustainable society is making our cities bigger. Inner city dwellers take up less space due to residential high rises effectively 'stacking them'. Also, urban residents can make more informed environmental decisions from the accumulated information captured by embedded sensors which track movements, pollution or energy use.

In stark contrast to McHarg, Lomborg notes that if people become richer they live in cities and do not impinge on nature so much. In a nutshell, his view is that 'if you have unrestricted poverty, then people will slash and burn to feed their kids. If you are rich, however, you go and become a web designer in the city.' Lomborg believes that modern industrial production is one of the main ways to reduce our footprint. So by this measure, the increasing rate of urbanisation in China and India is a good thing. Their inhabitants will consume less energy than they otherwise would, had they remained in rural areas or in smaller cities.

While many countries have chosen sustainability as an overarching goal, it is not inevitable. In Russia, the planning system still focuses on nature protection rather than sustainability. New Zealand chose to embody the biophysical environment in its aim for sustainable management. It just didn't encompass social or economic matters (Ryser & Franchini, 2015). Also, the inadequacy of traditional 'environmental sinks' (i.e., dumping grounds) can be acknowledged without embracing sustainability.

Retrofitting is more expensive than protecting natural areas. Yet natural areas with much lower states of dynamic equilibrium than equivalent ones elsewhere are often protected. For example, there's a marked difference between the biodiversity of England's countryside compared to South American rainforest. The former receives more protection. This reflects different values. It also reflects the different context for the regime administrating environmental protection. There is a balancing act needed between the regulatory 'burden' placed on different areas. Swaths of higher value (more natural) sites may receive disproportionately less protection than small sites with comparably little ecological value. The latter may happen to be relatively rare for their local area.

One mechanism to address this is 'biodiversity offsetting' once options to (1) avoid, (2) remedy and (3) mitigate the on site impacts have been exhausted. The goal is to make sure that a development results in no net loss. This is calculated by assessing the development's residual environmental impact on habitat. Biodiversity gain is given on another piece of land along with its long term management plan. Damage is decoupled in space and time from compensation. Arable land for sustainable housing is not forced to produce a poor quality nature reserve. Development funds released are spent on land with greater wildlife potential.

Another aspect of urban greening is urban agriculture; from allotment gardens to urban farms. Maintaining the agricultural surplus in land around settlements first allowed cities to develop. Most of this land is 'shut off' by the nature of land ownership and intensive modern farming practices. This started when the English agricultural economy turned industrial. Since then common land and small holdings were enclosed for commercial agriculture and direct family connection with food producing land broke down. This was partly due to the competitive nature of agriculture and the influence exerted by retail giants to keep food prices down. In other countries, there has been an even greater transition to industrial agriculture. The United States leads the way. It grows Genetically Modified (GM) crops on huge green chequerboard and geometrical fields. Almost no country is fully internalising the full environmental costs of its food production.

The increasing role of urban farming is reflective of decreased numbers of rural inhabitants making a living off the land. Urban farming is unlikely to ever replace the need for farming in rural areas but globally it has a lot of momentum behind it (for example Cuba, see Altieri, 1999). Urban agriculture is estimated to produce 15 to 20 per cent of the world's food supply and could play a major role in achieving global food security. Interestingly, it results from completely different circumstances.

In developed countries, urban agriculture plays only a minor role in improving the food security of an area. There's no incentive to farm the land around the private suburban house. Lack of available 'public' space and the absence of economic incentives also limits interest in the inner city. There are marked differences across the spectrum. In the United States, urban farming can be traced back to 1970s community gardens. Often it occurs in particularly volatile neighbourhoods. These have evolved to become a living network of small, dedicated groups. Many are pursuing some form of social utopia. Urban agriculture has become a means of converting private property—such as an abandoned lot— into a public domain.

Productive gardens do not need large parcels of land but management is important. The state can help the creation of these gardens by offering unused plots of land to groups for little or no money. In Germany and the UK, it is often local councils that give the land, set up a water system and eventually fence the area. The gardeners pay a small rent for the plot and have to attend to certain duties within an association.

Urban farming has the potential to bring communities together and alleviate some social needs. The main goal is to improve community integration and build on existing informal social capital. These gardens could help make sure that basic nutritional needs are met and possibly give extra income for those most in need in the community.

Elsewhere, such as in Havana, Buenos Aires and many other developing cities, urban agricultural production is not just a trend. It makes up a large part of the total food supply. It is a crucial part of the economy and a basic means of survival. Production and security of urban crops in developing countries is limited. This is because of both the illegality of urban farming and the effects of pollution, which cut crop yields. Future production levels and the security of urban agriculture are uncertain. This is due to the encroachment of urban sprawl onto farm lands (Corbould, 2013).

The Purpose of the Countryside

Measures to address the supply problems experienced during the Second World War were embedded in the 1947 UK planning system. In particular, versatile soils were protected from urban encroachment. Despite the potential for more intensive forms of agriculture, Britain still only produces around 60% of its food needs.

The importance of self-sufficiency in national agricultural production has been debated by commentators. Lomborg argued that the 'Malthusian' view, which the Earth Policy Institute subscribes, is outdated. New technologies allow humans to produce food from less land. The population can thus grow food without further harming wildlife. As the memories of the Second World War fade, the weight given to versatile soils under the planning system has been downgraded.

Neo-liberals have long argued that countries with a comparative advantage in agriculture should specialise in that sector. If they need, for instance, high-technology 'widgets' then these things can always be imported from developed countries. In their view attempts to achieve self-sufficiency are a misallocation of resources. It makes other industries less competitive and reduces overall welfare.

The reality is that 'developing' countries, whose economies are based on agriculture, have lagged behind developed countries. In the long run this has resulted in a polarisation of wealth. Worse still, the global market system forces many economically weak countries to concentrate on cash crops. These include coffee and cotton. Such products are useless to those in their communities who are starving. In the Third World, people have been pushed from rural areas, as farming and agriculture have failed to offer viable economic livelihoods. Aid programmes, aimed at rural areas, have been ineffective. As described earlier, this has significantly added to the amount of urbanisation in the Third World.

Many industrialised countries produce food surpluses because of protectionist agricultural policies. This includes the EU. In the UK, such policies have mainly been intended to preserve rural food production as a strategic priority. On the Continent, there have been concerted efforts to retain 'people on the land.' Peasant smallholdings have been retained to a far greater degree than in the UK. For these holders it meant they could eat straight from the land, providing not only fresh food but also a social basis to keep a rural culture. On the Continent, a lot of these measures worked because of state subsidies.

Of all countries, the Chinese, through their Hukou system strived hardest to keep rural workers in the countryside. By restricting the potential for mass migration from the land to the cities it avoided large slum areas developing. It was also justified to ensure structural stability. By regulating labour, it made sure that there was an adequate supply of low cost workers to state owned businesses. It also allowed the state to give preferential treatment to industrial workers and intelligentsia. They were more likely to protest and even revolt during periods of unrest. It wasn't until the 1990s that the Chinese government finally accepted that it was impossible to have industrialisation without urbanisation. In doing so it abandoned its policy of 'leaving the land but not the villages; entering the factories but not cities.'

The function of the countryside, and its traditional association with food production, has declined in the West. Barriers between town and country have been broken down changing its meaning. This has been attributed to the depopulation of the countryside, coupled with mass mobility through use of the private motor vehicle. In 1900, it may have been substantially correct to equate 'rural' with 'agriculture' in the UK. Today 'rural' may signify habitation at low densities, but no longer does it signify a particular way of life, centred on farming.

There still remains a belief in the connection of rural land with certain types of crop varieties and animals. Nature and surprise were alien concepts on The Continent. The English preference was for natural, wild, romantic settings and the avoidance of straight lines (Joseph Addison, 1711). The Picturesque movement,[118] was followed by Coleridge, Keats, Shelley and Romantic Poets all extolling the English countryside.

Landscapes are illusory and often they are erroneously regarded as being independent of human use. In America, food production and scenic beauty are different things. This is not so in England, where the countryside gives a deeper source of identity (it is no coincidence that their economy is not as dependent). In Australia and New Zealand, the approach is somewhat in between. Both these economies are heavily dependent on maximising rural production. Rural idealisation happens less often in countries that stay essentially rural. They are places for working farms not leisure activities.

In a similar way that there has been a move to the countryside, or at least the garden city concept, there has also been parallel moves to coastal areas. Scarborough was the first seaside town in England. It came about from the late 17th Century ideas[119] on the health giving properties of the sea. The

---

[118] Movement followers, such as William Gilpin (1770s), had a passion for ruins and unmanicured nature.
[119] For example, Dr Witte's 1660s Scarborough Spa.

Victorians clearly thought living by the coast could bring benefits to their health. Access to the countryside was the reside of the wealthy. The beach huts and promenades built at beautiful locations along the UK coastline were intended for the middle classes. Even today, the latest census data reveals that people living near the sea are happier than those inland. Explanations for this include the practical, such as the sea giving us both a source of food and access to trade. There are also more controversial theories, such as the aquatic ape hypothesis. Strong cultural associations may also be at play in improving our sense of wellbeing. This includes the mental and physical health effects of looking at 'blue' or watery environments (Stewart, 2013).

Given the prevailing trend for urbanisation some thought has been given as to how the countryside might be integrated with the city. One such proposal was the 'agricultural city' designed by Kurokawa in 1959. It proposed 'mushroom houses.' These would sprout above farm fields on pilings supported by a massive grid structure. This would have left the surrounding ground clear for crops (Graham, 2016). Interestingly, Kurokawa's earlier idea of a linear city has also been re-invented as a means to give residents easy access to greenspace for urban food production. This is referred to as the Linear Ecocity (Gyr, 2010).

In Anglo-American countries, within the last two decades, there has been a small countertrend of relatively wealthy people moving to both the countryside and coastal areas. The greater the numbers, the more this trend undermines the values of those already living there. The effect of reverse sensitivity on port areas was discussed earlier. Firstly, the landscape is changed through the introduction of new dwellings. Secondly, people moving there for leisure also have different perspectives to those who depend on the countryside for their livelihood. They are not willing to endure as much congestion, noise and light pollution from economic activities as those who live and work there.

Landscapes are a type of cultural resource, but one that will be undermined as soon as its appropriated for cultural ends. The more marketable such items become, the less unique and special they end up. So wild or aesthetically desirable places succumb in much the same way as inner city, gentrified areas. The more value accrued to a protected place, the greater the pressure that's applied for tighter planning controls. Many people may wish to live in the countryside, but they can't do so without first transforming it into something nobody wants.

The purpose of countryside around cities is a very twenty-first century question for advanced economies. It remains pertinent given the economic logic to expand onto greenfield land and the irreversibility of this process. In urban growth scenarios, the logic of capital, demands more land supply. Land ownership decides whether there is take up or not. The cashing in of the land 'asset' replaces a constant, perpetual, ongoing source of revenue from agriculture with a single payment or benefit. The former may be attractive to the site developer, but less so to farmers. They see their business as a way of life, thus taking a longer term view. Most farmers have a deep-seated concern for the land which prevents them from seeing it strictly as a commodity.

Differences between urban and rural populations are represented in politics and the media. The media is dominated by an urban cultural bias. Even when rural issues are reported, the focus is often upon environmental issues, rather than agricultural food production. American Presidential elections show a marked urban and rural split in power bases between the two main parties. The Democrats tend to hold power over urban areas while the Republicans have greatest sway in rural areas. The urban population typically comes off best. Indeed, most political bases and ideologies, both on the left and right, have emerged from urban settings. Regardless of whether it's seen as positive or negative, urban elites tend to impose their will on rural communities. The imposition of measures includes environmental controls (for example, pesticide use), planning controls (on what can get built) and cultural controls (for example, the English fox hunt ban). Another example of the latter is the Nordic concept of Allemanstratten. It gives the public the 'freedom to roam' across the countryside. By law, all natural areas are considered public space for recreation so long as no damage or pollution is caused (Ryser & Franchini (ed) 2015).

Rural Planning

Planning for the rural environment is tied to the politics of cities. Unsurprisingly, the encroachment of buildings and structures are to be avoided in favour of the following:

- Agricultural production;
- Maintaining other open space values;
- Containing the growth of cities; or
- Preserving the size of existing villages and settlements.

All the above can fall under the category of protecting the countryside for its own sake. This shouldn't be regarded as merely anti-development but intended to complement the needs of urban life. Britain has personified the role of planning in the protection of the countryside. The aim of the 1947 Act,[120] seems to have been the preservation of a traditional way of life and a traditional economy 'whatever the cost.' (refer to Hall et al., 1973).

Alan Evans (1988) wryly commented on the paradoxical attitude of the British middle classes. 'Those who travel outside Britain do not seem to think that the landscapes of Tuscany, Umbria, Brittany or the Loire Valley have been irretrievably ruined by piecemeal development. On the contrary, they seem to be pleased that villas exist which are relatively cheap and which allow them to live in rural surroundings.'

There will always be those who find cities distasteful or disagreeable and so seek to leave them. Historically, the wealthy fled Mediterranean cities in summer to reside in country villas thus creating a two house system. Even within the same class, different cultures behaved differently. Continental aristocracy sought an urban court. In England, the country estates remained central and power diffused into the regions. For the cosmopolitian classes there is a cycle of new wealthy workers in the city moving back to the countryside. This contrasts to the slum dwellers that Turner was describing. The question is whether policies should help certain groups to move to the countryside. It is preferable, in setting rural policy, to encourage people to stay on the land in the first place.

Rural planning policies that protect the countryside for its own sake will always face pressure in the form of 'heated' urban land values and attempts to circumvent the system. Any developments allowed over time give justification for further departures from the original purpose of the restriction. For instance, the openness of a site may be able to accommodate the transparency of a glasshouse. Then, in turn, this may later justify a shed. Over time, an activity done in the open justifies a more permanent structure for example, for security or management reasons. In other systems, for example, New Zealand, a 'permitted baseline' must be considered which is used to justify further development. If one can erect a hedge or fence for screening, as of right then what further harm is there in erecting a low profile building behind it?

There is a degree of balance. Rural farm practices may need new structures. The preservation of open views is considered a private interest that the law is not intended to protect. The strictest examples of controlled localities are typically 'national parks' designations. These apply to landscapes that resonate in the national psyche, even by those who may never visit. These 'freeze' further development and management of the landscape to

---

[120] The approach was developed by the wartime Scott Committee.

a particular stage of progress or period. Any further change is seen as undesirable. It applies to new structures, or changes to existing ones, rather than to machinery that can be used. Hidden technologies like mobile towers or different agricultural uses, are generally acceptable. An exception would be a dramatic shift, such as between open landscape to forestry or woodland (or vice versa). Regulations that limit the competitiveness of farming operations can only be sustained if they add to their revenue. One means is through business activities that are related, such as tourism or state subsidies.

Containment of the City

The containment of towns and cities has traditionally related to the defence needs of the urban population. Infrastructure may have been as basic as the city walls themselves. Yet it was often inadequate to keep up with urban growth. This resulted in 'urban spill' beyond the old city into unwalled suburbs.

It is also possible to be so relaxed with zoning that it hardly places any greater restriction than if controls didn't exist at all. This occurred in the UK during the 1930s.[121] This approach could be regarded as pro-growth in the current housing crisis debate. Yet it resulted in all of the 'usual problems' associated with unplanned development. Capital for urban development is finite and urban expansion. Without direction from the public sector it results in an excess land supply. The private sector responds by attempting to exploit cheap land and existing public services in an inefficient manner. An example of this is 'ribbon development.' This is growth in the countryside along main highways. The effects of this were soon questioned starting a series of ad hoc legislative controls later in the 1930s that culminated in the 1947 Act.

The 1947 Act ended up placing controls on most forms of development beyond urban areas. This was the start of growth boundaries. Based on free-market ideology it amounts to 'supply restriction' using Brueckner's (2008) classification. The intention was to gain public benefits through restricting the uptake of land and channelling monies (both private and public) to where it can best deliver market demand. Trying to match demand and supply can be frustrated by land being taken up too quickly, wastefully or not being taken up at all. Co-ordinated decision making can also be hampered by political boundaries set up between the existing urban boundaries and the countryside.

---

[121] It was estimated in the Barlow report (1940: para 241), that in the half of the country covered by draft planning schemes in 1937 there was sufficient land zoned for housing to accommodate 291 million people.

Each authority typically stands for different community needs. This is essentially the accusation directed towards the semi-permanent boundaries of the English metropolitan greenbelt - now being blamed for the housing shortage.

Stanilov (2007) claims that for most cities under socialism, the focus by planners was placed on the periphery of the city. This is where residential high rises were concentrated. The 1993 Constitution of the post-Soviet Russian Federation set the boundaries for Moscow. Having reached its regional limits for growth, development had to turn inward, rather than continuing to expand outwardly, as was the strategy during the Soviet era. This drove up the cost of land within Moscow's official boundary (Makhrova and Molodikova, 2007). 'New Russians' (i.e. the nouveau riche) continued to expand outwards. They took over areas that used to hold dachas[122] and turned them into gated communities (Alden and Crow, 1998).

The original aims of London's greenbelt are for example, agricultural production and landscape protection. The current perceived issues over the use of this 'planning tool' reflect a failure within capitalism to disperse growth evenly across England, rather than failure of the mechanism itself. One might as well stifle London's ongoing growth,[123] as to try and set new industries within northern towns and cities. It exists for its own sake and to restrict urban uses, thereby promoting more intensive brownfield development. It doesn't necessarily achieve the goal of bringing the countryside to the city. The greenbelt is hardly within walking distance for most residents. Being a half hour train ride away doesn't bring trees into the average day of a commuter. Yet the alternative of having sprawling areas of low-density housing and potentially epic commutes is clearly undesirable as well. The almost sacrosanct nature of the greenbelt belies its cultural status. Not all of it is of scenic merit. Yet with so much of the rest of the country having been transformed by market forces, migration and ideological tinkering, the greenbelt remains a quintessentially English entity.

Islamic countries do not have the same rural / urban tradition of greenbelts. In contrast, the Ministry of Land and Resources (MLR) in China prepares land use plans mainly for the protection of agricultural land. They bear some similarity to zoning and the stopping of certain developments within specific boundaries. Yet control is achieved through a simple but effective mechanism of allocating a quota to local governments. The quota specifies the quantity of agricultural land that can be converted into the built-up areas.

---

[122] Simple recreational, detached housing,

[123] Cynics might well say that the greenbelt is ensuring just that.

The issue with London's greenbelt is that it is a fixed regulatory tool continuing to serve its purpose against a context of high population growth and increased societal mobility. It doesn't allow a more flexible approach to remove land from the greenbelt and replace it elsewhere. Removing one piece sets a precedent that could speed up the overall removal of the whole. This is especially so for authorities who find it easier to retain the whole than risk being seen to favour any one landowner over another. In England, garden cities are deemed the way forward. There's nothing inherently wrong with 'garden cities.' They are preferable in many ways to the creation of a sprawling urban conglomeration. Yet they must have access to effective public transport, retain sufficient density and balance between employment and residential uses. They are inevitably going to cater better for the middle classes, but that is the group best placed to endure the resulting travel costs.

There are two ways of looking at the same issue defined by the administrative context. If London's Mayor can't resolve growth problems, then the logical response would be to 'escalate' the matter to the next tier of authority. It is central government in this case. High tiers of authority have broader geographic remits. They will inevitably see the issue as being spatial in nature and therefore seek to apply spatial solutions. This might re-examine the cross-boundary administrative problems limiting supply. The greenbelt is an easy target. Yet if London was seen as a land-locked entity, or chose to see itself as such, it might approach its constraint problem differently. If it had enough powers of competency, it could look to apply the sorts of non-spatial mechanisms available to Hong Kong or Singapore, such as a land tax.

PART VII:
CRISIS PLANNING

1.0 Crisis, Natural Hazards, Disasters and Resilience

The need for an agricultural surplus around each settlement has been replaced by globalised food production and increased productivity. This is a result of the Green Revolution. Yet the super-efficiency of our increasingly 'just-in-time' food production system brings increased risk. This is from potential disruption resulting from the increased vulnerability to economic, social and environmental shocks across the globe.

Commentators have noted strong links between changing climate, environmental practices, ecosystem decline, the agricultural surplus and even societal collapse. The scientist and author Jared Diamond (2006) has been most alarmist about the latter. He has focused on the parallels between modern society and the collapse of the Roman and Mayan Empires. His theories have been backed up by subsequent research (Yuhas, 2015).

Both Roman and Mayan civilisations were hardest hit in their urban centres. The city of Rome was looted by invaders in the fifth century and half-abandoned. In the case of Mayan civilisation, cities in the Yucatan peninsula such as Tikal, ended up as abandoned ruins. This was sometime during the 8th or 9th Centuries. Both civilisations lingered on in simplified, 'mediaeval' forms. For Ancient Rome, the brunt of the environmental cost was borne in the Mediterranean basin. It's thought to have resulted in the shift of power to the more northern peripheral areas. These included the ethnic states of Goths, Franks and English.

Environmental decline is inevitably greater in the Third World where funding for high standards of infrastructure is notably less. With so many cities built around current sea levels, the issue of melting polar caps and rapidly changing sea levels has the potential to cause massive disruption. In parts of the Western World, the increased risk of flooding is putting strains on insurance companies. They are increasingly aware of increased local risks. So landowners are increasingly restricted from obtaining mortgages for new and existing houses in marginal land. Even in established urban centres, storm events are putting pressure on authorities to respond with bigger, better and more expensive solutions. An example, was Hurricane Sandy in New York, Nov 2012. Sea level rise may spur the need for the radical planning of settlements in the future.

For many cities, current water supplies are inadequate placing pressure on their local environment. Erkens (2014), identified regions of the globe where the abstraction of water is resulting in the ground water level falling 10 times faster than water levels are rising. In Jakarta, Indonesia's largest city, the population has grown from around half a million in the 1930s, to just under 10 million today. This heavily populated area is dropping by almost two metres, as groundwater is pumped up from the Earth to drink.

The same practice led to Tokyo's ground level falling by two meters. In Venice, commercial extraction compounded the effects of natural subsidence caused by long-term geological processes. Land subsidence, together with sea level rise, are both contributing to the same problem. That is larger and longer floods and greater inundation depths of floods.

The best solution is to simply stop pumping groundwater from local sources. This approach taken in Tokyo and Venice during the 1970s resulted in land subsidence more or less stopping. In other places, such as the Third World, finding an alternative source of (affordable) water remains a problem. It's a wicked problem. Cities have to be able to afford the technologies that avoid the need for unsustainable levels of abstraction in areas susceptible to subsidence.

In drier countries, climate change will be even more challenging. Arabic architecture has been associated with what is termed as bioclimatic urbanisation. That is naturally cooled without energy cost. It is achieved with the skilful use of climate-responsive courtyard houses and narrow, winding streets. Despite these benefits, events in recent years have severely affected several countries. The is the so called 'heat dome.' With temperatures soaring to well above 50 degrees Centigrade electricity and water supplies have been exacerbated. This has forced Officials to call public holidays.

Technology has made possible the go ahead for large, wealthy urban conurbations in 'inhospitable' places (as described in Part II). Increasing global temperatures are likely to make some areas unsustainable. Numerous Australian outback towns may disappear within 20 years due to climate change and the threat of bushfires. Tourists may have to avoid Spain and Italy in summer months. German researchers at the Max Planck Institute (reported 4 May 2016) suggest that prolonged heatwaves and desert sand storms could make some regions in the Middle East and North Africa uninhabitable. This would clearly contribute to migratory pressures in surrounding countries.

The history of whole nations and empires has been dramatically altered by natural hazards and disasters striking urban centres. This is due to the concentration of resources within, both human and physical, making them vulnerable to crisis. Natural hazard events can be biological in origin such as plague, or geophysical such as floods, earthquakes and volcanoes. They have devastated countless cities during the ages. Many people complain that England is over-crowded. As the sixth most densely populated major country in the world it has 401 people per square kilometre. Yet with forgiving weather (i.e., no extremes) and its distance from major tectonic plates, it's ideally placed as a centre of population.

Systematic collapse may sound alarmist but modern society often has high supply chain dependencies. This was shown during the 2011 floods in Thailand. The floods inundated the industrial estate factories of Japanese automobile manufacturers and Western Digital. Western Digital is the producer of one-third of the world's hard disks. Modern society also depends on technologies with high potential risks. The Chernobyl disaster of 1986 resulted from weaknesses in its design and insufficient technical skills. There were deficiencies in safety training and regulation of the personnel. It happened during a test after all. The release of radiation from the Fukushima plant, in Japan 2011, resulted from an earthquake and tsunami event. These disasters were greater in magnitude than the design standard of the facility to cope with. The issue is not just the risk from operational radioactive accidents. It's dealing with nuclear facility decommissioning which needs the maintenance of a functioning society for generations to come!

Society has also become dependent on intelligent technologies. In the past, the role of electromagnetic pulses from solar activity was merely of scientific interest. Now, because of our dependency on electronic systems, it's become a key test of global resilience. For decades, disease has been held in check by powerful antibiotic drugs. Over prescription of these drugs has resulted in rising drug resistance. It now poses a significant threat to urban populations.

Collapse of economic and social structures can and has happened in modern times. This is particularly in traditional, one employer towns, tied to a single company. The abandoned Hashima Island made the set of the James Bond movie, Sky Fall (2012) and became a UNESCO World Heritage site in July 2015. The island's abrupt demise in 1974 is a story of coal production, depletion and finally mass exodus. Leon Krier has made the point that some cities are more adaptable than others. Milton Keynes cannot survive an economic crisis, or any other kind of crisis. It is planned as a mathematically set social and economic project. If that model collapses, the city will collapse with it. If peak oil should push the use of the private motor car out of the reach of most in society, then only compact urban forms are going to survive or prosper. Their residents will be able to walk or use cycles between different destinations, and public transport may still be practical.

Wars and disasters have in the past given unique opportunities to rebuild. After the Great Fire of London, the architect Sir Christopher Wren sought a new plan. This was for a series of wide boulevards radiating from the new St Pauls Cathedral, interconnecting in a straight lined grid. This was fought by private landowners and developers who realised this would cut across the pre-fire boundaries of their building plots. Whereas Haussmann succeeded in the 18th Century in widening Paris's boulevards, these landowners succeeded in preventing the realisation of Sir Christopher Wren's grid plan for London. Yet some lessons were learned. This included the use of permanent materials in building construction which would limit the potential for similar, future events occurring.

In a free society, there is a choice as to whether preparation for civil emergencies is planned (communal) or individual. An example of the latter is the 'preppers' movement in the United States. Often natural hazard management resourcing is imbalanced in its focus. In Latin America and the Caribbean, 90 percent of international funding for natural hazard management is spent on disaster preparedness, relief, rehabilitation, and reconstruction. This leaves only 10 percent for pre-disaster prevention.

Cutting disaster risk is heavily associated with either design standards or avoidance of hazards altogether. The imposition of controls to prevent hazards from arising can affect the viability of certain developments. Within the Third World, concrete structures offer the possibility of hurricane and earthquake-proof dwellings. The emerging cities of the Third World are vulnerable, especially informal settlements. This vulnerability is extremely high in Caribbean nations and the Mexican and Central American Atlantic coast. They face acute challenges from hurricanes and other natural disasters. In 2004, Hurricane Jeanne left 2,400 dead in Haiti and nearly one quarter of a million people living in the slums of Gonaives, homeless.

There's a truism that earthquakes don't kill people but rather it's the collapse of buildings around them. Relatively simple measures could protect millions of people at risk of death in the Pacific mid east belt cities. One means would be standards requiring the greater use of strengthened concrete at a 10% additional building cost. Another is constraint planning, for example, delineating no build areas around fault lines, to limit damage.

Tehran[124] lies on at least 100 known fault lines and could be hit by a major earthquake at any time (Harrison, 2005). The UN rates Iran as the number one

---

[124] The capital of Iran, with a population of 12 million people.

country in the world for earthquakes. That is whether measured in intensity, frequency or the number of casualties. It has been calculated[125] that there is a 90% chance of an earthquake measuring 6 on the Richter scale hitting Tehran and a 50% chance of an earthquake measuring 7.5 striking the capital. Almost 80% of total buildings in Teheran are extremely vulnerable. This is due to their un-reinforced masonry and partial frame construction. Few of the buildings have been made to withstand even an earthquake measuring 6 on the Richter scale. So far, government efforts have focused on training exercises. Scientists have considered how a risk based approach should apply. They have concluded that the city should either be comprehensively rebuilt or moved. Historic buildings would need to be strengthened to reinforce them against earthquakes. A catastrophic event would cause millions to be killed or injured. They believe the capital needs to be moved somewhere else. If not, then at least steps are needed to decrease the population and make Tehran more resistant to earthquakes. According to one of the scientists, the best way is to move the government out of Tehran. It could be accommodated where there is still space to build satellite towns, in safer areas. If some government ministries move outside the capital, other employers will be drawn out. The suggestion for relocation is the best intentions being applied within a technical and rational world view. Yet, as in all other planning matters, there is no avoiding the socio-political aspects of such proposals. With belief slower to change than science, various arguments against taking action have emerged. Firstly, there is the concern of going too far in alarming the community. Secondly, there is insufficient money to rebuild their homes and offices. Thirdly, is the psychology of disasters and the fatalistic approach of residents, who act against rectifying the situation. Finally, is the lack of freedom of speech in which to engage with the authorities. Perhaps the most notorious recent example of the way in which disaster mitigation laws have been applied is that of Turkey's Law 6306, passed in 2012. Any area under risk from a particular disaster falls under the jurisdiction of the government and results in the commencement of demolition processes. Residents have only 30 days to go to court to dispute the findings of any assessment (Ryser & Franchini, 2015).

The paradigm of post-modernism is comfort, safety and security. Protecting the city may be paramount, but efficiency and short-term gain define how far planning can go in avoiding or mitigating natural hazards. After disaster events, (democratic) governments are forced to act. If politicians are accountable, relief funds and resources will, in theory, get to

---

[125] By the International Institute of Earthquake Engineering and Seismology at Tehran University.

where they are needed. When things do go wrong planning can be reactive, in the form of setting up new (planned) settlements for refugees. 'Needs must' and planning restrictions maybe set aside or suspended. The significant loss of inner city office space in Christchurch, New Zealand following the 2010 and 2011 earthquakes is one such example. Companies were allowed to disperse their teams into the suburbs, due to a relaxation of planning rules.

The current mantra is to make cities 'resilient.' What this means is contextual. Each city has specific vulnerabilities. The Rockefeller Foundation has devoted significant resources to a research programme (100 Resilient Cities network). It awards 100 cities that it feels 'have shown a dedicated commitment to building their own capacities to prepare for, withstand, and bounce back rapidly from shocks and stresses.' The motive for the competition may only be to score each cities' speed with which they can return to the desired status quo of capital accumulation. Yet it at least raises the profile of natural hazards which are too often ignored in short term political cycles.

Natural hazards result in disruptive change, 'disorientation' and the 'removal of 'identity.' With resilient cities and disaster management, the issues start with authorities having to worry about a specific natural hazard. The bigger issue is with the overall effect on social cohesion.

2.0 Security, Crime and Warfare

Crime and Public Space

Crime and disorder also affect social cohesion and are disproportionately urban issues. Some crimes come down to meeting immediate physiological needs. In theory, the welfare state should reduce the incidence of property crimes. Inevitably, poor people, such as migrants to urban centres, bring other 'social problems of poverty' with them. In the many informal communities of the Third World this is invariably worse and extends to violence and drug trafficking.

It was noted in earlier sections, that social division can be apparent without the symbolism of structural separation. Yet the design and layout of physical space, such as public areas, does have a profound influence on social order. William Whyte (1980, 1988) observed that off-peak use of public space gives the best clue as to how the function of such spaces is viewed. A low proportion of women indicates that something is wrong, as women are more discriminating in their choice of public space. Society creates the city, not vice versa (Tueni, 2000). Yet once the built environment is constructed it has both harmful and beneficial impacts on social dynamics.

There is a strong link between the spatial form of the settlement and ways in which encounters are produced and controlled. This is particularly along public street space as was the case in the markets of the Middle Ages. In organic towns and settlements, particularly those based on foot traffic, urban streets were placed axially. These sped strangers on their way to the urban markets or squares. Once there, they were slowed down. The grouping of the inhabitant's houses gives urban safety. The system cleverly works by strangers policing the space, while inhabitants police the strangers.

As noted earlier, modern design principles have, in contrast, been notorious for their inadvertent segregating effect. The re-engineering of inner cities in the United States, after the urban uprisings of the 1960s, just happened to create major physical highway barriers. These became moats in effect between high value, downtown property and impoverished inner-city neighbourhoods.

As mentioned earlier, crime and the perception of crime has resulted in societal change. Childhood itself has changed greatly in the West during the past generation. 'Free range' childhood started becoming less common in the 1980s. This is where kids weren't chaperoned by adults. Gated communities sprang up geared towards personal safety. They featured electronic means of control, such as bar-code swipes for entry. Newman (1973) notes that residents in these communities have a stronger sense of ownership when there are barriers, security and exclusivity. The overall result is that the city becomes a maze of restricted places, streets and neighbourhoods. The need for safety, security and protection flows into other areas of society as well. Sport Utility Vehicle sales proliferated before the credit crunch in Western cities. Such vehicles were based on military designs, such as the Hummer, yet warfare had not been heard of for generations in these places.

The importance attached to private property shaped the level of resources by the State to protect it. There were those like Locke (Part I) and at another extreme was Lenin. After establishing his regime in Russia after the First World War, Lenin considered the existing criminal class as potential allies. Crime was viewed as being inextricably tied to 'social excesses' resulting from capitalism.

In the Modern West, crime policy has become oriented towards responses to crime rather than the processes that might prevent it. Politicians, driven by the interests of social cohesion, address the everyday issues of local crime, anti-social behaviour, racial intolerance and community breakdown. The focus of debates is whether to increase police forces and / or prisons. The potential of citizens to prevent crime through urban design is overlooked. During the 1990s, the Mayor of New York achieved a 45% increase in police force levels to combat crime. Some states are also increasingly looking to modern surveillance technologies to oversee and control the public zone. At national borders, regular travellers can use hand-scan biometrics to bypass immigration controls. This is while 'illegal' immigrants face increasing scrutiny in their attempts to cross boundaries.

The 'war on terror' has pushed militarised debates about 'security' into every walk of life. Security theorists have pushed the extension of airport-style security surveillance systems into encompassing cities. Urban politicians are applying Third World cordons and formal 'security zones' found around strategic cores and Government districts, into the likes of 'congestion charge zones' in the West (Graham, 2010).

GPS and mobile phone systems track the time–space trails of everything from cars to electronically-tagged offenders. Mass ownership of mobile phones gives an international personal tracking system by stealth. Automatic speed cameras are used to fine drivers through licence-plate recognition. The police make use of computerised statistical systems to see where crime is taking place and respond accordingly (for example, New York Police's CompStat). Strategic urban sites, such as global financial centres and airport cities, are now surrounded by 'smart' Closed Circuit TV systems. These automatically scan traffic for stolen cars. In addition, the tens of millions of analogue CCTV systems on city streets are rapidly being digitised and computerised. This is to automatically scan for 'unusual' events. They will also identify the scanned-in faces of those deemed to be dangerous by the state, the police or local security officers. A street embedded with CCTV may look the same as one without, but it will be a different sort of place. Increasingly, this is changing genuine culture. The city-saturating, culture of control involving CCTV is forcing society to adjust its behaviour, just in case 'they' are watching!

Public space has always been symbolic in political demonstrations. The settings of Tahrir Square (Cairo), Syntagma Square (Athens) and Puerta del Sol in Madrid served as the platform for political unrest in recent years. Additionally, in 2011, the indignados ('the outraged') occupied plazas in cities across Spain. They protested against the effects of the financial crisis and were followed days later by the aganaktismenoi in Greece. The disturbances in Istanbul in 2013 were sparked by plans to develop Gezi Square. Without the intervention of armed forces, such mass protests can rapidly escalate into full-scale revolt.

In the past, city walls and gates were the most visible aspect of social control. City walls served as both a form of infrastructure and military technology. Yet by the late 18th Century they were being phased out, increasingly redundant as a technology against external threats. Domestically, Haussmannian style boulevards were still deemed as useful to punch through neighbourhoods of insurrection.

When it comes to restricting internal dissent and protests, behavioural restrictions based on location are applied. Think of modern day buffer zones around Abortion clinics. For internal conflicts, the use of walls and gates remains. It's just the terminology that has changed to identity checkpoints, blast walls, and the general robotisation of defence measures.

Institutional prisons are the last resort for social control. Enforcement success has correspondingly resulted in soaring population numbers in prisons. There is the need for ever greater scales of penal institutions. The United States 'broken windows' theory of policing calls for strong penalties, even for minor infractions. Indeed, the United States has created a 'prison economy' for facilities around this policy. U.S. Statistics reveal that the United States holds 25% of the world's prison population, but only 5% of the world's people. From less than 300,000 inmates in 1972, the jail population grew to a peak of 1,615,487 inmates in 2009, before starting to fall.

Even if jails don't reform criminals, they do at least keep them off the street. There have been significant attempts to make the system pay for itself, in the form of cheap labour that's potentially available. The United States is once again an attractive location for investment which was originally destined for Third World labour markets thanks to prison labour. Yet the extensive use of 'free' labour does not always pay off. Despite the enthusiasm for its use by authorities, the Soviet Gulag system was an overall drain on the economy. This is despite the system being designed to extract natural resources from remote and often hostile parts of the country.

With the Cold War over, perhaps the biggest threat of war in the twenty-first century is internal disintegration. Even nations with no significant external threats may find themselves in decline because of acute ethnic, racial or class conflicts. This is particularly where there is economic disparity among groups and where groups are geographically isolated. Where communities identify themselves in terms that are not shared by their neighbours it weakens the State. As happened in the former Yugoslavia and also in Syria, Lebanon and Nigeria today, it fell apart at the first serious blow.

When city communities fall apart internally due to unresolvable tensions communities adapt through the built environment. Walls and other partitions often go up having the effect of reducing the normal internal circulation. Getting them back down can take concerted time and effort. This is particularly if it's accompanied by a power vacuum at regional or national level. Civil society relies upon municipal authorities. This is not only in the sense that they issue policies and salaries. It is also because they alone have the authority and capability to consolidate the control of contested territory (Calame & Charlesworth, 2000).

Where the State has fallen apart, or its authority undermined, other options may become necessary to restart a transition back to peace. In Beirut, an experiment to use market forces was instigated. A private company guided postwar, urban reconstruction. A red line was placed around the ruined Central Business District. Relinquishing highly contested urban territory to the vagaries of the market was unprecedented. In the end though, it was successful.

War Campaigns

The nature of warfare may seem out of place in a book on planning. Yet warfare is a highly planned activity in its own right; particularly, about weaponry and logistics. There is a high correlation between large society, central government and warfare.[126] The larger the scale of war in the industrial era, the greater has been the tendency towards (central) planning. This is in the production of anything and everything- including construction. During the Second World War, the German minister Speer, noted that 'total war' was concentrating even their building industry. Standardisation was deemed necessary. This saved skilled technical manpower and created rational, serial production methods. It raised productivity and resulted in large scale building projects. Wars also have implications for different planning systems, including justifying the nationalisation of property (seizure) and potentially replacing the planning system with that of the victors.

The War economy had an important influence on the UK planning legislation as well. The limitations of the 1909 Planning Act to accommodate munition workers during the First World War was quickly appreciated. This

---

[126]   The only civilisation that has been suggested for having achieved a utopian mix of sophisticated cities, in a seeming absence of government and warfare, is the Indus Valley (2600 to 1900 BC) (reference: Andrew Robinson).

spurred a more economically, interventionist stance to the housing sector. It began with the Housing Acts in 1914 and 1915 and finally came to fruition through comprehensive planning after the Second World War.

Most wars have geographic goals. The defence of nations is, politically at least, linked to the control of territory. Military campaigns focus on cities as centres for power and control. In the twenty-first century the spectre of natural resource depletion will result in new wars over natural resources. In a way that Nietzsche would have appreciated, it's felt necessary for military planners to destroy in order to create.

Warfare is clearly anti-planning in the sense that it seeks to bring destruction upon an enemy. The aim of campaigns against enemy states is to disable the enemies' military. Often this is associated with the destruction of the social cohesion of that society by:

- Fragmenting communities
- Sowing confusion
- Denying access to resources
- Destroying resources and infrastructure (for example, scorched earth policy)
- Disrupting the efficiency of an enemy's communication and transport system.

In warfare itself, military strategies distinguish between urban and non-urban areas. In Ancient times, the capture and destruction of cities, generally by siege, was the main aim of combatants. Mao's victorious rise to power in 1940's China used a strategy whereby occupation of the countryside allowed his forces to encircle and finally capture cities. The countryside was vulnerable, allowing communist forces to establish bases. Cities and main lines of communication were strong points, occupied by imperialists and reactionary allies. Cold War military doctrine similarly stressed the imperative of bypassing cities. This was based on the nightmarish spectre of Stalingrad-like, house-to-house combat with severe casualty rates observed during Second World War.

Modern, hard, urban infrastructure is vulnerable. Described as, 'tightly coupled,' problems in one piece of equipment can cause problems in all. Electricity is a key dependency. In the end its failure decimates the entire urban system, unless enough back up can be maintained. Such tactics have been played out in modern Palestine. The modernity and connectivity of the urban fabric has been undermined by the Israeli army in its attempts to control territory. Water tanks have been deliberately riddled with bullets, electronic communications jammed, roads dug up, water mains smashed, electricity transformers destroyed, media transmitters bulldozed and hospitals bombed. The strategy, in effect, is to holistically deny the right of inhabitants to an urban modernity. At the same time, the demographic and urban coherence and contiguity of the Palestinian people is being impeded by the implantation of modern, barricaded, Jewish settlements. These are connected by infrastructure systems both to each other and to the main Israeli territory. This includes water, roads, highways, telecommunications and electricity. They bypass, or drive wedges between, surrounding Palestinian neighborhoods. The manifestation of geopolitical conflict, as a clash of urbanist styles, has rarely been so stark.

The technological dimension of progress and modern science has been strongest about weaponry. As such, science has become a complimentary accessory to mass destruction. Warfare technology has come a long way, such as the use of aerial bombings to devastate cities. These began with the First World War raids conducted by German Zeppelins. It quickly escalated to the use of aircraft technology to destroy buildings. By the end of the Second World War, techniques had been refined with such devastating effect as that which took place in Dresden (1945). The high explosive bombs first exposed the wooden frames of buildings. Incendiary bombs would then ignite the wood. Finally, firefighting efforts were hampered by a range of explosive devices. By the NATO bombing of Yugoslavia (Serbia) in 1999, the mass destruction methods had been replaced, by precision, guided munitions. Civilian deaths were significantly reduced yet such tactics proved effective at removing the modernity and connectivity of the urban fabric. This included bridges, TV stations, electricity and the like.

When civil disaster or war results in the breaking down of urban supply networks the plight of residents quickly deteriorates. Popular culture is obsessed with the possibility of collapse (*Sci-Fi movies*). Pillaging of supplies and resources occurs in almost any desperate community. This even occurred in Europe during the closing stages of the Second World War. Residents cut down the public Tiergarten forest in Berlin and burned timber cladding for firewood taken from private houses in Amsterdam. It also continues at a less spectacular rate in shrinking cities around the world, where crime is associated with the plundering, stripping, scrapping and vandalising of vacant buildings.

City planning has the potential to reduce the impacts of external threats on cities. Yet the nature of war, and how it impacts on cities changes more quickly than that of the evolving urban fabric. There are no city walls for protection. New threats to those living in densely populated cities are terrorism, bombers and missiles. A little known factor shaping Le Corbusier's architectural thinking was to minimise the vulnerability of urban spaces. His 1930s high rise building plans were intended to reduce the impacts from the emerging techniques of aerial bombardment and gas attack. Post-September 11th, Le Corbusier's skyscrapers are now considered to be extremely vulnerable.

The United States terrorism attacks, in 2001, exploited the intensely concentrated logic of global city development. Indeed, some involved in the attack were qualified urbanists, opposed to Western architectural modernism. It instantly reversed the iconic power of the skyscraper as a symbol of urban 'progress' and modernisation. From an icon of power, progress and the dynamism of urban America, it became a symbol of fragility. It plunged the cityscape into a new era of vulnerability. Despite this, it did not stop skyscraper construction continuing apace with so many new proposals coming forward.

Just as cities were once seen as sinful, and Marx saw the 'urban masses' as the catalyst for revolution, there are disturbing parallels with the way urban elites now view cities. They are seen as places that concentrate acts of subversion, resistance, mobilisation, dissent and protest (Graham, 2010). Davis (2006) notes a United States study into how demographic changes will affect future cities. The underlying theme is that poverty in urban areas will drive the ground bed of future insurgencies.

The response of urban authorities in areas under the threat of warfare has been the use of concrete structures for protection - for example, bunkers. The planning and design of Western cities is, once again, being scrutinized from the point of view of military vulnerability. The key may lie in the ability to limit the ability of groups and individuals to use infrastructure as a means to project resistance and violence. This includes the postal, electricity, internet, finance, airline and transport systems.

Even the internet is making us more vulnerable, given the increasing number of connected devices in our lives. Society is ever more dependent on the small pool of internet companies who 'mine' our stored personal data for profit. The current version of the internet is also reliant on a relatively small number of server farms. This makes it both easier for government agencies to access us without our consent. Equally, we are an easy target for hackers. The internet also has a darker side, the so called dark web. This allows the linking up of criminal activities beyond the reach of government surveillance.

Urban sprawl was once seen as compatible with reducing the United States' vulnerability to a pre-emptive Soviet nuclear attack, during the Cold

War. The interstate highway system was likewise supported as a 'defence highway' system. In the Post-Cold War era, the potential threats from unconventional warfare, asymmetric struggles and global insurgencies discourage centralised, technological systems. Decentralised urban configurations are viewed as having greater inbuilt 'resilience' (Graham, 2010). These use compartmentalised power, water and communications grids. In a similar way, splitting up files and sharing them across a network reduces our virtual world vulnerability. It makes it harder for others to access our data.

CONCLUSIONS:
A VIEW TO THE FUTURE

The West is accustomed to high levels of urbanisation. Fifty percent of the population in the United Kingdom lived in cities by the mid-1880s and a similar percentage in the United States by 1920. Cities before and during these periods were places of stress, conflict and sometimes actual misery. High density living, often in cramped, unsanitary conditions, was the only housing available to the urban masses.

Urban authorities' have had to make technology-policy decisions to improve living outcomes. These have been successful over time, even if the motives were not always altruistic. Yet as has been covered in Parts V – VI, urban professionals still got criticised for many of their past decisions. These included their support of segregation, tower blocks, ring roads, urban highways and out of town shopping centres. This reflected the context and priorities of the time that society is starting to come to terms with now. In particular, the faults and imperfections of the 'modernist project'.

Most of the planning debate over the last century has focused on acceptable standards for living space. This has been within a context of generally increasing material standards. As I have sought to show, standards for space are relative to other factors they must be traded against. In reacting to the industrial revolution, more open space amenity was seen as being desirable to improve urban conditions. This stance has now been reversed as part of the gradual realisation of a number of pressures over time. These include continued growth, issues of affordability (sometimes seen as disproportionately affecting minorities), distance from employment, infrastructure costs, dependence on fossil fuels, changes to demographics and concerns over emissions of greenhouse gases. With some exceptions, smaller land 'units' are accepted as creating more compact cities.

There are parallels between the living conditions of industrial city inhabitants in the West, and those now experienced in the Third World. The solutions presented to resolve Third World issues have focused on the role of capital and open markets in wealth generation. What is often overlooked is that many of the rights found in the West have only been gained over time. These have been through struggle and sacrifice and include democracy, equality and environmental protection. Industrialisation, rather than open markets better explain the phenomena of urbanisation.

There remain intractable issues for the Third World to raise the living standards of its slums. Due to its association with extremism, global urban poverty should be considered as much a concern as climate change. The general wealth levels of these residents need to be improved. Also, there is a need for better physical infrastructure, provision of minimum building and sanitary standards that aren't prohibitive for inhabitants. In the end, Third World authorities need to take more of a planned approach to their economies (refer to the UNCTD 2016 report; page 246). Also, we in the West need to review our most damaging patterns of consumption.

As it is, the trajectory of progress now experienced in Western nations now appears to be unravelling. We can expect in the near future, at least, greater scarcity of natural resources, a changing climate and declining public sector resourcing. In respect of the latter, the public sector may be able to adapt through new information technologies.

De-industrialisation and 'casino capitalism' was never part of the economic vision for success. Inequality has worsened and new issues are arising. These new issues include technological artificiality, environmental degradation and social division. These have replaced the earlier, more life threatening concerns of industrial city life. The built environment now suffers from disconnected peripheries, dysfunctional public space, gated communities, virtual escapism and increasing insecurity. The past successes of the welfare state and planning controls have, in some cases, caused or reinforced the rise of these new issues.

Governments have never given sufficient priority to reviewing the effectiveness of past intervention measures. Rational and reasonable approaches get sidetracked in the post-modern era by media driven controversy. A collusion of political players in the West, has allowed homelessness to increase at the same time as social realms have been commodified. These are as diverse as drug taking, prostitution, elderly care and childcare. The secondary and cumulative impacts of these activities on society as a whole too often get ignored. Such activities may be subject to compliance with 'performance or effects based' regulations, but these measures are always going to be limited. These limitations may well parallel those of similar systems in built environment outcomes, however, assessing these are beyond the scope of this book.

To Intervene or Not – That is the Question

Regulation is no longer a favoured tool given the drive to cut 'red tape.' This is even more so with planning controls that are geographic in nature. They have the potential to be pervasive across many economic sectors. The case for minimum building standards give a certainty that the use of a structure won't cause injury from collapse. This directly benefits their inhabitants. Only confident builders of structures, or the few with insufficient resources to meet the standards specified, would seek to scrap building codes altogether.

In contrast, the benefits offered by the planning system are generally more subjective and indirect. This may explain why it's relatively rare for countries to integrate spatial planning with building standards. Planning controls benefit the surrounding community, rather than those proposing the development itself. As such, there is more of a challenge to explain the reason for the process when those being restricted can see little benefit. It's easy to agree that land use controls are needed for facilities that could pose significant risks to the community (for example, nuclear power stations). It's harder for subjective, residential 'design' controls (for example, addressing the impacts of an oversized dwelling). Both types of proposal may have equally 'unacceptable impacts' for those potentially affected. Neither group has to objectively weigh up which of the two situations is worse overall.

At an international level there has never been greater recognition and understanding of urban issues and their solutions. One inherent problem with intervention is whether the mandate to engage (e.g., legislation) is fit for purpose. Enacted legislation needs to be flexible so its administrators can deal with changing economic times across different areas. Any amendments would be derived from a lifecycle approach to the monitoring and care of the regime itself (known as 'regulatory stewardship').

Should reform of the planning system be found necessary, then it needs to be addressed as part of a much wider legislative review. This would cover human rights, social welfare, building standards, infrastructure, environmental management and aligning property taxation with land use aims (admittedly a formidable task). Environmental sustainability is best served by having relevant goals incorporated into sectoral pieces of legislation for the development of infrastructure and transport.

Another inherent problem is the nature of urban issues being global in scope, but perceived and responded to locally. The stance of the national government on the economy, environment, population growth and migration, in particular, sets the scene for local land use and planning. Too often there is a disconnect between the level of control exercised between the different tiers of government.

Even if legislative drivers are set at the national level, urban codes (regulation) have to be applied at the local or city level. That is because they are spatially contextual rather than universal in nature. There are now much better technical (in some cases utopian) solutions to urban issues. Yet while the legal means to carry them through still exists, there is far less political will. It's difficult to gain public backing when the only part of the community that engages in such debates is the one that believes it has the most to lose.

When setting the balance between technocratic input and public participation in decision making, the culture and level of democratic engagement of society as a whole needs to be taken into account. It's a catch-22. Often the length of time needed for public consultation processes can mean evidence is dated before the Plan is even implemented. Neither less participation, nor direct democracy on specific issues, necessarily results in better decision making.

Institutionalised planning is thus mired in much wider issues around representative democracy and declining public sector capabilities. What is needed is the ability to quickly shift intractable local issues up to higher tiers of government for resolution. This won't happen if higher tier authorities are, or are perceived to be, less trusted and accountable than others. This was illustrated in the United Kingdom's BREXIT referendum result over the EU.

Planning Trade-offs and Outcomes

Decision makers face the dilemmas of trade-offs and setting priorities. Institutional levers are applied to economic, social or environmental problems. Most typically these include setting standards on the freedom of individuals to undertake activities.

Higher standards for (new) urban design make infrastructural investment more attractive. High standards refer, for instance, to promoting growth within restricted acceptable locations. Yet, unless specifically provided for, lower value uses may get pushed out. These include start-up enterprises, manufacturers, warehouses and waste operators. Higher environmental standards may promote retail, culture, certain technologies (IT) and tourism. Those other sectors that can't meet such high standards, such as industry, may be forced out. This occurred late, last century throughout The West. Higher standards may benefit the existing labour force through the setting of minimum wage and health care. This may attract migrants. Yet labour intensive industries may feel they must move away. This is the case with the West's 'hidden work' which is effectively done in 'sweatshops' found in The East. This pattern even applies to variances in social freedoms. Unless strong cultural norms exist, greater personal freedoms may encourage people to move to such areas. The result is a less cohesive society. All of this suggests that there are two categories to choose between for economic growth; creative or productive cities. Too often the choice taken is dictated to at the national level of government.

Creative, high income cities may benefit from denser urban forms across most land use types, high environmental standards but looser restrictions over individual freedoms (for example, encouraging movement). In this context, comprehensive planning approaches are best (using techniques of masterplanning). They'd promote mixed use developments within dense, central city locations. There would also be discretion to grant permissions.

Taxes on capital and investment must be kept low and expensive environmental standards avoided in productive cities. Competitiveness is important with authorities undercutting regulations relative to other cities, whilst avoiding a 'race to the bottom' (a form of Malthusian anarchy). General wages and standards for workers are also driven down by the increased supply of new workers through either internal or external immigration. While it may also seem tempting to 'water down' land use controls across the board, this should be resisted. Where restrictions on higher value uses are removed from areas of production it will mean that firms 'making' things will be driven out. This is particularly the case for the less productive, service sector. If capital flows can be directed to employment areas, it enables economies of scale and a more co-ordinated approach to infrastructure.

Areas of production can be as large as necessary to give flexibility for employers with extensive land use activities. They also benefit from low amenity standards and/or high public subsidisation. They would cater to start-up firms and those specialising in low carbon activities. The latter include product repair, maintenance, upgrading and remanufacturing which also tend to be more labour intensive than those extracting raw materials.

The history of British planning that followed the Second World War aspired towards productive cities. A comprehensive planning approach was applied rather than that suggested above. Yet as noted earlier, development was being undertaken in a different context. It assumed relatively higher levels of state land ownership and funding than is commonly acceptable today. As it became apparent, the system was systematically amended in the decades that followed to encourage growth. The introduction of special economic zones was the best example of this.

There remains a moral imperative for urban policies to make sure that the centre of cities allow poorer communities to reside, close to jobs. This is both for creative and productive cities. Those with this mandate need to make sure that the use of public infrastructure and funds does not, in the end, serve the wealthy.

The Sustainable City

Sustainability has become the cornerstone of the modern western planning system. It's based on the hard evidence around resource depletion and the threat to society as a whole. Yet the pursuit of sustainability does carry with it the following ramifications:

- It's outcome focused: Evidence, monitoring and technical professionals are important for the wider public interest. Evaluation needs to be institutionalised within planning authorities. Free markets, democratic choices, social freedoms, open information and social media are all good things in themselves, but they are process orientated. They don't always bring about desired outcomes without intervention;

- It's not about GDP: There's a cost in achieving strong sustainability. It can be so high that economic competitiveness can be put at risk. In practice, planning systems typically deliver increases in economic and social capital (economic growth). This comes at the cost of natural capital. Whether this allows our society to avoid the fate of the ancient Sumerians and Incas (see Part II) will only be known in time;

- It challenges the logic of capitalism: Even if cities do become 'sustainable' the world won't if the processing of natural resources, used in consumer products, continues at the same rate. The ecological footprint of the Western World needs to be lowered overall. Yet a higher standard of living is currently the main belief that unites The West (Part I). This includes its energy use and supply chain distances to cities through more renewable energy, recycling and lower consumption of scarce resources;

- Community buy in is essential: While sustainability may not refer to the ability of Western democracies to resolve class and social conflict, it can't escape from the need for social cohesion entirely. Inter-group mediation and compromise has to be able to continue, just not dominate. The question for politicians and technocrats is which of Fuller's (2007) quadrants, discussed in Part I, are we aiming for.

There are many different design solutions to make sure of equality and environmental outcomes within the urban fabric. The linear city was one such concept. The lessons of history are that new designs don't in themselves reform their inhabitants. The English model village, Soviet communal house and Le Corbusier's Unit T style tower blocks show this. Nor is it practical to fix an existing, poorly laid out urban environment by rebuilding it. Changes within the domain of public authorities, such as roads, are usually the slowest and most expensive to make.

The best investment for public authorities to promote sustainable urban practices is through economic incentives and other mechanisms for behavioural change. Policy co-design or co-creation initiatives allow for policy to be based on a real understanding of the values of each local community. Unfortunately, these forums are typically expensive to run. Design thinking principles are especially applicable to resolving 'wicked problems'. This is where both the problem and the solution are unknown at the outset of the problem-solving exercise (Part IV).

In saying the above, there are still fundamental choices to be made in the direction taken to urban form. The biggest concern is the continued growth of mega-cities. They are by nature inherently unstable, with large population movements and social divisions. They contrast with cities that score highly for liveability. These include Nordic countries, with their high incomes, smaller population sizes and cohesive societies. Mega-cities may allow some talented people to better fulfil their potential, but often that's at the expense of other values, cohesion and local culture. The logic of growth management in such settings, lends itself to area specific legislation to derive solutions. Yet in doing so it risks fragmenting national urban and socio-economic planning.

The power of big industry results in calls for a corporatist approach to government. The global economy leads to calls for global government. It shouldn't therefore be a surprise that over-urbanisation reinforces the need for heavy, ongoing state intervention. The larger cities are, the less they can be allowed to operate as 'complex, adaptive systems.' The effective administration of mega-cities creates tension with local democracy, cultures and even private ownership. Without a clear form or ethic of global solidarity, the logic of urbanisation reinforces ever more hierarchical and complex forms of management. This is evidenced by the increasing role of supra-national organisations such as the UN and EU in urban affairs.

Planning controls end up as just another set of regulations. They are meant to promote social cohesion and address the consequences of societal fragmentation.

'Ordinary' towns and cities are optimal. Such places don't receive the same attention at the national level of government. This is probably due to the economic and political clout of their larger urban rivals. Yet ordinary towns and cities are better placed to serve humanity. They can do this by encouraging 'place based' communities that are tied to their urban identity. In these settings, different values need to be emphasised. This includes retaining existing historic heritage, land marks and generally supporting the relationship of communities to their culture and traditions.

General Principles

Ethics and morality teach us that pursing economic gain without weighing up the social and environmental costs is flawed. An independent decision maker is needed to rigorously assess the social and environmental impacts of development. Informed discussion over the true costs and benefits needs open forums, backed up by the public equivalent of a R&D department. What's proposed (for example, housing numbers) has to be shown to be deliverable. This is in light of recognised social and environmental constraints.

Divergent views need to be 'front loaded' at the beginning of the preparation process. In contrast, the scope for challenging a finalised Plan should be reduced. Discretion to grant planning permission can be useful to respond to changing circumstances. The problem is that it reinforces the disconnect between policy makers' aspirations and what's carried out 'on the ground.'

The significance of land tenure is underappreciated. Democracy is generally enhanced when there are high levels of private ownership. Yet this does not mean that the public domain should be eroded by large, corporate interests.   The debate over privitisation is now too narrowly focused on central, pedestrianised 'meeting' points. Too often the benefits of public sector ownership are realised by private businesses. In reality, the benefit of a public High Street and a private retail mall can be a subtle one for a consumer.

In the United Kingdom, housing has become the land use that trumps all other needs through the planning system. This has more to do with economic growth theory than any right of the urban poor to adequate housing. Enshrining a right to housing might be useful, but this would be inevitably countered by the right of property owners to use their land as they see fit. As with any matter of human rights, beyond Walzer's minimums, there are issues. First, deciding which right or value takes priority. Second, how to take into consideration unrepresented rights, such as in this case, future generations.

Housing delivery dominates and distorts the national economy, even at the expense of more productive uses. The housing market is small and tightly controlled by landowners and construction companies. Policy makers have not only failed to address this. They have compounded the problem by their well-intended demands for higher density living and environmental standards. These have raised the cost and technical complexity of building projects.

Setting aside areas for self-starter homes, and employing other measures to encourage greater competition in the construction market (even assigning builders as key workers) are useful mechanisms. Helping community ownership would be the ideal solution. Existing options include the community right to buy (for example, land, buildings or infrastructure). This is where having registered an interest, the community gains first right of refusal when the asset comes up for sale. Community land trusts and housing co-operatives can help community development that's sustainable and protect against land speculation.

It may be valid for the state to interfere in the land market when investors are failing to invest enough. This is by means of control, allocation and if necessary, designation of land for critical needs. Given the speculative value of land ownership, discussed earlier in Part I, greater taxation incentives based on the site's locational value are needed. This would encourage site development of under-used land. Such taxes can be a substitute for those on production and consumption, which impede an economy. If this is insufficient, then recourse may be necessary to public sector house building programmes.

Ideas that sit outside the urban code

The issues around urban form have significant implications for our society. As this book has shown, solutions revolve around a much broader political and economic context. There are certain aspects worth debating that avoid any fundamental re-think of the current economic and social systems.

First, is the issue around defining growth on GDP whereas natural capital would be more suitable. Second is the inefficient use of privately owned resources. While Marx may have been mistaken in view to alleviate the suffering of the poor by exploiting the natural environment, resource not labour efficiency is preferable. As a society, we need to develop a model that goes beyond Rostow's 'fifth stage' to a sustainable sixth. Within this sixth stage, taxes would be lowered on work and increased on the consumption of non-renewable resources. That is virgin raw materials, land and fossil fuels. It is also necessary to shift from the exclusivity of private ownership to a more collaborative consumerism. In terms of chattels, access by demand and performance rather than outright ownership is one means to promote more efficient use. This would see greater use of lease based models of ownership. They encourage the designing in of adaptability and extension of product life. Resident or non-profit groups can promote greater sharing or bartering of private assets, such as houses and transport, through the use of web based technologies. Under-used urban land should be used to directly address housing shortages. The compulsory purchase of land by the public sector may have to be used to make sure development occurs in the right place and at the right time. That is not-with-standing the tension this may create between elected public bodies and private property rights.

The state can support under-performing areas by assisting local communities to help themselves. The effort and expense of rebranding underperforming areas as 'cultural' or 'exciting', through so called 'cultural' programmes, is misplaced. It would be better to concentrate on encouraging simpler and more sustainable living practices. They don't have to be any less educated. These practices could be incentivised by universal, basic income that is targeted at those committed to remaining within deprived areas.

Third, is giving people in cities greater possibilities to re-connect with their surrounding countryside. Concerns about the future availability of energy, water and environmental resources for cities are well recognised. What remains under appreciated are the benefits of rural communities in maintaining small-scale agricultural practices.

If the culture is too heavily urbanised further access for urban dwellers to the countryside won't enhance positive connections. There need to be incentives to interact with the real world, rather than people spending increasing time on social media and games. It is necessary to give people a real stake in living off the land to nurture independence and allow citizens to take care of themselves and others.

As paradoxical as it may sound, the State may need to give additional support to local communities. This could be powers to designate under-used land to set it aside for new, temporary activities (allotments and the like). Every family needs the option of gaining access to an allotment, if desired.

More radical would be a proposal for a fairer redistribution of the ownership of countryside for the inhabitants of this nation. This is most relevant around the urban periphery. It's a means of redressing the wrongs of history discussed in Part I. Such an approach would see the return of physical 'commons'. These would be locally used, provide natural resources and even construction materials for long term public benefit.

Fourth is the role of the state about the introduction of new technologies that impact on the environment. Technology may not be good or bad, but nor is it neutral.[127] It is not only the technology itself that's important but who wields it and for what aim. Broad principles need to be agreed internationally. This has already happened with the banning of CFCs. There would also be the need for independent, centrally funded research to assist policy makers. A more sophisticated, ethical approach at the supra-national level is needed around new technologies. Even when new technologies are deemed helpful to the wider society they can pose risks when we become dependent upon them. This is particularly when they are centralised or dominated by a few corporate companies.

Society needs to consider the pervasive role that automation technologies will play in the future. Solution-based thinking is needed to consider how a majority of the population can continue to find meaningful work. Workers can support their own cause in this respect. They can purchase goods that have been produced by other workers, rather than by automated processes. A global balance of primary, secondary and tertiary employment is socially beneficial. At the very least, workers need to be offered a liveable wage.

Fifth, there is an issue around social cohesion and place based identity. Low levels of owner-occupation, modern transportation systems and welfare dependence reduce the perceived value of spatially derived relationships. Few in The West feel the need to invest time with their neighbours. Paradoxically, more effort is put into remote, virtual and non-spatial relationships. This makes modern society uniquely vulnerable to disasters and disruption. Even when disasters bring survivors together, this can result in conflict with authority (Mooney & Neil, 2009).

Finally, effective urban design and provision of large infrastructural projects need to be achieved without evoking Big Government. Too often planning problems do not fit neatly within existing government structures and arrangements, encouraging additional tiers of administration. In fact, nation states are no longer the best framework for tackling some of our problems; we may need to go more local and more global at the same time.

Command-and-control systems will linger on in The West despite trends towards more distributed power and public sector constraints. These are especially applicable to sub-national or regional tiers of government. The

---

[127] Refer to Kranzberg's first law.

long term legitimacy of such intermediate tiers of government may at times be precarious. They are in theory better placed to address specific issues. These include commuter and watershed catchments, and genuinely different forms of spatial community, for example, communal and travelling groups. There will always be tensions with the more strategic goals of higher levels of authority. Overriding local aspirations should be the exception rather than the norm.

In England, neighbourhood planning can put genuine, non-cosmopolitan 'culture' centre stage. By being able to sit outside existing institutional arrangements it can side step any ongoing local government restructuring. Plan making would be done in a more flexible and adaptive manner by engaging local government politicians, landowners, community groups and individuals early on in the setting of planning rules. They would work together on solutions including using on-line tools and forums for group decision making. Agreed mechanisms would give the local community substitutes for public finance, such as development contributions. The development management system would be less costly and may avoid 'private sector accredited agents' if less discretion is allowed.

Instead of telling developers to 'build over there,' planners may end up much like network administers. They would be appointed to various roles. These include maintaining electronic online participatory systems. They would set the parameters for community initiated changes. There's also an important role of maintaining transparency and common understandings of meanings. In essence, they would make sure the system works seamlessly at different scales. Most importantly, they would help resolve conflicts. Knowledge should be freely available and globally shared. The public sector's role would be to fund planners and evidence gathering. It would make inventories of pollution release, land sale, valuation and registers of the controlling interests in land accessible. Data on wage levels, energy consumption and the like would also be provided. A national agency would oversee compliance and monitoring.

The growth and development of cities over the past few decades has encouraged the segregation of social groups, with little or no social mix. Theres a need to create positive culture through life lessons. This could involve activities as diverse as environmental enhancement, building construction and taking care of people. These could be delivered by non-government and/or religious groups. Alternatively, it could be through a new form of national service. Alongside this is the need to invest in public space, support services and amenities close to communities and ensure there are high standards of physical connectivity. This is especially for those without cars (including access to rural areas).

The Ideal Community

There's a lesson that we can draw from the credit crisis, subsequent recession and ongoing ramifications to global market economies. It is that such turmoil stands for far more than just a crisis in neo-liberal economics. It challenges the aspirations of liberal social structures and ideology; particularly their 'means' rather than 'ends' connected goals. You will recall from Part VII that if the principles used to build successful local communities are reversed it damages or destroys them. This can come from an enemy but could also be a 'well-intentioned' government authority. Promoting grass-root community identity and non-commercialised culture is better than a creeping form of 'managerial totalitarianism.' The importance of place and belonging is inherent within us (Wilson, 2014). That is clear from the democratic choices made by communities on BREXIT and the 2016 US election. It thus makes sense that local communities be allowed to develop their own practices, way of life and cultural norms. This may echo the UK's 'Big Society' project. Wise leaders are always needed at different tiers of government, but artificial standards of urban based elites should not override local community choice (MacIntyre; 1981).

There are many mechanisms by which local communities could promote their local culture and values in an outward looking way. In doing so, the worst measures associated with gated communities are to be avoided. Planning tools are only part of the equation. There should be an ability for local communities to opt in or out of certain taxes and regulations imposed at a national level. Real power won't have been transferred unless they can specify their own boundaries and decide where their tax payments are spent.

Societies' long term success in interacting with both ourselves and the environment is going to come down to some sort of moral covenant. This may be supported by, but would sit outside of, the public sector. Imposed solutions and savy, social media campaigns that aim to 'bring us together', until we get tired of them, are inadequate. Rather, we need something that can engage the body, mind and spirit. It's less about where to build, and more about how to work together effectively. The future is going to be challenging. It may be necessary to adapt to the fallout of wars, climate change and natural disasters which may need unprecedented relocations of existing populations. Such a re-configuration of our urban fabric will present opportunities for humanity to remedy the mistakes of over-urbanisation. Most importantly, we need to move beyond the artificiality of progress, as it's now framed. Rather we need to discover who our neighbours are.

SOURCES

Part I

Acemoglu, Daron & Robinson James; *Why Nations Fail*; Crown Business (2012)

Beijia Ma; as reported by the Guardian '*Robot revolution: rise of 'thinking' machines could exacerbate inequality*' https://www.theguardian.com/technology/2015/nov/05/robot-revolution-rise-machines-could-displace-third-of-uk-jobs (2015)

Bell, *Communitarianism and Its Critics*, Oxford: Clarendon Press (1993)

Castells, M.; *The Informational City: Information Technology, Economic Restructuring and the Urban-Regional Process*; Oxford & Cambridge: Blackwell Publishers; (1989)

Chang, Ha-Joon ; *23 Things They Don't Tell You About Capitalism*; Penguin Books Ltd *(pg140 and 145)* (2011)

Davis, V. H; *The Oldest Divide*, City Journal Autumn 2015, Manhattan Institute (2015)

Durkheim, Emile (1893) *The Division of Labour in Society*; Translated by W.D. Halls, New York. The Free Press (1984)

Feng Jicai; as reported by Ian Jonson in 'Once the Villages are Gone the Culture is Gone'; New York Times (Feb 1 2014)

Foucault, Michael, *Power: The Essential Works of Michel Foucault* 1954-1984: Forbes Magazine; Putting a Price Tag on Unpaid Housework by Bryce Covert (30 May 2012)

Garza G.; *Global Economy, Metropolitan Dynamics and Urban Policies in Mexico; Cities* 16:3 p154 (1999)

Gerber, T.P; '*Russia's Population Crisis: The Migration Dimension.*' Policy Memo #118, Program on New Approaches to Russian Security, Harvard University. (2000)

Gerber, T. P. and Hout, M. '*Tightening up: Declining class mobility during Russia's market transition,*' American Sociological Review, 69(5): 677-703. (2004)

Giles, C.; *In economics consumption is for life, not just for Christmas*; www.ft.com/cms/s/0/3d4b5196-6739-11e3-a5f9-00144feabdc0.html (Dec 18 2013)

Glaser, Edward; *Triumph of the City: How Urban Spaces Make Us Human* (*pg 129*) Pan Macmillan (2012)

Gorz A.; *Capitalism, Socialism, Ecology*; Verso (1994)

Gray, J; *Black Mass: Apocalyptic Religion and the Death of Utopia*; Penguin (2007)

Harvey, D; *The Condition of Postmodernity*, Blackwell (1990)

Harvey, D. *Rebel Cities: From the Right to the City to the Urban Revolution* (*pg 40 and 46*) (2012)

Kondo, M. *The Life-Changing Magic of Tidying Up: The Japanese Art of Decluttering and Organizing* Ten Speed Press; (1st edition 2014)

Lewin, M; *The Soviet Century*; Verso Publishers (2005)

Mann, Dr Sandi; from the University of Central Lancashire (July issue of Reader's Digest) (2013)

MacIntyre, A. *After Virtue*; University of Notre Dame Press (1981)

Mills, C. Wright; *Letter to the New Left;* as reported by David Burner, C. (1960)

Merrill Lynch - Bank of America; *Robot Revolution – Global Robot & AI Primer* (2015)

Monacle; Affairs/Urbanism – Most liveable city: Copenhagen. Retrieved from: https://monocle.com/film/affairs/most-liveable-city-copenhagen/ on 30.03.2016.

Oxfam, *Richest 1% will own more than all the rest by 2016*; http://www.oxfam.org.uk/blogs/2015/01/richest-1-per-cent-will-own-more-than-all-the-rest-by-2016 (19 Jan 2015)

Pollard, Sidney; *The idea of progress: history and society* (1968)

Putnam, Robert D. '*E Pluribus Unum: Diversity and community in the twenty-first century*'. Scandinavian Political Studies (Wiley) 30 (2): 137–174. The 2006 Johan Skytte Prize Lecture. (2007)

Richardson, Celia & Halliwell Ed Boiling Point: *Problem Anger and What We Can Do About it*; Mental Health Foundation (2008)

Roscoe, Philip; *I Spend therefore I Am: The True Cost of Economics*; Penguin Book (2014)

Rostow; *The Stages of Economic Growth: A Non-Communist Manifesto* (1960)

Sacks, Lord Jonathan '*Multiculturalism has had its day. It's time to move on*' http://www.thetimes.co.uk/tto/faith/article3846453.ece (19/8/2013)

Sacks, Lord Jonathan; Chief Rabbi Lord Sacks says society is 'losing the plot' http://www.bbc.co.uk/news/uk-23825465(25/8/2013)

Schouls, Peter A. *Descartes and the Possibility of Science*; Cornell University Press (2000)

Spencer, Herbert (1896) *An Epitome of the Synthetic Philosophy*; Cornell University Library (2009)

Taylor C; *Sources of the Self: The Making of the Modern Identity*, Harvard University Press (1990)

Tonnies F; *Community and Society; Gemeinschaft & Gesellschaft*; NY: Transaction Publishers (1988)

UN Habitat, *The Challenge of the Slums: Global Report on Human Settlement* London (2003) pg3;

Walzer, *Interpretation and Social Criticism*, Cambridge: Harvard University Press. 24; (1987)

Walzer; *Thick and Thin, Notre-Dame*: University of Notre Dame Press (1994)

Wilson, Edward O; *The Meaning of Human Existence*'; Liveright (2014)

World Health Organisation; Report: *Air pollution levels rising in many of the world's poorest cities* (2016)

World Bank - World Development Report '*Digital Dividends*' (Jan 2015)

Whyte; *Organisation Man*, Simon & Schuster (1956)

Wright, R. *A Short History of Progress*; Canongate Books (2006)

Part II

Acemoglu, Daron & Robinson James; *Why Nations Fail*; Crown Business (2012)

Barr and Hashagen; p23 *ABCD Handbook: A Framework for Evaluating Community Development, Achieving better community development*; Community Development Foundation (2000)

Barthelemy and Rémi Louf; 'Journal of the Royal Society Interface – study based on mathematically modelling 131 cities (2014)

Beckerman, Wilfred; *Small is Stupid, Blowing the Whistle on the Greens*; London Duckworth (1995)

Carson, Rachel (1962) *Silent Spring*; Publisher: Penguin Books (1972)

Cohen, M.A. *The hypothesis of Urban Convergence: are cities in the North and South becoming more alike in the age of globalization?* in Cohen et al. (eds) Urban Future: Global Pressures and local forces (Washington DC) (1996)

Crowther et al; *Mapping tree density at a global scale*; published in the Journal Nature (2015)

Dear 2000 and Lees 2002 in *Urban Regeneration in the UK* by Andrew Tallon (2013)

Davies E.; *Endangered Elements - Critical Thinking - As our supply of some essential elements dries up, it's time to start urban mining.* Chemistry World (Jan 2011)

Diamond, Jared; *Collapse: How Societies Choose to Fail or Survive*; Penguin (2006)

Douglas J. McCauley, Malin L. Pinsky, Stephen R. Palumbi, James A. Estes, Francis H. Joyce, Robert R. Warner; *Marine defaunation: Animal loss in the global ocean* (16 Jan 2015)

Easton, Mark, *Bustling market towns hold the secret of happiness*- BBC – 24650757 (24 Oct 2013)

Ellen MacArthur Foundation, *Towards the Circular Economy* https://www.ellenmacarthurfoundation.org/ (2013)

Engels; Supplement on Proudhon and the Housing Question - from Marx K, *The Communist Manifesto* (1872)

Friedman, John; *The World's Cities: Contrasting National, Regional and Global Perspectives* by A.J. Jacobs; Routledge; 1 edition (August 11, 2012) Fuller B. The New Sociological Imagination; Sage Publications (2007)

Hall P, *Great Planning Disasters*; Wiley (1992)

Harvey, D. *The Urban Process Under Capitalism: A Framework for Analysis,* (1984)

Harvey, D. *Rebel Cities: From the Right to the City to the Urban Revolution* (2012); (pg630) (pg63)

Hayes, P (2012) Liberated from the 'idiocy of rural life' Spiked Online http://www.spiked-online.com/newsite/article/12023#.VyR_S1L2bIU (pg59)

Heim C., *Structural Changes: Regional and Urban.* In: Stanley L. Engerman and Robert E. Gallman (eds.) (2000)

Henshaw D., *Cancer cases in children 'up 40% in under 20 years*; as reported by The Sunday Telegraph; Children with Cancer UK (2016)

Hook, Lesley *China Faces Rubbish Problem* http://www.ft.com/cms/s/0/3ac0fc10-7ed7-11e1-b009-00144feab49a.html Financial Times (pg77) (10/4/2012)

Jenkins, Simon; *Crisis, what housing crisis? We just need fresh thinking*; Guardian (30 September 2015)

Lewin, M; *The Soviet Century*; Verso Publishers (2005)

Markusen, A. *Sticky places in slippery space: A typology of industrial districts.* Economic Geography 72(3): 293-313. (1996)

Marshall, A; *Principles of Economics* Macmillan and Co., Ltd (1920)

Maugeri, L; Oil: *The Next Revolution - The Unprecedented Upsurge of Oil Production Capacity and What It Means for the World*; Discussion Paper 2012-10, Belfer Center for Science and International Affairs, Harvard Kennedy School (2012)

Neslen A. *New rules to regulate Europe's hormone-disrupting chemicals* https://www.theguardian.com/environment/2016/jun/16/new-rules-to-regulate-europes-hormone-disrupting-chemicals (16 June 2016)

Newman, P. and Thornley, A.; *Urban Planning in Europe*: International competition, national systems and planning projects (London and New York: Routledge) (1996)

Papayanis, Nicholas; *Planning Paris Before Hausmann*; The Johns Hopkins University Press (2004)

Piers Mitchell (9/1/2016) *How Roman Toilets (And Fish Sauce) May Have Helped Spread Parasites Across Europe*; https://www.washingtonpost.com/news/speaking-of-science/wp/2016/01/08/how-roman-toilets-and-fish-sauce-may-have-helped-spread-parasites-across-europe/ Cambridge University

Raftery, Prof Adrian; *World population to keep growing this century*, hit 11 billion by 2100; Science Journal - University of Washington (2014)

Rostow; *The Stages of Economic Growth: A Non-Communist Manifesto* (1960)

Sachs, J - *Global food crisis looms as climate change and population growth strip fertile land*; http://www.theguardian.com/sustainable-business/2014/jun/17/climate-change-advocates-your-focus-on-food-insecurity-is-backfiring (17/6/2014 Guardian)

Sassen, S. *'Cities in a World Economy'* in Readings in Urban Theory Fainstein and Campbell, eds. Oxford, Blackwell (2002)

Saskia Sassen ; *The Global City: New York*, London, Tokyo Princeton University Press (1991)

Sklair, Leslie; *Sociology of the Global System*, Baltimore, MD: John Hopkins University Press (1991)

Schwartz, P & Randall, D; *An Abrupt Climate Change Scenario and its Implications for Unites States National Security*; Pentagon-commissioned analysis US Department of Defense, 10/2003; Fortune, 2/9/2004; Observer, 2/22/2004

Toon, Donald; agency's director of economic crime command at the National Crime Agency (25 July 2015)

Wilkinson, Richard. *Unhealthy societies: the afflictions of inequality*. London New York: Routledge (1996).

Wilkinson, Richard G.; Marmot, Michael; *Social determinants of health* (2nd ed.). Oxford New York: Oxford University Press. (2006) [1999].

World Wildlife Fund; *Living Blue Planet Report-species, habitat and human well-being* (2015)

Part III

Acemoglu, Daron & Robinson James; *Why Nations Fail*; Crown Business (2012)

Adams and Watkins; *The Value of Planning*; RTPI Research Report (2014:36)

Alterman R et al, *Comparative Perspective on Land Use Regulations and Compensation Rights* - Published in 2010 by ABA Press (2010)

Alterman (2014) *Planning Laws, Development Controls, and Social Equity Lessons for Developing Countries* - Edited by: Hassane Cissé, N. R. Madhava Menon, Marie-Claire Cordonier Segger, Vincent O. Nmehielle © 2014 International Bank for Reconstruction and Development / The World Bank

Gywn Topham, *Ryanair to become first airline to fly to Spain's Ghost Airport* - The Guardian 10 March 2015

Beattie, Alan, *False economy – A Surprising Economic History of the World*; Penguin (2010)

Blower, *The City as a Social System* Milton Keynes : Open Univ. Press; (1973)

Bounds, Michael; *Urban Social Theory city self and society*; OUP Australia & New Zealand (2004)

Brindley, Rydin & Stoker; *Remaking Planning: The Politics of Urban Change: Politics of Urban Change in the Thatcher Years* (1996)

Brindley, Rydin & Gerry - *Remaking Planning: The Politics of Urban Change* Routledge (1996)

Brown, W.A. *Piecework bargaining.* London: Heinneman (1972)

Castells, M; *The Urban Question: A Marxist Approach*; MIT Cambridge (1977)

Chan, 2003 from Reeves D. *Planning for Diversity: Policy and Planning in a World of Difference* (RTPI Library Series) (2005)

Clarke and Newman; *The Managerial State.* London: Sage, (1997)

Davidoff, *Advocacy and Pluralism in Planning* (1965)

Department of Communities and Local Government; Technical consultation on implementation of planning changes (Feb 2016)

Denhardt, R.B.; Vinzant Denhardt, J.; *The New Public Service: Serving Rather than Steering,* Public Administration Review 2000, November.

De Vreeze; oningbouw inspiratie en ambities; Kwalitatieve grondslagen van de sociale woningbouw (Housebuilding, *Inspiration and ambitions; qualitative bases of social housing construction*), National Woningraad, Almere ; (1993)

Doorn, J.A.A. van (1955) Wijken stad, reële integratiekaders? (*About integration in city and neighbourhood*), in: Prae-adviezen voor het congres over sociale samenhangen in nieuwestadswijken, 17 december, Amsterdam.

Du Gay; *The Values of Bureaucracy*, Oxford: Oxford University Press (2005)

Clarke and Newman; *The Managerial State*, London: Sage, (1997)

Cowan, R; *Ninety-four per cent of masterplans fail*, UDS Blog (2012)

Fainstein, S *The City Builders: Property Development in New York and London, 1980-2000* (Studies in Government and Public Policy) (2001)

Faludi A, *Planning Theory,* Pergamon Press (1973)

Faludi, 1987, p.43 in Allmendinger *Planning Theory*, Palgrave, New York (2002).

Furedi, F; *Can Humanity Live Without Borders*; Spiked Online (2016)

Fuller, S. *Knowledge Book: key concepts in philosophy, science and culture,* McGill-Queen's University Press, (2007)

Hall, Peter, Price Cedric, Banham, Reyner New Society, *Non-Plan: An Experiment in Freedom*; New Society (1969)

Hagman and Misczynski, *Windfalls for wipeouts : land value capture and compensation American Society Planning Association*, (1978)

Hallett, G. (ed.), *Land and housing policies in Europe and the USA: a comparative analysis*, London, Routledge (1988)

Harvey, *The condition of postmodernity*. Urban Forum, 2. pp. 122-124 (1989)

Harvey, D. *Rebel Cities: From the Right to the City to the Urban Revolution* (2012)

Hollis, Leo *Cities Are Good for You: The Genius of the Metropolis* Bloomsbury Paperbacks pg 75 / 213 (2014)

HM Treasury & Department for Business, *Innovation & Skills*, UK Summer Budget July 2015 – Productivity Plan (2015)

Killian Pretty Review, *Planning Applications: A faster and more responsive system*; London, DCLG. (2008)

Klosterman, 2003) – from *The Planning Process in the US and Germany*: A Comparative Analysis STEPHAN SCHMIDT_ & RALPH BUEHLER International Planning Studies, Vol. 12, No. 1, 55–75, February 2007 (pg109)

Klosterman, R *Arguments for and Against Planning;* Town Planning Review 56: 5-20. (1985)

Kolossov, V. and O'Loughlin, J., *How Moscow is becoming a capitalist mega-city.* International Social Science Journal, 56: 413–427 (2004)

Le Corbusier '*Contemporary City of three Million People'* Exhibit at the Salon d'Automne in Paris (1922)

Le Corbusier *La Ville Radieuse - The Radiant City* (1933)

Lefebvre, Henri (1968) Le Droit à la ville 2002. *The right to the city and its urban politics of the inhabitant'*

Leon Krier (1993) in Carmona M et al, *Public Places Urban Spaces Public Places* - Urban Spaces: A Guide to Urban Design; Architectural Press (2003)

Leunig T.; *Community land auctions working towards implementation*; CentresForum November 2011

Lipsky M; (1983) *Street Level Bureaucracy: Dilemmas of the Individual in Public Service;* Russell Sage Foundation (2010)

Merrifield, Andy *The New Urban Question* – PlutoPress (2014)

Mintzberg, H. *Structure in Fives: Designing Effective Organizations*, Prentice-Hall, New Jersey (1983).

Minxin, Pei, *China's very success could cost the regime dearly* –– Financial Times 26 (May 2014)

Montgomery C. *Happy City – Transforming Our Lives Through Urban Design*; Penguin (2013)

Newman & Thornley, *Urban Planning in Europe: International Competition, National Systems and Planning Projects* – Routledge (1996)

Odum WE *'Environmental degradation and the tyranny of small decisions'* BioScience, 32(9):728–729. (1982)

Olson, M. *The Logic of Collective Action – Public Goods and the Theory of Groups*; Harvard Economic Studies (2002)

Peckitties, Tom *Capital in 21st century*; Harvard University Press (2013)

Rittel, Horst, and Melvin Webber; *'Dilemmas in a General Theory of Planning,'* pp. 155–169, Policy Sciences, Vol. 4, Elsevier Scientific Publishing Company, Inc., Amsterdam, 1973. [Reprinted in N. Cross (ed.), Developments in Design Methodology, J. Wiley & Sons, Chichester, 1984, pp. 135–144.]

Ruble B.A. B. A. Ruble, *'The Rise of Moscow, Inc.,'* Wilson Quarterly (Spring 1998): 84-85. 9

Rydin Y *The Purpose of Planning: Creating Sustainable Towns and Cities*; Policy Press (2011)

Ryser J; *International Manual of Planning Practice*, ISOCARP, International Soc. of City and Regional Planners 2008 edition

Ryser J & Franchini T.,; *International Manual of Planning Practice*, ISOCARP, International Soc. of City and Regional Planners 2015 edition

Salter, W. E. G.: *Productivity and Technical Change*, Cambridge University Press (1963).

Sanandaji, N., *'Debunking Utopia: Exposing the Myth of Nordic Socialism'* WND Books (2016).

Siegan, B.H. *Non-Zoning in Houston*, 13J.L. & Econ. 71, 142 (1970)

Terpstra, J. and Havinga, T., *Implementation between tradition and management: structuration and styles of implementation, Law & policy*, 23(1): 95-117. (2001)

Wragg, R. and Robertson, J.: *Post-War Trends in Employment, Productivity, Output, Labour Costs and Prices by Industry in the United Kingdom,* Department of Employment Research Paper No. 3 (1978)

Slavitt, Lesley Deborah , Reconstruction & WWI – *Internationalism and the Idea of the Expert, A Study in City Planning & Rebuilding* – Columbia University1994

Smith N. and Dumienski Z (November 2015) *A land value tax could fix Australasia's housing crisis* -- The Conversation 9 Nov 2015; Saudi land tax could raise $13bn a year – report, Arabian Business, Ed Attwood 22 (pg127) Stanilov, K. (2007).

Stanilov, Kiril (Ed.) *The post-socialist city: urban form and space transformations in Central and Eastern Europe after socialism:* Springer Berlin. (2007)

Sweetwell & Maxwell, *Encyclopedia of Planning Law and Practice* (2015)

Van der Heijden, Manon; *Civic Duty: Public Duty in Early Modern Low Countries* (2012)

Wagenaar C, *Town Planning in the Netherlands since 1800*; Responses to Enlightenment Ideas and Geopolitical Realities (2011)

Esping-Andersen, G, Sassen S and Lewis R., *Towards a New Welfare State*, WRR (2005)

Yelling J.A. *Slums & Slum Clearance in Victorian London*; Allen and Unwin (1986)

PART IV

Acemoglu, Daron & Robinson James *Why Nations Fail*; Crown Business (2012)

Alterman R. *Planning Laws, Development Controls, and Social Equity Lessons for Developing Countries* - Edited by: Hassane Cissé, N. R. Madhava Menon, Marie-Claire Cordonier Segger, Vincent O. Nmehielle © 2014 International Bank for Reconstruction and Development / The World Bank (2014)

Arnstein, S., *Ladder of Citizen participation*. Journal of American institute of planners vol 35 no 4 July 1969

Ashton K. (2009) *That Internet of Things*; http://www.rfidjournal.com/articles/view?4986 (pg165)

Ayres, Ian and John Braithwaite; *Responsive Regulation: Transcending the deregulation debate*. New York: Oxford University Press (1992)

Bauman (1989) in Du Gay *The Values of Bureaucracy*. Oxford: Oxford University Press (2005)

Diefenbach T. *New Public Management in Public Sector organisations: the dark side of managerialistic* 'enlightenment' Public Administration 87 (4), 892-909 (2009)

Dowie, Mark - *Losing Ground: American Environmentalism at the Close of the Twentieth Century* (MIT Press, 1996), American Foundations: An Investigative History (MIT Press, 2001).

Duyvendak, J. W., Knijn, T., & Kremer, M. (Eds.). *Policy, people, and the new professional. de-professionalisation and re-professionalisation in care and welfare*. Amsterdam: Amsterdam University Press. (2006)

Freidson, E. *Professionalism: The Third Logic* (London, Polity Press). (2001)

Hartley, D. *Re-Schooling Society* – Falmer Press (1997)

Harvey, D. *Rebel Cities: From the Right to the City to the Urban Revolution* (2012)

Hambleton R., *Leading the Inclusive City: Place-Based Innovation for a Bounded Planet*, Policy Press (2014)

Head, B., *Toward More "Evidence-Informed" Policy Making?* Public Administration Review, Vol. 76, Iss. 3, pp. 472–484. © 2015

Jacob J. *The Death and Life of Great American Cities* Random House New York (1961)

Jones, Rhion & Gammell, Elizabeth *The Art of Consultation*; Biteback (2009)

Kamarck E. *The End of Government... as we know it*: Making Public Policy Work (2007)

Kendall, L and Reed, S MP; *Let it Go: Power to the People in Public Services Progress* (2015).

Kirkpatrick, I., Ackroyd, S. and Walker, R., *The new managerialism and public service professions,* Basingstoke: Palgrave. (2005)

Kuhn *The Structure of Scientific Revolutions*; University of Chicago Press (1962)

Majone, Giandomenico. *Evidence, Argument, and Persuasion in the Policy* (1989)

Process. New Haven, CT: Yale University Press.
Ministry for the Environment; *Improving our resource management system: A discussion document* Wellington (2013)

Parker, G. & Doak, J. *Key Concepts in Planning*, Sage, London. (2012)

Ormerod, Paul *Why Most Things Fail: Evolution, Extinction, and Economics* Faber and Faber (2005)

Terpstra, J. and Havinga, T., *Implementation between tradition and management: structuration and styles of implementation, Law & policy*, 23(1): 95-117. (2001)

Vegara Dr A. *Reflections on City Regions*, RTPI Planner July 2015 (2015)

US GAO *Environmental Protection: Overcoming obstacles to innovative state regulatory programs*. GAO-02-268. Washington, DC: US General Accounting Office, p19 (2002)

Webber M. (1960) in Wingo, L. (ed). *Cities and Space: The Future Use of Urban Land*. John Hopkins Press, Baltimore.1963:54 (1963)

Wu F, Zhang F. & Wang Z.. *Planning China's Future: How planners contribute to growth and development* RTPI Research Report no.12 December (2015)

Part V

Adams & others; *Urban Development and Planning*. London (1994)

Alden, J. & Crow, S. *Moscow: Planning for a world capital city towards 2000*. Cities, 15, 361-374. (1998).

Atkinson and Moon, *Urban Regeneration in the UK* by Andrew Tallon (1994)

BBC, *Le Corbusier works named as UN world heritage sites* http://www.bbc.com/news/world-europe-36820119 (17 July 2016)

BBC, *Giant Mao statue 'removed' from Henan village* http://www.bbc.co.uk/news/world-asia-china-35262798 (8 Jan 2016)

BBC (Ash, Lucy), *Risking death at sea to escape boredo*m; http://www.bbc.co.uk/news/magazine-33986899 (20 August 2015)

Ball, 2011; In research for DCLG

Barras R. *Building Cycles – Growth and Instability*; Wiley-Blackwell. (2009)

Boddy, Martin; *Building Societies*, London Macmillian (1980)

Carmona, M et al; Public Places - Urban Spaces: A Guide to Urban Design Architectural Press (2003)

Chang, Ha-Joon; *23 Things They Don't Tell You About Capitalism*; Penguin Books Ltd (2010, 219)

Condon M. *Seven Rules for Sustainable Communities Design Strategies for the Post Carbon World*; Island Press (2010)

Clapson M. *Suburban Century: Social Change and Urban Growth in England and the USA*; Berg (2003)

Condon P, *Seven Rules for Sustainable Communities: Design Strategies for the Post Carbon World* – Island Press (2010)

Crang, M.; *Cultural Geography* 116-117 (Routledge (1998)

Cullen, G. *Townscape* (Architectural Press, London). (1961)

Daniel A. Bell & Avner de-Shalit *The Spirit of Cities: Why the Identity of a City Matters in a Global Age;* Princeton University Press (2011)

Davis M. *Planet of Slums*; Verso (2006)

Dowall, D. and Monkkonen, P.. '*Consequences of the Plano Piloto: The Urban Development and Land Markets of Brasilia.*' Urban Studies, 44:10, pp. 1871-1887. (2007)

De Botton, *Architecture of Happiness*; Penguin (2007)

Daily Mail; http://www.dailymail.co.uk/news/article-3138099/26-Romanians-three-bed-house-near-Stratford-s-Olympic-Stadium.html (26 June 2015)

D.o.E in *Women and Planning: Creating Gendered Realities*
By Clara H. Greed (1972)

Domosh, M; *Symbolism of the Skyscraper: Case Studies of New York's First Tall Buildings 1988* - Journal of Urban History (1988)

Dovey, p44 and Huxtable 1997, p3 in Public Places, Urban Spaces: The Dimensions of Urban Design; Elsiever (1999)

Ehrenhalt, A., *'Community and the Corner Store: Retrieving Human-Scale Commerce,'* The Responsive Community, 9(4): 30–39. (1999)

Fainstein, S., *The Just City*; Cornell University Press (2010)

Florida, Richard; *The Rise of the Creative Class: And How it's Transforming Work, Leisure, Community and Everyday Life* Paperback; Basic Books (2003)

Ford in Public Places, *Urban Spaces: The Dimensions of Urban Design*; Elsiever (2000)

Forrester, J: *Urban Dynamics*. Pegasus Communications (1969).

Forty A.; *Concrete in Culture – A Material History*; Reaktion Books (2012)

Gentile, M. & Sjoberg, O. Intra-urban landscapes of priority: *The Soviet legacy.* Europe-Asia Studies, 58, 701-729. (2006).

Geoghegan, Tom; *Why do so many Americans live in mobile homes?* (24 September 2013)

Glaeser Edward *Triumph of the City: How Urban Spaces Make Us Human* (2012)

Hall, P. and Tewdwr-Jones, M. *Urban and regional planning.* (2010)

Hall, 2006 p 100 in Urban Regeneration in the UK by Andrew Tallon
Routledge (2013)

Heathcote ,Edwin *Why Art Galleries Are Moving Back into Domestic Settings*
Financial Times (3 Oct 2014)

Heyden Tom 10 Sept 2014 - *The Era of Radical Concrete* BBC
http://www.bbc.co.uk/news/magazine-29082338

Hillier B *The Social Logic of Space*; Cambridge University Press (2008)

Heinrich Hubsch's; *welchem Stil sollen wir bauen? In What Style Shall We
Build* (1828).

Hillier B; *The Social Logic of Space*; Cambridge University Press (2008)

Hollis, L; *Cities Are Good for You: The Genius of the Metropolis* Bloomsbury
Paperbacks (24 April 2014)

Hoyt, H. 1933. *One hundred years of land values in Chicago*. Chicago:
University of Chicago Press. (pg284)

Hurley, A., *Diners, Bowling Alleys and Trailer Parks Chasing The American
Dream In The Postwar Consumer Culture* (2002)

Jasper van der Lingen, of Sheppard & Rout Architects; Critics slate 'bizarre'
new cathedral http://www.stuff.co.nz/business/rebuilding-
christchurch/8516549/Critics-slate-bizarre-new-cathedral (2013)

Jenkins, Simon Crisis, *What housing crisis? We just need fresh thinking* —
Guardian (30 September 2015)

Journal of Planning and Environmental Law (2013 – Issue 6)

Jacobs, J *The Death and Life of Great American Cities* (Harmondsworth:
Penguin). (1965)

Jargowsky P; *Poverty & Place*; Russell Sage Foundation (1997)

Kaplan & Kaplan, *The Experience of Nature: A Psycological Perspective* Cambridge University press (1982)

Kirkman, R – *Ethics of Metropolitan Growth for future of our built environment* 2010; pg 11

Khrushchev 7 December 1954 to All-Union Conference of Builders, Architects and Workers in the Building Materials Industry (1954)

Kendzior S. *Expensive cities are killing creativity: New York City, a traditional incubator for artists, has now become a 'gated citadel' for creativity.* http://www.aljazeera.com/indepth/opinion/2013/12/expensive-cities-are-killing-creativity-2013121065856922461.html

Le Corbusier; *Immeubles Villas* (1922)

Legner M.(ed) 'From cultural quarters to creative clusters: creative spaces in the new city economy.' *The sustainability and development of cultural quarters: international perspectives.* Stockholm: Institute of Urban History: 32-59 (2009)

Lynch, Kevin; *The Image of the City*; MIT Press (1960)

Mazumbar, (2000) in *Public Places, Urban Spaces: The Dimensions of Urban Design*; Elsiever (pg278)

Moore R. *Why we build*; Picador (pg214; 282) , pg 300 (2012)

Naser, Jack L. *'Does Neotraditional Development Build Community?'* Journal of Planning Education and Research23: 58. (2003)

Nedoroscik, J.; *The City of the Dead: A History of Cairo's Cemetary Communities,* Westport p 43 (1997)

Ooi, CS; *Creative industries and tourism in Singapore* – in Richards, Wilson Tourism, creativity and development (2007)

Overvelde Johannes; Harvard Universities (11/03/2016)

Packard V. *The Hidden Persuaders*; Ig Publishing; Reissue Ed edition (10 Oct. 2007) (1981)

Pine, J. and Gilmore, J. *The Experience Economy*, Harvard Business School Press, Boston (1999)

Planning Resource; reporting decision by Inspector Isobel McCretton, in Planning 19 April 2013 (pg229)

Neale J; *Improving Housing Quality: Unlocking the Market*, RIBA (2009)

Randviir, Anti (2002) *Space and Place as Substrates of Culture*

Ridge P. *Is Shared Living a Solution to the Housing Crisis*; The Planner (April 2016)

Randviir Anti, *Space and Place as Substrates of Culture* ; Proceedings of the Estonian Academy of Arts 10, 2002. lk 140–154

Rodríguez, G *Is Honduras heading for the privatization of parts of its territory? The Tico Times* (18 January 2015)

Rolf Pendall, Robert Puentes, & Jonathan Martin, *From Traditional to Reformed: A Review of Land Use Regulations in the Nation's 50 Largest Metropolitan Areas* (Research Brief, Brookings Institution, Aug. 2006).

Ritzer, 1999 in *Eventful Cities: Cultural Management & Urban Revitalisation* by Greg Richards, Robert Palmer; Elsvier (2010)

Royal Institute of British Architects; Ministry of Works, *Post-War Building Studies* no 18 The Architectural Sue of Building Materials (1946) (pg282)

RTPI; *Why places need to be at the heart of policy-making in the twenty-first century*; Spatial Publication Planning: Horizons; (2014)

Shuman, M. H., '*Community Corporations: Engines for a New Place-Based Economics,*' The Responsive Community, 9(3): 48–57. (1999)

Soja E. (1995) *The Community of the Weak: Social Postmodernism in Theological Reflections* by Hans-Peter Geiser; Wipf and Stock (2013)

Sperling & Gordon - *Two Billion Cars Two Billion Cars: Driving Toward Sustainability* Oxford University (2010)

Storper, M. & Venables A. (2003) *December Buzz: Face-To-Face Contact and the Urban Economy*

Storper, M.. *The regional world: territorial development in a global economy,* New York: Guilford Press. (1997)

States, Richard – *Iconoclastic Currents in the Russian Revolution: Destroying and Preserving the Past – Bolshevik Culture: Experiment & Order in Revolutionary Russia* ed Peter Kenez, R. States (Bloomington 1985)

Szelenyi, I., 'Cities Under Socialism and after,'.in Andrusz; G; Harloe, M. and I. Szelenyi (eds), Cities after Socialism, Oxford, Cambridge: Blackwell Publishers, 286-317. (1996)

Tallon A, *Urban regeneration in the UK,* Routledge (2010)

Turner J, Housing, *Priorities, Settlement Patterns and Urban Development in Modernizing Countries*; Journal of American Institute of Planners 34 (1968) pp354-63.

Verbeek J. (2014) *Lead Author of Global Monitoring Report* 2014/2015

Venturi, R., Brown D.S. and Izenour, S.; *Learning from Las Vegas: The Forgotten Symbolism of Architectural Form* (1977)

Voith, Richard P; '*Do Suburbs Need Cities?*' Working Paper No. 93–27/R, Federal Reserve Bank of Philadelphia. (1994)

Weclzwowicz G. 'From Egalitarian Cities in Theory to Non-egalitarian Cities in Practice (2002)

Westin *Privacy and Freedom*; The Bodley Head Ltd (1967)

Whyte, W.H. *City: Rediscovering the Center*. New York: Doubleday. (1988)

Yueh, Linda *Can De-industrialisation be reversed?* BBC (16/2/15)

Zukin S. *The Culture of Cities*; Wiley-Blackwell (1995)

PART VI

Alden, J. & Crow, S.; *Moscow: Planning for a world capital city towards 2000. Cities,* 15, 361-374. (1998)

Alker Tripps Road Traffic & Its Control (1938), *Town Planning and Road Traffic* (1942)

Allen K; *UK housing policy leads to loss of 6m sq ft of offices in year*; Financial Times p4 9/9/2015 http://www.ft.com/cms/s/0/aeb3ba3e-55fe-11e5-a28b-50226830d644.html (pg299) (2015)

Altieri, M.A. *The ecological role of biodiversity in agroecosystems.* Agriculture, Ecosystems & environment, 74(1):19-31(1999)

Baumeister, R. *Stadterweiterungen in Technischer, Buupolizeilicher und Wirtschaftlicher Beziehung*, Berlin, Ernst and Korn, 1876 and Stübben, Joseph, Der Stadtebau, Darmstadt, Bergstrasser, 1890. See also Bangert, Wolfgang, op. cit., Chapter 4 (pg306)

Bressey report; *The Highway Development Survey*, for Greater London, (1937)

Brueckner, Joseph Gyourko, Albert Saiz & Anita Summers, *A New Measure of the Local regulatory Environment for Housing Markets: The Wharton Residential Land Use Regulatory Index*, 45 Urban Studies 693 (2008)

Claire Corbould; *Feeding the cities: is urban agriculture the future of food security? Future Directions International* (1 November 2013)

Creswell, Place: *A short introduction* (short Introductions to geography) Oxford: Wiley-Blackwell (2004)

Cullingworth & Caves; *Planning in the USA*; Routledge (2003)

Duany, A., Plater-Zyberk, E. and Speck, J. *Suburban Nation: The Rise of Sprawl and the Decline of the American Dream.* New York: North Point Press. (2000)

Ducas, Sylvain; *Case Study of the City of Stockholm and the Greater Stockholm Area: Municipal and Regional Organization*, Urban Planning Tools and Issues, Planning of Transportation and the Green Network, Housing Issues : Summary : Research Report; La Ville de Montréal (2000)

Engel, B; *Public space in the 'blue cities' of Russia - The Post-Socialist City* (pp. 285-300): Springer. (2007)

European Centre for Environment and Human Health, looking at Abi Scott from the University of Exeter Medical School (*Oh, why do we like to be beside the seaside?* By Lorna Stewart BBC- 28/9/2013) (pg316)

Evans, G.W., Lercher, P., Meis, M., Ising, H. and Kofler, W.W. *Community noise exposure and stress in children.* Journal of the Acoustical Society of America 109(3), 1023-1027. (2001)

Evans, A. W.; *No Room! No Room! The Costs of the British Town and Country Planning System,* London: Institute of Economic Affairs (1988)

Forty A; *Concrete in Culture – A Material History*; Reaktion Books (2012)

Global Commission, *Better Growth, Better Climate*: The New Climate Economy Report (2014).

Hall et al; *The containment of urban England* vol Two (London: George Allen and Unwin) (1973)

Jones, P., Hillier, D., & Comfort, D, *Putting which town centres first?* Town and Country Planning. Retrieved from http://www.highbeam.com/doc/1G1-119444895.html (2004).

Le Corbusier, *Toward an Architecture Frances Lincoln* (1929)

McHarg, Ian; '*Design with Nature*; Wiley (1969)

Lomborg B. *The Sceptical Environmentalist*; Cambridge University Press (2001)

Molodikova, I., Makhrova, A. '*Urbanization Patterns in Russia in the post-soviet era.*' In K. Stanilov (ed) 'The Post-Socialist City: Urban Form and Space Transformations in Central and Eastern Europe After Socialism,' Springer, Dordrecht, pp. 53-70. (2007)

Minton A, Ground Control – *Fear & Happiness in the 21st Century City*; Penguin (2012)

Montgomery C.; Happy City – *Transforming Our Lives Through Urban Design;* Penguin (2013)

Morgan J. & Mitchell P *'Employment and the circular economy: job creation in a more resource efficient Britain*'; WRAP & Green Alliance (2015)

Pahl, R. '*Managers, technical experts and the state.*' In: Captive Cities: Studies in the Political Economy of Cities and Regions, Michael Harloe (ed.), Wiley, London; New York, pp. 49-60. (1977)

Paxton; presented to the Parliamentary Select Committee on Metropolitan Communications in June 1855

Victor Moore & Michael Purdue - *A Practical Approach to Planning Law* - 12th edition (2012)

Sitte, Camillo *City Planning According to Artistic Principles* (1889)

Stanilov, K. *The post-socialist city: urban form and space transformations in Central and Eastern Europe after socialism*: Springer Berlin (2007)

Siegelbaum, *The Socialist Car: Automobility in the Eastern Bloc*; Cornell University Press (2011)

Slone D. & Goldstein D. *A Legal Guide to Urban and Sustainable Development for Planners,* Developers and Architects (2008)

Smart, A; *Making Room: Squatter Clearance in Hong Kong* (Hong Kong: Centre of Asian Studies, The University of Hong Kong, (1992).

Talen, Emily - *City Rules: How Regulations Affect Urban Form* (2012)

United Nations Conference on Trade and Development, Trade and Development Report, http://unctad.org/en/PublicationsLibrary/tdr2016_en.pdf (2016)

Uyttenhove P., *The Garden City education of Belgium planners around the First World War;* Planning Perspectives 5:3, 277 – Journal of Planning & Environmental Law Issue 5 2015 A Fit Country? The Impact of the Great War on Town & Country Planning – Gregory Jones QC & Charles Streeten). (1990)

Wagenaar, C; *Town Planning in the Netherlands since 1800: Responses to Enlightenment Ideas and Geopolitical Realities* (Rotterdam) (pg309; 319) (2011)

PART VII

Climate Change Exodus: *North Africa, Middle East Could Become Uninhabitable By 2050 Due To Severe Heat*;
http://www.techtimes.com/articles/155557/20160503/climate-change-exodus-north-africa-middle-east-could-become-uninhabitable-by-2050-due-to-severe-heat.htm#sthash.N6WJoFrs.dpuf

Allaire, J.; '*Neighborhood Boundaries,*' Information Report No.141, published online by the American Society of Planning Officials, 1313 East 60th St. Chicago Illinois 60637; resource retrieved 9/04/11 (1960)

Corbould, C.; *Feeding the Cities: Is Urban Agriculture the Future of Food Security?* Future Directions International team; Australia (2013)

Davis (2006) – reporting Peters R. (1996) *Our Soldiers, Their Cities*; Parameters Spring 1996.

Diamond, J *Collapse; How Societies Choose to Fail or Survive*; Penguin (2006)

Doug Bolton *Climate change could see tourists avoid Spain and go to Latvia for summer holidays*, EU study finds; http://www.independent.co.uk/travel/climate-change-could-see-tourists-avoid-spain-and-go-to-latvia-for-summer-holidays-eu-study-finds-10454643.html (14 Aug 2014)

Graham, W, *Dream Cities: Seven Urban Ideas That Shape the World* Amberley (2016)

Gyr, K; *Linear cities could lead to 100% global sustainability* http://www.altenergymag.com/article/2010/03/linear-cities-could-lead-to-100-global-sustainability/629/ (2016)

Calame J., & Charlesworth E., *Divided Cities*: Belfast, Beirut N Jer, Mostar & Nicosia (2012)

Erkens G, Deltares *Sinking coastal cities* Research Institute in the Netherlands Utrecht University (May 2014)

Graham S. *Cities Under Siege: The New Military Urbanism*, Verso (2010)

Harrison (2005) *Quake experts urge Tehran move* http://news.bbc.co.uk/1/hi/world/middle_east/4346945.stm reporting International Institute of Earthquake Engineering and Seismology Teheran University

Landry C. in Collaboration with City of Helsinki Urban Facts; *The Digitized City: Influence and Impact*; Comedia (2016)

Newman, Oscar; *Defensible Spaces: People and Design in the Violent City*; Architectural Press (1973)

NHS; https://www.england.nhs.uk/ourwork/innovation/healthy-new-towns/ (2016)

Peyer R., *Tube network 'to be put out of action within 15 years' due to soaring population*, London Standard (12 June 2016)

Smart, A; *Making Room: Squatter Clearance in Hong Kong,* Centre of Asian Studies, University of Hong Kong p. 63 (1992)

Tueni in *Divided Cities: Belfast, Beirut, Jerusalem, Mostar, and Nicosia* By Jon Calame, Esther Charlesworth (2000)

William W; *The Social Life of Small Urban Spaces*; Project for Public Spaces Inc (1988)

William W; City: *Rediscovering the Center*; University of Pennsylvania Press (1988)

Yuhas; *Great Blue Hole off Belize yields new clues to fall of Mayan civilisation*; http://www.theguardian.com/world/2015/jan/03/great-blue-hole-belize-clues-fall-mayan-civilisation (2015)

CONCLUSION

MacIntyre, A. *After Virtue*; University of Notre Dame Press (1981)

Mooney, G. and Neal, S. (eds) *Community: Welfare, Crime and Society,* Maidenhead, Open University Press/Milton Keynes, The Open University (2009).

Lightning Source UK Ltd.
Milton Keynes UK
UKOW01f2306060917
308723UK00002B/203/P